Christian Liturgy: Theology and Practice

I. Systematic Theology of Liturgy

Edward J. Kilmartin, S.J.

Sheed & Ward

Sheed & Ward is a service of National Catholic Reporter Publishing
Company, Inc.

Library of Congress Catalog Card Number: 87-61262

Published by: Sheed & Ward
                   115 E. Armour Blvd. P.O. Box 414292
                   Kansas City, MO 64141-0281

To order, call: (800) 333-7373

Contents

PART I

The Modern Context: The Theological And Anthropological Dimensions Of The Liturgy

The first part of this book provides an overview of some of the valuable contributions of modern theology and the human sciences toward the deepening of the understanding and pastoral practice of the worship of the Church. It serves as an introduction to a systematic theology of liturgy, which is set in the context of the history of salvation (Part II). The mystery of the Christian liturgy is the theme of Part III. The concluding section (Part IV) formulates a theology of the seven sacraments of the Church in dialogue with the central insights of the traditional theology and dogmatic teaching of the churches of the East and West.

Chapter 1 of this introduction describes key aspects of the history of theological reflection on the liturgy, and it identifies basic concepts which determine the modern approach of systematic theologians to all aspects of liturgy. Chapter 2 reviews the contributions of the human sciences to the understanding and practice of Christian worship and, at the same time, indicates their limitations.

1

Chapter 1
History Of The Theology Of The Sacraments: Salient Features

The ancient churches of the East and West, as well as high church elements of the Reformation churches, agree on the number of the chief liturgical rites of the Church of Christ. In the traditional enumeration of the Western churches, they are: baptism, confirmation, Eucharist, sacraments of reconciliation and of the sick, orders (diaconate, presbyterate, episcopate), and matrimony. These rites play analogous roles in the life of the Christian community. No one rite can serve the purpose of the others. While a certain resemblance exists between them, there are still greater differences. However, all relate to the one economy of salvation. Hence a Christian interpretation of the chief rites must take into account the peculiar function of each, as well as their ordering to one another.

A systematic elaboration of the meaning of the central liturgical celebrations of the Church, attuned to the level of maturity of Christians at various stages of development, has an important pastoral function. It furnishes the kind of knowledge that enables more active, fully conscious participation, as well as commitment to what is being celebrated. But it is also pastorally useful to have at hand a theological synthesis that identifies common aspects of the rites and, from this starting point, develops general principles applicable to them all.

This more comprehensive theology of the sacraments is possible, provided that theologians do not make the blunder of attempting to construct their syntheses on premises which are foreign to the rites themselves. Rather, a theology of the sacraments should derive from reflection on the forms of celebration of each rite. Once theological explanations of individual sacraments have been sufficiently developed, the more abstract, systematic ordering of general principles can be undertaken.

The credit for the initial attempts to develop a systematic theology of general principles, applicable to the chief rites of the Church, belongs to Western theologians. The historical roots of "Principles of Sacramental Theology" (*De sacramentis in genere*) go back to St. Augustine of Hippo. He taught the Western churches that these rites should be included under the category of the *sacramenta* of the economy of salvation. His understanding of *sacramentum* as a holy sign (*sacrum signum*) of a saving grace (*res sacramenti*) was taken over by early scholastic theology. The word became a technical term for the chief rites of the Church with the birth of systematic treatises on the subject. Twelfth-century scholastic theologians applied it to all the major rites in order to indicate their analogous roles. At the same time, these theologians developed principles which could be predicated of all of them.

Theologians of the high scholastic period of the thirteenth century consolidated the earlier findings, and contributed significantly to a deeper understanding of the theology of the sacraments. By the end of that century the main lines of *De sacramentis in genere*, as well as the theology of particular sacraments, was well established. A common systematic approach was found in all Catholic schools of theology. The authority of this system was so great that the official teaching of the magisterium of the Western churches, and its preaching, became more and more determined by the language and content of school theology. This had the effect of constraining theologians to work within a system which was the creation of school theology itself.

Further limitations on the space required for creative reflection on the sacraments was occasioned by the sixteenth-century reaction of the Reformers to the traditional Catholic sacramental theology. The Council of Trent, attempting to answer objections to Catholic doctrine, touched on a variety of aspects of classical sacramental theology. But it never intended to present a complete exposition of the late medieval teaching, much less of the high scholastic synthesis. The procedure was always the same: a list of objectionable positions of Reformation theologians was drawn up on the subject of individual sacraments, and on general principles of sacramental theology. Those opposed to traditional Catholic belief were rejected.

In the post-Reformation period, these same doctrinal issues remained alive because the Reformers were not satisfied with the Tridentine decisions. In this situation Catholic theologians turned their attention to the exposition of the teaching of Trent, and to a defense based on whatever support could be mustered from the sources of Christian tradition. For the most part, the structure and content of treatises on sacramental theology were dictated by the Reformation agenda. These tracts had a characteristically apologetic bent, were often marred by a polemical tone, and employed anachronistic interpretations of proof texts drawn from Scripture and other sources of theology. Moreover, the absence of a critical edition of the *Acta* of the Council of Trent made the task of establishing the correct interpretation of the conciliar decrees extremely difficult in many cases. At the same time, this lacuna contributed to the development and cultivation of narrow, literal interpretations of conciliar decrees that have since proven not to correspond to the intention of the fathers of the council.

Two other characteristics of Catholic theology, from the seventeenth to the twentieth century, are noteworthy. First, despite intramural differences between various schools, the systematic treatment of theological themes was remarkably alike. Second, Catholic theological circles showed little sensitivity to the limitations of the scholastic methodology. On the contrary, they displayed excessive optimism concerning their basically uniform treatment of all aspects of the revealed truth. The sacramental theology of the last four centuries is a good example of this.

However, the history of theology makes clear that theological reflection is always conditioned by a variety of cultural and historical circumstances. At one time, the questions provoked by a particular religious experience may so highlight certain aspects of revealed truth that others, which previously received attention, are neglected. A new age, on the other hand, may rediscover these forgotten truths, make its own special contribution and, at the same time, overlook many valuable insights of the immediate past.

The process of thinking through the meaning of revealed truth has not always resulted in new gains on all fronts. Sometimes it has taken place at the cost of considerable loss of ground in areas of vital importance. But this should not come as a surprise. The principle of intelligibility in Christian theology is the relationship of one aspect of the economy of salvation to all the others. A systematic theology of any of the revealed truths, by its very nature, intends to take account of all the factors which contribute to the understanding of the single truth under analysis. However, it is difficult to imagine that any theologian, or school of theology, could command such a grasp of the real content of the whole of Christian revelation as to be able to formulate a completely satisfactory, contemporary theology of any aspect of this revealed truth.

The formulation of a theology of the chief rites of the Church is particularly difficult. These rites are the expression, in practice, of all that goes to make up the life of faith. Hence it is no wonder that the attempts of the past to develop a comprehensive exposition of their meaning have always failed to reach the desired goal. History teaches us that we must not expect too much from the contemporary work of systematic theologians. However, history also teaches us that a sacramental theology can be developed which corresponds to the particular spiritual needs of an age, provided the theologian is attuned to the cultural and historical context and asks the right questions.

I.
Salient Features of Scholastic Theology of the Sacraments

The birth of scholastic theology can be traced back to the eleventh-century controversy over the relationship of the Eucharistic bread and wine to the risen body of Christ. The systematic tracts, "Concerning the Body of the Lord," occasioned by this debate were linked to similar treatises on the other "major sacrament," baptism, in the early twelfth century. This nucleus formed the basis of early scholastic systematic theology of the sacraments. The introduction, "Concerning the Sacraments in General," gathered together principles that could be applied to all sacraments. In this latter tract theologians attempted to get at the heart of the problem: What constitutes a chief rite of the Church? As a result of their efforts, this commonly accepted brief description emerged: A sacrament is a sign instituted by Christ to confer the grace which it signifies. But the full meaning intended by formulas of this type can only be grasped by reading the treatises in which they are found. For example, Hugo of St. Victor (d.1141) employs a succinct definition of sacrament, set in the context of his particular understanding of the history of salvation. He begins with the question: Since sacraments are intended for human beings, what is the actual situation of humanity in the history of salvation? Only by supplying a response to this question could he make sense out of the role of sacraments in the life of faith.

The early scholastics, as well as those of the high scholastic period of the thirteenth century, had great powers of synthesis. They used them in the attempt to shed more light on the significance of sacraments in relation to the whole economy of salvation. These theologians recognized that an adequate grasp of the principal rites of the Church could only be achieved by situating them within God's activity in history, and in relation to the human condition of sinfulness. Above all, the sacraments had to be linked to the incarnation and life of Jesus Christ, as well as to the Church of which he is the Head.

Sacraments were understood as "efficacious signs of grace," a concept derived from the liturgical experience of being graced. They were treasured as the outstanding medium by which the Father, through Christ in the Holy Spirit, bestows and deepens the new life of faith. However, another part of the whole tradition, grounded in the same liturgical experience, teaches that sacraments are efficacious in the measure of the grateful response of the subjects, made possible by the gift of faith. Consequently, scholastic theology was challenged with the task of explaining how the divine initiative and the response of faith come together, and are related in the celebration of a sacrament. The synthesis, achieved by the twelfth- and thirteenth-century theologians, is impressive. Despite its limitations, this systematic theology of the sacraments was not equaled in the late medieval period, nor in the following centuries down to the modern era.

We have already mentioned that the doctrinal synthesis of the Council of Trent on the subject of sacraments lacked the fullness of a true systematic treatise. The Reformers had criticized many of the traditionally unassailable doctrinal positions relating to this aspect of the life of faith. Accordingly, Trent was forced to take a stand on several important issues. These included the number of the sacraments instituted by Christ, and the relation between sacramental celebrations and the bestowal of the grace signified by them. Post-Reformation Catholic theology was greatly influenced by the limited doctrinal teaching of Trent and, therefore, by the Reformation critique which dictated the subject matter of the conciliar decrees. This is not the place to discuss, in detail, the neoscholastic theology of the sacraments. Only those peculiar traits can be mentioned which determined the more common Catholic understanding of the chief rites of the Church up through the first few decades of the twentieth century.

This school theology describes sacraments by the model of objective means of grace, instrumental causes of grace, confided to the Church by Christ. While sacraments are portrayed as signs and causes of the grace, the sign function is relegated to a marginal place. It serves to distinguish one sacrament from the others, and to awaken in the recipient the appropriate response to the particular grace offered in each sacrament. Hence the problem of explaining how sacraments cause grace is situated at the level of an analogy with instruments of art, and not with that of the instrumentality of signs. Within this conceptual framework no consensus was possible, among Catholic theologians, on the subject of causality of sacraments; for theological reflection on the "physical causality" of sacraments turned to philosophical principles far removed from the concrete liturgical celebrations.

The connection between Church and sacraments is also very weak in the neoscholastic system. The sacraments are not identified precisely as acts of the Church itself, but rather as acts of the minister of Christ. Since the minister represents Christ, the head of the Church, he can also be said to represent the Church. Here again, as in the case of the analysis of the sign and causal functions of the sacraments, this school of theology could do no better than establish an extrinsic link between the community of believers, as such, and sacraments. In other words, the sacraments are depicted as ministerial acts of the priest, who is minister of the Church and acts as a representative of Christ in the administration of sacraments. Therefore, sacraments appear to be means of grace located within the sphere of the Church, but not precisely acts of the Church.

It is especially noteworthy that this theology treats the sacraments almost exclusively from the standpoint of their mystery dimension, that is, under the aspect of the divine movement toward believers. The anabatic dimension, the aspect of worship or the movement of the liturgical assembly toward God, is confined to the liturgical prayer and symbolic action surrounding the "essential sacramental gestures and the accompanying formulas."

Typically, this theology only affords a marginal consideration of the role of Christ, his activity in the liturgy, except in the case of the Eucharistic sacrifice. Even less attention is paid to the role of the Holy Spirit. The latter characteristic is due to the traditional Catholic scholastic teaching that the sanctifying work of the Trinity is common to all three persons, except for the case of the incarnation in which the humanity of Jesus is assumed by the Word in hypostatic union. The texts of Scripture as well as the teachings of the Fathers of the Church which speak of the sanctifying work of the Spirit, are interpreted to mean that the Spirit is sanctifier only by way of "appropriation," that is to say, because the work of sanctification accords with the name "spirit."

The absence of pneumatology, the theology of the Holy Spirit, in Western systematic theology had a profound influence on the understanding of the nature of sacramental grace. Nevertheless, other presuppositions more directly contributed to an infra-personal concept of this reality. Sacramental grace, the grace proper to each sacrament, is conceived in neoscholasticism as including sanctifying grace. This latter grace, a supernatural entity, is described as a divinely bestowed disposition that qualifies the recipient of the sacrament for union with uncreated grace, that is, the indwelling Trinity. After the Council of Trent, Catholic theology, following the lead of an earlier tendency, developed the distinction between created grace (supernatural elevating grace) and uncreated grace (God's self-communication). This was done in such a way that a certain disjunction was either postulated or presupposed between the two realities of grace. In other words, the simultaneous presence of both graces in the soul of the just person was considered to be a fact. However, absolutely speaking, the presence of the dispositive grace did not imply the presence of the uncreated grace. Rather, the uncreated grace was perceived as more or less the complement of the created grace.

II.
Twentieth Century Catholic Theology of the Sacraments

Twentieth-century Catholic theology continues to recognize the valuable contributions of the scholastic treatises on principles of sacramental theology. At the same time, modern scholarly researches in the fields of biblical exegesis, history of dogma, liturgy, systematic theology, and the human sciences have brought to light the limitations of this theological synthesis. They have demonstrated the need for a thorough rethinking of the traditional outlook. Some of the major contributions to the renewal of sacramental theology made prior to, or shortly after, the completion of the Second Vatican Council, are described below.

A. Grace

Neoscholasticism conceives humanity as coming forth from God in an act of creation, a purely gratuitous gift. As created being, humanity is ordered to a destiny that corresponds to its corporeal and spiritual perfections. This humanity could have been granted the fate of an eternal, natural bliss, without frustrating the act of God by which it was created. However God intervened, in a second act, to confer on humanity a supernatural finality. To accomplish this, God bestowed a created grace as an addition. Thereby humanity was elevated to a new level of existence, disposed for a participation in the divine life of the Trinity.

Both the so-called conservative and progressive wings of modern Catholic theology severely criticize this theological outlook, insofar as it postulates the real existence of humanity, closed in on itself and granted a natural finality. The idea that humanity ever existed in a state of pure nature, and had a corresponding nature destiny, is reckoned to be without historical foundation. This does not mean, however, that the supernatural destiny of humanity corresponds to the exigencies of human nature as such. It does mean that God determined created humanity from the outset, by a purely gratuitous act, for a fate that transcends the human condition. Consequently, recent Catholic theology affirms that grace, by which humanity is elevated to a supernatural destiny, was conferred from the beginning of the existence of humanity. This divine grace, the self-communication of God, in the Spirit, is always and everywhere present to human beings, orientating them toward personal communion with the divine Trinity. Grace-events, which occur at definite moments in time and space, are instances of the acceptance of God's self-communication by the historical, free acts of human beings. From this point of view, actual graces are explained as the dynamic aspect of the divine saving presence seeking to evoke the free response of humankind. These actual graces are called "only sufficient" insofar as they meet with rejection on the part of the free person. They are called "efficacious" insofar as they meet with acceptance. In other words, actual graces are not described as "sufficient" or "efficacious" from the viewpoint of the divine initiative, but from the standpoint of the openness of the human person to God's loving invitation.

The modern Catholic understanding of grace, an instance of the recovery of a neglected or forgotten truth, has important consequences for the theology of the grace-event of the sacramental celebrations. Sacraments do not appear to be isolated instances of God's saving actions in space and time. Rather, they are understood as special moments of an activity occurring always and everywhere, when human beings respond to God in accord with their understanding of the true meaning of their existence. Sacraments supply the special context in which God's self communication can be more fully accepted.

B. Faith and Sacraments

Neoscholastic theology describes sacramental celebrations as events in which something is offered for consumption to more or less passive subjects. The sacrament is "administered" by the presiding minister to the "recipient." The necessary conditions for a fruitful reception of the sacrament, by an apt subject, are the intention to receive the grace signified and the habitual dispositions which correspond to the purpose of the particular sacrament. Thus the subject of a sacrament is depicted as having less than an active role in the communication of grace.

The rethinking of the relationship between faith and sacrament has led in modern times to a more personalistic approach to the "recipient" of a sacrament. It is now more clearly seen that the active response of the subject is an intregral part of the liturgical action. On it depends the grace-event of the celebration. In other words, the personal offer of grace by the Father, through Christ in the Spirit, requires a corresponding personal response on the part of the adult subject. This way of explaining the matter of efficacy of the sacraments corresponds to the orientation of the whole liturgical tradition. Moreover it offsets a possible misunderstanding that sacraments automatically confer grace on those who are habitually disposed to receive that grace.

C. Church and Sacraments

The modern stress on the importance of the active participation of the subjects of sacramental celebrations has contributed to a new view of the relationship between Church and sacraments. In the neoscholastic outlook, sacraments are seen as special gifts confided to the Church and administered by the qualified minister in the name of Christ. More precisely, they are described as acts of the competent representative of Christ, which take place *within* the Church. Consequently, the Church is understood to be the dispenser of sacraments, through its ministers who are authorized by Christ. From this point of view, it is not altogether clear why sacraments, absolutely speaking, could not have been entrusted to some other institution.

Modern Catholic theology provides the reason why sacraments can only be celebrated in the Church. Returning to the patristic understanding of the relation between Church and sacraments, Catholic theology has recovered the truth that sacraments are acts of the Church itself, not merely acts which, by Christ's will, take place only in the Church. The Church can be said to dispense sacraments. But this means that these celebrations are acts by which the Church actualizes itself as agent of Christ. In short, sacraments are acts that flow from the very nature of the Church.

D. Christ

Modern Catholic theology has brought to the foreground, in a new way, the central message of the Christian tradition: the permanent, active presence of the risen Lord and his saving work in the whole scope of the life of the Church. Neoscholastic theology stressed the personal presence and activity of Christ in the celebration of the Eucharistic sacrifice, with special attention given to Christ's unique mode of presence in the Eucharistic species. Current Catholic theology displays a greater awareness of the personal and active presence of Christ in all liturgical activity. The recovery of this neglected truth has brought with it a new consciousness of the mystery dimension of each and every aspect of a liturgical celebration. Christ's active presence is associated not only with the essential kernel of a sacramental celebration. Rather the surrounding liturgical prayers and symbolic actions, the scriptural readings and homily, are all more consciously valued as complementary ways in which the Lord communicates with his Church.

E. Holy Spirit

The teaching about the active role of Christ in the whole of the liturgical celebrations of the Church is complemented by the growing concern of Catholic theology to work out a better explanation of the role of the Holy Spirit in the liturgy. It is commonly recognized that one of the main tasks of sacramental theology is the rethinking of the implications of the patristic teaching about the personal mission of the Spirit to the Church, and the consequences that follow for the theology of the sacraments.

As yet the pneumatological dimension of the sacraments has received only marginal attention in Catholic theology. This is easily demonstrated by a perusal of the table of contents of recent contributions. With notable exceptions, references to the Holy Spirit are incidental. Only infrequently is the attempt made to integrate the missions of both the Word and the Holy Spirit into a sacramental theology in a systematic way.

F. Human Sciences

Especially since the Second Vatican Council, a growing interest has been manifested by Catholic theologians in the potential of the human sciences to contribute to a modern theology of liturgy. There seems to be a general awareness of the importance of employing, at every stage of theological reflection on sacraments, the findings of these disciplines on the subject of symbolic activity, ritual conduct, conditions for the experience of transcendence, and the role of celebration in human life.

All the more recent insights described above provide the basis for a new systematic approach to Christian liturgy and, in particular, to the chief rites of the Church. There is need of a new version of the old scholastic *De sacramentis in genere*. Partial syntheses by theologians of the first rank have provided valuable contributions toward this goal. But they are often substituted by less gifted disciples for the more comprehensive, if imperfect, scholastic treatises. There is even a surprisingly common tendency to use one word to describe the nature of a sacrament, which is favored by some influential theologians, to express a par-

result in the cult of certain theses, which foster an even narrower understanding of sacraments than that of neoscholasticism; the second contributes to the nurturing of a form of nominalism even worse than that of
late scholasticism.

III.
Second Vatican Council[1]

The Second Vatican Council was strongly influenced by the solid
gains of modern liturgical scholars and systematic theologians, and it attempted to integrate many of these contributions within its doctrinal approach to the liturgy. *The Constitution on the Sacred Liturgy*
(*Sacrosanctum Concilium*) refers to the relationship between the
participants' faith and the fixed liturgical forms of expression of this
faith in such a way as to challenge theologians to think more deeply
about the intimate relation between faith and sacraments (59). The
Church is described as a sacramental reality (26). Hence the Church's
relation to the sacraments is placed in a new light. *The Dogmatic Constitution* on the Church (*Lumen gentium*) develops more fully the concept of the sacramental nature of the Church (1; 48). This constitution
introduces the profound notion that the Church is not only made by the
sacraments but also *makes the sacraments* (26; 11).

Sacrosanctum Concilium repeatedly mentions the importance of the
active participation of the whole liturgical assembly, priest and laity (11;
14; 27; 48; 50). It points out that the implementation of this ideal can
only be realized through personal communication among the participants. Employing the language and principles of the science of communication, the constitution emphasizes the need for understandable
rites (34; 72) and linguistic exchange (36; 54). In this way human communication is identified as pertaining to the essence of Christian liturgy.

The constitution on the liturgy affords an insight into the relationship
between what the community does and what God does in liturgical
celebrations. The communication between the human participants of
the liturgy has a depth dimension, known only by faith. At this deeper
level, an exchange takes place between God and his people: "For in the
liturgy God speaks to his people, and Christ is still proclaiming his
gospel. And the people reply to God by song and prayer" (33). In short,
the liturgical expression of the faith of the Church is construed as an ap-

peal of God, in Christ, to the liturgical assembly. This is understandable because of the nature of the liturgy. The Spirit inspires the Church to express its life of faith in fixed forms that correspond to the very content of the life of faith: the self-communication of the Father, through Christ, in the Holy Spirit.

The liturgical celebration is a response of faith of the community to the inner-word of faith. This response to the hidden self-communication of God, which is experienced in the depth of the existence of believers, is prayer. But this prayer is made in union with Christ who, in the power of the Holy Spirit, is the source of the prayer of faith. Christ, in the power of the Spirit, is the source of the real communication between the liturgical assembly and the Father of all.

Sacrosanctum Concilium refers to the active presence of Christ and his saving mysteries in the Church, "especially in her liturgical celebrations" (7). The risen Lord is described as the chief speaker and actor of the liturgical assembly, who communicates with his members through the expression of the faith of the Church of which he, in the Spirit, is the vital source. As a result, the faithful are aroused and made capable of interacting with the Lord, of addressing the Father through the one mediator between God and humankind.

The idea that the liturgy is the expression of the faith of the Church is well expressed in a passage of the constitution that links faith to the chief rites of the Church. It is said of the seven sacraments that "They not only presuppose the faith, but through words and things also nourish it, strengthen it and express it" (59). This outlook furnishes the basis for understanding the formulas of the essential sacramental rites, the so-called *forms of the sacraments (forma sacramentorum)*, as primarily a *prayer.* Thus a relatively new concept of the dynamics of sacramental celebrations, new at least for scholastic theology, is made available. In this perspective, the essential sacramental gestures and formulas are not interpreted exclusively as signifying a movement from God to the subjects of the celebration. Rather, they point also, and in the first place, to the movement of the liturgical assembly toward God.

This brief description of some of the contributions of Vatican II toward the reformulation of a new theology of the sacraments may serve to indicate the overall approach of the council itself. The council refrained from issuing dogmatic definitions, while seeking to grasp the meaning of the liturgy, under all its aspects, from a pastoral point of view. Consequently, the conciliar reflection on the liturgy begins with the liturgy itself. This approach enabled the *Sacrosanctum Concilium* to speak more concretely about the immediate subject of the liturgical celebration. An opening was provided for a corrective to the neoscholastic concept of the subject of liturgy.

In traditional Catholic school theology, the immediate subject of the liturgy includes the holy members of the Church throughout the world who unite themselves with the presiding minister by their intention. Currently, Catholic theologians seems to be more open to the idea that the holy members of the Church are correctly seen as implicated only mediately in the concrete liturgies of the universal Church, through the prayer which they make for the strengthening of the faith of each liturgical assembly. This point of view seems to correspond best to the whole tradition of the East and West, which identifies the direct subject of the liturgy as the local assembly of believers.

IV.
The Relationship Among the Four Sections of This Book

The proven contributions of modern Catholic scholarship to the theology of liturgy, and the orientation of Vatican II on the same subject, provide a valuable blueprint for the work of constructing a new systematic theology of liturgy. Some of the more important elements that must be integrated into this synthesis are elaborated in the following chapters.

Chapter 2, which also serves an introductory function, completes Part I. It describes contributions of the human sciences to the understanding and practice of Christian worship. Part II situates the liturgy within the broader context of the history of salvation (Ch. 3), and the relation between divine revelation and the experience of transcendence (Ch. 4). The concluding chapter treats the role of liturgy in the whole of the life of faith (Ch. 5). Part III contains a systematic theology of liturgy, grounded on a theology of the economic Trinity (Chs. 6-12). Part IV provides a systematic treatment of principles of sacramental theology, with special reference to traditional theological problems linked to the seven sacraments (Chs. 13-19).

Notes

1. H. Volk, THEOLOGISCHE GRUNDLAGEN DER LITURGIE (Mainz: Matthias-Grünewald, 1964); A. Bugnini & C. Braga, eds., THE COMMENTARY ON THE CONSTITUTION AND THE INSTRUCTION ON THE SACRED LITURGY (New York: Benziger, 1965); W. Barauna, ed., THE LITURGY OF VATICAN II, 2 vols. (Chicago: Franciscan, 1966); J. A. Jungmann, Commentary on SACROSANCTUM CONCILIUM in DAS ZWEITE VATICANISCHE KONZIL. Commentaire I. LEXIKON FÜR THEOLOGIE UND KIRCHE, Supplement (Freiburg im Br.: Herder, 1966); F. McManus, SACRAMENTAL LITURGY (New York: Herder, 1967); E. J. Kilmartin, "The Sacred Liturgy: Reform and Renewal," in C. Last, ed., REMEMBERING THE FUTURE: VATICAN II AND TOMORROW'S LITURGICAL AGENDA (New York: Paulist, 1983) 33-47.

Chapter 2

Human Sciences and

Sacramental Theology

Catholic theology assumes that the final arbiter in the matter of interpretation of the meaning of liturgical activity of the Church is the understanding of the Church, based on the knowledge of faith. The global perception of the life of faith, which impregnates and structures the lives of believers, gives rise to the interpretation of liturgy. Those who have the office of teaching in the Church have the chief responsibility for articulating this understanding. Guided by the Holy Spirit, the teaching office formulates the conviction of believers. This teaching, given in the form of solemn definitions intended to evoke the unqualified assent of members of the Church, always tends toward the full expression of the truth about the aspect of the liturgy under consideration. Catholic theology takes for granted that such statements furnish a true perspective on the mystery of the liturgy. Hence it is axiomatic, for Catholic theologians, that the interpretation of liturgy is logically irreducible beyond that given by the community of faith, aspects of which are sometimes proposed in the form of solemn dogmas. However, this does not mean that the sciences, which study the human being under all the modalities of human existence, are incapable of contributing significantly to the fuller practice of the Christian liturgy.

Christian liturgy has a depth dimension, graspable only through the knowledge of faith. On the other hand, liturgy is an activity of the earthly Church, living under the laws of historical, human existence. Human sciences can contribute to the clarification of those presuppositions for an effective celebration of the earthly liturgy, which comes under the laws governing the existence and growth of human communities. These sciences can also provide information about the role of liturgy in the event of personal communication between the saving God and the community of believers.

Human sciences base their findings on the objective evidence which they are able to measure by their particular methods. They analyze the human side of the liturgy, leaving the question open about the truth of faith's claim to a transcendent dimension. The data that these sciences furnish to the theologian is indispensable for a realistic approach to liturgy. Only by taking account of the laws that govern effective human communication, in the sphere of celebrations of the communal life of stable communities, can the temptation to construct an esoteric theology of worship be avoided. There is always the danger of a tendency to isolate liturgical practice from the so-called profane sphere of human existence, and even from the religious sphere of Christian daily life.

God communicates with his people in and through history, in and through historical forms of human communication. The human sciences analyze the laws governing this communication. They furnish data, which should accompany and support theological reflection at each stage of its progress in the interpretation of liturgy. Some of the contributions of these sciences to the theology of liturgy are described below.

I. Modern Anthropology [1]

Modern anthropology takes as its point of departure the description of the human being furnished by phenomenology, that is, the human being as it appears to the senses in its moods and presuppositions. From this perspective, an understanding of the human person is derived which differs considerably from an older view. The human person is no longer seen as a kind of self-contained spiritual being that employs the body to communicate itself to the world. The idea is abandoned that humankind has a twofold nature, in which the spiritual side is able to come into operation independently of the corporeal. Rather than conceiving the human being as spirit enclosed in the body, the body is understood to be the real symbol of the human spirit. The unity of being between the spiritual and corporeal components is such that the human being must be described as *embodied spirit*. As such, the spirit of the human person depends on the body for its contact with the world. The spirit does not turn by itself, in a second act, to others and things. On the contrary, it is by bodily contact that the human spirit is activated to turn itself toward the surrounding reality.

Spirit and body are so intimately united that human development is conditioned by their interaction. This exchange affords the possibility of progressive development in the areas of consciousness, liberty, and love. The human being develops through the exercise of the freedom with which it is endowed. But in order to develop, one must go out of oneself in a process initiated by bodily contact with surrounding reality.

As a being of the cosmos, humankind is dependent on the surrounding world of realities for biological and human growth. Human persons differ from animals through understanding. But they do not generate ideas from themselves alone. For this they are dependent on the power of conception, and so are referred to the sensible world. The human being has the capacity to react to non-verbal and verbal stimuli. This assures the comprehension of objects and their correlations. Humans also have the linguistic capacity to control and codify information. This verbal thinking undertakes the analysis of the connections between things and their appearances by a series of successive operations.

In the process of reaching out to the world, the human being continually uses words to work with images, or to associate images. But the effort to penetrate the meaning of realities runs up against the problem of distinguishing, and relating, the variety of the real. Consequently, a world of symbols is developed in order to establish connections between the plurality, a connection which cannot be seen or touched.

The world of symbols derives from images, originating in the direct perception of external reality. These symbols transcend the purely physical data and, at the same time, bestow meaning on it. The symbol "man" or "woman" contains characteristics which enable the thinking being to apply it to a variety of men and women. These symbols can also be referred to other physical beings, which manifest particular traits of men or women.

The relation between image and word is one of dependence. They always belong together and, in turn, are dependent on a specific context. The word is provoked by the image, and the image is interpreted by the word. The working together of image and word yields a system of symbols, which enable the thinking human to bestow meaning on the realities of the cosmos.

A. Outward and Inward Perception

So far we have pointed out the fact of the mutual dependence of the human spirit and body. But it has also been shown with the same data that human beings have the experience of outward and inward perception. They experience an outward perception, an outward seeing and hearing. But there is also the inward perception, an inward seeing and hearing, which enables the creation of a world of symbols. The inward seeing and hearing corresponds to the outward seeing and hearing. The outward perception remains at the surface of things; the inward penetrates to the depth of realities in varying degrees. Consequently, there is also a way of speaking which remains at a superficial level, and another way of speaking which opens up the depth dimension of reality for those who have the capacity to hear the message.

All human beings have the experience that what is essential is seen with the heart, and is not perceived merely with the eye. What is seen at first glance has a deeper meaning not yet revealed. The coupling and crossing of the outward and inward, at play in perception and speaking, reveal the essential structure of the human: embodied spirit. Because of this structure, humans are able to penetrate beyond the superficial, to make connections between things and establish meaning. This structure is the ground for what is called authentic human communication, communication in which meaning is exchanged between people through bodily contact. In this process, the human body's role cannot be adequately described as the instrument by which the human spirit moves out to the world of persons and things, dependent only on its own dynamism. Rather the body is best described as a *real symbol.*

1. Body as Real Symbol

The original Greek word *symbolon*, in its verbal form, means "to throw together." Initially the noun signified a sign of recognition between two person: Two broken pieces of a coin, for example, when joined together, produce a whole, indicative of some form of relation between the possessors. The term "real symbol," can be used in contradistinction to a particular understanding of sign. From this point of view, a sign signifies a reality with which it is not joined in unity of being. In other words, there is no complete correspondence between being and meaning, so that the distance between the signifying and signified reality is not fully overcome. For example, signs of peace between nations can exist, but this does not guarantee the reality of peaceful coexistence. The term real symbol, however, is used where unity of being exists between the signifying and signified reality. A symbol of this type is given where there is unity of being between matter and spirit. Man, embodied spirit, represents an instance where the body is real symbol of the whole person. According to Catholic traditional belief, another example is the eucharistic species, the sacrament of Christ's body and blood.

The human way of existence is corporeal. Through the body, the human being gains consciousness of self as a being in the world, and in relation to others and the things of the cosmos. The body is the most original manifestation of the person to self, and the source of self-knowledge. However, as the original symbol of the human being, the body is not static. It is caught up in a process of growth. The body is not only the most original epiphany of human beings, the most immediate way by which they are revealed to themselves and to others. The body is also the primordial act of the human, by which self-knowledge is generated.

From the moment of birth, the body begins to grow. Eventually, it waxes, wanes, and succumbs. In this biological process the body is a realizing sign: It corporealizes, realizes, and so signifies the mystery of the human person. In this process, one moment is not simply like another. There are special junctures of the biological life, which become new sources of self-knowledge.[2] There are situations of the biological life in which the whole of human existence is condensed, where past and present, the meaning and non-meaning of human existence are at issue. Here human beings are referred symbolically beyond themselves. Such junctures are puberty, sickness, the infirmity of old age. They reveal that the human person is an open question to which no ready answer can be given. In such situations, humans experience themselves as referred beyond themselves to some mysterious finality, which remains undisclosed. Along with the experience of being unable to extricate oneself from the concrete situation of crisis, there is also that of being a free being able to assume a stance concerning the meaning and direction of one's life.

The situations described above can be called "boundary situations"[3] because, despite the freedom of the human being to make changes and to manipulate things and other people, this particular kind reveals one's inability to control one's own destiny. These situations, which cannot be manipulated but must be accepted and endured, manifest the finitude of the human being, and so raise the question about the meaning of life.

The biological junctures are potentially symbolic. But for them to become symbols, there is needed intentionality: a spiritual, conscious activity. They become symbols when the person does not ignore them. To the extent that one recognizes their significance, these situations become sources of self-knowledge. There are also analogous situations in the sphere of social life. The call to make a decision about the course of one's adult life, or about coming to the aid of others who make unconditional demands in their absolute need, cannot be manipulated. These situations can be set aside, ignored for a time, but they remain, and call for a human response. How is one to answer?

We owe the experiences mentioned above to our human condition. Our human spirit penetrates the biological and social situations of crisis in which we find ourselves, and seeks to clothe them with meaning. However the search for meaning is never conducted in isolation from one's social context.

2. The Human Being as Being of History

The boundary situations in which humans find themselves call for a response about the meaning of life. But they are not experienced in a vacuum. For the normal human being belongs to a community in which such situations are already given interpretations. The fundamental, common situations of human existence, of the biological and social order, occur in a context of traditional interpretation. Human existence is mediated in and through human history, or, more precisely, the meaning of human existence, under all its aspects, is mediated through the tradition of a human community.

The society in which we live provides us with a word, a timely word, which interprets these situations, and which includes or excludes different possibilities of meaning and choice. Here the word exercises its most original function. Evoked by the situation, the word of tradition illumines it and qualifies it. The word does not merely give information. It enlightens the human situation and thereby furnishes the key to the response that must be made in order that one can give meaning and direction to one's life.

In short, the timely word, the word spoken at the right time, determines the meaning of a boundary situation. Furthermore, the word not only has the power to shed light on a given situation of crisis, it can also create and change a situation. Through the word spoken at the right time, a present historical context, without apparent eventful potential, can become a human situation which calls for a decision.

This consideration of the relation between word and human situation enables us to appreciate the solid anthropological grounding of the Christian sacraments. Sacramental rites employ doxological and rhetorical language, enriched by images drawn from a variety of spheres of human life. Together with symbolic actions, these forms of verbal expression signify a human and social situation. At the same time, the word announces that God's saving presence is to be found in these situations, and how the participants of the celebration should respond. In this type of activity, a particular human situation is no longer referred to an undetermined, impersonal, and dark transcendence, but to God's love. The situation is proclaimed to be filled with God's presence, and the participants are instructed about the appropriate response.

The foregoing insight into the relationship of mutual dependence between word and palpable human situations which call for decision, allows us to view the sacraments in an analogous way. However, caution should be exercised when it is a question of identifying analogies, drawn from daily life, which can be applied to shed light on events of the life of faith. Walter Kasper, dependent on Gerhard Ebeling's explanation of the relation between word and human situation[4] that was given above, applies it to the sacraments. He concludes that sacraments represent human primordinal situations, and make them, through the word, situations of salvation, times of grace and signs of God's grace for believers.[5]

This approach cannot be faulted insofar as it identifies a possible analogy taken from the world of daily life, which is applicable to sacramental celebrations. But the analogy is weak. Lurking behind Kasper's analysis is a concept of sacramental word too closely identified with the preaching of the word of God. The difference between the two instances of word of God is not sufficiently appreciated. If, following Karl Rahner's description, we can speak of the sacramental word as the highest instance of the word of God spoken in the Church, there still remains the question: What is the nature of the sacramental word, which gives it this peculiar status? Scholastic theology could easily agree with Rahner's explanation, assumed by Kasper, that the sacramental word has this peculiarity because it is a word spoken by the Church, organ of salvation, in favor of the individual in special situations of the life of faith. For scholastic theology tends to view the essential symbolic gesture and formula of the sacraments as having an exclusively katabatic, or downward, direction, from God to the recipient.

If we remain with Kasper's analogy, the impression is given that the sacramental word has the exclusive function of interpreting how the individual is to respond to the human and social situation, which calls for the decision of faith. The preaching of the word of God has the function of providing instruction about the way in which one is to respond to God in the variety of human situations in order to live a life conformed to the gospel. The sacramental word, by its very nature, also has the function of orientation, that is, it supplies instruction about the appropriate response to the human situation that is being celebrated in favor of a subject. But the sacramental word is essentially a *prayer* addressed to the Father, through Jesus Christ in the Holy Spirit, made by the community of faith on behalf of the subject of the sacrament. In the case of the adult subject, it is presupposed that previous instruction has led to the request for the sacrament. We will return to this subject later on. For now it suffices to note that it is ultimately a theology of prayer which determines the depth of meaning of the sacramental word.

B. Efficacy of Human Engagement

Under the general theme of anthropology, it is worth noting another consideration that sheds some light on the dynamics of sacramental celebrations. The experience of love, beauty, truth, etc. is conditioned by truly human activity, the engagement of the whole person. Such engagements lead to a humanizing experience, the depth of which is measured by the intensity of the human involvement. But the experience of truly human values does not find its most profound source in the human engagement itself. The human engagement does not simply create the experience by itself. Rather the experience is mediated through the encounter with what is of human value. The experience comes as a gift.

The human activity, through the dispositions accompanying it, makes possible the occurrence of the humanizing event.[6]

This observation has an important application in sacramental theology. In the liturgical action a human engagement of faith takes place through the ritual action. Likewise, in the same ritual action, a divine intervention occurs in favor of the participants. But the dynamics of this process does not differ from the essential structure of any authentic human engagement, which results in the experience of truth, through meditative reading of the Scriptures, the experience of the beauty of autumn foliage, etc. The law of correspondence between the human engagement and the resulting humanizing event is applicable to the matter of the conditions necessary for fruitful participation in the sacraments.

In sacramental celebrations there is no question of two agencies, divine and human, producing an effect by a conjoint action, which is greater than the sum of the effects of the two agencies taken separately. This concept of "synergism" must be excluded because the human and divine agencies do not enter the process as independent partners. On the other hand, the two agencies should not be so contrasted with one another that the idea of cooperation is given only marginal consideration.

In other words, the activity of God and the activity of the subjects of sacramental celebrations should not be conceived in this way: The divine activity gains in intensity in the measure that the human activity in faith is impaired, or lessens in intensity in the measure that the human engagement increases. This way of conceiving the efficacy of the sacraments is typical of scholastic theology, which stresses the objective efficacy of the sacraments to the neglect of the importance of the active, personal engagement of the subjects. In order to grasp the presuppositions for a fruitful engagement in a sacramental celebration, one that results in the event of communication of the grace signified, it is useful to introduce the concept of the correspondence between authentic human engagement with the world of persons and things, and the humanizing event that follows and is perceived as a gift. For, in the case of sacramental celebrations, there is the matter of human engagement, albeit an engagement of the life of faith. Therefore, the effect that follows is measured by the intensity of the involvement of the participants of the liturgical activity.

C. Symbolic Perception

Symbolic perception, the ability to penetrate beyond the superficial appearances of reality, is essential for the living of a fully human life. All the more does this power serve an irreplaceable function in the life of the Church, especially in corporate worship. It is axiomatic that the Church exists in a community to the extent that the members perceive God's presence in the midst of the liturgical assembly. For the communal response to God's hidden address, the prayer of faith, is constitutive of the community of faith. If the community does not pray, it does not believe in the One who has called it to be church, and cannot be called the church of God.

The symbolic language and gestures of liturgy are calculated to appeal to the symbolic perception of the participants, to enable them to perceive Christ's saving presence, to arouse them to engage themselves in, with, and through Christ in the worship of the Father of all. Those who are conditioned to perceive the concrete world as symbol of transcendence and of the transcendent God himself, find in the ritual celebrations of the Church an important opportunity to share in the mystery of the community's life in Christ.

However, this modern industrial age has been conditioned to think of the real world as that which can be verified by instruments of measurement under human control. To the extent that this has become a habitual disposition, it becomes increasingly difficult to perceive the external world as a sign of non-measurable reality over which human beings have no control. Correlatively, there reigns the suspicion about all experience of transcendent reality.

There is some truth to the often heard saying that modern technological humans are conditioned to define the reality around them in terms of objects in themselves, that is, as that which is measurable and can be manipulated. The meaning of the world that lies beyond its immediate usefulness tends to be overlooked. The old biblical and patristic idea, that all creation is through the Word of God and bears the mark of truth, is in the Spirit of God and bears the quality of goodness, is largely neglected. The notion that all reality has been given meaning by God, and is a medium of encounter with God, has given way to the conviction that it is up to humankind to give meaning to the world.

The loss of perception of the multidimensional levels of reality has its effect on the quality of Christian involvement in the liturgy. To the extent that the community lacks the power of inward perception, a serious pastoral problem exists. What can the human sciences be expected to contribute to remedy this situation?

1. Psychology and Sociology

We can begin a response to this question with a brief description of what can be expected from psychology and sociology. These thematic sciences provide information about techniques, based on statistically calculated laws. Psychology investigates how symbols are formed and function in the psychic life of individuals and groups. This discipline explains how symbols are linked to fundamental needs of the human being, and how their perception can be conditioned. Sociology analyzes social institutions and clarifies their role in the social life of humankind. This science is concerned with symbols as social institutions.

Psychology offers many valuable insights on the subject of *symbolic competence*, the capacity to link traditional symbols with one's own adult personal symbols. The application of the findings of psychology, in this matter, to the task of promoting more effective liturgical participation is illuminating. It can be shown that a catechesis of the sacraments must take into account the modern condition of human existence and its influence on the life of faith. Also, concrete contexts are identified, to which participants of the liturgy may be expected to respond in a religious way.

Sociological studies commonly define the moods and motivations of people in modern industrial civilization as those whose underlying drive is toward rational attainment of goals through the individual achievements of members, using persons and things as the means. Therefore the conclusion is drawn that an alternative disposition is needed, if the symbolic dimension of reality is to be experienced. This disposition is described as *appreciative consciousness:* the ability to experience something or someone in itself. The development of this ability, which orientates humankind toward the mysterious dimensions of life, obviously requires the development of the attitude and practice of contemplation.

Sociological research has called attention to the modern experience of transcendence associated especially with the common sharing of the human condition. This experience is related more generally to everyday situations, and less with extraordinary events and circumstances.[7] Above all, this experience appears not to be orientated toward the domain of official, institutional religion. To the extent that the analysis of sociologists is correct, a special challenge is offered to those who must take responsibility for promoting effective Christian liturgy. To be effective, communal worship must be conducted more consciously as the activity of a community; its relation to concrete daily life must be manifested in a more explicit way.

2. Phenomenology

While psychology and sociology provide valuable information regarding the means of promoting effective liturgy, these thematic sciences presuppose what has become problematical: the meaningfulness of the gospel message, and its liturgical expression for modern people. Phenomenology has a special contribution to make in this regard. This science describes the being of the human person as a whole, in its thought, moods, and presuppositions. Phenomenological studies show that the experience of the holy belongs to situations in which the question of ultimate meaning is raised. The distinction between the sacred and profane is placed at the level of understanding. In other words, everything profane has a sacral dimension, if its deepest meaning is penetrated. The study of those areas in ordinary daily life, where questions of meaning are raised, can lead to a sharper view of where experiences may grow which enable the modern person to newly articulate the names of the holy.

The data of phenomenology provides a clue to the way in which the catechesis of the sacraments might begin. At the outset, there would be introduced some reflection on how one relates to oneself, to concrete things, and people. Contemplation is needed, which brings the awareness that life is not only to be lived but pondered. A phenomenological introduction to the doctrine of the sacraments is gaining in popularity today. The audience may be invited to recall their experiences of the depth of meaning in daily happenings. This approach can also take the form of the narrative of one's own discovery of meaning in routine living, and the subsequent experience in sacramental celebrations. Through this method it is possible to show convincingly that anything can be cognized as a symbol of something transcendent, and even of the transcendent God himself. In this way a broad experiential basis can be cultivated, as preparation for the active participation in the liturgy.

II.
The Science of Liturgy and the Human Sciences

The science of liturgy is concerned with a specific form of communal activity of a particular stable community. The problem for the liturgist corresponds to the formal object of this science, that is, the Church insofar as it accepts the saving work of Jesus Christ and responds prayerfully to the Father of all blessings. Consequently, this fundamental question is posed: What form of liturgy enables the worshipping assembly to enter into saving dialogue with the God who continually works among his people? Since the assembly is composed of individual members, an answer to this question entails inquiry about the person who is being formed by the liturgy, and the conditions under which the formation is realized. At this point the anthropological sciences make their contribution.

Psychology informs us that liturgy is effective to the extent that the participants are enabled to make connections between the adult, personal symbols through which they carry on their daily lives, and the traditional, fixed symbolic expressions of Christian faith. Studies in this field also formulate laws that must be taken into account if any form of communal activity is to be effective in promoting the life of the stable community. Sociological research underscores the need for cultivating appreciative consciousness in modern civilization, and provides helpful direction toward the development of the alternative disposition to the typical moods and motivations of the present technological age. The findings of phenomenology are particularly relevant to the promotion of liturgical celebrations that make a difference in the lives of believers.

After the general inquiry about the person who is the subject of the liturgy, the liturgist has this further question to answer: What forms of liturgical activity are effective for the community of believers as such? An adequate response to this question is not possible without knowledge of the nature of the Church. This knowledge is gained by knowing what the Church has been in the past. Since knowledge of what the Church has been in the past derives from what the Church has done in the past, it is evident that the study of the history of the Church's activity is indispensable for the gaining of knowledge of what the Church is. Correspondingly, the history of the liturgy is relevant to the determination of what the Church is, and what forms of liturgy can be expected to support and develop the life of faith in the modern world. In other words, the liturgical life of past generations provides laws of liturgical communication, which enabled Christians to experience God's saving presence and to name God in their response of praise and thanksgiving. These laws are applicable to the Church of today. Here we can only mention a few examples.[9]

The Old and New Testaments record the initial and normative encounters of the creature with the God of revelation. These sources provide a wealth of information about God's names, actions and ways of speaking, as well as the conditions under which an appropriate response can be given. Concrete laws are reflected, apart from which no nearness of God is experienced in the public forum.

The form of address of God to the people, through the mouths of the prophets, is one example: "Thus says the Lord, your God." This corresponds to the statement of the letter of the Council of Jerusalem, which was sent to the Christian community at Antioch: "It is the decision of the Holy Spirit, and ours too..." (Acts 15:28). The Old Testament psalms supply many forms of expression of the experience of the absence of God which, nevertheless, include petition for God's help (Ps 10; 13; 102, etc.). The psalms are particularly useful as models for fashioning liturgy in the midst of modern society which, itself, experiences God as the distant God.

The Old and New Testament provide material and norms both for examining the quality and potential of the renewed liturgy, and for promoting the experience of God speaking and acting in the midst of the assembly. Phenomenology, the works of painters, poets, musicians, offer a glimpse into those spheres of human life where the experiences are nourished which enable the articulation of the names of the ground of human existence in a new and more effective way. But even more can be learned from the sources of revelation about where God can be discovered, and how he is to be addressed.

Above all, the Cross of Jesus Christ, the primary symbol of Christian faith, should serve as the model of the liturgical expression of this faith. This symbol represents, on the one hand, the inhumanity of human beings toward the incarnate Son of God; on the other hand, it represents the victorious love of God for all humanity. It calls under judgment all attempts to subordinate the human being to the limited goals of worldly power and, at the same time, guarantees the meaning of every activity aimed at the removal of whatever contributes to dehumanization of the children of God.

Since liturgy continually announces the liberation of humanity through the Cross of Christ, especially in the celebration of the Eucharist, the forms of liturgy should be fashioned and celebrated in such a way that they contribute to the disclosure of concrete conditions of daily life that retard human growth. As celebration of the life of faith, liturgy aims at the development of the whole person, a centered-self, freed to affirm one's own inviolable worth and to contribute to the human growth of others. The ideal liturgy is one in which the participants find the opportunity to play out their resolve to live a life worthy of children of God. Where this ideal is approached, the liturgy becomes the *practice* of that hope, which alone sustains the daily life of faith.

III.
Phenomenology of Religious Worship

Christian liturgy falls under the category of the worldwide phenomenon of religious worship, the communal expression of the basic interests and value relations of a stable religious community. What is commonly called "authentic religious worship" has certain common characteristics. This form of expression of social life comes under the broader heading of a category of communal activity of social groups of a secular character, by which the identity and purpose of the group is represented. The latter type of activity is located at what can be called the horizontal level of human life. It has a purely functional role to play at the level of the human, social reality, and makes no claim to aim at, or include, a dimension that transcends the purely human.

Traits common to the forms of communal activity that represent the identity and purpose of a secular or religious group, provide valuable information about the origin, structure, meaning and function of Christian worship, as well as the laws governing its effectiveness. This theme can be presented in various ways. The path chosen here begins with the concept of culture and the derivative subculture. Then the connection between these two realities, and what is called cult, is examined. From there we proceed to the analysis of the common characteristics of cult,

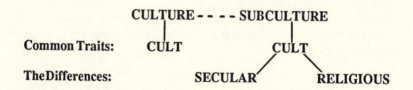

as applied to the variety of social groups, and pass on to the question of the differences between secular and religious worship. The following diagram illustrates how the presentation is organized.

A. Culture—Subculture

We have already observed that the human being is a symbol-maker. To accomplish the task of distinguishing, identifying, and relating surrounding reality, a world of symbols is developed. Humans regularly employ symbols to bestow meaning on, and to derive it from, the world. The capability of symbolization is the presupposition for the possibility of human communication and the establishment of social groups.

Social groups live in what we call a *culture*. The word culture, according to Vatican II's *Pastoral Constitution on the Church in the Modern World, (Gaudium et spes)*, "refers to all those things which go to the refining and developing of man's diverse mental and physical endowments" (no.53.2). For our purpose, a more technical definition can be cited.

> Culture denotes a historically transmitted pattern of meanings embodied in symbols, a system of inherited conceptions, expressed in symbolic forms by means of which men communicate, perpetuate and develop their knowledge and attitude toward life.[10]

A cultural field is constituted by a coherence of images, codes, and rites; of rules concerning reading, speech, and conduct, founded on language. This system enables an individual to take a stand in space and time in a signifying way, to identify oneself and to realize oneself as in the world and as a fellow human being alongside others. All cultures express a particular world of meaning, which may not coincide with that of certain social groups within the milieu. A dominant culture furnishes material for the formation of a differentiated system of rules by which such groups may carry out their common life in a way that corresponds to their grasp of reality. These subcultures make a selection from the symbolical material at hand, and integrate it into a new synthesis, a cultural model that governs their style of life.

B. Cult

Cultures, or related subcultures, serve as the regulative background for specific symbols or symbolic actions, which crystallize the governing interests and value relations of a social group. Such basic symbols are required for the constitution and preservation of human communities. They structure the reality of the experience of the community, make it accessible, and establish norms for daily activity. These symbols define the community vis-à-vis other groups and enable the members to recognize one another and to communicate with one another. Above all, the world of meaning peculiar to the community is condensed in them. They shed light on everyday reality and its tasks, and provide direction for its mastery. These symbols contribute significantly to the uncovering and interpretation of situations of routine living which call for decision, if human growth is to be realized. Such symbolic expressions of spiritual values fall within the category of cult.

The Indo-European root of the Latin word *cultus* signifies moving oneself around and in. The Latin root has the general meaning of inhabitant or cultivate (*incola; colere*). In the area of worship, *cultus* refers to the homage rendered to the gods. It is employed in modern ecclesiastical language for liturgy (*cultus publicus*), or private worship (*cultus privatus*). In classical usage *cultus* has a field of meaning which pertains to the properly religious. However, it is extended in modern times to the profane sphere of life. It can refer to the value relations of any culture or subculture.[11]

1. Common Characteristics of Cult

All social groups have forms of ritual behavior, more or less fixed. These stable forms of communication, known to all, favor and foster the engagement of members and their communication with one another. The experience of belonging to the group, of sharing the same goals and hopes, is made possible by such institutional behavior. What we have described as the cult of social groups displays this ritual shape. It also pertains to the type of human activity called *celebration*.[12]

In order to maintain and promote growth, human beings spontaneously turn away from routine living at regular intervals to engage in the celebration of life under one or another of its aspects. In this activity ordinary forms of expression of daily life are stylized in order to serve as the mirror for the profound realities hidden in day-to-day living. Celebrations are intended to bring to the surface of consciousness the enduring spiritual realities that support human and humanizing existence. These communal events contribute to a better understanding of such realities, enable them to be lived in the way peculiar to celebration, and thereby influence decisions in daily conduct. Their efficacy is conditioned by experiential knowledge of what is being celebrated, and the experience of what is being celebrated in the ritual activity itself.

Finally, we should note one last characteristic of the cult of social groups, already sufficiently implied in the above description. The celebration of the governing interests and value relations of the group marks a new beginning; it is *generative*. A new sense of the unity of the group, the sharing of the same goals and hopes, a new resolve to live out this social identity day by day, is the effect of this activity.

2. The Cult of Secular Social Groups

Stable, secular groups come together at regular intervals, as a means of maintaining their identity. Their cohesion is preserved by fixed ritual activity, which recalls the original action of persons who founded the organization, and which images forth the common day-to-day life of membership in the organization. The repetition of the charter, defining the limited goals and hopes, and the symbolic actions, expressive of the social unity, effect a kind of new beginning. A new joining together of the participants takes place, as they become vitally conscious of their opportunities and tasks of a practical kind.

3. The Cult of Religious Societies

Religious communities live within broader cultural contexts. They form subcultures, dependent on the surrounding culture for the formulation of the particular symbolic field in which their religious lives are conducted. The style of life of these communities takes visible form through the language and symbols drawn from the surroundings. Through a selection of material appropriate to their understanding of reality, these communities establish a system of rules for daily life. In a further step, this system of rules is further refined, stylized, and integrated into forms of communal expression of their religious life. The resulting ritual forms the unique representation of the basic interests and value relations of the society.

This religious cult cannot be identified with the spontaneity of the daily exercise of religion. It highly stylizes a world of meaning and understanding of reality, allowing the permanent values that support the group to come to the surface, and be lived in a intense way. Religious communities need cult. By it they are continually constituted and held together. Cult defines a community, sheds light on its tasks, and furnishes the basis for the interpretation of situations of daily life that call for a decision.

But the forms of religious worship that once satisfied the needs of a community may, in the course of time, lose much of their power of communication. The initial correspondence between the system of rules that regulates the daily life of the group and the cultic expression is not maintained when the religious subculture undergoes developments due to changes in the ambient culture. The evolution of a dominant culture affects the understanding of reality. The meaning of language, symbolic action and ways of relating between persons is altered. Naturally this has an effect on the religious subculture, which must live within a cultural milieu. Also new historical situations of the religious community give rise to new questions, changing tasks, etc., which contribute to an evolution in the community's self-understanding, and grasp of the meaning of all reality.

The cult of a religious society may remain fixed, as it is passed on to succeeding generations. But new cultural and historical situations of the community effect changes in the meaning of the cultic expression. Also the world of meaning, crystallized in the cultic symbols, is subject to change due to new questions, new commitments, etc., which arise from the concrete historical situation.

When a crisis occurs in a culture, it affects the external expression of the life of the religious subculture, as well as its understanding of itself and the world around. Adjustments are called for, when this situation obtains. The preservation of the connection between the world of meaning constitutive of the community, and its crystallization in the community's basic symbolic activity, so that the link is recognizable to all, is of the highest importance. If the correspondence is gradually obscured, if the cultic activity no longer communicates effectively, then the community itself is threatened with loss of identity. If the symbolic expression of cult, whose function is to establish the identity of the group and mediate meaning, is scarcely recognized as such, if the shape of meaning of all reality, expressed by cult, is less clearly perceived, then the acceptance will be substantially affected.

a. Functions of Religious Worship[13]

Religious worship, in general, may be described as the celebration of the transcendent good of the collective life of a community. It formulates the communal experience of overcoming the negativity of daily life, and being able to affirm the good. It is a means of social integration and authorization of the social order. It links the insecure constructs of the realities of the earthly society to an external and higher reality, the divine order.

From the phenomenological standpoint, three major functions can be assigned to religious worship: *orientation, expression,* and *affirmation.* Forms of corporate worship represent the *orientation* of a religion. They provide instruction about the nature of the world, relations between the human and divine, ethical perspectives. Authentic religious worship is a medium in which the participants are able to *express* their relationship to the divine ground of all being. Ideally, communal worship enables the community to shed a variety of bonds of suppression, which prevent the freeing experience of being saved. Anxiety and guilt are set aside, and unrestricted elevation of the heart and mind takes place. The goal of religious worship is the *affirmation of the participants in their quest for renewal.* It aims at overcoming death, serving as medium of healing a sinful state and broken communion, providing a share in the new life.

Of course, the effectiveness of religious worship depends on many factors. As a means of integration into the social order, all depends on the character of the religion, and the measure of its autonomy in a concrete situation. While it can be an articulation of an advanced understanding of human dignity, it can also serve to mask over social injustice in the interest of the powerful. Cult enables the community to express its religious life to the extent that the cultic verbal and gestural language can become the expression of the adult, personal symbols by which the participants carry on their daily life. The effectiveness of the function of affirmation depends on what "new life" is affirmed, what certainties supported, and how reconciliation between the human and divine, and humans among themselves, is understood. Forms of religious worship can be feasts of liberation for, or instruments of suppression of, authentic human development.

b. Normative Concept of Religious Worship

From a phenomenological point of view, the uniqueness of religious worship lies in the intention to bring to the surface of the lives of the community not one or another human value on which human development depends, such as human love, fidelity, or patriotism. Rather, it aims at coming into contact with the ground of all reality, God. That is what is peculiar about religious worship. The three major functions of religious worship considered above pertain to the horizontal dimension of the phenomenon, to the affective, social side of an activity which is intimately linked to the whole range of the life of the religious society. However, a normative concept of religious worship cannot be limited to this aspect. All religious worship has a so-called vertical dimension. It aims at being the medium of a new advent of the divine ground of existence, which changes all things through its coming.[14]

The history of religions provides useful data concerning the uniqueness of religious worship.[15] From the beginning of recorded history, the human being manifests itself as uncomfortable with its finitude. The desire to overcome the basic human condition is displayed in the construction of a hierarchy of activities, which form a unity and represent a value system. With the help of this hierarchy of values, which differ in the variety of cultural contexts, humanity seeks to rise above the sameness of daily life. Studies in the history of religions show that the search to transcend earthly conditions is accompanied by a sense of the presence of the numinous, the other-worldly, originating in the experience of liberation from the confining conditions of routine living. This experience was expressed, from the outset, in the form of symbols, myths, and ritual behavior.

Eventually the archaic experience of the presence of some transcendent reality was rationalized, with the result that it was situated above the world of change. Height, the distance above the level of the earth where humans normally live, became the symbol of liberation from the human condition and the sphere of participation in the life of the numinous. The mountain is identified as the place where the gods dwell. This way of thinking is exemplified in the account of the ascent of Moses "to the mountain of God" (Exod 24:13). The point of contact between the higher and lower worlds, the axis of the world, is imaginatively depicted in various ways, of which Jacob's ladder is one example (Gen 28:10-22).

The symbolic way of describing the world of the numinous, and its point of contact with the human world, reflects the inability of humankind to really penetrate the mysterious ground of all being. At the same time, it manifests the awareness that the value of human activity is dependent on participation in the world of the numinous. At some unrecorded time in human development, this insight led to the view that cultic activity is effective to the extent that it repeats, through imitation, an action of gods, heroes, etc., which represents a victory over the finite possibilities of humanity. The repetition of such an action allows human beings to transcend earthly conditions and share in the original victory over earthly laws won by a transcendent personality in mythical time.

Nearly all theologies of ritual activity of world religions are based on this fundamental principle: Every religious ritual action that mediates salvation has a divine model. Correspondingly, religious communities gather together in the hope that their cultic activity will be the medium of the advent of the transcendent reality. This ritual activity is the confession that the community is dependent on higher powers. It announces that the community does not possess all truth. It is the practice of the hope that the community can learn anew, from the advent of divine truth itself, the deepest meaning of human existence. Since religious worship announces the advent of the divine that renews the lives of the participants, it says something about the value of human works. The worshipping assembly is taught that it should not base its expectations on human powers, but on that source which alone can give meaning to all responsible human effort. In this way religious worship wards off discouragement based on human failure and the pressure to succeed, and, at the same time, reveals new possibilities for daily living.

The foregoing description of what is unique about religious worship must be kept in mind when the attempt is made to construct a normative concept of this activity. However it would be a mistake to limit a normative concept to this aspect. The affective, social side of worship must not be neglected. If religious cult serves as medium of a divine epiphany, it also has other functions. The limiting of religious cult to this one function reduces human activity to the exclusive role of serving as organ, or instrument, of the advent of the divine. It fosters a theory that places worship outside the scope of critical evaluation. A realistic appraisal of concrete forms of worship includes an evaluation of their effectiveness in promoting the threefold social functions mentioned above. A normative concept should furnish the basis for a judgment about the value of forms of worship along the lines of the Old Testament prophetic criticism of externalized, heartless religion.[16]

c. Christian Cult

The foregoing general remarks about religious worship are applicable to Christian liturgy. In the first place, Christian communities do not begin at zero-point to create a completely new symbolic field in which to live out their life of faith. Rather they draw on elements of the surrounding culture in a selective way, fashioning a new synthesis in which different meaning is given to the symbolic material regarded as appropriate to the Christian subculture.

The system of rules which organizes the daily life of the Christian faith is the visible expression of a mystery, of the new relation between God and humanity. This mystery of salvation is represented and realized in the spontaneous exercise of concrete, routine living within the Christian subculture. In other words, the daily life of the community of faith, lived in the variety of persons and events, is *sacramental* insofar as this practice represents and realizes the life of communion with God and among the faithful. However, the broader symbolic field of Christian daily life is not sufficient to meet the demands of communal expression of the community's self-identity. Hence the system of rules undergoes scrutiny in the light of faith. A selection is made from the forms of communication of daily life with a view to the creation of a ritual expression of the life of faith.

The resulting symbols and symbolic actions are ultimately tied to some broad cultural background. They represent cultural goods, filtered through the life of faith and put to the service of the community's worship. These basic symbols crystallize the fundamental realities, which support the life of faith, in the peculiar way of symbolization. Employed in the communal expressions of the liturgy, they have the function of establishing and maintaining Christian identity, and mediating the meaning by which the community is held together and grows.

1. The Functions of Christian Worship

From the point of view of phenomenology, Christian worship is an activity in which the Church manifests and realizes itself in the public forum. It is a symbolic communication of the Christian experience through the medium of the biblical and ecclesiastical tradition. As celebration of the life of freedom from sin, reconciliation with God, and communion with those who are in Christ, Christian worship has the functions of all authentic forms of religious worship. But its specific character raises problems, when it comes to the question of the concrete efficacy of the liturgy in the variety of historical and culturally conditioned situations.

a. Orientation

Communal forms of worship have a didactic function. They provide direction for daily life. This aspect is especially relevant today because the Church lives in a society where Christian values are set aside. However, worship is also the place where the historical heritage of the Christian expression of faith is met in a living way. This tradition needs interpretation. Hence the Church has the task of renewing the liturgy constantly, so that a bridge is provided between the biblical and past history of the Church and the modern world. This renewal will be successful to the extent that it is the fruit of a dialogue between past and present questions and answers.

b. Expression

As symbolic expression of the life of faith, the liturgy employs the rich treatures of the past experience of faith. The intention is twofold: 1) to supply the best possible means of a corporate response to what God has done and is doing for the community through Christ in the Spirit; 2) to enable the individual to express a unique prayer of praise, thanksgiving, and intercession. But this intention is often frustrated by the inability of many modern Christians to engage meaningfully in the gestures and speech belonging to another age. This situation offers a special challenge to those bearing an official responsibility for the promotion of a vital liturgy: the task of providing instruction about inherited rites and, as occasion demands, the creation of new forms of worship more appropriate to the contemporary needs.

c. Affirmation

The goal of Christian worship is the affirmation of believers in their quest for the meaning of their existence. Liturgy always proclaims the promise of salvation, and liberation from the anxiety and guilt which the participants experience in their daily lives. But the message is communicated through a historically and culturally conditioned form of expression of a particular experience of liberation and reconciliation, of salvation and redemption. Therefore, the question of the capability of the traditional forms of liturgy to respond to the needs of new situations of life and contexts of experience must be continually raised.

2. Efficacy of Christian Worship

We have already noted the peculiar generative efficacy of communal celebrations of social groups. All religious communities have an analogous set of images of their common life, which are displayed in worship, and an analogous efficacy.[17] Christian worship, in particular, is the means by which the community is newly constituted as the Body of Christ. This communal activity recalls the original action of Christ and his followers, by which the Church was founded and the meaning of membership determined. Consequently, it generates a new beginning of the community each time it gathers together. But, as with the communal expression of the identity of all social groups, the effect is conditioned by the active involvement of believers. As communicative activity, the Christian liturgy brings to the surface of consciousness of the participants the gifts which are already given with the life of faith: the saving presence of God, personal union with Christ in the Church by means of the power of the Holy Spirit. But this activity is needed because the members of the Church live in and through history and so must continually celebrate their common life of faith lest they lose the awareness of their identity.

3. Christian Symbols and Christian Identity

We have already discussed how the cultic forms of religious communities communicate the corporate identity. The same holds true for the Christian community. The loss of correspondence between the

Christian community's self-understanding and its liturgical expression endangers the existence of the community.

The link between Christian forms of liturgy and the ways in which the life of faith is understood and practiced in routine living, is maintained by numerous spontaneous adjustments in the different cultural settings and historical situations. More substantial changes in forms of worship may also be required to preserve the quality of this basic activity of the life of faith. But, because of the intimate relation between liturgy and daily life, forms of worship should never be changed or corrected over the head of surrounding culture. Ritual conduct cannot be simply identified with the spontaneity of the daily expression of the life of faith. Some detachment is necessary to create ways of expressing the abiding spiritual realities undergirding routine living in order that they may be lived in a celebrative way. However, innovations introduced without due regard to the natural source of liturgical expression, the surrounding culture, should not be expected to contribute to liturgical renewal.

a. Inculturation

The last remark relates to an important consideration which is receiving special attention today. The relation of revelation, Christian life, and worship to cultures took on particular significance at Vatican II, as the council struggled with the problem of liturgical reform.

The revelation of God and the various ways of expression of the response of humankind to that revelation are necessarily bound to a culture. But there exists no overarching, superior culture which transcends and, at the same time, includes all other cultures. This fact leads to the conclusion that the full reception of Christian faith, conveyed in the clothing of one culture, by those of another culture, entails inculturation.

> Inculturation may be described as follows: (It is) the integration of the Christian experience of the local church into the culture of its people, in such a way that this experience not only expresses itself in elements of this culture, but becomes a force that animates, orientates and innovates this culture so as to create a new unity and communion, not only in the culture in question but also as an enrichment of the Church universal.[18]

Inculturation first took place when the gospel was implanted in the Palestinian milieu. Later on the faith was received by the surrounding peoples and expressed in the dominant culture of the Mediterranean lands. When the Church had to articulate its life in other ways than that of the Hellenistic culture, it could do so only through some specific culture. New ways of expressing the faith, suited to different cultures, are not merely desirable. Human beings are deeply bound to their cultures, which are elements of their identity and personality. Hence inculturation is a basic requirement for a full life of faith.

The principle of inculturation of Christian faith is receiving special consideration in the so-called third world countries. Long dependent on European colonial powers, these nations are now experiencing along with political freedom a new self-identity, which includes a rediscovery of the values of their own cultures. As the process of inner growth of the developing nations continues, questions are raised about the limitations of the culturally conditioned versions of Christianity which they have received as a European export.

The Christians of these nations are beginning to pay more attention to their native cultures which are interwoven with religious elements possessing great significance for Christian life. In many ways, and with greater confidence, they are affirming that pluralism of ecclesiastical life, based on inculturation, is no danger to the unity of faith. Rather it is a source of strengthening of this unity, as the lesson of history shows.[19] For inculturation is simply the embedding of the one faith, in a way that is connatural and congenial, within the culture of a people, determining that people to live the one faith in the best way possible for them.

Vatican II touched on this subject in *Sacrosanctum Concilium.* Here it is recommended that the liturgy be "adapted170 to the particular character and tradition of different peoples and that their cultural heritage be taken into account in the process. Regulations for adaptation were established (37-40). *The Decree on Eastern Catholic Churches (Orientalium Ecclesiarum)* recalls that the different rites, developed on the grounds of cultural differences in the course of centuries, are to be awarded similar rights and the same honor (2-6). *Lumen gentium* teaches that the universal Church is called from all peoples and that particular churches possess characteristic cultural values which are to be treasured as an enrichment of the whole body of faithful (13). Above all, *Gaudium et spes* explores the relation between faith and culture (42, 44, 58 [53,56]). Stress is placed on the fact that the Church is bound to no culture, embraces all cultures, and has used in her preaching the discoveries of different cultures to spread, and explain, the message of Christ to all nations, to probe and more deeply understand it, and to give it better expression in liturgical celebrations and in the life of the diversified community of the faithful (no. 58.2).

What can be said about religious societies in general, concerning the relation between culture and cult, is applicable to the Christian Church and its liturgy. The Christian community must live in a cultural milieu, and expresses best its life of faith, including worship, in and through elements of the native culture. It goes without saying that the process of inculturation is the responsibility of the individual churches and their members. For it is a question of expressing their experience of the life of faith in a way that is congenial to them. They are the cutting edge at which the universal Christian values and the particular cultural riches meet. They alone are capable of making the suitable synthesis that could provide a genuine contribution to the catholicity of the whole Church.

b. Human Communication and Liturgy

The renewed theology of the word of God has had an impact on the understanding of the dynamics of the liturgy. Also the ecclesiological insight that liturgy is the "self-expression of the Church," as well as the christological understanding of liturgy as the medium of encounter with Christ, "sacrament of God," grounds the possibility of rethinking the question of the sacramental dimension of Christian worship. Alexandre Ganoczy's book, *An Introduction to Catholic Sacramental Theology*, provides a good example of how the gains in the field of sacramental theology can be fruitfully exploited through a "communications theory" of sacraments [20]

A modern theory of communication offers a description of how an event of human communication takes place through speech and symbolic action. When it is integrated into the depth dimension of Christian liturgy, it offers the possibility of a better understanding of sacraments and, at the same time, provides pastoral norms for a more effective style of celebration.

Ganoczy's analysis has the advantage of introducing the human dimension into the global vision of the sacramental economy from the outset of his theological reflection on the liturgy. He begins at the level of the anthropological character of the human being, along the lines described by the various human sciences which we have considered above. Briefly, human beings allow access to themselves by free self-communication, through the body. But they communicate through already established symbol systems. Through these systems they communicate themselves and receive communication from others. As both communicator and communicant, individual persons are located in a context that exercises controlling influence over all the parties involved. But in the case of liturgy, there is the mystery aspect that does not allow it to be conceived and interpreted merely as an exercise of group dynamics.

Ganoczy offers this working description of a sacrament:

> The sacraments can be understood as systems of verbal and non-verbal communications through which those individuals who are called to Christian faith enter into the communicative process of the ever concrete faith-community, participate in it, and in this way, borne up by the self-communication of God in Christ, progress on the path of personal development.[21]

Vatican II's *Sacrosanctum Concilium* encourages this way of thinking by describing the liturgy in terms which are reminiscent of the language of modern sciences of communication. It is said that in the liturgy, "God speaks to his people, and Christ is still proclaiming his gospel, and the people reply to God by song and prayer" (no.33).

It is clear that the fixed forms of the liturgy are the expression of the lived faith of the Church. The liturgy does not have forms of expression which can be construed as a direct address of God, or Christ, to the community. The liturgical expression is, rather, a form of witness to the event of saving revelation. In the biblical sense, the event of saving revelation is the event of the new relation between God and the believer. It includes the self-communication of the Triune God and the act of faith accepting God's offer of love. The event of this new relation is conditioned by historical forms of communication, in and through which God enables the human being, by the gift of faith, to recognize that God is offering the invitation to enter into personal communion with himself.

The Scriptures are a witness to this saving revelation, not the revelation as such. The liturgy is also a form of witness. The peculiarity of liturgy lies in the fact that it is a corporate response of witness to the saving action of God, a confident response to what God is doing now in accord with the meaning of the particular form of liturgy. Consequently the liturgical constitution describes sacraments, from this standpoint, as "sacraments of faith" (59), that is, in them the conviction of faith of the Church is expressed.

The liturgical formulations of the witness of faith are necessary so that all may perceive, hear, and respond to the content of faith (*fides quae creditur*), that is, the self-communication of the Triune God. Since liturgy is the expression of the response to God's offer of his grace, it is not primarily aimed at doctrinal instruction. Rather, the liturgy is primarily a prayer. This makes understandable why the liturgical constitution stresses the type of activity that moves the participants so that "their minds are raised to God" (33).

In the liturgy the participants are placed in the midst of a system of speech, ritual, gesture, etc., that makes claims to be accepted or rejected. This system of communication, enabling a human sharing, exercises a steering effect on the relations of the interacting participants. Comprised of doxological and rhetorical language, along with symbolic actions, the liturgical activity allows the individuals to express their special needs and particular religious experiences. But the liturgy is primarily the expression of the global perception of the faith of the whole Church. Those who share the same faith are able to express it in a common or similar way. In fact, what each one brings of personal faith to the assembly is helped by the common expression of faith to transcend one's own limited appropriation of the depth of the whole life of faith. In other words, the individual is able to respond more fully to God by participating in the experience of the faith of the Church expressed through the liturgy, and by sharing in the experience of faith expressed by the other participants.

The liturgy, expressing what God has done and what God is doing in the lives of believers, is the means by which God's self-communication occurs in a personal way. Through the experience of the liturgy, believers are led to the conclusion that the fixed forms of expression of faith, as well as the personal faith expressed by the assembly, are supported by Christ himself: the High Priest of the worship of the Church. In the language of the science of communication, Christ can be described as the chief speaker and actor of the event of communication. Present to the assembly, and united with them in the one Holy Spirit, Christ enables the faithful to interact with him through the common prayer and song. The word of the liturgy, in its various forms, is a response of faith. It is made in union with Christ. Christ is the Word of God in person, sent as the address of the Father to humanity. But as the *incarnate* Word of God, Christ is the receiver of the Word of God, and likewise the chief responder to the Father in his humanity.

For the eyes of faith, Christ is the sender, receiver, and the medium of the dialogical event of the liturgy. This explains why the Church believes that Christ instituted the sacraments, empowers the Christian community for their celebration, and is the principal actor. As the unique Mediator between God and humanity (1 Tim 2:5; Heb8:6), he acts in the liturgy through the expression of the faith of the Church of which he, in the Spirit, is the living source.

This way of looking at the structural foundation of the liturgy in general, and the sacraments in particular, offers a new way of understanding the peculiar efficacy of all forms of Christian liturgy. This topic is discussed in the last part of this book. For now it suffices to observe that, from the point of view of a communications theory of liturgy, the whole central activity of the liturgy assumes the character of prayer, and this includes the kernel of the chief rites of the Church. The efficacy of this prayer derives from the fact that the High Priest of the liturgy of the Church is Christ himself. In other words, the Church's claim that the sacraments are an infallible offer of grace finds its deepest source in the liturgical experience of the truth of the Lord's promise: the certainty that the Father will respond to the prayer made by the Church of God "in the name of Jesus."

c. Semiotics

The subject of liturgical communication raises the question about the contribution which semiotics might make to a better understanding of the function and effectiveness of liturgy. Semiotics studies a wide variety of things insofar as they enter into a relationship of standing for something, e.g., a word, a gesture, facial expressions, etc. But this science does not merely study these entities in themselves. Semiotics investigates how interpreters actualize the potential semiotic relations that exist in the universe. It attempts to explain what a symbol is, how it is structured, and how it symbolizes or transmits its message.

The application of the methods of semiotics to Christian liturgy can lead to new insights into the dynamics of liturgical communication.[22] While this subject deserves a much fuller treatment, we are constrained to limit our remarks to some of the results of a structural analysis of Christian sacramental rites which are particularly relevant to the material of the final section of this book.

The analysis of the elements of a sacramental celebration shows, in the first place, that the visual, verbal, tactile, gestural, and olfactory media are intimately linked. They are so structured that they convey a unified message. Second, sacramental celebrations belong to the order of practice. A real human and social situation is being celebrated, one that makes demands on the participants. At the same time, what is being done signifies something else at a deeper level. In other words, the meaning directly signified, the denotation, connotes something else not perceived or known independently of the meaning of what is denoted. Third, there is the matter of the fundamental context that removes the native ambiguity of the symbolic action and enables the activity to convey the message intended. This fundamental context is the Christian community itself. The message is only operative in relation to a context accessible to the reciever. The fundamental context of all liturgical rites is the community assembled in the name of Jesus. The truth of the social situaltion, expressed by the rite, must be present if the sacramental celebration is not to be falsified. Hence when a sacramental celebration is imitated on the stage in a dramatic play, the necessary social context is absent.

In each instance, the analysis of sacramental rites shows that the elements constitutive of the framework of the rite have, by themselves, a significative function found in religious rites of other religious groups. Taken together, however, they express one meaning: something social and interpersonal, located at the level of human experience. The symbolic action and interpretative word, chosen to enable the participants to live out this human situation, convey understanding of a deeper dimension that cannot be denoted: a spiritual reality, experienced only through the gift of faith.

A rather significant consequence follows from this analysis; it is not always given enough attention in treatises on sacramental theology. It is necessary to respect the order of signification of sacramental rites, precisely because they pertain to the order of practice of the faith. The rites signify a human and social situation to which the subjects of the rites are called on to commit themselves in accord with the special demands of the gospel. These rites do not directly signify the gift of grace. A direct representation of such a spiritual reality can only be dramatized. But sacramental rites are not mere mythical gestures, expressive of some desire. They are practices that signify human commitment to the claim of God in specific human and social situations of the life of faith. An important pastoral consequence follows from this: *Sacramental rites should express as clearly as possible the social and interpersonal dimension into which the subject is being integrated.*

The analysis of the various levels of signification of the rite of initiation is given below. This schema can serve as a model that is applicable to the other sacramental rites.

	BAPTISM	**CONFIRMATION**	
Symbolic Activity:	Profession ofFaith	Bath and Prayer	Imposition of Hands and Prayer; Anointing
Signifies:	Engagement ofFaith	Purification; Passage from Death to Life	Consecration to Christian Life
Taken Together, They signify:	Incorporation into the Community of Christ: a social and interpersonal reality, located at the level of human experience.		
And Connote:	Incorporation into the Body of Christ, through the gift of the Holy Spirit.		

N.B. The whole process of symbolization is directed by the Holy Spirit, the living source of the life of faith of the Church and of its expression.[23]

Conclusion

We have been considering ways in which the human sciences can contribute to a better understanding of the meaning of liturgy, and the laws governing its structure and effective practice. Since liturgy is one way of living out the life of faith under the conditions of history, the data of the human sciences should be continually reckoned with in the formulation of a theology of liturgy worthy of the name pastoral theology.

However, the life of faith is a life in Christ. Ultimately it is only understandable from the background of the whole of the divine plan of salvation for the world, stretching from creation to the fulfillment of the Kingdom and having its high point in the life, death, and glorification of Jesus Christ. It is only by situating the liturgy within the framework of the totality of human existence, sanctified by the redeeming work of Christ, that the specific character of liturgy can be understood.

Notes

1. H. Demolder, "Orientations de l'anthropologie nouvelle," REVUE DE SCIENCES RELIGIEUSES 43 (1969) 149-173.

2. This theme, as related to the anthropological basis of sacraments, is developed by J. Ratzinger, DIE SAKRAMENTALE BEGRUNDUNG CHRISTLICHER EXISTENZ (Meitingen-Freising: Kyrios, 4th ed., 1974 11ff.; Confer also: W. Kasper "Wort und Sakrament," in O. Semmelroth, ed., MARTYRIA, LEITOURGIA, DIAKONIA (Mainz: Matthias-Grünewald, 1968) 275-277; A. Schilson, "Katholische Sakramententheologie auf neuen Wegen," HERDER KORRESPONDENZ 33 (1979) 572-573.

3. K. Jaspers, PHILOSPHIE II: Existenzerhellung (Berlin: Springer, 3rd. ed., 1956) 203.

4. GOD AND WORD (Philadelphia: Fortress, 1967).

5. "Wort und Sakrament," 277.

6. C. Traets, "Orientations pour une théologie des sacrements," QUESTIONS LITURGIQUES 53 (1972) 112-113.

7. P. Berger, RUMOR OF ANGELS: MODERN SOCIETY AND REDISCOVERY OF THE SUPERNATURAL (Garden City: Doubleday Anchor Books, 1970).

8. For example, T. Schneider, ZEICHEN DER NÄHE GOTTES: GRUNDRISS DER SAKRAMENTENTHEOLOGIE (Mainz: Matthias-Grünewald, 1979) 17-20; A. Schilson, "Katholische Sakramententheologie," 574-575.

9. A. Häussling, "Die kritische Funktion der Liturgiewissenschaft," in H. B. Meyer, ed., LITURGIE UND GESELLSCHAFT (Innsbruck: Tyrolia, 1972) 103-130, offers a more extended treatment of this subject.

10. Charles Geertz, THE INTERPRETATION OF CULTURE (London: Oxford, 1975) 89. Confer also: A. Kroeber, CULTURE: A Critical Review of Concepts and Definitions (Cambridge, Mass.: The Museum, 1952); idem, THE NATURE OF CULTURE (Chicago: University of Chicago, 1952); F. Schupp. GLAUBE, KULTUR, SYMBOL: Versuch einer kritischen Theorie sakramentalen Praxis (Düsseldorf: Patmos, 1974) 9-17.

11. A. Gaillermou, "Du sacré au profane: Variations sémantique sur quatre thèmes, célébration, cérémonie, rite, culte," LA MAISON-DIEU 106 (1971) 93-94.

12. For further remarks on the subject of the phenomenon of celebration, confer: B. Langemeyer, "Die Weisen der Gegenwart Christi im Liturgischen Geschehen," in O. Semmelroth, ed., MARTYRIA, LEITURGIA, DIAKONIA, 295-299; E.J. Kilmartin, "A Modern Approach to the Word of God and Sacraments of Christ: Perspectives and Principles," in F.A. Eigo, ed., THE SACRAMENTS: God's Love and Mercy Actualized. Proceedings of the Theological Institute of Villanova University 11 (Philadelphia: Villanova, 1979) 91-94.

13. P. Cornehl, "Theorie des Gottesdienstesein Prospect," THEOLOGISCHE QUARTELSCHRIFT 159 (1979) 178-194.

14. R. Schaeffler, "Kultische Handeln. Die Frage nach Proben seiner Bewährung und nach Kriterien seiner Legitimation," in R. Schaeffler - P. Hünermann, ANKUNFT GOTTES UND HANDELN DES MENSHCEN. Thesen über Kult und Sakrament. Quaestiones disputatae 77 (Freiburg im Br.: Herder, 1977) 9-50.

15. R. Hotz, "Religion-Symbolhandlung-Sakrament: Die christliche-theologische Bedeutung des kultische Symbolhandeln," LITURGISCHE JAHRBUCH 31 (1981) 36-54, offers a useful schematic presentation of man as symbol maker and of the function of symbol in the arena of religious worship in history, with special reference to Christian symbolic activity.

16. R. Schaeffler's formulation of a normative concept of religious worship stresses, in a one-sided way, the function of medium of advent of the divine. His apologetic approach, in reaction to the attempt to reduce the meaning of worship to the affective social side, by an appeal to the essential laws of cult itself, is incomplete. (P. Cornehl furnishes a good critique of the limitations of Schaeffler's "Kultische Handeln," ["Theorie des Gottesdienst," 183-184]).

17. On this theme, consult: P. Hünermann, "Sakrament—Figur des Lebens," in R. Schaeffler - P. Hünermann, ANKUNFT GOTTES UND HANDELN DES MENSCHEN, 51-87.

18. Ary R. Crollius, "What is New about Inculturation? A Concept and Its Implications," GREGORIANUM 59 (1979) 735.

19. J. Mühlsteiger discusses this matter with reference to the history of Church law ("Rezeption-Inkulturation-Selbstbestimmungsrecht," ZEITSCHRIFT FÜR KATHOLISCHE THEOLOGIE 105 [1983] 261-289).

20. (New York: Paulist, 1984) 142-182 [Trans. from EINFUHRUNG IN DIE KATHOLISCHE SAKRAMETENLEHRE (Damstadt: Wissenschaftliche Buchgesellschaft, 1979)107-135].

21. INTRODUCTION TO CATHOLIC SACRAMENTAL THEOLOGY, 156.

22. M. Amaladoss, "Semiologie et sacrement," LA MAISON-DIEU 97 (1973) 7-35.

23. This means that a clear-cut distinction between "merely ecclesiastical rites" and rites instituted by divine intervention is untenable. The Greek Fathers recognized a pyramid of antitypes, which participate in the prototype, Christ and his saving work, in different degrees, But all were viewed as grounded on the Spirit (R. Hotz, SAKRA-MENTE—IM WECHSELSPIEL ZWISCHEN OST UND WEST [Zürich: Benziger, 1979] 288-289). In the West, Augustine's teaching about SANCTA MATER ECCLESIA being the subject of the liturgical activity kept this idea alive. But later on Western theologians formulated a sharp distinction between sacraments, properly so-called, and liturgical actions of the Church. This distiction contributed to a distinction between SACRA-MENTS and SACRAMENTALIA, the latter being conceived of as ecclesiastical rites, efficacious because of the prayer of the Church.

PART II

History of Salvation and Christian Liturgy

Christian liturgy has the shape of a dialogue. The observable phenomenon manifests that the worshipping community is open to an engagement with the Triune God. The community itself knows, with the certitude of faith, that its liturgy is the privileged place of divine-human encounter. At the same time, the Christian is enjoined to pray always, since God is present in all situations of life, calling for a response to his grace of self-communication.

God works in and through history to communicate his saving grace, and this means in and through human communication in the individual and social spheres. But there is also the matter of God's special revelation, culminating in the Christ-event, and the sending of the Holy Spirit to establish the Church. Within the life of faith of the Church, the event of the new relation between God and humanity is continually realized in a unique way. This holds especially for the liturgy of the Church.

In order to gain deeper understanding of the special place of communal worship in the life of faith, it must be viewed from the background of the whole history of salvation, begun with creation and to be brought to final fulfillment with the second coming of the Lord. An initial approach to this subject is given in the next three chapters. An introduction to the concept of the history of salvation (Ch. 3) is followed by some observations on the nature and content of the experience of transcendence associated with the communication of divine grace (Ch. 4). This paves the way for an analysis of the specific character of Christian liturgy in relation to other basic acitivities of the life of faith (Ch. 5).

Chapter 3
History of Salvation

Life events, happenings of some importance, have a meaning that goes beyond the moment in which they occur. Events are not something that simply happen to a person; past events leave their mark. Human growth occurs through the experience of events; through such happenings human potential is actualized. There is no need to dwell on this point. Proverbs such as, The child is father of the adult, bear out what is the universal human experience. But what is worth noting here, a subject to which we will return later on, is how this phenomenon demonstrates the essentially relational nature of the human being. Through actualizing itself in relation to the world of things and other persons, the human being grows in personhood. Since past events are determinative of the personal identity of the individual, they remain in the present in their effect.

The events experienced by social groups have a similar efficacy. They have a constitutive meaning for these groups in the present. It is well known that a community defines itself by its actualized potential. In other words, a community knows what it is from that it has been. And it knows what it has been by what it has done in and through the past ways in which it has reacted within relational contexts. But no social group can limit its potential simply to what has already been actualized. For the history of the stable societies shows that they came to be what they are through the discovery of their possibilities *and* the courage of past generations to take a stand in new situations, to meet the challenge of the moment.

The new circumstances in which a stable community finds itself offer objective situations that are pregnant with meaning and values, that raise new questions and call forth answers. Through the interplay between the subjective working of the mind and heart with these objective situations, life events are realized which contribute to the development of the individual and the community as a whole.[1]

The dialogue structure of human history has a depth dimension, the divine grounds of all existence.[2] God's activity, in and through history, is not a graspable event, in the sense that it occurs as an event *alongside* the ordinary events of human history. Rather, God has bound himself to the history of humanity in a very intimate way. He himself is present and active in the concrete process of the ordinary life events of individual and society. The earlier acts of God, discerned in these events, reveal the direction in which God moves humanity toward a goal, a direction which becomes clearer in God's later acts.

I. Theology of Creation.[3]

God's involvement in history begins with creation. According to Genesis, God's working and activity is a speaking. Creation is a happening in and through the word. It is speech of God, derived from his will. Creatures, coming into being by God's freely speaking out of love, are the expression of God's love. The breath of love by which the word goes forth is the creative power of God. Since God speaks to be heard and accepted, creation attains its meaning when God is heard and accepted. When creation perceives itself as gift, and accepts with thanksgiving, it is turned back to the Giver and obtains its full meaning.

All created things, coming from God, speaks of God not out of self and from self, but from God. Creatures have more to say than what they are in themselves. They also announce that they are from God. In other words, created things are the personal expression of God; for nothing exists from God by way of apersonal necessity. All being derives from the free, personal act of God.

Individual creatures have the potential to express something more of the mystery of God when they are brought into new relational contexts of meaning by human beings. It belongs to the personal creature to activate this potential of created being. Humans have the power to express themselves in another creature. They can mediate new meaning and, therefore, being to another. They can activate the passive potentialities of thingly creatures so that they mediate what is properly human. This happens, for example, in the creation of music, poetry, paintings. Through this kind of activity, humans are able to communicate with one another, on condition of the conscious opening of the other to communication.

But what is being realized through the human power of bestowing meaning, and conveying it to others, is not simply human communication. More is said than a human being can say about oneself. The rational creature does not simply speak from, and out of, oneself, but also from God. Human communication is a medium by which God communicates with rational creatures.

As embodied spirits, human beings are a kind of symbol of the world; for in them traits of the various levels of created being are found. As beings of the cosmos, they can respond in thanksgiving for the gift of creation on behalf of all created reality. The meaning of the world is fulfilled through acceptance of God, the Giver, and this happens through created personal being, the crown of the universe.

Humans attain their meaning, and that of the cosmos, by entering into a dialogical relation with God. They are created for partnership with God. Gen 1:26-28 speaks of rational creatures as created according to the "image of God" and awarded "dominion" over the rest of creation. But there is more. They are partners with whom God enters into a personal relationship. In the Hebrew Scriptures it is said of the Israelites that they must not "degrade yourselves by fashioning an idol" (Deut 4:16). New light is shed on the description of human beings as image of God with the revelation of the Triune God. If God is Trinity, his symbol in the world must be Trinitarian. Traces of the Triune God should manifest themselves in all authentic human activity; for the Triune God is present and personally working in and through the human image of God.

A. Trinitarian Concept of Creation

All creation comes from God the Father. As gift of the Father, it manifests the Father's love. But according to the New Testament, all creation originates through the personal Word of God (John 1:1ff.). This witness of faith allows us to say that creation is the expression of the Father's love through his one and unique Word, who is the self-expression of the Father from all eternity, the one object of the Father's love.

As a speaking of the Father through his one Word, revealed in the economy of salvation as Son, creation is a participation in the nearness of the Word to the Father. Creation exists through the Word in the sense that it is spoken in love on the ground of the personal relation of the Father to his Word. On this account creation is holy because it is from God through the Word, who is "the light" (John 1:4,5,9ff.).

Creation is also "in the Spirit of God," that is, in accord with the Spirit of God. This means that the Holy Spirit is communicated in creation and is active in creation. In the Spirit, the Father creates, orders, guides and animates created being. As the Spirit of the love of the Father for the Son, and of the Son for the Father, the Holy Spirit is the source of harmony and personal communion. Consequently, the Spirit establishes and maintains personal relations between God and creatures, and of creatures among themselves. The Spirit is the love of the Father expressed in creation through the eternal Word. Hence creation bears the stamp of God's love. Since the Father created the world in the Spirit of love, love characterizes the basic relation between creature and creator. This explains why the going out of creation from God does not entail estrangement from God. The Spirit grounds a togetherness of creature and creator that enables the theologian to speak of real relations of God to creatures extending beyond that of dependence of creaturely existence on God.[4]

The possibility of the "spiritualization" of created things, through the powers of personal creaturehood, is grounded on the bestowal of the Spirit of God in creation. Through the Spirit the original possibility of communication in truth and love between personal creatures is established, as well as the possibility of communication between the Triune God and human beings in history.

History has a dialogical structure that can be described as the interplay between the subjective working of the mind and heart and objective situations that bear meaning and value. But at its depth, history is a dialogue of salvation between the Trinity and humanity. The created world, and all its meaningfulness, is God's address to humankind. The verbal character of creation and all its manifestations derives from God's Word. The experience of inner-wonder and inner-welcome of meanings and values discerned in objective situations, which we judge to be God's own, has its source in the Spirit of God. The Spirit moves us to desire and welcome such spiritual goods in order to be true to ourselves, and conformed to God's will.

II. Theology of Redemption

The history of God's relationship with humanity is a history unfolded according to a consistent plan. The Pauline and Deuteropauline writings employ the word "mystery" to describe the one divine plan (1 Cor 2:7), which includes creation, redemption, and eschatological fulfillment. God, who created all things and guides them toward fulfillment, is not deterred by the Fall of man. God wills the reconciliation of humanity with himself, despite humankind's continued efforts to be something else than what God had intended. To this end, in what we call "salvation history" in the strict sense, God established a covenant with Israel and remained faithful to it despite the shortcomings of the covenant partner. And, in his own good time, he effected a new, definitive covenant through his Son, Jesus Christ.

The mystery of redemption consists in the Father's acceptance of sinners through the mission of the Word. The Word of God was always present to, and active in, the world from the outset of creation. But now the Word gains a new presence through the incarnation. Assuming the concrete humanity of Jesus of Nazareth, the Word of God now became present in person under the conditions of history. But there is more. He became present in the situation in which humanity finds itself. The Word did not assume a humanity in the form originally created by God. Rather he took flesh in the form which humanity had become, namely, deformed by sin.

The Father wills that the redemption of humanity be accomplished by "...sending his only Son in the likeness of sinful flesh" (Rom 8:3). Therefore it can be said that "We have...a High Priest who...in every respect has been tempted as we are, yet without sin" (Heb 4:15). The incarnation involves the self-emptying of the Son of God in the fullest sense: the setting aside of the glory he has at the right hand of the Father and the entrance into the form of servant, "being born in the likeness of men" (Phil 2:7). In this condition, his obedience and love become the response made on behalf of sinful humanity and accepted as such by the Father. But for this work of salvation to bear fruit for free human beings, they must follow his way, become conformed to "the image" of God's Son (Rom 8:29).

Although the mystery of salvation is realized in a definitive way in Jesus Christ, it continues to be realized in the world after the glorification of Jesus. For Jesus offered himself to the Father, not just to receive the meaning of his existence from the Father of all blessings, but also for the salvation of the world. Therefore, the risen Lord sends the Holy Spirit from the Father to establish the new people of God.

The Church is the "mystery" of God, derived from the mystery of God, Jesus Christ. This new people is the historical, social manifestation of the mystery of God's plan of salvation, called to grow into the fullness of Christ by obedience to the Cross and by receiving into their midst those who accept "the word of the Cross" (1 Cor 1:18). Through the Church's basic activity of preaching, service of love, and liturgy, the union of believers with the Triune God is deepened, and others are drawn to join their ranks.

These basic activities fall within the category of "mystery," insofar as they manifest and realize the one divine plan of God for the salvation of the world. Just as the Father willed that the redemption of the world be accomplished by the Word in the likeness of sinful flesh, so now, in the time of the Church, he also wills that the community of believers, heirs of a sinfully disposed humanity, be a special organ of salvation. The activity of the Church, carried out through the members, bears the marks of a humanity deformed by sin. The various forms of this activity display that imperfection which is the result of the inheritance of the historically determined, sinful tendencies. The true *kenosis*, or self-emptying, of the divine saving activity in the activity of the Church, derives not merely from the fact that God's self-communication is mediated through human communication. Rather, it is grounded on God's free decision that the divine action be communicated through that of the sinfully disposed Church, with all the imperfections that this implies.

The sending of the Spirit, following the death and glorification of Jesus, entails a new presence of the Spirit in the world. Always present to the world from the beginning, the Spirit now has the mission to experience a new presence and activity, in and through the Church. The Spirit gained a new presence in the world in the incarnation, being sent by the Father to effect the binding of the fruit of Mary's womb to the Word of God. The same holds true for the Spirit's personal presence in the Church. In both cases something new and unheard of takes place. But after the initial creation of the world, the Spirit works with what is at hand. In the case of the incarnation, the Spirit does not sanctify a new humanity untouched by the generations of the past. "God sent his Son in the likeness of sinful flesh as a sin offering, thereby condemning sin in the flesh." Therefore, those "who are in Jesus Christ...live, not according to the flesh, but according to the Spirit" (Rom 8:1-4). In the time of the Church also, the new working of the Spirit is in continuity with the past.

The Holy Spirit establishes the social structures of the Church, but they are structures that correspond to the human condition in the yet not fully redeemed world. What can be said about the Church's social structures and its activity, in a general way, holds also for its various forms of worship. At the depth of the liturgical celebrations, the content is the one mystery of the divine self-communication. To this extent the forms of liturgy are simply holy because of the mystery symbolized: the real event of personal communication between God and the believing participants. But the form of the liturgy, insofar as accomplished through the activity of the Church, derives from the yet not fully redeemed new people of God. These forms originate in the language and gestural ways of communication available in different cultural and historical settings in which the Church must live.

The variety of rich liturgical traditions, through which the life of faith is manifested and realized, are only relatively appropriate to express what is proper to the event signified: a saving encounter between God and his people. The Church knows this instinctively and, therefore, does not award any liturgical tradition absolute value, or even pride of place. Rather, the Church is conscious of the fact that the Spirit, who is the ultimate architect of all authentic liturgical tradition, works with what is at hand. In new situations, it can be expected that the Spirit will inspire changes in forms of celebration in order that culturally and historically conditioned believers may be enabled to respond more fully to God's invitation to personal communion, and the consequences it implies for the daily life of faith.

Notes

1. T. Dunne, "Theology and History," THEOLOGICAL STUDIES 45 (1984) 139-152; B. Lonergan, "Mission and the Spirit," in P. Huizing and W. Basset, eds., EXPERIENCE OF THE SPIRIT., Concilium 99 (New York: Seabury, 1976) 69-77.

2. J. Splett, "Die theeologische Dimension der Geschichte," ZEITSCHRIFT FÜR KATHOLISCHE THEOLOGIE 100 (1978) 302-317; W. J. Hill, "The Historicity of God," THEOLOGICAL STUDIES 45 (1984) 320-333.

3. R. Schulte, "Die Einzelsakramente als Ausgliederung des Wurzelsakraments," MYSTERIUM SALUTIS IV.2 (Einsiedeln: Benziger, 1973) 46-155.

4. This subject is discussed at length in Part III, Chapter 10.

Chapter 4
The Experience of the Transcendent Ground of All Being

By definition the transcendent ground of all earthly reality is not accessible to human beings in the way that earthly reality is experienced and known through the senses. Human beings, beings of the cosmos, acquire knowledge of earthly realities by observation. Moreover, possessing a common nature, they can communicate with one another. This unity of the human species enables communication between persons at various levels, even down to the depth of that interpersonal communication where one addresses the other, as other, in the openness we call love.

Indeed, it is at the level of loving communion that human beings find the possibility of human growth. However, God is not a structure of human existence, although he is the ground of this existence under all its aspects. The experience of finitude, briefly touched on in Chapter 2, enables the rational creature to discern, however darkly, the transcendent reality on which existence depends. But the possibility of a personal, dialogical relation between humankind and God is not a purely *a priori* given. If it is at all possible, it must be the result of a divine initiative. On the other hand, if God enters into such a relationship with human beings, it is conditioned by laws governing human communication itself; for there is no other way human beings can be so engaged and still remain human beings.

This present chapter offers some reflections on the subject of the experience of the transcendent God, confessed by Christians as a personal God who invites humanity to enter into personal communion with himself as ground and goal of human existence. A brief analysis is given of the process by which growth in human personhood is achieved. From this background the conditions of God's self-communication are identified, and the content of the experience of saving revelation is described. Concluding remarks are made on the subject of the sociological conditions that contribute to the experience of God's personal, saving presence.

I.
Human Growth in Personhood

The remote condition for the possibility of experiencing a personal God, as the ground and goal of human existence, is given with the ability of a human being to become present to self in subjective consciousness. This consciousness of self originates in the process by which the human spirit goes out to the world through the body and returns to self by means of the external world. In order to be conscious at all, there must be some objective content of consciousness by which self-consciousness is mediated. The discovery that one has concepts, however unreflective, is the experience of one's otherness. In a further step, one becomes conscious of being a human person among other persons by being addressed by them as a *thou*. Through this address one becomes simultaneously conscious of one's own personhood and that of the speaker. This initiates the movement by which the addressee goes out to the other, as other.

The movement by which the person goes out to the other as other begins the completion of the circle of presence-to-self and presence-to-other. It is fulfilled when the other accepts the invitation to a dialogue in love. In such a dialogue, the uniqueness of the other is affirmed, and wonder and thanksgiving are felt because of the access which the other has allowed to his or her personhood. Through this process the lover and the beloved grow as persons. The beloved is made aware of his or her otherness and unique value. Thereby the beloved is freed from the compulsion to self-assertion and self-justification. One is enabled to turn aside from preoccupation with self and to live "for others." This means that the beloved is on the way to adulthood; for the human being is essentially relational, and realizes self in relation-to-others.

On the other hand, the lover uncovers his or her own mystery in the discovery of the ability to bestow meaning on the beloved. In short, one develops self by offering self in loving; for the loving I, in loving a thou, learns to love one's own love and so oneself. The recognition of one's own inviolable worth is the result of the experience of the creative power of one's own love, that is, the power to awaken the knowledge of self-worth in the beloved.

Self-knowledge of one's own mystery, and the otherness of another human being, affords a shadowy glimpse of the ultimate source of otherness. It can lead to reflection on the deepest mystery of the otherness of the human person: the ultimate source of all otherness, the absolute Other.

From the foregoing anthropological considerations it can be concluded that human existence involves a process of reciprocity between subject and object. There is a mediation of the world to the individual person, and of the personal being to the world, in which occurs a process of mutual determination. The highest level of the reciprocity is human encounter, through which growth in human personality is made possible. It is within this context that the specifically divine-human personal communication takes place.

II.
Transparency of Transcendent Reality in Immanence: The Notion of Sacrament

Revelation of the ground and goal of human existence, the awakening of knowledge of this ultimate depth and meaning of human life, is God's act. Human beings have this knowledge because God reveals self personally. But this revelation takes place through the historically acting God. God, who is beyond history, manifests self in and through concrete, historical events. Events of this kind are the medium in which revelation occurs. Naturally, the revelation of God admits of degrees from the standpoint of the categorical historical engagements. They are made more transparent for the coming-into-play of God, in greater depth and intensity, as God identifies self with the fate of the people of the old covenant, with the fate of his only Son, Jesus Christ, and with that of the new people of God, the Church. God's self-revelation also admits of degrees from the standpoint of the openness of the human addressee to receive it. However what is being offered in saving revelation admits of no degrees. God's self-revelation is God's self-communication. And God does not offer simply a part of self, as do human beings in their interpersonal communication.[1]

The idea that God acts in and through history, makes himself personally available for loving communion in and through events of history, is not objectionable. But it needs to be developed.[2] It is more precise to say that God reveals self personally in and through human interpersonal communication. The being-in-of-God in this communication allows us to speak of its sacramental nature. In this sense, "sacramental" includes three concepts:

A. The self-communication of God is a "transcendental" act, namely, originating from a purely divine activity and not filtered through any human means.

B. This transcendental act is "categorialized," namely, given an expression that is graspable by human beings and enabling the appropriate response.

C. The transcendental act is categorialized on the ground of human interpersonal communication and, consequently, on the basis of human corporeality, historicity, and intersubjectivity.

III.
The Content of the Experience of Transcendence in Immanence

The content of the experience of saving revelation is best described with the help of the analogy of human love. The human being is constitutively ordered to the love of another and for another. To be the object, and the subject, of the act of love is a fundamental exigency of humankind. At the same time, human freedom enables a person to be open or closed to another. This exigency and this freedom mutually condition one another, and grow in their reciprocity. For, as the exigency is fulfilled in the unity of love, the other is not made the object of possession, but of affirmation as other. Hence the beloved is freed to be other. In brief, the otherness and differences of the I and the thou grow in the measure of their mutual love.

The mystery of this unity of love is the loving, personal God. God is the source of the otherness of the lovers, of their inviolable worth, of their freedom to be open to the other in selfless love. Consequently, the otherness of the other cannot be the ultimate object of human love. Rather the human expression of love points to the Other who alone is worthy of the full commitment of love. The other human being can only be loved in the love of the transcendent Other, the source of all otherness. But it is also true that the awareness of the love of God for human beings is conditioned by the experience of human love. One must have this human experience, at least at some level, to know that one is lovable.

The Christian finds this experience very radically in *the memory of Jesus Christ's life, death, and resurrection.* Christian faith claims that God, the Father, loves all humankind and calls them to live a life of interpersonal love with himself in which they will find their fulfillment. The proof of this love, for the eyes of faith, is Jesus Christ. In him the Father's love for the world is manifested.

The fundamental characteristic of Jesus of Nazareth, as described in the four Gospels, is his complete orientation toward his Father. The Fourth Gospel formulates this trait very pregnantly in words attributed to Jesus: "The Father and I are one" (10:30). This saying should be read in the context of such sayings as, "I am in the Father and the Father is in me" (14:11), and "I...live in his love" (15:10). Jesus and the Father are one in a profound dialogical unity of love.

The love of Jesus for the Father is unique. His human love, both of the Father and all the Father's children, is not to be compared to the love of the "saints" of all times, and granted merely a quantitatively superior intensity. It has a profound Trinitarian basis, to be identified in Part III, Chapter 11, of this book. Here we are only interested in pointing out the consequences of the unity of love of Father and the Son of God in his humanity.

Because of this love between the Father and Jesus, the Father abandons him to the death of the cross. This saying, attributed to Jesus just before his death, allows us to speak of the Father forsaking his beloved Son: "My God, my God, why hast thou forsaken me" (Mark 15:34). This text has been interpreted in various ways. As a matter of fact, it is a quotation from the opening verse of Ps 22, which closes with a confession of praise of the faithful God who exalts his faithful servant. But whatever may have been the intention of the Christian tradition, associating Ps 22:1 with the last utterances of Jesus, there is a profound theological sense in which we can speak of the Father abandoning the Son in the event of his crucifixion.

On the cross Jesus is placed, so to speak, over against the Father, as the other in the likeness of sinful flesh. This concept is well expressed in 1 John 4:10: "In this is love, not that we loved God but that he loved us and sent his son to be the expiation for our sins." This happens, according to the will of the Father, in order that Jesus might experience to the fullest extent possible, in his life of faith, his otherness vis-à-vis the Father. Therefore he is enabled to respond, to the highest degree of the limits of the possibility of human freedom, to the Father's love for him. In this unique instance, the unity of love between God and one who is "truly man" reaches its highest fulfillment in history. It is a unity in love, which entails the still greater difference of the purely divine love of the Father and the human love of him who is the incarnate Son of God.

The event of the Cross is the expression of the Father's love, who "hands over"[3] his Son to the point of fullest self-emptying. The Father gives himself to humanity in his Son on the cross in order to draw back the sinful world into his love. As representative of all humanity, Jesus opens the world to the Father's love. The believer comes to know the love of God and the only way of responding to this love. It is by opening oneself to the love between Father and incarnate Son, by uniting oneself in love to the love of Jesus for the Father in freedom of faith, that one arrives at the highest degree of specificity of creaturehood and freedom. In the measure that the rational creature becomes other, in the sphere of the personal love between Father and incarnate Son, the unity with the Father grows.

In this unity of love, the otherness of God and the otherness of creatures grows in the measure where love increases on the part of the latter. A unity, in a still greater difference, is realized to the extent that the otherness of God is affirmed by the creature in his or her otherness and freedom. This unity of love is not capable of indefinite development. It reaches a state of equilibrium in the blessed life of those who ascend with the risen Lord to share in the blessings of the fulfilled Kingdom of God. In the state of blessedness, the fully redeemed saints are enabled to respond to the fullest extent of their spiritualized existence to the otherness of the Triune God. For here the divine persons offer themselves to be known and loved in their personal distinctness without the use of the language and symbols of the earthly life of faith, and the blessed live not by faith but by vision.

IV.
Sociological Context and the Experience of the Transcendent God

The content of the experience of God's saving revelation is both the experience of being addressed by the Other *and* of being able to respond as other in the freedom of love. We experience salvation as the experience of being qualified by God to offer him a worthy response of praise and thanksgiving. All authentic Christian liturgical traditions confess that God is worthy of praise. For example, the traditional introduction to Eucharistic Prayers includes the exhortation by the presiding minister to give "thanks to the Lord, our God," and the assembly responds: "It is truly fitting and just." At the same time, the prayers themselves exude the confidence, born of faith, that the community can offer acceptable worship before God, through Christ.[4]

However, this confidence of the members of a liturgical assembly is not purely and simply the effect of the liturgical context itself. The awareness of personal dignity and worthiness to stand before God and address him in an acceptable way is intimately linked to the experience of the daily life of faith. This routine living, however, takes place in a variety of contexts of repressive structures which prevent human development. The pressure of achievement, for example, leads people to identify themselves too closely with their work, possessions and status in society, to lose the awareness of their native otherness and inviolable worth.

In the process of liberation of Christians from such sociologically conditioned repressive structures, the Church has an important role to play. As institution of social freedom, the Church has a responsibility to work for the transformation of the social order, so that it becomes a place where people can live a freeing existence. To this end, the Church should seek to display structures which respect the rights, duties, and freedom of all the members. In this way the community of faith becomes credible as a critic of the social order, provides a model of social reform, and furnishes a context in which the members are prepared for responsible engagement in the social sphere of daily life.[5] We need not pursue this topic further here. One aspect of this theme, which pertains to the vast field of spirituality, is discussed in Chapter 5: the responsibility of the Church to contribute to the transformation of society also through her liturgical celebrations.

Notes

1. This subject is discussed in Part III, chapter 10. For now, it suffices to note that, from the Trinitarian point of view, the Father communicates self to humanity though the mission of the Word and Holy Spirit. Strictly speaking, it is incorrect to refer to self-communications in the case of the Word and Spirit. The concept of three "self-communications" is not compatible with the traditional Trinitarian doctrine of processions. However, this doctrine does not entail a denial that Work and Spirit are actuating in relation to humanity's obediential potency for union with the divine.

2. A. Gerken, OFFENBARUNG UND TRANSZENDENZERFAHRUNG: Kritische Thesen zu einer künftigen dialogischen Theologie (Düsseldorf: Patmos, 1969) 24-25; Idem, THEOLOGIE DER EUCHARISTIE (Munich: Kösel, 1973) 197, n. 59; T. Schneider, ZEICHEN DER NÄHE GOTTES, 31, n. 15.

3. The accounts of the institution of the Eucharist, in the Synoptic Gospels, are a valuable witness to the conviction of Jesus himself, that what he does, in his life for others, is based on the initiative of the Father. The more original source of the activity of Jesus is not expressed; it is hidden by the use of the passive form of the verb. The Pauline account speaks of "the night when he was handed over" (1 Cor 11:23); Lk 22:19 quotes Jesus as saying: "This is my body, which is given for many."

4. The anamnesis-offering prayer of the Eucharistic Prayer of the Apostolic Tradition of Hippolytus derives from the third century. It serves as a model for the expression of the Church's intention in numerous liturgical traditions, and contains this explicit statement about the status of the community of faith: "We thank you that you have reckoned us worthy to stand before you, and serve you in the priestly ministry." (C. B. Botte, LA TRADITION APOSTOLIQUE DE SAINT HIPPOLYTE, LQF 39 [Munster: Aschendorff, 1963] no. 4, 16)

5. J. B. Metz, "Political Theology," in K. Rahner, ed., ENCYCLOPEDIA OF THEOLOGY. The concise SACRAMENTUM MUNDI (New York: Seabury, 1975) 1238-1243; F. Schupp, AUF DEM WEG ZU EINER KRITISCHE THEOLOGIE. Quaestiones disputatae 64 (Freiburg im Br.: Herder, 1974) 43-49; Confer also: J. B. Metz, GLAUBE IN GESCHICHTE UND GESSELSCHAFT (Mainz: Matthias-Grünewald, 1977).

Chapter 5
The Liturgy and Other
Basic Activities of the
Church

We have already explored the relationship between culture, cult, and religious worship. The phenomenon of cult was set within the wider horizon of the human communal life process, and Christian worship was shown to correspond, in its various functions, to all forms of authentic religious worship. Laws governing the relationship between culture and religious worship allowed us to formulate this important pastoral conclusion: Close attention should be paid to changes in culture which affect the understanding of religious symbols and, consequently, threaten the loss of the community's awareness of its identity (Ch. 2). The previous two chapters explained how the human laws governing the binding of liturgical practice to concrete culture come into play in the event of God's self-communication (Ch. 3), and the human experience of the historically acting transcendent God (Ch. 4).

The present chapter returns to a theme already introduced in Chapter 2: the place of worship in the life of the Christian Church. Only now it is considered under a new aspect. The life of faith is expressed in many ways, which can be brought under the general categories of preaching, service of the neighbor, and worship. Our inquiry is not concerned with proving that communal worship should be included under the general category of worship, as a basic activity of the Church. Rather, we ask: What special contribution does liturgy, as a basic activity, make to the full realization of Christian ecclesiastical life?[1]

I.
Christian Understanding of Life

Christians know that they are called into the new life through baptism. Dying and rising with Christ, they are set on the way of Christ (Rom 6:1ff) that leads to fulfillment of the individual personality. However, this discipleship is achieved in the context of a community of faith. The Son was sent by the Father to lay the groundwork for the establishment of the new people of God, in the midst of which the fullness of life is made possible: "I have come that they may have life, and have it in fullness" (J 10:10). The "they" is a community without geographical boundaries, "from every nation, from all tribes and peoples and tongues" (Rev 7:9). But the fulfillment of the promise of the new life requires the full assent of the members, in commitment to the way of Jesus Christ. The community as a whole, as well as the individual believers, must exert themselves on the path toward the fulfilled Kingdom. This effort requires, among other things, thinking over the pattern of social life that is conformed to the ideals of Christian Scriptures.

A. Basic Activities of the Life of Faith

The gift of the new life is described in various ways in the New Testament writings. According to the author of 1 John, it consists in "our fellowship...with the Father and with his Son, Jesus Christ" (1:4). This unity of Christian life derives from God, through Christ in the Spirit: "There is one body and one Spirit...one Lord, one faith, one baptism, one God and Father of us all, who is above all and through all and in all" (Eph 4:4-5). This life is not confined to one dimension of human existence. It embraces the totality of human life. It is lived in and through the body in the whole range of possible relationships: the relation to self, to others, and to the world of things. Paul expresses this idea well: "I appeal to you...to present your bodies as a living sacrifice, holy and acceptable to God, which is your spiritual worship" (Rom 12:1).

The whole field of Christian life can be differentiated according to the ways in which a person lives in relation to self, to others, and to the creator of all. The many forms of activity, as applied to the community of believers, are traditionally gathered under these general headings: 1. the preaching of the faith by word and deed (*martyria*); 2. the self-offering in the service of the neighbor (*diakonia*); 3. the celebration of the togetherness of God and his people (*leitourgia*). However, any Christian activity has the aspects of preaching, service, and worship. For the life of faith is a totality, embracing the whole of human existence, expressing itself fully in all the ways it is actualized.

Preaching of the faith, by word and deed, is a form of worship of God: "...the priestly service of the gospel of God" (Rom 15:16). The charitable service of the neighbor is also a form of worship: "Do not neglect to do good and to share what you have, for such sacrifices are pleasing to God" (Heb 13:16). Worship of God should include a service to all: "...I urge that supplications, prayers, intercessions, and thanksgivings be made for all men.... This is good, and it is acceptable in the sight of God our Savior" (1 Tim 2:1-3). Nevertheless, the various ways of actualizing the life of faith have their own special value. Preaching the word of God is not exactly the same thing as communal worship; communal worship is not equivalent to coming to the assistance of the neighbor in need of material help: "My brothers, what good is it to profess faith without practicing it?... If a brother or sister has nothing to wear and no food for the day, and you say to them: 'Good-bye and good luck!'...what good is that?" (Jas 2:14-16)

B. Liturgy as a Basic Activity

Vatican II's *Sacrosanctum Concilium* affirms that the liturgy is a fundamental activity of the Church. It has the whole tradition of the Church as a backing for this teaching. Jesus himself stresses the need for prayer (Mtt 6:5; Lk 18:1). After his death and glorification, Christians assembled regularly for communal worship. A few texts of the New Testament mention these assemblies. They are described as a "coming together" (1 Cor 11:17ff), or an "assembling together" (Heb 10:25). Paul's remark "If the whole church gathers in a place" (1 Cor 14:23) is equivalent to *the full assembly of the local community.* The Epistle to the Hebrews alludes to the responsibility of Christians to support one another through regular assemblies: "...not neglecting to assemble together...but encouraging one another..." (Heb 10:25). One of the main reasons for assembling was communal worship (Acts 2: 42,47; Eph 5:19-20; Col 3:16). In a relatively short time, the "first day of the week" (Acts 20:7; 1 Cor 16:2), "the Lord's Day" (Rev 1:10), or "the Lord's,"[2] was the regular day of assembly in most Christian churches.

The practice of Christians of all ages of the Church manifests the conviction of faith that communal worship is indispensable to the maintaining and strengthening of the Christian life. Some examples of this conviction, drawn from the ante-Nicene period will suffice. In the second century, Ignatius of Antioch, or Pseudo-Ignatius, bases the obligation on the need to give "thanks and glory to God,"[3] and judges that failure to assemble is a sign of weakness of faith.[4] The third century anonymous author of the Syrian *Didascalia* argues that since Christians are members of the Body of Christ they have the responsibility to assemble lest their absence "cause the Body of Christ to be short a member." The author recognizes that the Body of Christ lives from Christ the head. Therefore he concludes that Christians need to share in the assemblies "on the Lord's Day to hear the word of life, and be nourished with the divine food which abides forever."[5]

The earliest canonical legislation concerning Sunday attendance is found in the Council of Elvira (c. A.D. 309). Canon 21 states: "If anyone located in the city does not attend church three Sundays, let him abstain (i.e., from the eucharistic communion) in order that he may be rebuked."[6] This canon presupposes that an obligation exists. It merely provides a concrete sanction for non-observance of a practice rooted in the nature of Christian life, which may not be neglected for a long time (three weeks!) without serious consequences for the life of faith.

A contemporary document furnishes valuable witness for the understanding of the Christian obligation to participate in weekly services. It is *The Acts of the Martyrs, Saturninus, Dativus, and Their Companions.* These Christians of the town of Abitina, located about 150 miles from Carthage in the upper valley of the Mejerda River, refused to comply with the edict of Diocletian, signed sometime after February 23, 303, which outlawed the Christian religion. They were brought to Carthage for trial. During the interrogation by the proconsul, the presbyter Saturninus was asked why he disobeyed the precept of the emperor by holding assemblies in his house. Saturninus responded: "The *dominicum* cannot be neglected. Thus the law commands." While under torture, replying to the same question, he said: "Thus the law commands, thus the law teaches." Commenting on this, the Christian recorder of the *Acts* writes: "Even under torture, the presbyter proclaims the most holy law on behalf of which he has willingly undergone suffering." When the lector Emeritus was asked why he held assemblies in his house, he answered that he could not turn away his brethren because "...we cannot live without the *dominicum*." After this episode another Christian, Felix, asked why he attended the assemblies, states simply: "I am a Christian." Then the rest of those on trial exclaimed: "We are Christians; we cannot but observe the holy law of the Lord to the shedding of blood." Ignoring this interruption, the proconsul addressed Felix again: "I do not ask whether you are a Christian, but did you participate in the assemblies..." Commenting on this statement, the recorder of the *Acts* observes: "Do you not know, Satan, the Christian is constituted in the *dominicum* and the *dominicum* in the Christian, so that the one without the other does not stand."[7]

In the foregoing account *dominicum* refers to the Eucharistic assembly, a usage current in North Africa and Rome in the third and fourth centuries. These assemblies are related to a law: "the holy law of the Lord." This should not be understood to refer to a positive law about the holiness of Sunday. What is meant is the Law of the Gospel: the spirit of the Gospel which, in a comprehensive way, calls for the celebration of the Eucharist on the Lord's Day. The observance is referred to the law of Christ himself, and the practical observance of it is viewed as the distinctive mark of being a Christian.

The original law of Sunday observance derives from the implications of the Eucharistic celebration for the life of faith. It was not based on a natural law obligation of a community of like-minded believers to worship God together at specific times as a way of expressing their dependence as creatures on the Creator of all.[8]

II.
Nature of Liturgy

What is the peculiar nature of liturgy, in general, that differentiates it from other basic activities of the Church?

In the first place, liturgy involves the being together of like-minded people. It responds to a basic need of humans to be conscious of belonging to a community. Moreover, liturgy supports and deepens what is essential for the existence of Church. The Church is a community of three partners: God, the individual, and the community. In order to maintain this partnership intact, there must be a real, active, and continuous communication. This is a presupposition for all communities. Hence regular liturgical assemblies are relevant from the side of God, the individual and the community as a whole. But the special character of liturgy derives from the fact, not that it furnishes the occasion for assembly, but that it is a *celebration* of the life of faith.

Celebration is a primordial phenomenon of human life. It cannot be brought back to another category and explained through it. It is thoroughly itself, and can be known in its proper reality only in itself. In this respect, celebration is like love. One can speak meaningfully about love, and clarify what it is by reflection. But this can be done only because people already have experiential knowledge of love.

We all know what celebration is from our experience. As a humanizing event, it is primarily expansion of consciousness without the loss of contact with the real world. Human beings spontaneously turn from routine living at regular intervals to engage in celebrations of life. Here ordinary expressions of daily life are stylized to serve as mirror for profound realities hidden in day-to-day existence. We have already noted, in Chapter 2, that this way of acting is intended to bring to the surface enduring values, supportive of human existence, in order that they may be lived more consciously and explicitly. Celebrations of this sort have an important influence on daily conduct; they keep before the minds of the celebrants, the pattern of life that is worthy of them.

Liturgy enables the expansion of consciousness in a way that it proper to it. It includes joyful praise, the placing of serious questions for answers in the confidence of faith, thanksgiving for the benefits received, and communal prayer made "in the name of Jesus." Liturgy corresponds partially to the ordinary phenomenon of humanizing celebrations. But the expansion of consciousness transcends the experience of being accepted by community, and that of living out human values in a celebrative way.

The source of the liturgy is the life of faith, created by the active presence of the risen Lord, in the power of the Spirit, at the very core of the inner life of the faithful. Liturgy is the celebration of believers together in the sphere of the new life of faith, or, more precisely, the celebration of the new life in Christ. Consequently, it includes, in an eminent way, all the qualities of communal activity that support fixed convictions:

the courage to live a life worthy of the gospel; the joy of living; the consciousness of freedom from those compulsions which hinder human growth; the awareness of the dignity of men and women created in the image of the Triune God.

From the foregoing considerations, we can formulate this working definition of liturgy: Liturgy is primarily the exercise of the life of faith under the aspect of being together "in the name of Jesus" for the realization of communion, the sharing and receiving, between God, community, and individual, in a coordinated system of ministerial services. Communal celebrations of the faith are necessary because believers need this form of expansion of consciousness in order to secure their center, or to find it again. From this point of view, and in accord with the whole of authentic Christian tradition, the obligation to share in communal worship is not grounded simply on a natural law demand that creatures must recognize in the social dimension of human life the Creator on whom their existence depends. Rather the Christian obligation to worship in common at regular intervals is based primarily on the need to exercise one's faith in an explicit and social way, to affirm one's fidelity to God, to self, and to others in a communal setting, in order to gain the support to maintain this fidelity in the whole of one's life.

As celebration of the life of faith, liturgy draws on, and integrates, the other two basic activities, preaching and various forms of Christian service of love. As all of God's gifts to his people, liturgy involves the tasks of a grateful response of witness to the gospel, as well as service on behalf of others. All the members of the common priesthood (1 Pt 2:5ff) are called to participate in liturgical service in accord with their gifts and special ministries.

III.
Liturgy and Commitment to the Gospel

Liturgy is also the profound source of the mission of Christians. The essential effect of common worship is a deepening of communion between God and the participants, and of the participants among themselves. If one truly enters into the spirit of the liturgy, actively participates according to the real meaning of Christian worship, one is necessarily led to commitment to that common action by which the Church grows into the Body of Christ.

When I encounter a person, I experience a thou. The measure of the experience is determined by the intensity of the mutual openness of the one to the other. This experience necessarily leads to new action. An experience that does not express itself in a changed orientation of existence and some action, is no genuine experience. The activity, however, might not show itself exteriorly. It might remain for the present as a new focus because effective action is not yet possible.

Encounter always involves the notion of *engagement*: a commitment of one person to the other in the act of encounter.[9] Depending on what happens in the encounter, the engagement can result in the commitment of both parties to a common action. Some encounters lead to essential engagements of people, where the issues are concerned with fundamental interests and value relations of human existence. One thinks of the commitment to fostering social justice. Such engagements derive from the experience of the encounter. Liturgical encounter between God and believers and of believers among themselves, is calculated to issue in an essential engagement. Communal worship should lead to a commitment to the following of Christ in word and deed, a commitment derived from the liturgical experience itself.

Paul speaks from this perspective in the Epistle to the Galatians. Through his preaching of Christ crucified, the Galatians received the Spirit by hearing in faith: "O foolish Galatians! Who has bewitched you, before whose eyes Jesus Christ was publicly portrayed as crucified?... Did you receive the Spirit by works of the law, or by hearing with faith?" (3:1-2) This experience of being justified "by faith in Christ, and not by works of the law" (2:16) should not be in vain: "Have you experienced so many and so remarkable things all to no purpose?170 (3:4) Through baptism, the Galatians have put on Christ, assumed his character, become like him. As a consequence of this union of all with Christ, there derives a superior unity among Christians themselves. Differences disappear in virtue of the realization of the new unity: "For as many of you as were baptized into Christ have put on Christ. There is neither Jew nor Greek, there is neither slave nor free, there is neither male nor female; for you are all one in Christ Jesus" (3:27-28). In this new life, grounded on the Spirit, Christians are called to follow the lead of the Spirit: "If we live by the Spirit, let us walk by the Spirit" (5:25). This means observing the law of love: "...through love be servants of one another" (5:13). "Those who belong to Christ" (5:24), "Bear one another's burdens and so fulfill the law of Christ" (6:2).

The experience of the new relation to God, issuing from the hearing of the gospel and baptism, the experience of being able to say Father, animated by the power of the Spirit of Jesus Christ, is proof that one has received adoption as child of the Father: "And because you are sons, God has sent the Spirit of his Son into our hearts, crying 'Abba! Father'" (4:6). Living "by faith in the Son of God, who loved me and gave himself for me" (2:20), the believer displays this grace by a daily life corresponding to that of Jesus of Nazareth: "But the fruit of the Spirit is love, joy, peace, patience, kindness, goodness, faithfulness, gentleness, self-control" (5:22). "So then, as we have the opportunity, let us do good to all, and especially to those who are of the household of faith" (6:10).

The relationship between communal worship and daily life is a rich theme, deserving of more attention than is often given to it. A liturgical celebration that effectively proclaims the "death of the Lord" (1 Cor 11:26), one in which Jesus Christ is convincingly "portrayed as crucified" for the salvation of the world, will undoubtedly have a profound influence on the daily lives of the participants.

In addition to what has already been said above, three aspects of the relationship between communal worship and routine living call for special consideration. There is the question of the contribution that liturgy might make toward the transformation of social conditions in each culture; the reciprocal influence of liturgy and the daily life of faith; the relation between liturgy and politics in the narrow sense.

A. In the Service of the Transformation of Society[10]

The didactic function of liturgy, mentioned in Chapter 2, gives direction for living a freeing existence in the midst of the numerous circumstances of routine existence which tend to weigh down the spirit. The symbolic language, verbal and gestural, has a power of communication not available to the more discursive speech. In one way or another, Christian liturgy proclaims what Paul calls the vocation to freedom: "For you were called to freedom" (Gal 5:13). All forms of Christian communal worship witness, with thanksgiving, to the grace given to Christians to live free from the law of the flesh: a life of freedom from anxiety, self-seeking, and self-justification. Liturgy promises that, while those who do "the works of the flesh" (Gal 5:19) "shall not inherit the kingdom of God" (Gal 5:19), those who follow the "desires of the Spirit" (Gal 5:17) "will reap from the Spirit eternal life" (Gal 6:8).

Liturgy has the potential to contribute to a freeing existence through its eschatological orientation. The traditional liturgies of the Church, to a greater or lesser degree, all proclaim the hope of the coming Kingdom in which the whole cosmos, and humanity within it, will be fully renewed. Paul describes the longing for this new, changed earth:

> For the creation waits with eager longing, for the revealing of the sons of God... creation itself will be set free from its bondage to decay and obtain the glorious liberty of the children of God. We know that the whole of creation has been groaning in travail...and not only the creation, but we ourselves...groan inwardly as we wait for... the redemption of our bodies (Rom 8:19-23).

This hope should be maintained and fostered through liturgy in ways that contribute to a style of life worthy of those who are "God's own people" (1 Pt 2:10).

The theological reflection, in the churches of both East and West, has paid special attention to the eschatological significance of the use of material elements in the celebration of baptism and Eucharist. In the Christian traditions, which take seriously a theology of sanctification of matter, the material elements of the liturgy are understood to become bearers of "grace." Through the consecration of the water of baptism or the bread and wine of the Eucharist, accomplished by the Church as representative of Christ, and the sanctifying action of the Spirit, these earthly realities obtain a special, divinely willed relationship to the saving God. They become vehicles of the sanctification of the participants of the sacraments. At the same time, these consecrated elements signal the renewal of the whole cosmos. They represent prolepticly the time when the whole transformed cosmos will be the field of worship, when the fully redeemed human race will no longer have need of the symbols of faith to call to mind the mystery of creation.

Certainly this theological outlook has its value, as long as it does not contribute to a reification of saving grace. And there is no doubt that the consecration and sanctification of matter can arouse the Christian hope of the renewal of the world. In addition to this, the vision of the eschatological fulfillment is fostered by the variety of symbolic actions of liturgy, which represent the movement of the pilgrim Church on the way to the Kingdom. In this regard, one thinks of the Great Entrance of the Byzantine Divine Liturgy.[11] The Eucharistic meal is the most potent manifestation of the reality of the fulfilled kingdom; for the whole community shares, by way of anticipation, the banquet of the kingdom with the Lord, in the Spirit, unto the glory of the Father.

However the potential of the liturgy to contribute to the practice of hope is not exhausted by these considerations. Since the liturgy has the function of providing direction for the daily life of faith, it should serve to spotlight concrete socially-conditioned forms of slavery and suffering as a way of liberation of the faithful from the false promises and seductions of the age. Communal worship should support the participants in their quest for freedom from oppressive structures of society. Beyond this, it may be suggested that liturgical space be allowed for participants to express their freeing experience from these obstacles which prevent human development.

It is in keeping with the spirit of liturgy to seek ways in which the opportunity may be offered for the playing out of an anticipated, possible freedom from the daily experience of suffering and servitude. In this way liturgy could become a more effective laboratory of maturity: a place where historically and culturally conditioned forms of oppression, and the pressure to commit oneself to the achievement of limited goals, are revealed as not necessary, and so the place where the hope of the true life, promised by the gospel, is awakened. Through the enlightenment furnished by this kind of liturgy, a freeing existence can be nourished which, by way of anticipation, becomes a living symbol of universal redemption yet to come.

Christian liturgy has its model in the primary symbol of Christian faith, the Cross of Christ. This symbol protests against the subordination of the human person, or the churches of God, to any worldly power or material thing. At the same time, it guarantees the meaning of every employment undertaken for the removal of that suffering which contributes to the dehumanization of the person. Since Christian worship proclaims the liberation of humanity through the Cross of Christ, it should also be made to contribute in concrete ways to the disclosure of the common conditions in cultures which prevent the development of centered selves: people who are freed from the need to always seek their own advantage, and so freed for the service of others. Moreover, communal worship should be so conducted that the opportunity is given to the participants to express their freedom in Christ in all dimensions of the routine living, as a real anticipation of the "...end, when he

(=Christ) delivers the Kingdom to God the Father...that God may be everything to everyone" (1 Cor 15:24-28).

The basic law governing the orientation of Christian liturgical symbolism is succinctly summarized by Thomas Aquinas:

> The sacrament is both a commemorative sign of that which preceded, namely the passion of Christ; and demonstrative of that which is effected in us by the passion of Christ, namely grace; and prognostic, that is foretelling of future glory.[11]

Accordingly, the future of salvation should be highlighted in the liturgy. But the kingdom of God in its totality of meaning, which includes the transformation of the world and human society, has an essentially eschatological nature. Since it can only come to pass by God's action, the Church can only anticipate it by the symbols of faith. The proper place for the practice of the hope of a transformed world is in the daily life of social communication. But as the celebration of the life of faith in all its dimensions, the liturgy of the Church affords a precious opportunity to recall that the world is still far from the state of reconciliation with God, and it provides the context for the practice of the full breadth of the hope in things to come.

B. Liturgy and Politics in the Narrow Sense

We have been discussing the relationship between liturgy and politics *in the wide sense*, that is, a human and social activity concerned with the whole social dimension of the human endeavor. The broad concept of politics is inclusive of the variety of social conditions by which individuals and groups attain their fulfillment in a relatively satisfactory way. But there is also the question of the relation between liturgy and politics, where politics is understood to refer to government and the nature of the regime under which a community lives, as well as the way ordinary people share in it. On this latter topic, some brief reflections will have to suffice.[13]

We measure the concrete efficacy of liturgy by the extent to which it enables the community to transcend the present situation and live a more liberated life of faith, hope, and love. To this end, liturgy should communicate the two scriptural understandings of how God is Lord of history. On the one hand, God is described as one who works in and through history by special interventions in the individual and social spheres. On the other hand, he is identified as one who works in and through the historical activity of human beings.

If liturgy is to remain faithful to the normative witness of Scripture, it must include these two points of view. As a consequence, it may not be expected that authentic forms of Christian worship will offer easy solutions as to how political and social activity should be conducted. But what it offers through its didactic function is extremely important. Good liturgy points to basic values that must be respected in specific political projects: for example, love of poor and rejection of all forms of injustice. In the light of God's justice and peace, which liturgy always announces, the worshipping assembly is invited to inquire about its understanding of justice and peace. In the liturgical affirmation that God's justice is also his mercy, the community is made aware that there is a form of justice which transcends all human justice. This disparity furnishes the ground for a possible critique of all social systems and all earthly forms of authority.

What we call good liturgy highlights the recalling of the death of the Lord, the Cross of Christ: the symbol of the power of the weak. This liturgy awakens the knowledge of values that are more important than those associated with the power of the strong. By fostering the values of fraternity and compassion, communal worship contributes to a type of unity between Christians that is more a unity of trust and desire than one of uniformity in matters of political strategies and policies. In the context of political pluralism, good liturgy is an indispensable means of securing a unity among members of a Christian community that transcends legitimate differences; for it encourages mutual questioning, listening, and the openness to admit the inadequacies of one's own position on disputed issues.

C. Liturgy and the Ethical Life

We have discussed the place of liturgy within the basic activities of the Church and explained the connection between liturgy and a daily life of commitment to the gospel under the aspect of the effect of the experience originating from the liturgical encounter with God. The obverse is the dependence of the efficacy of liturgy on the basic commitment to Christ that the community brings to the liturgical assembly.

Liturgy is not something that takes place totally independent of routine Christian living. Rather, the daily life of faith conditions believers to engage themselves in communal worship in such a way that they are carried to a new level of religious experience, in and through the celebration of the faith, and are able to accept God's grace more explicitly and intensely.

The mutual relation of dependence between liturgy and other basic activities of the Christian life of faith is taken for granted in the Christian tradition. Any further discussion of this subject requires the analysis of the correspondence between the nature of liturgy and the other different activities of faith. One example is that of the connection between Christian worship and the social service of the neighbor.[14]

Liturgy signifies the offering of the whole of one's life as a living sacrifice to obtain from God the meaning of one's existence and to contribute to the salvation of the world by Christian service in the world. The gospel calls on believers to worship God and, at the same time, to assume the responsibility for the good of the neighbor. But the relationship goes beyond the mere juxtaposition of two essential commitments.

The heart of the liturgy is prayer. If we get behind a superficial understanding of prayer as something we do for God, we gain the insight that what we are doing is really something that God is also doing. Is not prayer really the active openness of the creature to God? And is not this openness made possible by God's action, secretly inviting the creature to enter into a holy communion?

Prayer is initiated by God, and through the prayerful response God is enabled to enter more intimately into his world. Thus a situation exists that corresponds to the ultimate goal of creation. This goal is the self-communication of God to his creatures. It reaches its highest fulfillment when the creature praises God for his goodness; for this response is the expression of the openness to receive God's gift in the freedom of faith. Human beings praise God when they make their intention, that for which God created the world. This means recognizing the offer of personal communion with God and accepting it. The response of the creature is praise of God, but it benefits only the creature. It amounts to letting God be God in our lives. Hence it is correct to say that the liturgy, or private prayer, has an anthropological goal from the side of God. From the side of the creature, it has a theocentric goal, that is, letting God be God in our lives.

The achievement of all genuine prayer is a kind of liberation of God to be what he intends to be in relation to his creatures. The proper effect is the birth of self-confidence in one's own dignity as son or daughter of the one Father and, as a consequence, self-forgetful love. In the measure that God is liberated by prayer in our lives we are moved to extend his coming into the full scope of our activity. This necessarily includes our liberating activity in society. By allowing God full rein in our service of the neighbor, God gains further entrance into his creation.

As Christians, we confess that the liberation of God was realized fully, in and through history, in the incarnation of his only Son. The Father was fully acknowledged and received as such by Jesus of Nazareth, and his saving, personal presence extended to others through Jesus' activity. The liberation of God to be the saving God in our world comes through our acceptance of our dignity as sons and daughters of the Father of Jesus Christ and, therefore, our identity as brothers and sisters of one another.

Both the concept of liberation of God and the idea of the identity of people as sons and daughters of the one Father challenge us to do something about the depersonalizing structures and relationships in society. The liberation of God in human history coincides with the understanding of the Kingdom of God preached by Jesus and inaugurated by him. This liberated presence is God's presence in love, in saving power and lordship. It is a power and rule that may not be restricted to the inward lives of believers. It should have an effect on the whole range of social life, though human cooperation.

The intimate link between worship and social activity is based on the concern of both for the coming of the Kingdom and its values. The connection between prayer and social activity should be relatively clear to Christians. The activity of social service is the concrete expression of our identity as children of the one Father. It is the practical recognition of Jesus Christ, the unique Son of God, in the deprived: a service on behalf of the kingly rule of God. Genuine Christian worship naturally opens out into this service in daily life.

However, there is a danger that the link between Christian service and prayer will remain only in the realm of discursive thought. If there is to be a real interaction between prayer and social service, there must be a deeply rooted, experienced connection. This experience is conditioned by the presence of the qualities demanded of humanizing social action.

In social action, the caring for others structurally and personally, the focus of attention and activity, is other human beings. The social worker is drawn into the world of the other. But the other always remains beyond one's grasp, a center of its own, caring and acting in its own right. The other is reached only by invitation freely given. Other persons place a claim on us to recognize their unique and inviolable personhood. They may be a matter of concern to us, but they should be also subjects who command awe and respect.

The recognition of another as a being of irreducible value takes on the qualities of thanksgiving, awe and respect. This way of encountering another as a thou can lead to the recognition of the source of human otherness, the absolute Other. When social activity is motivated by what we have described in Chapter 2 as the mood of "appreciative consciousness," that is, appreciating something or someone in itself, it evokes the qualities of thanksgiving, awe and respect, the very qualities of prayer. One is naturally turned in the direction of the source of all otherness, and so to prayer.

The qualities fostered by Christian worship, which reminds us that God is Father of all, are those which social service tends to awaken through the experience of the other as other. While worship is directed to the Other and the recognition of the otherness of human beings is a byproduct, social service focuses on the others and the recognition of the source of their otherness is a byproduct. The interaction of both experiences is the surest way to safeguard the authenticity of Christian worship and Christian service of love in daily life.

Conclusion

The life of faith is one, but it is expressed in differentiated basic activities. All these activities have the aspects of preaching, service of the neighbor, and worship of God. But they differ from one another insofar as one or other aspect comes to the foreground. Liturgy, according to its essence, is the event of the coming together of the members of a community of faith for the realization of the communication among three partners: God, individual, and community as a whole. It is the most important means of the continuous sharing among these partners, a condition for the maintenance and fostering of the existence of the Church.

However, liturgy makes its unique contribution because it is the communal celebration of the life of faith.

The potential of the liturgy to contribute to the daily life of faith can be discussed from numerous standpoints, beginning with the liturgical experience of the encounter with the Father of all, through Christ in the one Spirit. In this chapter the contribution that liturgy might make to ethical-societal activity was discussed. Also the dependence of the efficacy of liturgy on another basic activity of the Church was explained, namely, Christian social service.

Our concern has been with the anthropological, or horizontal, side of communal worship. The vertical side, the profound and ultimate basis of the relevance and relation of liturgy to the totality of Christian life, was only mentioned marginally. Liturgy is, above all, an event of the offering of the grace of God and a saving communication insofar as the worshipping assembly is open to God's gift. The theology of grace provides access to another approach to the relation between corporate worship and the routine life of faith. This subject deserves special attention and has been developed by others elsewhere. In the interest of brevity, we must be content with a summary observation on this theme. It serves as a conclusion to this chapter and an introduction to Part III, in which the mystery of the liturgy is considered in detail.

The world is God's world, graced from the moment of creation. In it God is always present to the innermost kernel of human existence, inviting humankind to accept his self-communication. In the broad sense, salvation history can be understood as the history of the acceptance of God's love through the exercise of human freedom. This happens wherever human beings live according to the truth of their existence as they see it. The point of time in which this history attained its most profound realization, never to be surpassed, was the sacrifice of the Cross of Christ. In this event what is of ultimate significance for the world is present: the Father's love for the incarnate Son and for all humanity in him. This love was expressly received by the crucified Savior, in his obedience of love unto death on a cross. Through participation in this "liturgy of the Cross," in union with Christ through the Spirit, each individual obtains the meaning of one's life and the pledge of future glory.

In the daily, routine living of the life of faith, Christians have to find ways of expressing their openness to receive the gift of God's love; for grace is offered always and everywhere. God's saving presence claims the response of believers, in freedom of faith, in all relational connections in which they live. The gospel is quite clear on this point. The life of faith is one lived according to the way of Jesus in the whole range of human existence. But Christians are also obliged to grant place and time for the celebration of the "liturgy of the Cross" in the social situation of corporate worship. In the liturgy of the Church, what happens continually and everywhere in all dimensions of human life is explicitly accepted in the praise and thanksgiving of the community of faith, that is, God's self-communication. In the liturgy, the divine depth of human existence is more clearly manifested and more decisively received in freedom of faith.

It is a mistake to conceive the liturgy as the event of a discrete intervention of the God of salvation in an otherwise graceless world. Liturgy is not the only place where the event of grace occurs. Rather, it is a particular holy place within the broad sacral sphere of the whole of human existence. It is the symbolical representation and realization of salvation history, which also becomes a real event wherever men and women of good will respond responsibly to claims made upon them to act in accord with their human dignity. Therefore, for example, the petition that the Holy Spirit be sent from the Father on the participants of the Eucharistic celebration should not be interpreted as referring to an inbreaking of the divine into the world. Rather, it should be understood as expressing the openness of the community to accept the self-communication of God, who is always and everywhere present at the depth of human existence with the offer of his grace.

If we can speak of the "liturgy of the world," a phrase employed by the late Karl Rahner,[15] as the variety of historical events in which God's self-communication is accepted in human freedom, then the high point is the liturgy of the Cross of Christ. The communal liturgy of the Church, the Body of Christ, can be described as the celebration of this liturgy of the world in its definitive expression. The thankful remembrance of the Cross of Christ, made in union with the one High Priest in the power of the Spirit, manifests and realizes the outbreaking of the universal and abiding self-communication of God, which occurs in the whole breadth of human existence.

Christian liturgy is not an odd, special sphere within an otherwise profane existence. It is not correctly described as a divine liturgy in the world, but as the divine liturgy of the world. Nourished by the daily life of faith, the community of believers assembles to explicitly accept in a celebrative mood what is given everywhere, and what alone affords meaning to human existence. The liturgy is needed especially because the mystery of life is too often obscured for the eyes of the dull, who tend to content themselves with the common things of life. Indeed, all Christians need to be reminded continually of the death of the Lord, which reveals this mystery in the public forum. Those who live by faith and not by vision require the constant support of the solemn proclamation of the "Lord's death, until he comes" (1 Cor 11:26).

Notes

1. H. Reifenberg, "Gottesdienst als wesenlicher Grundvollzug christlichen Lebens und seine Konsequenzen für Kirche und Theologie," MÜNCHENER THEOLOGISCHE ZEITSCHRIFT 28 (1971) 241-257.

2. DIDACHE 14.1; Ignatius of Antioch, Ep. to the Magnesians 9.1.

3. Ep. to the Ephesians 13.1.

4. Ep. to the Ephesians 5.3.

5. R. H. Connolly, ed., DIDASCALIA APOSTOLORUM (Oxford, 1929) Ch. XIII, p. 124.

6. C. J. Hefele, ed., HISTOIRE DES CONCILES D'APRES LES DOCUMENTS ORIGINAUX N (Paris: Letovzey et Ané, 1907) 222.

7. T. Ruinart, ACTA MARTYRUM SATURNINI, DATIVI, ET ALIORUM PLURIMORUM MARTYRUM IN AFRICA, P.L. 8. 705-713 (here 710-712).

8. Vatican II's CONSTITUTION ON THE SACRED LITURGY 106 grounds the observance of Sunday not merely on the traditional practice, but also on the meaning of the Eucharist. This text does not dwell on the obligatory nature of the weekly gathering. Rather it stresses the obligation of pastors to instruct the faithful about the meaning of the Eucharist in such a way that they may be led to a joyful participation.

9. H. Wagner, "Begegnung als theologische Kategorie," TRIERER THEOLOGISCHE ZEITSCHRIFT 86 (1977) 25-26.

10. F. Schupp, GLAUBE-KULTUR-SYMBOL, 201-287. This controversial book offers a critical theory of sacramental practice. The author develops the thesis that all Christian symbolic language and symbolic actions should ordered to, and subordinated to, the ethical-societal relations. This proposal is grounded on the Christian vocation to contribute to the transformation of society, as understood in the preaching of Jesus concerning the Kingdom of God. If this book is read as a comprehensive theology of sacraments, which is not the intention of the author, one can find much to criticize (e.g. the review of M. Schmaus in THEOLOGISCHE REVUE 73 (1977) 124-133). But there is no doubt that the presentation of the Catholic doctrine of liturgy, under all its various forms, would be improved if Schupp's insights are included (confer: C. Mayer, "Transformation

der Gesellschaft mit Hilfe der Sakramente," THEOLOGISCHE QUARTELSCHRIFT 155 (1975) 144-149).

11. R.F. Taft, THE GREAT ENTRANCE: A HISTORY OF THE TRANSFER OF GIFTS AND OTHER PREANAPHORAL RITES OF THE LITURGY OF ST. JOHN CHRYSOSTOM. Orientalia Christiana Analecta 200 (Rome: PISO, 1975).

12. SUMMA THEOLOGIAE III. q.60, art.3 resp.

13. D. Power, "The Song of the Lord in an Alien Land," in H.A.P. Schmidt & D. Power, eds., POLITICS AND LITURGY. Concilium 92 (New York: Herder & Herder, 1974).

14. The following exposition of this theme is dependent on the insights of Enda Mc-Donagh, INVITATION AND RESPONSE (Dublin: Gill and Macmillan, 1972) 96-108. A useful presentation of the relation between liturgy and ethics, including a good deal of bibliographical material, is found in G. Wainwright, DOXOLOGY: THE PRAISE OF GOD IN WORSHIP, DOCTRINE AND LIFE (New York: Oxford, 1980) 399-434.

15. "Zur Theologie des Gottesdienst," THEOLOGISCHE QUARTELSHCRIFT 159 (1979) 162-169.

PART III
The Mystery Of Christian Worship

The variety of forms of Christian liturgy of the several liturgical traditions are intended to express, in the manner peculiar to symbolic language, verbal and gestural, the totality of the life of faith. The difference among the traditional forms of liturgical activity, especially the seven sacraments, lies in the intention to awaken a response of faith centered on one or another aspect of this life in Christ. But the way in which that aspect is presented is conditioned by a global perception of the life of faith which impregnates and structures the life of the particular church. The differences between the ways in which the several liturgical traditions of the churches celebrate these types of liturgy originated in the culturally and historically conditioned ways of communication of the common faith.

The authentic Christian liturgical traditions are a unique source of understanding of the economy of salvation. As the expression of the complex world of meaning of Christian faith, liturgy is second only to the primary norm of interpretation of the saving revelation of God in Christ, namely Scripture.

A systematic theology of liturgy attempts to formulate a coherent, concise, and consistent interpretation of the content and meaning of this typical communal activity of the Church. But the systematic theologian cannot rest content with establishing the particular theological outlook reflected in the ritual celebrations of some particular liturgical tradition. The knowledge gained by this investigation is extremely valuable for the whole project. Still the liturgical traditions are not the only sources of knowledge of Christian faith. Liturgy itself, for example, must always be tested and evaluated in the light of Scripture, as well as the other basic sources of knowledge of the faith. This theme is the subject of Chapter 6.

Having identified the scope of the task of a systematic theology of liturgy, a further step is taken in Chapter 7. Here a corollary is developed that flows from the fact that liturgy is a comprehensive expression of the life in Christ. The life of faith is grounded on, and finds its fulfillment in, the economic Trinity. This truth leads to the conclusion that a systematic theology of liturgy can and must be brought back to a theology of the Trinity. But what theology of the Trinity should guide theological reflection on the deepest meaning of the liturgy? If the liturgy is a peculiar expression and realization of the economic Trinity, which grounds and structures all aspects of the economy of salvation, what understanding of this mystery should be presupposed?

The history of dogma is replete with theologies of the Trinity. Some have not survived the critical examination of the churches, while others are favored by one or other ecclesiastical tradition. A systematic theologian is always faced with the problem of selecting an approach to this heart of Christian theology. The theology of the Trinity preferred by this author is set forth in Chapters 8 and 9. An application of this theology to christology and grace is presented in Chapters 10 and 11. Chapter 12, the conclusion of Part III, outlines a presentation of theology of liturgy as theology of the Trinity.

Chapter 6

Theology as Theology of the Liturgy

The phrase "theology as theology of the liturgy" is open to more than one meaning. For example, one speaks of liturgy's theology, employing the subjective genitive. The witness of faith, in the form of the Church's liturgical prayer, is a speaking (*logos*) about God (*Theou*) in the form of a speaking to God. As such, liturgy is a source of theological knowledge. On the other hand, theological reflection on the content and meaning of liturgical practice can also be called "theology of liturgy," employing the objective genitive. Here it is a matter of theological understanding of liturgy, formulated by reflection on the liturgy as object of study.

Understood in the latter sense, two questions can be asked. Is there a sense in which all systematic theological reflection on various aspects of the economy of salvation should qualify as theology of the liturgy? The principle of intelligibility in systematic theology is the relation of one aspect of the revealed mystery of salvation to *all the others*. For example, a theology of grace would be deficient if it did not include the considerations drawn from Christology, pneumatology, etc. Correspondingly, a theological exposition of Christology would not be complete without reflection on the relationship of Christ to the liturgical activity of the Church. But to what extent should all systematic reflection of the various branches of theology be a theology of liturgy, that is, explicitly draw out the implications of their subject for a theology of liturgy?

The second question concerns the value to be awarded to liturgy as a source of theological knowledge. One might presume that liturgy is *the* unique source of knowledge, under which other traditional sources are to be subsumed. Or, liturgy might be considered among several sources, each of which has its particular and indispensable contribution to make to the understanding of the life of faith. How should the role of liturgy, as source of theology, be understood in the task of working out a systematic theology of any aspect of the economy of salvation and, in particular, a systematic theology of the liturgy?

A response to these two questions is given in this chapter. First, it is explained why all so-called branches of theology should endeavor to demonstrate the relevance of their particular subjects for the understanding and practice of the liturgy. Second, the relative value of the liturgy for the formulation of a systematic theology of the liturgy is discussed.

I.
Systematic Theology as Theology of Liturgy

An answer to the first question, posed above, follows as a corollary to certain anthropological observations already discussed in Chapter 2. The subject of the relationship between culture, cult, and religious worship, and the application of this data to Christian worship, need not be repeated here. It may only be noted that liturgy is the most important place in which the Christian community expresses its nature. Liturgy serves the indispensable function of establishing and maintaining Christian identity, mediating the meaning whereby the community is held together and grows.

It is a matter of the highest importance that the connection be recognized *by all*, between the world of meaning, constitutive of the community, and its crystallization in the basic symbolic language, verbal and gestural, of the liturgy. If the correspondence is gradually obscured, if the shape of meaning of the life of faith, expressed in the liturgy, no longer serves as the symbolic expression of the community's self-understanding, then the free acceptance of, and commitment to, the complex world of meaning of the Christian faith will be seriously affected.

From the consideration of the role of liturgy in the life of faith, this conclusion follows: Systematic theologians, working in all branches of theology, should consider it a matter of the highest priority to show how their subjects can contribute to a better understanding and practice of communal worship.

II.
Systematic Theology of Liturgy and Its Sources

A systematic theology of the liturgy differs from the various specialized fields of theology which focus on specific themes. Its object is the liturgical symbolic activity, which expresses in a synthetic way all that goes to make up the life of faith. In the liturgical symbolism all the themes of theology are brought together. The liturgical-sacramental practice implies a comprehensive interpretation of reality, which can be unfolded with constant reference to the practice itself. Hence it may be said that liturgical symbolism *per se* mediates the Christian global perception of the world of faith, and so Christian identity. But *per accidens* the practical connection may not be grasped.

The formulation of the relationship between the Christian perception of the life of faith and the practice of faith has been the subject of discussion in recent years.[1] The linguistic hybrid "orthodoxy-orthopraxies" was first formulated in recent years by Johannes B. Metz, a Catholic German professor of theology, to express this relationship. However the concept goes back to the patristic period and is perhaps best expressed by Maximus the Confessor: "Practice is the reality of the theory; the theory is the intimate and mysterious nature of the practice."[2] Here *ortho-* represents a quality proper to a theory which intrinsically affects practice, and is not the quality of a theory, previously established, of which practice is a casuistic adaptation. Maximus applies this principle to the spiritual life.[3] But it has important applications in the whole range of the practice of the faith, including liturgy.

The practical connection between the world of meaning of Christian faith and communal worship was established with the birth of Christian liturgies. In the patristic period, a good deal of effort was exerted in working out and communicating an ever deeper grasp of the meaning of the liturgical symbolic activity. This can be verified by reading the mystagogical catecheses of Cyril of Jerusalem, John Chrysostom, Theodore of Mopsuestia, and Ambrose of Milan. It is the task of a systematic theology of liturgy to maintain or recover this coherence and to do this by a consistent interpretation of the central symbolic activity of the liturgy.[4] It may be expected that a theology with this orientation will contribute to the building up of the life of faith, which is grounded on, and nourished by, the liturgy.

The study of the theology of liturgy can be undertaken in one of two directions. One may ask about the understanding of the faith reflected in a specific liturgical tradition at some stage of the past history of the Church. By analyzing the relevant data of the historical context in which the liturgy was formulated or used, the particular global theory that grounds the concrete practice can be worked out. A Catholic systematic theology of liturgy is not concerned directly with this kind of historical question. Rather it asks: How is one to explain the connection between the liturgical symbolic activity and the central mystery of the life of faith within the scope of the comprehensive Catholic tradition?

A response to this question requires taking into account the *law of prayer* (*lex orandi*), but also the other sources of theological knowledge. The help of a variety of sources of theology is needed besides the liturgical practice. Each of these sources has a particular contribution to make to the theological enterprise. We can learn much from the liturgy itself about the profound mystery which it represents. But discursive thought is required to bring to the surface the Christian potential of meaning symbolized in liturgy. Special attention must be given to the *law of belief* (*lex credendi*), understood as the doctrinal formulation of aspects of Christian revelation.

A. Lex orandi - Lex credendi

The axiom "law of prayer-law of belief" has become representative of two points of view, regarding the value of liturgy as source of theology. Odo Casel has to his credit the great merit of bringing to the foreground of theological thought the importance of understanding theology as theology of the liturgy. But he tended to make the law of prayer a law "unto itself." According to him, the truth of the faith is made accessible not simply in a unique way through the liturgical celebration of the faith of the Church. Rather the liturgical expression of the self-understanding of the Church, while not rendering other modes of expression of faith superfluous, is clearly superior from all points of view. The authentic liturgical traditions are not simply one among many sources of knowledge of faith, but *the source and central witness* of the life of faith and so of all theology. As a consequence of this one-sided stress on the value of liturgical-practical grounding of theological knowledge, Scripture, and the other sources of theology are placed in the background of his theological reflection.[5]

While Casel tends to formulate the axiom in the direction of "the law of prayer is the law of belief," Pope Pius XII's encyclical letter *Mediator Dei* reverses the accent: "Let the law of belief determine the law of prayer."[6] There is no doubt that he had in mind the problems raised by the reduction of the sources of theology to the law of prayer. His solution is to admit that liturgy is a source of the faith of the highest rank, but to accentuate, by reversing the axiom, the unique value of the law of belief, guaranteed by the teaching authority of the Church.

Both of these approaches, which tend toward an overdrawn identity between theory and practice, threaten to obscure the unique value of two different kinds of expression of faith. In order to avoid either extreme, it should be recognized that the traditional axiom itself is open to either accent in specific cases. The slogan "law of prayer-law of belief" leaves in suspense which magnitude might be the subject, and which the predicate, in particular instances. Consequently, it seems legitimate to state the axiom in this way: *the law of prayer is the law of belief, and vice versa.*

This latter formulation conveys the idea that the two sources of knowledge are neither independent of one another nor serve precisely the same purpose. On the one hand, the law of prayer implies a comprehensive, and, in some measure a pre-reflective, perception of the life of faith. On the other hand, the law of belief must be introduced because the question of the value of a particular liturgical tradition requires the employment of theoretical discourse. One must reckon with the limits of the liturgy as lived practice of the faith. History has taught us that forms of liturgical prayer and ritual activity, however orthodox, often had to be dropped or changed to avoid heretical misunderstanding. Moreover, in new historical and cultural situations, the question of the correspondence between the community's understanding of Christian truth, and its expression in the liturgy and that of the authentic whole tradition, must continually be placed. To respond responsibly to this problem, other sources of theology must be introduced along with the liturgical-practical grounding of the knowledge of faith.[7]

Conclusion

Theology, conceived as the systematic reflection on liturgical practice, can be developed in various ways. But the aim is always the same: to attain more precise knowledge of the depth dimension of all forms of Christian communal worship, as well as the peculiar significance of the various forms in which liturgy is celebrated. Since the mystery of salvation is one, and not many, the one and the same mystery is realized in all forms of the liturgy of the Church. Because this mystery is the ground and goal of all activity of the life of faith, it determines ultimately all aspects of liturgy.

Systematic theology, as systematic theology of liturgy, completes its task only when it demonstrates how the liturgy serves in its particular way as transparency for the mystery of salvation. The reduction of the theology of liturgy to the one divine plan of God is the aim of this theology. The one mystery of Christian faith is the Triune God in his self-communication to humanity. All classical liturgies confess this Trinitarian grounding and goal of the economy of salvation. In different ways, the forms of liturgy express the conviction of faith that the Triune God, in their economic activity, is the mystery of Christian worship. Consequently, theologians are challenged to show how theology of liturgy can be formulated as theology of the economic Trinity.[8] The concept of theology of liturgy as theology of the Trinity receives further attention in the next chapter.

Notes

1. P. Schoonenberg, "Orthodoxie und Orthopraxie," in DER ANTWORT DER THEOLOGEN (Düsseldorf: Patmos, 1968) 29-34; O. Semmelroth, "Orthodoxie und Orthopraxie: Zur wechselseitigen Begründung von Glaubenserkennen und Glaubenstun," GEIST UND LEBEN 49 (1969) 359-373; C. Dumont, "Orthodoxie vor Orthopraxie?" THEOLOGIE DER GEGENWART 13 (1970) 184-191; T. Schneider, "Orthodoxie und Orthopraxie: Überlegungen zur Struktur des christlichen Glaubens," TRIERER THEOLOGISCHE ZEITSCRIFT 81 (1972) 140-152.

2. QUAESTIONES AD THALASSIUM 63 (PG 90.681).

3. I. H. Dalmais, "La doctrine ascétique de s. Maxime le Confessor d'après le LIBER ASCETICUS," IRENIKON 17-39; L. Thudberg, MICROCOSM AND MEDIATION: THE THEOLOGICAL ANTHROPOLOGY OF MAXIMUS THE CONFESSOR (Lund: G. Leerup, 1965) 355-356; 360-363.

4. A. Schilson, THEOLOGIE ALS SAKREMENTENTHEOLOGIE: Die Mysterien-theologie Odo Casels. Tübinger Theologische Studien (Mainz: Matthias-Grünewald, 1982) 19-21.

5. A. Schilson, THEOLOGIE ALS SAKRAMENTENTHEOLOGIE, 128-131.

6. AAS 39 (1947) 540: "Lex credendi legem statuit supplicandi."

7. On the subject of the original meaning of the axiom: LEX ORANDI - LEX CREDENDI, confer: P. de Clerk, "'Lex orandi-Lex credendi.' Sens originel et avatars his-torique d'un adage équivoque," QUESTIONS LITURGIQUES 59 (1978) 193-212. Also K. Lehmann offers a good analysis of the problem of the relationship between dogmas and liturgical expression of faith: "Gottesdienst als Ausdruck des Glaubens," LITUR-GISCHES JAHRBUCH 30 (1980) 197-214.

8. L. Lies, "Trinitätsvergessenheit Gegenwartiger Sakramententheologie," ZEITSCHRIFT FÜR KATHOLISCHE THEOLOGIE 105 (1983) 290-291, notes the im-portance of the reduction of theology of liturgy to a theology of the Trinity in a critical review of several new contributions to the theology of sacraments.

Chapter 7

Theology of the Liturgy as Theology of the Trinity

According to Scripture, as interpreted by the traditional theologies of the East and West, salvation of rational creatures is a participation in the divine life of the Holy Trinity. This sharing in the life of personal communion with the three divine persons is a grace added to the grace of human existence. Since it is a matter of personal union between creature and Creator, there is required the free acceptance on the part of the creature.

The nature of the grace of union between divine persons and human beings cannot be fully grasped because creatures can never penetrate fully the mystery of God. Hence the concept of creaturely participation in divine life, or "divinization," is interpreted differently in the various traditional theologies. But always the analogy of human interpersonal communication is employed. The difference between human interpersonal communication, and that between humans and the divine persons can be described as the difference between partial and total self-communication. Since humans have only the immediately measurable experiential knowledge of being able to communicate a part of themselves to others, or of being the communicants of the limited share in the personal life of others, the full import of the divine self-communication remains a mystery, even when revealed in the experience of the life of faith.

The revelation of the transcendent goal of human existence is given to creatures in history, in the experience of personal communion with God. The authoritative interpretation of this experience is found in the witness of Scripture and the Tradition of the Church. The Church confesses that those who accept God's invitation to loving communion are already sharers by faith in a mystery that will be fully grasped in the light of glory by the blessed in heaven.

What the Church confesses about the nature of the grace of salvation, already bestowed on those who accept it in faith, can be described as Trinitiarian self-communication. A more extended treatment of this topic is given in Chapter 10. For now it suffices to note that self-communication, as applied to the Trinity, means a Trinitarian communication of divine life. According to Christian revelation, the Father communicates self since the Father is the source of all. But he communicates self through his Word and his Spirit to his creatures. Word and Spirit do not simply communicate themselves. However this does not exclude the idea that the Spirit and Word actualize the potential of a human being for personal communion with the Father.

The self-communication of the Father, outside the inner-Trinitarian life, always includes the communication of the Word and the Spirit. If the Word alone assumes the humanity of Jesus of Nazareth, there is also a sanctification of that humanity through the communication of the Spirit. In the instance of ordinary human persons, the Spirit is the source of sanctification by which they are brought into personal union with the Word, the essential image of the Father, and so into union with the Father.

One other aspect of the Father's self-communication may be noted here. Precisely because it is self-communication which has a Trinitarian structure in its content and execution, the experience of the Trinitarian grace is the experience of how God exists in God's self. Therefore the knowledge of faith, derived from the experience of the Christ-event, penetrates to the inner-Trinitarian life. There is a real correspondence between the way God exists in God's self and the way God reveals self in the economy of salvation, through the life, death, and glorification of Christ and the sending of the Spirit to establish the Church. It is axiomatic in Catholic theology that the economic Trinity is the immanent Trinity. What God reveals of self in the history of salvation corresponds to the way God is in God's self.

Further elaboration of this axiom need not detain us here. It is the subject of Chapter 8. However we can anticipate one important conclusion that follows from the identification of the economic and immanent Trinity, and which is pertinent to the theme of the theology of liturgy. Liturgical celebrations are a medium of participation of the faithful in the economic Trinity, a medium of Trinitarian self-communication. Liturgy is, above all, the work of the Trinity in its *execution* and *content*. What the community does is made possible because of the gift of the life of faith, a life lived in communion with the Father, through the Son in the Holy Spirit. Therefore, all three divine persons have an active role in the execution of the liturgy of the Church. Correspondingly, the efficacy of the liturgy is also, at its depth, a participation in Trinitarian life.

I.
Trinitarian Theology of the Liturgy

The mystery of the liturgy has a Trinitarian structure in its execution and content. From this axiom it can be concluded that a systematic approach to the theology of the liturgy has the task of demonstrating how the liturgy can be conceived as a realization of the economic Trinity. In other words, the identity between the mystery of liturgy and the mystery of the economic Trinity is the fundamental principle that should guide the attempt to work out a systematic elaboration of the theology of worship. A theology of worship must be concerned with showing how this real identity is to be understood and what consequences follow from this.

The reduction of the theology of liturgy to the theology of the Trinity is not only possible, it must be the goal of any theology of Christian worship. The dialogical structure of the liturgy, address of the Triune God and response of the believing community, shows that liturgy is a reality of the life of faith in which the economic Trinity is symbolically represented and communicated. The liturgical activity of the Church is a "real symbol" of the economy of salvation, that is, of the mystery of God's plan of salvation for the world, which reached its fulfillment in Jesus Christ and which is being further realized through the mission of the Spirit in the time of the Church. A systematic theology of worship must include, as the central theme, the explanation of the identity between this mystery of the economy of salvation and the mystery of the liturgy.

The idea of theology of liturgy as theology of the Trinity is hardly new. But there have been very few attempts to work out such a theology in a systematic way. Since there is a scarcity of proven models that might serve as a solid basis for further reflection, this project represents a real challenge. In recent times, some theologians have introduced the theology of the Trinity into their systematic reflections on the sacraments.[1] But generally the references to the Trinity serve only as a helpful means of pointing out what must be included in a comprehensive theology of liturgy.[2] Corresponding to liturgical prayer, which confesses that the liturgy is a medium of communication of Trinitarian life, a reference is always found to the Trinity in Catholic works on the theology of the liturgy. However the integration of a Trinitarian theology, so that it serves as more than a marginal aid to the understanding of the Christological and pneumatological dimensions of the liturgical event, frequently remains unfinished business.

Part of the problem can be traced back to the inadequate grounding of the Trinitarian dimension of all aspects of the economy of salvation: creation, history, humankind, grace, incarnation, mission of the Spirit, and Church. All aspects of the economy of salvation are realizations of the economic Trinity and must be brought back to this mystery. To the extent this endeavor is successful, the formulation of a theology of the liturgy as theology of the Trinity becomes possible.

II.
A Typical Modern Catholic Approach to the Mystery of the Liturgy

A typical modern Catholic approach to the mystery of liturgy can serve as an example of the problem involved in developing a theology of liturgy as theology of the Trinity. This approach is guided by the concept of liturgy as encounter with Christ, and displays the following traits.[3]

A. Presuppositions

The presentation presumes the procession model of the immanent Trinity, without developing a specific Trinitarian theology, even in the sense of the Eastern and Western options concerning the procession of the Spirit from the Father "through the Son" (East) or "and the Son"

(West). A distinction between the Trinitarian work in creation and sanctification (Trinitarian self-communication) is taken for granted. But the question of attribution of sanctification to the Godhead as such (a Western tradition) or to the personal mission of the Spirit (Eastern tradition) is not explicitly treated.

B. Anthropological Point of Departure

The anthropological basis of liturgical symbolic activity is described. The human being is real symbol, embodied spirit, and also symbol-maker, who creates symbols and communicates through them. To this anthropological basis is added a consideration of the fundamental principle of theological anthropology, namely, that human beings are created in the image and likeness of God and find their meaning by growth in this likeness through free acceptance of God's self-communication. From this beginning the presentation moves to Christology, then to the ecclesiological aspects of the economy of salvation, and finally to the liturgy, conceived as activity of the Church that takes place in union with that of Christ.

C. Christology

The attempt to formulate a theology of liturgy, applicable to the seven chief rites of the Church, begins with the mystery of Christ. He is the God-man. His humanity, joined in unity of person with the divine Word through his human spirit, is real symbol of God. Jesus Christ is simply the primordial sacrament of salvation; in him the divine prototype and the human image of God are united in unity of being, through the divine person of the only Son of God. As such he reveals and communicates the divine life to those who accept him in faith.

Because of the hypostatic union, resulting from the assumption of the humanity of Jesus of Nazareth by the Word sent from the Father, the Word himself bestows the Spirit from the Father on his own humanity. Thereby the humanity of Jesus receives the fullness of created grace; for the Spirit is the principle of sanctification of human beings.

In virtue of Jesus' obedience, grounded on the love of the Father and consummated in the event of the Cross, the humanity of Christ is raised to new life by the Father "in the power of the Spirit." In this new mode of existence as risen Lord, Jesus Christ is filled with the Spirit. In the pneumatic state, and in virtue of his redemptive work, Christ sends the

Holy Spirit from the Father as the divine principle of the life of the Church.

D. Ecclesiology

The establishment of the Church is a process of life, which includes the mystery of the incarnation, life, death, and glorification of Christ together with the sending of the Spirit to establish the new people of God. The grace of the Church is the gift of the Spirit, made possible by Jesus' human obedience. Through the gift of his Spirit, Christ shares his glorified existence with the members of his Body, the Church on earth.

The earthly Church is essentially a kind of broadening of the mystery of Christ within the history of humanity. The earthly Body of Christ corresponds structurally to the divine-human unity of Jesus Christ. Hence the Church can be called a "comprehensive sacrament" because of its unity with Christ. As a visible sign and instrument of the mystery of Christ, the Church is always dependent on Christ. Consequently, Christ's saving work, his life, death, and glorification, are always present and effective in the essential activity of his Body, the Church. All genuine works of the Church are works of Christ, who is present and active in and through these activities "in the power of the Spirit" whom he possesses in fullness.

The Spirit, whom Christ bestows on the Church, is the principle of the life of faith. In this sense, the Spirit may be called the "soul" of the Church. This implies that the establishment, maintenance, and growth of the Church depend on the *communication of the Holy Spirit*. But the idea that the Spirit is the soul of the Church should not be understood to imply that the Church can be called "sacrament of the Spirit." As "soul of the Church," or the ultimate depth of the life of faith of the Church, the Spirit resists corporealization. What is corporealized is the effect of the work of Christ. However, the Church is the place of the working of the Spirit, who conforms the Body of Christ to its Head.

E. Liturgy

The Church precedes the liturgy, even as the seven sacraments, in the logical order; for the liturgy, in all its forms, is the manifestation and realization of the Church as the Body of Christ. In the liturgy, and through it, the participants are taken up into Christ, "in the power of the Spirit," and through the encounter with Christ salvation is effected. This salvation is the self-communication of the Triune God. Hence the economic Trinity stands behind Christ, the primordial sacrament, who is encountered in the worship of the Church. In other words, the saving grace, derived from the redeeming work of Christ, is mediated through the encounter with Christ in the liturgy. The encounter with Christ culminates in the bestowal of the Spirit and his gifts. Since Christ is met in the liturgy and the believing participants accept Christ, they are brought into communion with the Father and become "another Christ" in the Spirit of adoption.

The acceptance of the grace of Christ is realized when the participants "give back" the saving work of God in Christ to the Father by prayer of praise and thanksgiving; for no work or word of God, among his people, reaches its goal unless there is this response of thankful confession of total dependence on the Triune God.

1. Critical Evaluation

The model described above stresses the unity between Word and Spirit; the implications of the differentiation are scarcely developed. As a consequence, the economic Trinity is placed behind Christ who, as primordial sacrament of salvation, stands in the foreground. The impression is given that a partially achieved unity of believers with Christ results from the liturgical encounter, and the role of the sanctifying Spirit is to fully actualize this unity.

The weakness of this systematic approach can be traced, at least in part, to the lack of a Trinitarian grounding of symbol,[4] that is, one that takes into account not only the unity of the divine persons but also the real distinction between them. In the immanent Trinity, the Father and the Word are identically the divine essence. Therefore we can speak of the divine immediacy of the Word to the Father, that is, the absence of any intervening reality. On the other hand, the Father is the source of all. The Word of God is spoken by the Father, who does not speak another Word; for all that can be spoken is said in this one Word. Proceeding from the Father eternally, the Word is the essential image of the Father. From this point of view, one must speak of the *divinely mediated immediacy* of the Word to the Father.

The Word is "real symbol" of the Father. A real symbol exists where there is unity of being between the symbol and the symbolized and yet the symbol is really distinguished from the symbolized. As essential image of the Father, the Word is identically the divine essence. But the fact that the Father and Word are identically the divine essence does not mean that the Word is the Father. Rather, the Word is from the Father, really distinguished from the Father as essential image of the Father. If one can agree that this Trinitarian grounding of the relation between "real symbol" and symbolized is valid, in an analogous way, for the order of grace, then this axiom should be acceptable: *The relation between symbol and symbolized always involves a mediated immediacy.*

This axiom can be recognized at work in the old patristic theology's analysis of essential aspects of the economy of salvation. In christology the principle of mediated immediacy is expressed very explicitly in the teaching, based on the Spirit-christology of the New Testament, that the Spirit binds the humanity of Jesus to the Word in hypostatic union. The Spirit is not a medium between the humanity and the person of the Word. In ecclesiology the unity between Christ and the Church is also conceived as the work of the Spirit who, as Spirit of Christ, is also the Spirit of the Church. The Spirit binds the Church to Christ, but is not a medium between Christ and the Church. In the order of grace the just person is understood to be united to the Father "in the Spirit," but immediately. No thing or person, not even Christ himself, stands between the just person and the Father. Also the active presence of Christ in the liturgy of the Church is not conceived as simply unmediated. Rather, it is the effect of Holy Spirit who binds the participants to Christ, though not as a medium between Christ and the worshipping community.

The model of a systematic approach to the theology of liturgy, which we are evaluating, includes a reference to the three divine persons. But no attempt is made, from the outset, to supply a genuine Trinitarian grounding of symbol. For the rest, the tract on the Trinity is only marginally introduced.[5] A Trinitarian theology of the incarnation, death, and glorification of Jesus is missing, as well as a Trinitarian ecclesiology. This theology of the liturgy takes the first step, that of bringing the liturgy back to the theology of Church and then to christology. But the second step is not attempted, namely, that of showing how the liturgy can be brought back to the economic Trinity and under all its aspects. Therefore the synthesis remains unsatisfactory. A Trinitarian anthropology, christology, pneumatology, and ecclesiology make possible a Trinitarian theology of the liturgy. Without this background, the elements of a theology of the Trinity, which are always included either explicitly or implicitly in a Catholic theology of the liturgy, necessarily remain unintegrated.

The example of a theology of liturgy which we have been considering is at home within the traditional scholastic theological synthesis. The key to the development is a notion of "real symbol," that is, a signifying reality that enjoys unity of being, given or achieved, with the reality signified. As such, the real symbol always communicates what it signifies. The Incarnate Word's humanity is real symbol of the divine Word. The Church is real symbol of Christ, and so its activity is real symbol of Christ's activity.

In this traditional Catholic outlook, the unity between the risen Lord and the Spirit is stressed. The differentiation between the two, and the consequences of this for the understanding of the dynamics of the economy of salvation, do not come to the foreground. Since the personal mission of the Spirit in the economy is dealt with equivocally or neglected, the impression is given that in the order of nature, not in priority of time, the Word assumes the humanity of Jesus and then bestows the Spirit, and the gifts of the Spirit, on that humanity. The same order of priority holds for the Church. The risen Lord unites his disciples to himself and then bestows the Spirit as "soul" of the Church. The liturgy of the Church is awarded the same structure. In the liturgical celebrations, the faithful encounter Christ, who draws them into union with himself "in the power of the Spirit."

In the conceptual framework of this model, the Spirit appears to be the instrument whereby Christ fully actualizes the union of believers with himself. This outlook is at home within the traditional scholastic approach to the theology of the Holy Spirit. According to the longstanding Western teaching, the work of sanctification of humanity is conceived as the work of the Triune God in an undifferentiated way. It is attributed to the Spirit, but only in terms of "appropriation," namely, because the Spirit signifies divine life. It is not predicated of the Spirit because of the personal mission by which the Spirit exercises a personal role in the economy of salvation, with divine sovereign freedom, though always in harmony with the personal mission of the Word.[6]

Conclusion

A theology of the liturgy as theology of the Trinity should begin with a theology of the Trinity. The personal missions of the Word and Spirit should be taken into account. In christology the immediate problem is the explanation of the personal roles of the three divine persons in the incarnation. The Second Vatican Council offers some guidance in this regard. The council does not present any new official teaching on the subject of the immanent Trinity that goes beyond that of the Council of Florence.[7] However, the conciliar teaching about the mission of the Son (*Lumen gentium* 3) and the complementary mission of the Spirit (*Lumen gentium* 4) offers encouragement for theologians to explore the nature and consequences of the personal mission of the Spirit in the economy of salvation.

What we know about the immanent Trinity is known from what took place in the world with the God-man Jesus Christ.[8] Therefore, the theology of the immanent Trinity, to be employed in a theology of liturgy, should derive from below, from christology. This means that the revelation of the Spirit, given in the Christ-event, determines our understanding of the Spirit in the inner-Trinitarian life. Beginning with a theology of the Trinity derived "from below," which nevertheless does not remain below, the task of constructing a theology of liturgy as theology of the Trinity can be undertaken.

Next there is the problem of formulating the inter-relationship between Christ, the primordial sacrament of the Triune God, and the Church, the comprehensive sacrament of Christ. The solution to this problem must be sought in the event of the Cross and resurrection; for it is the dead and risen Christ through whom we are given a share in the Trinitarian life.

At this juncture, the subject of pneumatology should be introduced; for the sharing in the mystery of Christ takes place "through one and the same Spirit" (1 Cor 12:13). The Spirit is the principle of sanctification in the individual and corporate life of the Church. The Spirit is the bond of union between the primordial sacrament Jesus Christ and the Church. In virtue of the presence of the Holy Spirit, the Church is a mystery intrinsically related to the mystery of the incarnation. The Church is like the mystery of the incarnation in that the social structures of the Church serve the Spirit of Christ, just as the humanity of Jesus serves the divine Word as organ of salvation.[9] The Church has it own proper structures. It is a mystery that has something to do with the economic function of the Spirit. This social reality is sacrament, made so by Christ, who shares his life-giving Spirit with his disciples and through his Spirit makes his Body, the Church, the social organ of communication of the Trinitarian life.[10]

In all the activity of the Church, the believers encounter the Triune God through the "service of the Spirit," who refers the community back to the original Christ-event through the authentic witness to this event given in the apostolic preaching, and leads the community into the full dimensions of this mystery through the response of faith to new situations in the life of the Church, which are to be answered in the light of Tradition.

In the Trinitarian approach to liturgy, the God whom Christians encounter in the worship of the Church is the Triune God. The Trinitarian God does not stand behind the risen Lord, who is present to his community assembled in his name. Rather the risen Lord is present to the assembly as its Head "in the Spirit." The Spirit, whom Christ possesses in fullness, whom Christ promised to his Church, is possessed by the holy assembly. The one Spirit, in Christ and in the Church, is the personal agent through whom the Lord is united to his Church, the personal source of divine power by whom the Lord is personally present, uniting the worshipping assembly to his eternal worship.

Notes

1. T. Schneider, ZEICHEN DER NÄHE GOTTES, 36-48, offers a partial synthesis of this type. He includes an integration of pneumatology and christology, beginning with the pentecostal event of the personal mission of the Spirit. But a thoroughgoing systematic presentation of the relation between the economic and immanent Trinity, and its relevance for a theology of liturgy, is not carried through.

2. The important contribution of E. H. Schillebeeckx to the history and theology of the sacraments, DE SAKRAMENTELE HEILSECONOMIE. Theologische bezinnung op s.Thomas' sacramentenleer in het licht van der traditie en van de hedendaagse sacramenten problematiek (Antwerpen T'Groeit: Nelissen, 1952) is marked by this deficiency, as is his more popular systematic theology of the sacraments, CHRIST, SACRAMENT OF THE ENCOUNTER WITH GOD (New York: Sheed and Ward, 1963).

3. The model employed here is quite typical of modern Catholic theology, and serves as the background for the recent contributions of L. Scheffczyk, "Jesus Christus—Ursakrament der Erlösung," and "Die Kirche—das Ganzsakrament Jesu Christi," and P. Kuhn, "Die Sakramente der Kirche—siebenfältige Einheit," which are found in H. Luthe, ed., CHRISTUSBEGEGNUNG IN DEN SAKRAMENTEN (Kevelaer: Butzen und Becker, 1981) 9-120 (Scheffczyk), 121-200 (Kuhn). This summary corresponds, in part, to the one found in L. Lies' critical appraisal of Luthe's book ("Trinitätsvergessenheit," 291-295).

4. Lies, "Trinitätsvergessenheit," 294-295.

5. The marginal treatment of the Trinitarian grounding of the theology of sacraments in Scheffczyk's essays is surprising. This author has made several contributions to the

theology of the Trinity. In his latest article on this subject, he demonstrates a good grasp of the German theological literature, and reports that the theology of the Trinity has become a focal point of theological interest: "At present, it is considered of the highest significance for faith and theology" ("Uneingelöste Traditionen der Trinitätslehre," in W. Breuning, ed., TRINITÄT: Aktuelle Perspektiven der Theologie. Quaestiones disputatae 101 (Freiburg im Br.: Herder, 1984) 47-72 [citation: 47]).

6. The traditional Western theology of "appropriation" leads logically to the conclusion that the Spirit is "soul of the Church" only by extrinsic denomination. The soul of the Church is really the activity of the Godhead as such. When the idea of soul of the Church is linked to a personal mission of a divine person, through which the establishment, continued existence, dynamism, and future directedness of the Body of Christ is realized, the only choice is to call the risen Lord the soul of the Church. Odo Casel, who is inspired by the pneumatology of the Alexandrian tradition before the fourth century and therefore before the development of the classical theology of the Holy Spirit, precisely says this: "Jesus Christ became KYRIOS CHRISTOS and as such, as the PNEUMA, is the soul of the Church, his Mystical Body" ("Mysteriengegenwart," JAHRBUCH FÜR LITURGIEWISSENSCHAFT 8 [1929] 155.) Confer: A. Schilson, THEOLOGIE ALS SAKRAMENTENTHEOLOGIE, 311.

7. DS 1300, 1330-1332.

8. W. Kasper, JESUS THE CHRIST (London: Burns and Oates, 1976) 180: "Our whole thinking moves from the world to God.... We never conclude from the Trinity to Christ and his Spirit given to us, but always the other way around."

9. This analogy is developed in Vatican II, LUMEN GENTIUM 8. In this way the council affirms that the unity between the Church and Christ includes the difference. The Church is a mystery, which has its own proper structure. Through a theologically differentiated way of speaking, the council corrects the view that the Church is simply the continuation of the incarnation: "As the assumed nature (the humanity of Jesus is meant) ...serves the divine Word as living organ of salvation, so in a similar way, the social structure of the Church serves the Spirit of Christ who vivifies it, in the building up of his Body."

10. The application of the Trinitarian structure of the economy of salvation to all aspects of the life of the Church is recognized by many theologians as a primary task of systematic theology. On the subject of "Trinity and Church," confer: E. Salmann, "Trinität und Kirche: Eine dogmatische Studien," CATHOLICA 38 (1984) 352-374. A recent contribution of Orthodox theology to this subject, which takes some account of the Catholic theological contribution, is found in the essay of G. Larentzakis, "Trinitarische Kirchenverständnis," in W. Breuning, ed., TRINITÄT, 73-96. The application of the model of the Church as mystery of the twofold mission of the Word and Spirit to canon law is made by R. Sobánski, "Modell des Kirche-Mysteriums als Grundlage der Theorie des Kirchenrechts," ARCHIV FÜR KATHOLISCHE KIRCHENRECHT 145 (1976) 22-44.

Chapter 8
The Economic and
Immanent Trinity

"Jesus Christ is true God and true man." This confession served many generations of the early Church as the adequate expression of the mystery of the relationship between Jesus of Nazareth and his Father, the Father of all. However, christological controversies, beginning in the fourth century, necessitated a more ample formulation in order to maintain the truth of the original creedal statement. A new formula was approved at the Council of Chalcedon, October 22, 451.[1] The council taught that in Jesus Christ the divine and human natures (*physis*) are "unconfused" and "unseparated," and that the center of unity is the one person (*mia hypostasis*) of the Word of God. The limitations of this dogma are well known. The difference is not brought out between the relation of the one hypostasis to the divine nature (a relation of identity) and the relation of the hypostasis to the humanity of Jesus (real distinction). Also, the question is left open as to how the humanity is assumed by the Word.

The history of the "reception" of Chalcedon is a complicated question and need not concern us here. The teaching of the council was the occasion for division in the communion of churches. However the churches that remained in union with Constantinople and Rome have made the symbol of Chalcedon a cornerstone of official christology. The other cornerstone of christology, understood in the limited sense, is the teaching of the Council of Constantinople III, September 16, 681, which rejected Monotheletism and, at the same time, defined that Christ had a human will.[2]

From the standpoint of this official christology of Byzantium and Rome, which has undergone practically no development in the subsequent centuries, the following may be said: On the ground of the one divine person in Jesus Christ, his personal and human reality has entered into a unique union with God from the outset of his existence. Jesus of Nazareth is the Father's ultimate, never to be surpassed, gift to the world. It may also be added, as a corollary, that the psychological unity of Jesus of Nazareth with the Father has its ultimate ground in that communication of being, of subsistence, from the Father to the humanity of Jesus, which constituted him as Son of God in his humanity. Jesus of Nazareth, in his person and activity, is the fullness of revelation of God in the economy of salvation.

The full access to the mystery of God's selfhood comes only through the incarnate Word of God. This means that what we know about God, as Triune God, derives from the knowledge communicated through the revelation of God in Jesus Christ. The way God reveals self in Jesus Christ is the way God exists in God's self.

The correspondence between the way God reveals self in the incarnation, and the way God exists in God's self, is the subject of this chapter. Having shown how the intimate relation between the revelation of God in Jesus Christ and God's inner-divine life is to be understood, a conclusion is drawn that has special relevance for a systematic theology of the Trinity.

I.
The Economic and Immanent Trinity

The term "economic Trinity" has a field of meaning that includes the free decision of God to go out of self in creation, the concrete arrangement of this project, and its execution. Above all, it refers to the ultimate goal of creation: God's self-communication to humanity, which began with the creation of humankind, reaches its fullness in the incarnation, and is extended to all humanity in a new way through the mission of the Spirit at Pentecost. The term "immanent Trinity" refers to the mystery of the inner-divine life of Father, Son, and Spirit, the source of the economic Trinity. Concerning the relation between the two, Karl Rahner has formulated this axiom: *The economic Trinity is the immanent Trinity, and vice versa.*[3] This formula serves as the point of departure for the following reflections on the relation between God's self-revelation and the inner-Trinitarian life.

A. The Economic Trinity Is the Immanent Trinity

The first part of this axiom can hardly be challenged by Catholic theologians. Through the mission of the Word in the incarnation and the complementary mission of the Spirit after Christ's glorification, salvation is revealed to consist in the self-communication of the Triune God, originating from the Father. Because the economic Trinity is the *self-communication* of God, what is revealed and communicated is God as God exists in God's self. Given the consistency of God, it follows that the economic self-communication of God is a real revelation of the inner-Trinitarian mystery. The self-communication of the Father, through the missions of the Word and Spirit, would not be self-communication, if what God is for us in the Word and the Holy Spirit is not proper to God in God's self.

B. The Immanent Trinity Is the Economic Trinity.

What does the second part of the axiom, "and vice versa," add to the first part? What did Rahner intend by it?[4] It could be employed to express the idea that what is involved in the economic Trinity corresponds to the immanent Trinity both in the *effect* and in the *execution*. The effect is the self-communication of the Father through the missions of Word and Spirit. The execution, according to Eastern theology, corresponds to the real distinction between the two processions in the immanent Trinity. Therefore, Eastern theology awards to the Holy Spirit a personal mission in the role of sanctifier. Traditional Western theology, on the other hand, has assumed that there is one personal mission in the economic Trinity, that of the Word. The work of sanctification is attributed to the Godhead as such, and to the Spirit only by way of "appropriation," that is, insofar as the name "Spirit" corresponds to the sanctifying activity of the Trinity. Rahner, among other Catholic theologians, has shown some dissatisfaction with this "appropriation" theory.

Rahner's may have used "vice versa" to exclude the Hegelian doctrine of the Trinity, namely, that God must come into Trinitarian self-possession through the otherness of the world! In line with traditional Catholic theology of the Trinity, Rahner opposes the Hegelian position, and has emphasized more than once that God is Trinity from eternity in the highest freedom. In short, the "vice versa" seems to be intended to affirm, at the very least, the necessary priority of the immanent Trinity. It must be stressed that Rahner does not intend the second part of the axiom to mean simple identity. He clearly states that the concepts and realities do not simply coincide. The immanent Trinity is the presupposition for the economic Trinity, the condition of its possibility.[5] However, he did not spell out all the implications of the second part of the axiom. Other theologians have added important qualifications. Yves Congar, for example, observes that the axiom should not obscure the fact that the revelation obtained through the economic Trinity in history is not to be equated with the knowledge to be granted through the beatific vision.[6] No doubt Rahner would have agreed with this. The objection of another theologian to Rahner's "vice versa" is even less illuminating. William J. Hill argues that it implies simple identity, and has drawn out the consequences of such a view.[7] A discussion of Hill's over-reaction to Rahner's proposal need not detain us. He does not pay sufficient attention to Rahner's theology as a whole, nor to what Rahner actually says in *The Trinity*, the work to which Hill refers.

II.
Piet Schoonenberg's Qualifications of Rahner's Axiom

Piet Schoonenberg's critical evaluation of Rahner's axiom deserves some attention. It is made from the background of his own understanding of the economic Trinity. Schoonenberg readily agrees with Rahner that the economic Trinity is the immanent Trinity. But he distinguishes between the pre-Christian and Christian economic and immanent Trinity. This creative, and sometimes controversial, Dutch theologian maintains as probable that in the pre-Christian immanent Trinity, the Father alone can be called person, the Word and Spirit being radiations of the Father. However, in the incarnation of the Word, both the Word and Spirit become persons. This means that, henceforth, the economic Trinity is a Trinity of persons, and this has consequences for the immanent Trinity. Now it can be said that the Trinity is Trinity of

Father, Son, and Holy Spirit, in which a triolog obtains both at the level of the economic and immanent Trinity. The economic Trinity (of persons) is the immanent Trinity (of persons).[8] While Schoonenberg agrees with Rahner that there is no mutual I - Thou relation in the immanent Trinity before the incarnation, he maintains its existence after the incarnation. This latter view is rejected by Rahner.[9]

The second part of Rahner's axiom is also explained by Schoonenberg from the background of the distinction between the pre-Christian and Christian Trinity. The immanent Trinity of Father, Son, and Spirit, relating to one another in interpersonal ways, is the economic Trinity. But this is the consequence of the incarnation in which the Word and Spirit become personalized.

Schoonenberg postulates a real "becoming of God." Remaining identically himself, God becomes himself by his active relating to humanity. God does not move from potency to act, but from act to act. The unchangeable and eternal Trinity of God changes himself in his self-gift, "at least in the Christ-event."[10] The Word personalizes the humanity of Jesus and, at the same time, the Word *personalizes self* by becoming man. The Spirit personalizes the humanity of Jesus, since the humanity is conceived in the power of the Spirit. Likewise the Spirit personalizes self in the fullness of the Christ-event, since the Spirit becomes the Spirit of the Son. Both Word and Spirit personalize themselves vis-à-vis humanity as a whole: The Word becomes speaker of God; the Spirit becomes advocate vis-à-vis the world, etc. In addition, the Word and Spirit personalize themselves in relation to the Father: In Jesus, the Word becomes response to the Father; the Spirit becomes one who prays to the Father in Jesus and in the believers. Finally, with the glorification of Jesus, the Word and Spirit personalize themselves vis-à-vis each other: The Son sends the Spirit; the Spirit sighs for the coming of the Son in the prayer of the faithful. The Father, who was always person, personalizes self in the sending of the Word and Spirit to personalize themselves. He becomes Father of Jesus, and the Father of humanity in Jesus; he becomes God of the Spirit, who leads humankind as his children.[11]

At the term of his exposition, Schoonenberg makes some cautious observations concerning his thesis. He suggests that two options are open. Either the Word and Spirit are not to be conceived as persons in their existence before the Christ-event, or are to be conceived as having a personal existence that becomes more sharply defined in relation to the Father and to one another after the Christ-event.[12] He is especially concerned with the danger of an uncritical use of the concept "person" for the Trinity. In his judgment, Word and Spirit in the pre-Christian Trinity must not be conceived as persons in such a way that a human personal being is eliminated in the case of Jesus, or that the personal influence of Word and Spirit in the incarnation conflict with one another.

The way out of the first problem is to admit that the Word in his divinity has the shape that excludes the possibility of a dialogue relation between the Word and the humanity of Jesus and, at the same time, enables the Word to form with the humanity, in the creative assumption, "one unique person."[13] The solution to the second problem is arrived at by thinking together the influence of the Word and Spirit on the humanity of Jesus in such a way that two possibilities are avoided: a twofold hypostatic union or the attribution of a merely accidental effect to the mission of the Spirit, namely, the communication of created grace to the humanity already united to the Word in hypostatic union. The answer lies in the thesis that the Word is not person, in the eternal Trinity, in such a manner of being that a personalizing influence of the Spirit in the incarnation is excluded, nor the human personal being of Jesus suppressed.[14]

Most Catholic theologians find difficulty with the idea that the personalization of Word and Spirit occur only in the Christ-event, that only at this juncture interpersonal relations exist in the Trinity.[15] Are these new interpersonal relations a new perfection in God? An affirmative answer seems to imply that God is in potency to a new perfection. A negative response raises this question: What reality do the postulated interpersonal relations in the immanent Trinity have? Further discussion of this issue need not detain us here. It is taken up in Chapter 10.

One other aspect of Schoonenberg's thesis is noteworthy. He argues that a mutual I - Thou relation exists in the immanent Trinity as a consequence of the Christ-event. Many other Catholic theologians also agree that such a dialogue, or rather triolog, exists in the immanent Trinity. But they postulate its existence from all eternity. Rahner, and others within the Thomist tradition, teach that no such dialogue can be postulated *on the basis of primary Trinitarian data.*[16] According to Rahner, the Word is spoken and does not speak; the Spirit is breathed forth and does not breathe. Hence he holds that the address to the Father by

Word and Spirit, in the economy of salvation, presupposes a creaturely point of departure.

Schoonenberg agrees about the creaturely starting point for the Thou directed to the Father by Word and Spirit. But this dialogue is judged to have inner-Trinitarian consequences. The Logos prays in Jesus, when Jesus prays; the Spirit prays in Jesus and believers, when they pray to the Father. Because of the correspondence between the economic and immanent Trinity, Schoonenberg concludes that an interpersonal relation must exist in the immanent Trinity, but only in, and since, the Christ-event. This question of interpersonal relations in the immanent Trinity, an essential aspect of the theology of the Trinity, is treated more fully in Chapter 10.

III.
Hans Urs von Balthasar on the Subject of the Correspondence Between the Immanent and Economic Trinity

The Swiss theologian Hans Urs von Balthasar has made the correspondence between the immanent and economic Trinity a foundation stone of his theology. But he follows a different path from that of the classical treatments previously considered. He judges that the Thomistic synthesis, as well as the whole Augustinian psychological turn, labors under insuperable difficulties. For it cannot make understandable that the relations in the inner-divine life are relations between persons. Also the concept of the divine self-gift must be limited, in that perspective, to the work of the Trinity outside itself in creation; for, in the classical scholastic synthesis, the Son goes forth from the Father primarily by way of knowledge, and the Spirit primarily by way of love. According to Balthasar, this understanding does not correspond to the New Testament revelation that God is Love. Since this revelation of the mystery of God in Jesus Christ corresponds to the inner-Trinitarian life, what consequences can be drawn from it, for the fuller understanding of both the immanent and economic Trinity?

The philosophical starting point for Balthasar's Trinitarian theology is the relational nature of persons, as I and thou; a relational connection that is realized by the human being experiencing the address of "thou." In this way, one becomes capable of addressing another as an I to a thou. This relation between persons provides the insight that the un-created person is a pure relation to a Thou.

Having situated the relations between persons in the first rank of images of the essence of God, Balthasar takes a second step, enabling him to conceive divine persons and their relations in a more concrete fashion. He stresses that there is a most intimate link between the immanent and the economic Trinity. This does not mean that the two are simply identified. There is still the greater difference that the eternal Trinity is the source of the economic Trinity. But the unlocking of the mystery of the immanent Trinity is made possible through Jesus Christ. Only through christology can knowledge of the immanent Trinity be derived. [17]

The way of access to this mystery of God is identified as the most significant event of the earthly life of Jesus, the event of the Cross. Here the inner-Trinitarian relations between persons are very concretely expressed. The Logos became incarnate by letting go of his glory, and by the Father not holding on to the Son.[18] On the cross, the fullness of this self-emptying is revealed. For the Son of God really died, while remaining God. This divine way of acting, the letting go of glory, is also the way of the Christian. We subsist and "become" in going out of ourselves to others and to God.

The event of the Cross corresponds to the way in which God exists in God's self. It is the revelation that the eternal generation of the Son, and the procession of the Spirit, must be understood as self-emptying.[19] As absolute Love, the Father gives away all, and the Son is generated. The Son, in turn, responds with an eternal thanksgiving, a total self-giving. "Proceeding from both, as their subsisting 'We,' breathes the 'Spirit,' who seals, at the same time leaves open (as the essence of Love), the infinite distance, and bridges it, as the one Spirit of both.[20]

Balthasar relates the historical exteriorization of the Trinitarian mystery to the eternal exteriorization. He postulates a mutual I - Thou relation in the eternal Trinity, and conceives the inner-Trinitarian relations more precisely as the eternal *kenosis* of the Father, Son, and Spirit. The correspondence between the immanent and economic Trinity is such that the economic Trinity is the one possibility within the immanent Trinity open for actualization. The Cross, the death of the Son of God, is the highest possibility of the exteriorization of the eternal triune being and life of God.

Balthasar's thesis about the historical exteriorization of the eternal exteriorization of the Trinitarian mystery affirms the essential difference between God's action "in the drama of the world" and God's divine being and life. But it also includes the idea that what Jesus Christ suffered in his humanity, the Word of God did and suffered. Whether this teaching can be reconciled with the dogma of the Council of Chalcedon remains an open question. Does it harmonize with the teaching that the humanity of Jesus and his divinity are "inseparable," but also "unmixed"?[21] This question is given further consideration in Chapter 10.

IV.
A Consequence of the Identity of the Economic and Immanent Trinity

The various approaches to the relationship between the economic and immanent Trinity, which we have reviewed, are in agreement that the confession of Trinity of persons made by the Church corresponds to the same three who relate as Father, Son and Spirit in the inner-divine life. In all cases, the common starting point for reflection on the mystery of God is the Christ-event. Once the implications of the economic Trinity for the immanent Trinity are established, a further step can be taken. One can move from the immanent Trinity to the economic Trinity to further elucidate the mystery of the economy of salvation.

A. Descending and Ascending Christology

The process of moving from the economic to the immanent Trinity can be carried out in two ways. One can begin with the fact of the missions of the Word and Spirit in the economy, concluding to the two processions in the immanent Trinity. Corresponding to the economic mission of the Word and the role of the risen Lord in the sending of the Spirit, the generation of the Word precedes the procession of the Spirit in the immanent Trinity. In turn, the eternal Spirit must be understood to proceed from the Father in such a way that some role is attributed to the Son, who is the *essential image* of the Father.

The procession model is then employed to shed light on the economic Trinity in all its dimensions. It is used to order a theology of Jesus Christ, Church, grace, etc. Somewhat different results have occurred when the Eastern interpretation of the procession of the Spirit, and then the Western version, is employed. According to traditional Eastern theology, the Spirit proceeds from the Father "through the Son." This phrase is interpreted in numerous ways, but always so that the concept of co-principle is not attributed to the Son. The Western version reserves the dignity of ultimate or unprincipled principle to the Father. Nevertheless the Son, receiving all from the Father, is also understood to be co-principle of the Spirit together with the Father. Hence the procession of the Spirit from the Father *and* Son (*Filioque*) is confessed.

The Eastern view can lead to excessive emphasis on the role of the Spirit in the time of the Church, to the neglect of the continuance of the mission of the risen Lord. The Western version can lead to excessive emphasis on the role of Christ in the economy of the Church, to the neglect of the mission of the Spirit. History shows that both one-sided views have existed. Still the two traditional ways of viewing the mystery of the Trinity need not lead to unbalanced theologies, nor to theologies which are in conflict on essential aspects of the economy of salvation. When the procession model is used correctly, that is, when new data are not introduced that go beyond what can be derived from christology, it can order other aspects of revelation so as to bring more intelligibility to the whole.

There is also another way of approaching the inner-Trinitarian mystery. It begins with the Christ-event, but from a different standpoint than that of the procession model. It asks about the process by which the Word became man. The accent is placed on the event of the assumption in which the Word and Spirit play a role. This point of view has been labeled "ascending christology.170 It differs from the type of theological reflection that places the accent on the incarnation, grasped as a fact. This latter outlook has been labeled "descending christology." It gives birth to the procession model of the immanent Trinity.

The data derived from reflection on the process by which the Word became man has implications for the understanding of the immanent Trinity, as well as for the understanding of other aspects of the whole economy of salvation. The becoming of the Word incarnate, as an activity of the Trinity, is a revelation of the inner-Trinitarian life. It may provide knowledge beyond what is immediately available from reflection on the incarnation and bestowal of the Spirit at Pentecost, conceived as factual realizations of the economic Trinity. It may also furnish knowledge about other aspects of the economy of salvation that do not come to the foreground from the vantage point of descending christology.

Schoonenberg's thesis about the incarnation as a process led to the conclusion that the immanent Trinity becomes three persons, existing in interpersonal relations through the personalizing of Word and Spirit. However, his proposal is based on a highly problematical concept of ontic change in God. In a less adventuresome way, it can be shown that reflection on the becoming of the incarnation tells us something about the immanent Trinity that is not yielded by the procession model and its descending christology. This other approach reckons with the fact that the economy of salvation has two decisive phases in all its aspects: the becoming and realization, or formation and constitution. Through the analysis of both phases it can be expected that greater intelligibility of the mysteries of the Trinity, Christ, grace, and Church will result.

Ascending christology depends on the data of revelation. As long as it is confined to this source, it can serve the function of ordering the variety of aspects of the revelation of God in Christ. But it cannot be divorced from descending christology, and the procession model of the immanent Trinity. Rather it functions as a complementary aid to that traditional synthesis. Chapter 9 describes in some detail the two basic ways of access to the mystery of the economy of salvation. The yield of both is discussed in Chapters 10 and 11.

Notes

1. DS 301-302.

2. DS 553-559.

3. "Der dreifaltige Gott als transcendenter Urgrund der Heilsgeschichte," in J. Feiner & M. Lohrer, eds., MYSTERIUM SALUTIS. Grundriss Heilsgeschichtlicher Dogmatik, II (Einsiedeln: Benziger, 1967) 328 [Eng. trans.: THE TRINITY (London: Burns and Oates, 1970) 21-24].

4. P. Schoonenberg has provided a succinct and more satisfactory analysis of the second part of Rahner's axiom than most authors who have discussed its implications ("Zur Trinitätslehre Karl Rahners," in E. Kling & K. Wittstadt, eds., GLAUBE IM PROZESS: Christsein nach dem II. Vatican [Freiberg im Br.: Herder, 1984] 473-475).

5. "Der dreifaltige Gott," 358, 365, 367.

6. JE CROIS EN L'ESPRIT-SAINT. III: La fleuve de vie coule en orient et en occident (Paris: Cerf, 1980) 41-43.

7. THE THREE-PERSONED GOD: THE TRINITY AS A MYSTERY OF SALVATION (Washington, D.C.: Catholic University, 1982) 141; 258, n. 18.

8. "Zur Trinitätslehre," 483-490. A brief development of this thesis is also found in an earlier essay of Schoonenberg: "Trinität—der vollendete Bund. Thesen zur Lehre von drei personlichen Gott," ORIENTIERUNG 37 (1973) 115-117.

9. "Der dreifaltige Gott," 366, n. 20. Schoonenberg thinks that Rahner should accept the inner-Trinitarian dialogue as a corollary to his axiom concerning the correspondence between the economic and immanent Trinity. In other words, if Jesus Christ addresses his Father, as Father, this should have a correspondence in the inner-Trinitarian life ("Zur Trinitätslehre," 478).

10. "Zur Trinitätslehre," 483-484. Confer also his book, THE CHRIST: A STUDY OF THE GOD-MAN RELATIONSHIP IN THE WHOLE OF CREATION AND IN JESUS CHRIST (New York: Seabury, 1971) 83-86.

11. "Zur Trinitätslehre," 485-486.

12. "Zur Trinitätslehre," 486.

·13. "Zur Trinitätslehre," 487-488.

14. "Zur Trinitätslehre," 488.

15. E.g., Y. Congar, JE CROIS EN L'ESPRIT-SAINT III, 38-41.

16. B. Longeran holds the same position as Rahner (DE DEO TRINO II. Pars systematica seu divinarum personarum conceptio analogica [Rome: Gregorian, 3rd. ed. 1964] 196). Y. Congar explains that New Testament texts, which point to an I - Thou relation between Jesus and the Father, refer to a human psychological I and the Human consciousness and liberty of Jesus. But he postulates a kind of proleptic presence of the human response of Jesus to the Father in the eternal Word, since the Son is eternally conceived as "INCARNANDUS, IMMOLANDUS, before being made flesh and sacrifice" (JE CROIS EN L'ESPRIT-SAINT II: Il est Seigneur et il donne la vie" [Paris: Cerf, 1980] 290-291). Congar's proposal sheds no new light on the problem.

17. THEODRAMATIK II/2: Die Personen in Christus (Einsiedeln: Benziger, 1978) 466.

18. In this context Balthasar appeals to Phil 2:6-7, without ever giving a thorough exegetical treatment of the pericope.

19. In this matter Balthasar borrows the insight of Sergej N. Bulgakow (1871-1944), who understands the processions of Word and Spirit as a self-emptying of the Father (DU VERBE INCARNÉ (Paris: Aubier, 1943). Confer: W. Löser, "Trinitätslehre Heute. Ansätze und Entwürfe," in W. Breuning , ed., TRINITÄT, 43.

20. THEODRAMATIK III: Die Handlung (Einsiedeln: Benziger, 1980) 300.

21. W. Löser discusses the difference between Balthasar and Rahner on this issue ("Trinitätslehre Heute,170 44).

Chapter 9
The Procession and
Bestowal Models

The history of reflection on the mystery of Jesus Christ shows that the starting point has been either with the fact of the incarnation of the Word and the mission of the Spirit, a consequence of Jesus' saving work, or with the event of the incarnation, in which the Word and Spirit play a role. Both ways of approaching this mystery are authorized by the New Testament. The Fourth Gospel begins with the idea of the descent of the Word of God: "The Word became flesh and dwelt among us" (Jn 1:14). At the outset of the Gospel according to Luke, the becoming of the Word incarnate is attributed to the action of the Holy Spirit on Mary, the mother of Jesus: "The Holy Spirit will come over you, and the power of the Most High will overshadow you; therefore the child to be born will be called holy, the Son of God" (1:34-35).

The first way of thinking about the mystery of Christ has been labeled Logos christology, or "descending christology." The second, which highlights the special role of the Spirit in the event of the elevation of the fruit of Mary's womb to unity of person with the Son, is called Spirit Christology, or "ascending christology." These complementary christologies lead to two models of the immanent Trinity, two ways of conceiving the processions of Word and Spirit from the Father. In other words, the missions of Word and Spirit, corresponding to the ways in which the Word and Spirit exist in the inner-Trinitarian life, are conceived in different, yet complementary ways, through reflection on the process or the fact of the incarnation. The Logos Christology grounds the procession model of the Trinity; the Spirit Christology grounds the bestowal model of the Trinity.

In this chapter the two models of the immanent Trinity are described. They serve as a means of organizing, in a systematic way, the various aspects of the mystery of Christ and its consequences. The yield of these models is the subject of Chapters 10 and 11. In order to illustrate the two models, use is made of the psychological analogy, popularized by Augustine[1] and further developed by Thomas Aquinas.[2]

I.
Procession Model

The procession model of the inner-Trinitarian life derives from reflection on the implications of the missions of Word and Spirit. The incarnation of the Word corresponds to the eternal generation of the Word from the Father; the sending of the Spirit corresponds to the eternal procession of the Spirit from the Father. Since the Word receives all from the Father, the Word has something to do with the procession of the Spirit. This aspect is formulated in the Eastern creedal statement as "from the Father through the Son." The traditional Western formula has "from the Father and the Son," acting as one principle.

The two processions include the communication of the divine substance; for the three persons are *homoousion* , identically the divine essence. There is one principle of operation rooted in this divine essence, not in the persons as such. This one operation, grounded on the unity of the divine essence, founds the idea of the interpenetration of the three persons. The unity and distinction between the divine persons is expressed in the Western axiom: All is one in God, except where the opposition of relation excludes this. Consequently from this point of view, the Father and the Son must be the one principle of the Holy Spirit, for there is no opposition of relation between Father and Son in this matter.

Aquinas begins with the traditional Western teaching just described. His systematic work follows the logical steps from the given Trinitarian processions, known from revelation. He moves in his thinking from processions to the implied relations, and then to persons. Though identical with the divine essence, Father, Word, and Spirit are really distinguished from one another. The distinction between the divine three consists in the pure ordering of the one to the other, resulting from the processions.

Aquinas conceives the divine three as relational, and the real distinction in God as that of a relational kind. Really distinct from one another, the three can be called "subsistent relations," that is, they subsist in the mode of subjects expressing pure regard of one another. Subsistent relation is understood both as distinguishing the divine three and constituting them as answering to the idea of subject, which is intrinsic to that of person. Hence Aquinas can employ the word person for the three, insofar as relation in God is regarded less under the formality of relating (pure order to another) than under the aspect of subsisting in itself.

In a further step, Aquinas takes up the Augustinian psychological analogy, and deepens it. It is useful, for Aquinas, at the stage where concepts are developing, but it does not penetrate to the essence of God. Accordingly, the Angelic Doctor switches to a new set of concepts when the mystery of the Trinity is met head on.[3]

In Aquinas' version of the psychological analogy, the prime analogue is the nature of the two acts of knowing and loving, which correspond to truth and goodness.[4] Aquinas reasons that knowledge is a perfection of the knower: self-knowledge, acquired through knowledge of the world. The world becomes known, and, at the same time, the process terminates in knowledge as an enrichment of the self, *a word*. The process of knowing terminates in an immanent term, the word being an endpoint contained in the operation itself, a term distinct from the operation. Here he finds an analogy with the procession of the Word from the Father; for this procession is an immanent term distinct from the operation. Aquinas calls this procession a *processio operati*, a procession of the thing operated.

The *processio operati* is distinguished from a *processio operationis*, procession of the operation. The latter type of procession has no immanent term, but terminates in something outside the knowing subject. There is some discussion among scholars concerning Aquinas' view of a procession of the Spirit, conceived as the mutual love of the Father and Son. Many hold that Aquinas, at least in his later works, taught that the Spirit proceeds as an immanent term distinct from the act of love, analogous to the distinction between the act of love and the immanent term of the act of love in the lover.[5] Others argue that Aquinas, at least in his earlier works, maintained that the Spirit is a *processio operationis*, and so distinct from the Word as the subsistent operation of love, and not as the immanent term of the divine act of love.[6]

Bernard Lonergan's analysis of the relevant texts of Aquinas' works led him to the conclusion that the Angelic Doctor viewed love as proceeding in human beings from the inner word of the intellect. Consequently, the procession of love itself does not produce anything as a term in which the act of love intrinsically consummates itself. The analogy is appropriate in that love depends on the inner word, just as the procession of the Spirit depends on the Divine Word. But there is no analogy between the procession of love and the procession of the Spirit in Aquinas' thinking; for he holds that the Spirit is the immanent term of the spiration from the Father and Son.[7]

Whatever might be said about Aquinas's view of the nature of love as *processio operationis* or *operati*, he applies the analogy of processions of intellect and will to God only *analogously*; for, in the divinity, intellect and will are only rationally distinct, being identically the divine essence. If one understands the procession of the Word from the divine intellect and the procession of the Spirit from the divine will, as univocal with the really distinct human processions of knowing and loving, this would imply a real distinction in God between intellect and will.

In the end, Aquinas transcends the psychological analogy, and teaches that the divine essence is the principle of divine generation. *As the Father's*, the divine essence is the potency by which the Father generates the Son; *as the Son's*, the potency by which the Son is generated; *as the Spirit's*, the potency by which the Spirit is spirated. This is the same thing as saying that, in recto, the potency of generating and spirating is the divine essence, but, in obliquo, the two potencies connote personal properties.[8]

Aquinas explains that the divine being, as pure act, prolongs itself into self-knowing and self-loving. At the heart of this prolongation, a Word breaks forth, which posits a speaker and spoken. In priority of order the speaker, as person, has the property of paternity, because of the identity with the divine essence as potency of generating. The self-expression of the Word releases love: *Ipse Amor procedens*. The mutual love of Father and Son bring forth the Spirit, as love proceeds in human beings. But whereas the word is an immanent term of the act of knowing in us, and the same thing can be said about the Word in the Trinity, a problem arises regarding the application of the analogy of human love to the procession of the Spirit in the Trinity. And it is not simply a problem of Aquinas' thinking on the matter.

Whatever may have been Aquinas' opinion about the existence of a *processio operati* in the act of love, it is doubtful that one can speak of a procession of a thing operated, which is a static term, a perfection of the operation and distinguished from it, in the case of the human act of love. The analysis of the phenomenon of human love shows that the movement is centrifugal. Its term is in the lover, but by way of formal causality. Love has no term in itself; its term is in the beloved.[9] Thus it differs from the word, which is an immanent term of the act of knowing.

Love is a procession of operation. But this does not exclude the possibility of an analogy between the procession of the Spirit and human love. The analogy can be sustained, if one grants that it is not necessary to conceive the Spirit as an immanent term in the Godhead in order for the Spirit to be conceived as immanent in the Trinity. This possibility should be conceded on two counts. In the first place, the concept of person, as applied to the Trinity of persons, is not univocal. The Father, Son, and Spirit are not precisely person in the same way. Second, it is not necessary to conceive the Spirit as immanent term in the Trinity in order that the Spirit be conceived as immanent in the Trinity. The immanence is secured because the Spirit is identically the divine essence.[10]

One other qualification of Aquinas' use of the psychological analogy is needed. He holds that the formal reason of the two processions in the Trinity, within the limits of the psychological analogy, is the essential operations of the divine intellect and will. According to Aquinas, the Son does not proceed according to the Father's knowledge, and the Spirit according to the mutual love of Father and Son. For this would necessarily introduce a factor which is incompatible with the analogy of one subject of the acts of knowing and loving. In other words, if the Father's knowledge is the formal reason for the generation of the Son, and the mutual love of Father and Son the formal reason for the procession of the Spirit, multiplicity of subjects is introduced, which finds no correspondence in the one human subject of the acts of knowing and loving.

Aquinas teaches that the formal reason of the processions, the exact and immediate explanation in the order of logical sequence, is the essential acts of knowing and loving. However, it is possible to conceive the matter in a different way. A distinction must be made between God's knowing and loving as identically God's being, and the "notional acts" of knowing and loving. *Notion* is a term that refers to the proper ideas by which we know the divine persons; *notional acts* are those that designate the origin of persons by processions. They are the acts performed by the Godhead, which are not common to the three divine persons. They are the Father's knowing, and the mutual love of Father and Son.

The formal reason for the generation of the Son, within the psychological analogy, can be conceived as the divine self-knowing, insofar as notional act of the Father. The divine self-loving can be identified as the formal reason for the procession of the Spirit, insofar as the notional act of Father and Son. This point of view does not conflict with the psychological analogy, which demands unity of subject; for the unity is guaranteed by the unity of the divine essence, with the corollary of unity of operation.

W.J. Hill takes this position, which goes beyond Aquinas.[11] Support is supplied by Eastern Trinitarian theology, which begins with the concept of person when responding to the question: Who is the subject of the originating acts of generation and spiration?[12] Building on this Eastern point of view, Hill argues that consciousness in God requires subjects who exercise consciousness. The three divine subjects know the divine essence, and so are known themselves and loved. This constitutes essential consciousness. On the other hand, the same consciousness is interpersonal: an activity of each person in relation to the others. This constitutes "notional consciousness." In short, in the single act of knowing, God knows, and at the heart of this knowing the Father utters the one Word in an act that is proper to him. Likewise, in the single act of loving, God loves, and at the heart of this loving the Father and Son breath forth the Spirit "in a notional activity common to them."[13]

II.
The Bestowal Model

David Coffey, the Australian Catholic theologian, has worked out an approach to the procession model which incorporates the Augustinian idea that the Spirit is the mutual love of Father and Son. It relates in part to the position of Hill. But Hill subscribes to the Thomistic thesis that there is a *processio operati* of love at the level of the human phenomenon and, within the psychological analogy, applies this to the procession of the Spirit. Coffey maintains that only a *processio operationis* can be predicated of human love. In the context of the psychological analogy, he argues that the procession of the Spirit is a *processio operationis*. The Spirit is identified as the "subsistent operation of love in the Godhead," and not an immanent term. Rather, the immanence of the Spirit is grounded on the Spirit's identity with the divine essence.[14]

Coffey, like Hill, goes beyond Aquinas' teaching that the Son and Spirit proceed from the essential acts of knowing and loving. The unity of the subject, required by the psychological analogy, does not represent an obstacle to the notional acts of knowing and loving being the formal reasons for the processions of Son and Spirit.[15]

Coffey explains that there is one psychological subject in the Trinity, with three subjectivities operating as one on the essential level and as distinct persons at the notional level. The one subject, one center of consciousness, one act of knowing and loving, can be conceived as performed by the Father alone, the Father and Son, etc. Coffey notes that while the only true notional acts are those of generation and spiration, still the two acts of knowing and loving, when specified in regard to subject and object, are constitutive acts, that is, constitute a divine person. Hence they can be called "notional."

The subject of the notional act of knowing is the Father; the subject of the notional act of loving is the Father and Son. The object of the notional act of knowing is the Father himself; the object of the notional act of loving is the mutual love of Father and Son. In regard to the object of the notional act of loving, there is an order of persons: The Father loves the Son; the Son loves the Father with the same love. This love is the Holy Spirit.[16]

According to Coffey, the notional act of loving is merely constitutive of the Spirit, and not productive in the sense of producing an immanent term. The Spirit is not the immanent term of a divine operation. The fact that the Spirit is a person does not require that he be an immanent term. One can argue that the Son is a person because he is an immanent term of a divine operation; for there are no accidents in God. But it is not legitimate to conclude that the Spirit is an immanent term because he is a person. For person in the Trinity is an analogous concept.[17]

The analysis of Coffey leads to the conclusion that the Father generates the Son by the notional act of knowing himself; the Father and Son spirate the Spirit as their mutual love. In the order of priority, the Father loves the Son with the Spirit, and, in turn, the Son loves the Father with the same Spirit. But there is one and undivided act of divine love, performed by the Father and Son in relation to each other: an act of mutual love, and not precisely an act of common love.

The presentation of Coffey, dependent on the psychological analogy, allows him to distinguish between the fact of the procession and the manner of procession of the Spirit. The Spirit, as constituted, proceeds from the Father and Son. But, in the manner of the bestowal, the Father bestows the Spirit on the Son and the Son bestows the Spirit on the Father as the answering love.

Conclusion

A. The procession model has a linear shape:

Eastern: Father $-\rightarrow$ Son ——— (through Son)$\rightarrow$ Spirit.

Western: Father $-\rightarrow$ Son ——— (and Son) $--\rightarrow$ Spirit.

This model does not state nor imply the purpose of the spiration of the Spirit. The direction is toward an infinite void.

The psychological analogy, applied to the procession model in the Thomistic synthesis (not necessarily the Thomist view, namely, that of Thomas Aquinas), offers the reason for the procession of the Spirit. The Spirit proceeds as the mutual love of Father and Son. But this application supposes that the Spirit is the immanent term of a divine operation and that there is a human analogue, namely, an immanent term of the operation of human love. The Spirit is distinguished from the act of mutual love, being the immanent term of this act. From this point of view, the Spirit could appear to be not precisely the bond of union between Father and Son, but a kind of bridge that stands in the way of the "mediated immediacy" of Son to Father.[18]

B. The bestowal model, within the psychological analogy, distinguishes the fact of the procession of the Spirit from the manner of procession, as in the Thomistic view: the Spirit proceeds as the mutual love of Father and Son. But the procession is viewed as analogous to that of human love, which terminates in the loved one. The human analogue is understood to involve only a *processio operationis* of love and not an immanent term in the one loving. The procession of the Spirit, conceived as only a *processio operationis*, is only *analogous* because the Spirit is immanent in the Trinity, identically the divine essence.

The procession of the Spirit closes the circle of presence-to-self and presence-to-other of Father and Son. But the Spirit is not to be conceived as a "bridge" between Father and Son. The Spirit does not obstruct the immediacy of Father and Son to each other. Rather the Spirit is the bond of communication of Father and Son.

Coffey gives the bestowal model this shape:

Perhaps a better visual representation be the following:

1. The Son proceeds from the Father.
2. The Spirit proceeds from the Father and is bestowed on the Son.
3. The Spirit is bestowed by the Son on the Father.
4. The "S" shaped curves signify the eternal act of communication of the Spirit as mutual love of Father and Son.
5. The intersecting lines signify: a. that the Spirit is not an immanent term of a divine operation situated outside the immediacy of the Father and Son to one another, but their bond of union; b. that the infinite distance between Father and Son is not closed by their mutual love.
6. The arrow pointing downward, from the intersection of the lines, signifies the possibility of the communication of Trinitarian life outside itself, precisely as the communication of the mutual love of Father and Son, the Holy Spirit.

The bestowal model is not dependent on the psychological analogy. We have only attempted to show the contours of this model through the application of the psychological analogy. The bestowal model finds support in the history of theological reflection on the Trinity on other grounds. This subject is taken up in Chapter 11. Moreover, as already stated, the bestowal model is not a substitute for the procession model. Rather it introduces a complementary notion concerning the purpose of the spiration of the Spirit, not stated or implied in the procession model.

The value of the bestowal model must be shown. What new knowledge of the economic and immanent Trinity results from the ordering of the data of revelation through the use of this complement to the procession model? This question is answered in Chapter 11, after considering the yield of the procession model, which is the theme of the next chapter.

Notes

1. W. J. Hill, THE THREE-PERSONED GOD, 53-62, provides a good summary of the Augustinian psychological analogy, Augustine developed the analogy between the spiritual operations in man and God. The triadic structure of human consciousness—memory, knowledge, and love—offered a useful tool to think about the three divine persons in one divine substance. Moreover, Augustine teaches that the ascent of the human spirit to God is grounded on the presence of the invisible missions of Word and Spirit, who proceed as knowledge and love in the immanent Trinity. Through the sending of Word and Spirit into the hearts of believers, the latter are initiated into the divine life. The experience of our love as divine gift is the experience of the love that binds Father and Son: the spirit of mutual love. Christian loving, experienced as a unitive force, is a faint reflection of the unity of Father, Son, and Spirit.

2. Hill, THE THREE-PERSONED GOD, 62-78, outlines Aquinas' theology of the Trinity. This passage should be read in connection with B. Lonergan's exposition of Aquinas' psychological analogy. The main difference between the two lies in Hill's thesis that the procession of the Spirit as love implies a procession within the will, which produces a term distinct from the act of love. Lonergan argues that, according to Aquinas, the second procession is "the procession in the will of the act of love from the inner word in the intellect" (VERBUM. WORD AND IDEA IN AQUINAS [Notre Dame: University Press, 1967] 100, n. 20; 201-205). According to Lonergan, Aquinas excludes the analogy between the human procession of love and the second procession in the Trinity because in his view the Spirit is IPSE AMOR PROCEDENS. Consequently, Aquinas relegates statements like "the Holy Spirit is the mutual love of Father and Son" to the level that is secondary to what can be deduced strictly from the analogy.

3. Processions are transposed to notional acts of generation, spiration, etc.; relations to personal properties (Lonergan, VERBUM, 213).

4. Thus it differs from Augustine's psychological analogy, which is based on WHAT THE HUMAN SPIRIT DOES, not on its proper reality. This self-referencing offers only a remote analogy as compared with that of Aquinas, based on the NATURE of knowledge.

5. This is the position of Hill, THE THREE-PERSONED GOD, 74-75; 263.

6. D. Coffey, GRACE, THE GIFT OF THE HOLY SPIRIT (Sidney, Australia: Catholic Institute, 1979) 12-15.

7. Longeran, VERBUM, 201-205.

8. Lonergan, VERBUM, 209-210.

9. Lonergan, VERBUM, 202-203.

10. Coffey, GRACE, THE GIFT OF THE SPIRIT, 14.

11. THE THREE-PERSONED GOD, 265.

12. THE THREE-PERSONED GOD, 268.

13. THE THREE-PERSONED GOD, 269-270.

14. GRACE, THE GIFT OF THE HOLY SPIRIT, 14-15.

15. GRACE, THE GIFT OF THE HOLY SPIRIT, 24.

16. GRACE, THE GIFT OF THE HOLY SPIRIT, 26-27.

17. GRACE, THE GIFT OF THE HOLY SPIRIT, 29.

18. The concept of "mediated immediacy" was discussed in Chapter 7.

Chapter 10
The Yield of the Procession Model: Incarnation and Grace

The procession model and its accompanying descending christology spotlight the very essence of God's mysterious plan of salvation for the world. This model originated through reflection on the consequences of the revealed missions of the Word and Spirit. The free decision of the Father to send the Word to assume the humanity of Jesus of Nazareth is revealed through the life, death, and glorification of the God-man. The sending of the Spirit, the result of Jesus' acceptable offering of himself for the salvation of the world, is revealed in the Pentecostal event. These two revelations, so intimately connected that the mission of the Word in the incarnation is only fully revealed through the mission of the Spirit, are the culmination of the gradual unfolding of the revelation of the mystery of salvation.

God always communicated self and continues to communicate self to all human beings who lived and who now live true to themselves, true to their understanding of what it means to be truly human. But the full revelation of the nature of salvation was only given in God's good time.

The special missions of the Word and Spirit in the Christ-event reveal that eternal life is personal communion with the Father through the communication of the Word and Spirit. Briefly, salvation is the acceptance by free human beings of the Father's self-communication which he makes through the communication of his one Word and his one Spirit. Because this self-communication corresponds to how God exists in God's self, the Church confesses that the Father is the source of all and that the Word and Spirit proceed from him eternally in the order unfolded in the two missions.

The procession model, derived from the reflection on the Christ-event, serves as a vantage point from which to gain additional knowledge of the mystery of salvation. Beginning with this theology "from above," what insights emerge concerning essential aspects of the economy of salvation? An answer to this question is the subject of this chapter.

We begin with the concept of God's self-communication. Here the analogy with human communication is employed as a helpful means of conceptualizing this mystery. In a second step the implication of this self-communication is introduced, namely, that real relations are established with human beings which transcend the relationship of dependence of creature on Creator. The fact of the new relational connection between God and creature, in turn, raises the issue of the nature of the receptivity of the unchangeable God to the response of the creatures who have been placed in the new personal relation to God. In other words, if God himself has established new personal relationships with his creatures, whereby they are made capable of personal communion with God, how does their response to God's offer of personal communion with himself affect God himself?

The subject of the third step is the unique character of the response made by Jesus of Nazareth to the Father. If this response has a creaturely origin, does it include a personal response of the Son of God in his divinity? Here the nature of Jesus' prayer comes to the foreground, an essential element of any theology of Christian worship. The fourth and final step explains the difference between the divine sonship, lived by faith, in Jesus of Nazareth and in fully constituted human persons. The last theme raises the important question about the nature of the grace of Christ, shared with redeemed humanity, and points to the limits of the yield made possible by the exclusive use of the procession model and its descending christology.[1]

I.
God's Self-Communication in the Immanent and Economic Trinity

In human personal communication the communicator goes out of self to the receiver in a centrifugal movement that involves simple efficient causality. Some kind of corporeal contact is needed as the condition for the possibility of sharing something of self with the other. The forms which are imparted begin the process by which the receiver is brought into the sphere of life of the communicator. This centripetal movement is made possible because the receiver is a person who can receive the form imparted in a personal way. For example, when a word is spoken to a person, it is received precisely as a word. It is received at the level at which it is communicated and not reduced in the reception to a level which is below that of personal communication. When a word is spoken to an animal, it is received as a signal, reduced to an impersonal level.

The assimilation of the form imparted in human personal communication takes place at the level of the intentional order. We may gain knowledge about the communicator, his or her attitude toward life, understanding of reality, openness to us, etc. The communication is always partial and is conditioned by the mutual activity of both communicator and recipient, as well as the capability of the one to communicate and the other to receive.

When we apply the concept of personal communication to God in the sphere of the immanent and economic Trinity, the following differences must be kept in mind. First, the simplicity of God excludes the possibility of a communication of something of God's self. God has no parts. If God communicates self, it must be the communication of the totality of God's self. But the depth of the reception depends on the capacity of the recipient. Since God's self-communication is the communication of the totality of God's self, we speak of God's *self-communication*. Properly speaking, self-communication can only be predicated of God. Others communicate something of self, but not self in a comprehensive sense. Second, God's self-communication does not necessarily require, from the outset, a personal activity on the part of the receiver. This is clear in the case of the processions of the Son and Spirit in the immanent Trinity.

God's self-communication to fully constituted human beings always involves personal activity on the part of conscious adults. Just as in the case of ordinary human personal communication, the receiver is not simply passive. The practice of infant baptism, according to the tradition of the Church, implies an exception. A faint analogy can be found between the inner-Trinitarian self-communication of God, God's self-communication in the incarnation, and infant baptism. In these three instances, there is no active reception on the part of the term of the communication. However, it may be noted in passing that a response of faith is needed to the offer of grace of regeneration in the case of infant baptism. It is supplied by the Christian community, which presents the infant for baptism and which represents the whole Church. The traditional practice of infant baptism sheds light on the social dimension of the human person and the role of the Church as organ of grace. It also witnesses to the initiative of God in all personal communication with human beings. Human beings never initiate the process of personal communication with God. God's communication of self necessarily begins with God!

A. Inner-Trinitarian Self-Communication

Reflection on the mystery of the inner-trinitarian self-communication necessarily begins with the Father, the source of all. As simply principle, without origin from elsewhere, the Father communicates self, and the Son receives self and the divine essence. The Father also communicates self in an activity in which the Son has a role as the essential image of the Father. As a consequence, the Spirit receives self and the divine essence. In both instances, the self-communication is from person(s) to person. There is no emanation from the Father. The Father is pure communicator; he does not receive himself from another, and is not received in the other. The Son and the Spirit, on the other hand, are not pure communicators; they receive self from another.

According to the procession model, the Son, as essential image of the Father, is communicated in the order of nature (not time) prior to the procession of the Spirit. Because the Son receives all from the Father, he must be assigned some role in the communication of the Spirit. Eastern theology conceives the procession of the Spirit as "out of the Father through the Son." Western theology stresses that the Son receives all from the Father, including the divine essence and operations, when it reflects on the procession of the Spirit. The Son is understood to receive from the Father in such a way that he becomes the "principled principle" of the Spirit. He is described as the co-principle of the Spirit, in a unity of activity in which the Father alone remains the "unprincipled principle."

These two views begin from different starting points: the Eastern version with the distinction of persons; the Western version with the unity of the divine essence. They cannot be made to coincide. As we have already seen the bestowal model provides a way of speaking about the procession of the Spirit in which the "through the Son" and "and the Son" are complementary ways of conceiving the origin of the Spirit. Further discussion of this matter is taken up in Chapter 11.

B. God's Self-Communication in the Economic Trinity

The Father is pure communicator in the immanent Trinity. He is not received in the communications of the Son and Spirit. The Son and the Spirit are communicated in a procession from person(s) to person. Consequently, if God chooses to communicate self to humanity, it can only be the two modalities of the self-communication of the Father that are received. The Son and the Spirit are received in such communications, and they become actuating in relation to humanity's potential for union with the Father.

What conceptual categories can be used to describe this self-communication of the Father? In the first place, the category of simple efficient causality can be introduced, insofar as interpersonal communication between God and creatures is conditioned by a centrifugal action whereby contact is established, as the condition for personal communication on the part of creatures. However, in itself simply efficient causality is exhausted in a centrifugal action.

The highest form of efficient causality is more useful, namely, formal causality. Formal causality involves the imparting of a form which is not reduced in the reception to a lower level in the recipient. The example mentioned above can serve to illustrate this. The human word is received as a signal by an animal; it is received as a word by a person, and so is not reduced to the lower level of impersonal signal. The word spoken by a person to another person has the potential of drawing the recipient into the intentional sphere of the life of the speaker. It includes the possibility of a centripetal action which, however, implies another category of causality: personal causality.

The characteristics of formal causality must be clearly distinguished from those of personal causality. It itself, formal causality does not presuppose any kind of activity in the production of the effect on the part of the object of the action, except passive reception. Since a form is imparted, the recipient is drawn into a new mode of existence. Formal causality exercises a centripetal activity. Examples drawn from scholastic philosophy are substantial form, the determinative principle of a composite being, or accidental form, a determinative principle of something which already has existence in itself.

Efficient causality, of which formal causality is the highest type, is determinative only from itself. The differentiation of effects is conditioned by the potential of different recipients. Formal causality, as distinguished from simple efficient causality, draws the recipient into the sphere of the communicator, in accord with the passive potential of the recipient. Formal causality exercises a centripetal effect. This also takes place in the sphere of personal communication, where the communicator imparts something of self, which is received as a form. However, in this latter instance, the completion of the centripetal action requires activity on the part of the recipient.

Personal communication has a dialogical structure. The imparting of the form, by which the recipient is introduced into the sphere of the personal life of the other and begins to share that life intentionally, is conditioned by the activity of the recipient. In short, the event of personal communication follows from the recipient's decision to allow something, or to be persuaded to do something, so that consequences follow from the free decision.

The term "personal causality" can be used to describe the process of personal communication in which the effect results from the causal activity of communicator and receiver. Formal causality describes the process by which the recipient is drawn into the sphere of the communicator by the reception of a form that is not reduced to a lower level in the recipient. Hence both formal and personal causality exercise a centripetal effect. But the completion of the centripetal movement, in the latter case, includes the recipient's determination to give self over to the communicator, in some way or other.

1. Causality and the Economic Trinity

The concepts of efficient, formal, and personal causality are not applicable to the immanent Trinity. Simple efficient causality implies physical contact between individuals separated by space. In the Trinity all persons are identically the divine essence. Formal causality, in the strict sense, also is excluded. The Son and Spirit do not receive a form from the Father; they receive themselves. Personal causality is not possible; for the Son and Spirit have no active role to play in the realization of their personhood. The processions are purely from person to person.

a. Sanctification of Human Persons

The notion of personal causality is applicable to the instance of Trinitarian self-communication to fully constituted, adult human persons. The communicator offers self for interpersonal communion, and the recipient does the same. The mutual giving of self realizes this personal communion. This self-communication of the Father includes the aspect of efficient causality, by which the recipient is determined in one's depth of being for the self-communication. Because God is not a structural element in the intrinsic constitution of finite human beings, one must speak of a transforming activity of God through which the individual is orientated to receive God's self-communication in the strict sense.

At the interior of the transformation, which is God's work, God communicates self in the totality of his divinity. This communication takes place through the communication of the Holy Spirit. But, by virtue of the *perichoresis*, the being in-one-another of the Father and Son and Spirit, the human being is united with the Son and the Father. Here the divine persons "communicate themselves" in the sense of offering themselves to be known and loved in their personal distinctiveness and in their relationality to one another. However, all three divine persons do not communicate themselves, in the process by which the human person is drawn into the sphere of the divine life.

Properly speaking, it is always the Father who communicates self. In the process of sanctification, in which the Son has a role, the Spirit is communicated from the Father. Just as in the immanent Trinity the Spirit is purely receptive and does not communicate, so also in the economic Trinity the Spirit does not communicate but rather is received. However this does not prevent the Spirit from being actuating in regard to the potency of the human person for unity with the Spirit, a potency actualizable only by God.

In the process of sanctification, the Spirit can be said to exercise a kind of divine formal causality; for the Spirit actualizes the human being's potential for personal communion with the Trinity. But the Spirit is not, strictly speaking, a divine form that enters into a type of hypostatic union with the human person and thereby determines that being in personhood. For the ordinary human being is already person. Rather, the realization of the personal communion with the Spirit requires the free personal response of the adult, in which one's human personhood remains fully intact.

b. Sanctification of the Humanity of Jesus

The category of personal causality is not applicable to the process of the sanctification whereby the humanity of Jesus was assumed by the Word. The Word, in divine freedom, accepted the mission from the Father, but the only human, personal response that played a role in the incarnation was that of Mary, the mother of Jesus. The assumption of the humanity of Jesus of Nazareth by the Word relates more to the category of formal causality. In relation to the humanity of Jesus, the Word can be called a kind of substantial form, in the sense that the entire being of Jesus subsists as that of the Son of God. As a consequence of this union, and in virtue of the *perichoresis,* the co-inherence or interpenetration of the three divine persons, the same humanity is in personal communion with the Father and the Spirit from the outset of its existence.

We may not say that the humanity of Jesus is united to the Spirit in virtue of divine formal causality; for this would entail two hypostatic unions. Thomas Aquinas raised the question about the possibility of such a twofold union,[2] but theologians generally have not pursued the matter further. In Western theological circles, the communication of the Spirit in the event of the incarnation is traditionally described as a consequence of the assumption of the humanity by the Word.

Heribert Mühlen, among modern Catholic theologians, has the merit of attempting to work out a new theology of the Spirit within the scope of the Western synthesis. Especially his elaboration of the fact and consequences of the personal mission of the Spirit represents a new phase in Western pneumatology. However, his assessment of the role of the

Spirit in the incarnation conforms to the old scholastic approach. Mühlen awards to the Spirit no other influence than the mediation of "habitual grace," which pertains accidentally to the "grace of union."[3] His outlook is determined by the exclusive use of the procession model, and the corresponding descending christology. Further discussion of this issue is found in Chapter 11. Now it is time to turn to the second topic of the chapter, real relations between God and humankind.

II.
Determination of God In and Through the Economic Trinity

We have seen that the procession model yields the notion that the Father, Son, and Spirit are subsistent relations. Applied to descending christology, the corollary follows that humankind is perfected through personal relatedness to the Trinity of persons. Consequently, relationality pertains to the essence of human personhood. Human beings are fulfilled through real relations to the Triune God. But does the Trinity have real relations to humankind and, if so, what consequences follow for the inter-Trinitarian life and the economic Trinity?

A. Real Relations of God to the World

The concept of real relations of God to the world has, in the past, provided difficulties for Catholic theology. However, now it is commonly recognized that the notion of real relation does not, in itself, imply dependence. In the immanent Trinity, there exist purely active relations. But there is no "divine dependency" of the Father on the Son or Spirit, and all are equal. Moreover there exist real causal relations between the Creator and creatures, pertaining to the category of efficient causality. They do not imply dependence of the Creator on the creature, except insofar as relations involve a logical dependence ceon a term. The Creator obtains no new perfection from creation, but the Creator really goes forth in creation. Also real relations exist between the Trinity and humanity in virtue of the self-communication of the Father in the missions of the Word and Spirit. How are these latter relations to be understood?

1. Changement in God

According to the New Testament, the Word became man. This means that the Word is changed by his self-relating to the humanity of

Jesus, and in his self-relating to all humankind. Can we describe this change as one in which the unchangeable Word merely changes in the other, that is, in the humanity? Karl Rahner provides this formula:

> The mystery of the incarnation must lie in God himself: in the fact that he, though unchangeable 'in himself,' can become something 'in another.'[4]

But is this way of considering the matter adequate? If the Word begins to be what he was not before the incarnation, can we speak of a change taking place in the Word of God himself?

We have already seen Schoonenberg's solution. He argues that God can change from act to act, though not from passive potency to act. In the incarnation, the Word personalizes himself, and the Spirit does likewise.[5] This seems to imply an ontic change in God that is not univocal with ontic changes in creatures; for creatures move from potency to act. William J. Hill rejects Schoonenberg's proposal because the notion of change from act to act is merely a "verbal sidestepping of the problem."[6] In its stead he suggests the idea of extrinsic change in God. When what God knows and loves changes, God's knowledge and love change relative to what has changed. Hill is representative of the point of view that has no fundamental difficulty with the idea of intentional change in God; it does not, in his judgement, seem to imply necessarily a change in "God's own ontic beingness." But he recognizes that intentional change in God might conflict with the ontic immutability of God.[7]

As a solution to the problem of how ontic immutability might be "reconciled with intentional change," Hill proposes a distinction between nature and person. God remains immutable in divinity, but wills to become, at the level of personhood, the kind of God he chooses to be *relatively*, that is, vis-à-vis free creatures. He wills this to the extent of choosing to accept determination from his creatures.

> Person means being as pure existential process, but occurring within the structures of what is known as nature or essence and in such wise as to leave the latter intact. If so it is possible to hold that God remains immutable in his divinity, while at the same time he wills to become at the level of personhood the sort of God he chooses to be relationally, i.e., vis-à-vis his free creatures—even to the point of choosing to accept determination from his creatures.8

But Hill is not completely comfortable with this explanation.

Elsewhere he admits that a becoming in God within the dimensions of intentionality, analogous to the personal becoming of the human being, may say too much.[9]

A position similar to that of Hill has been attributed to Karl Rahner. Wolfhart Pannenberg objects to Rahner's idea of change in God because it seems to imply that there is an inner sphere of God which is not touched by change.[10] However Rahner himself clearly states that "God...though unchangeable 'in himself,' can become something 'in another.' He himself, he in time."[11] This means that, for Pannenberg and Rahner, one has to take account of God's indivisible being. Because of the simplicity of God, there exists no inner sphere of God from which change is excluded, if change can be predicated of God at all.[12]

In the opinion of this writer, Hill's tentative solution to the problem of ontic identity and changement in God does not sufficiently contextualize the problem. The distinction between mutability at the level of personhood and immutability "in God's divinity" clashes with the notion of God's simplicity. The real difficulty with this solution is the starting point. The explanation of the mystery of God's changement is located at the level of an ontology of the natural being of God. Thereby the author abstracts from the context in which the problem should be considered, namely, the economic Trinity.

2. Missions and Receptivity

The proper way of addressing the dilemma of changement in the unchangeable God in the order of grace is to begin with the implication of the economic Trinity. The fundamental distinction that must be introduced is the one between the order of creation and the order of grace. God is simply unchangeable in the order of creation. At this level God remains as Father, the one who is eternal, omnipotent, the unchangeable pure act (*actus purus*). However, in the order of grace, in the economic Trinity, the Father determines himself to receptivity and historicity through the missions of the Word and Spirit.

Through the mission of the Spirit, a history is begun between God and his rational creatures which includes mutual recognition and response. Through the mission of the Word, there is a self-emptying of the Father in the self-emptying of his only Son. God himself becomes historically finite and weak in the weakness of love, capable of receptivity vis-à-vis his children. We learn from the economic Trinity that God, unchangeable according to his natural being as Father, has freely determined himself, in his Word and Spirit, to receptivity and historicity. The unchangeable God has made himself open to determination by finite, free rational creatures.

This self-determination of God is, therefore, a constitutive aspect of a Trinitarian ontology. This ontology is grounded on the natural being of God, as the unchangeable pure act. But it is also based on an ontology of love. God has revealed, through the creation of human beings and their calling to partnership and communion with himself, and particularly through the special missions of the Word and Spirit, that he has made himself open to the receptivity of human love. The offering of himself to be loved, through the missions of Word and Spirit, includes the capability of receiving the love of creatures; for, by its very nature, love is fulfilled in mutually exercised self-communication.

No doubt the thesis concerning the self-determination of the unchangeable God to receptivity and historicity needs further development. But the revelation of the economic Trinity forces Catholic theology to accept the conclusion that the unchangeable God is changeable, and vice versa. On this subject, Ludger Oeing-Hanhoff may be allowed a concluding word.

> The doctrine of the Trinity, with inclusion of missions, is the abrogation of this contradiction (namely, between the unchangeable and changeable God). To think dialectically of a God of this sort means to consider his receptivity, historical and weak finitude as his act, as essential trait of his self-mediation to rational creatures. Only so is a mutual real relation between God and creature possible.[13]

B. Relational Ontology

The essentially relational nature of God in the inner-Trinitarian life, and the relational link between God and rational creatures which, transcending the order of creation, opens out into that of mutually exercised self-communication, offers the theological basis for a relational ontology.[14]

An ontology is called relational because relation is conceived as a kind of transcendental, in the sense that it belongs to being as such.[15] In the perspective of relational ontology, as applied to human beings, a distinction is made between the existent standing-in-itself and standing-in-relation. The being-for of historical existents is realized by the act of relating. But there is a real identity, with a formal distinction, between the existent in continuity with itself and "becoming" through an "event," namely, a happening that is somehow unusual and of some importance to the person. The becoming through an event is a realization of the essentially relational existent.[16]

In relational, personalistic ontology the proper being of a person is the coming together of being and relation, of being and meaning for others. This outlook mediates between objectivity and subjectivity, between being and action. Hence the concept of person derived from this thinking is dynamic, essentially fluid.

The human person experiences itself as standing-in-relation from the beginning of conscious existence. Thereby the relationality of all reality is revealed; for the human being relates self, in principle and according to the possibility, to all being. Consequently an ontology of things is given with a personal ontology. This ontology falls under the category of the relationality that characterizes personal being. From this point of view where things are "for someone," they realize their essence. In a sense they begin to speak. The Old Testament concept of creation, which understands created things as speech of the Creator in relation to rational creatures, the crown of creation, can find its conceptual expression only in a relational ontology.

Relational ontology makes understandable how the historical, societal, biological, and physical aspects of personal being pertain to the realization of personhood. The essential relatedness of personal being to the world of things and persons requires that the relationality of a person be not limited to one or another relation, absorbed into one dimension of possible relations. Above all, rational ontology highlights the priority of the relation between creatures and the Triune God. Christian personalism places the gift of existence before the task. Our being is primarily a gift of God. Hence human beingness is always realized as a response, as a qualified thanksgiving for the gift of life. And it is necessary that this response be made, and maintained through responsible activity in all relations in world and society; for the response to God can only be made in and through history.

Relational ontology has important applications in all aspects of the economy of salvation. God has determined self to receptivity and historicity, through the missions of Word and Spirit. On the other hand, human beings realize themselves to the extent that they relate themselves to the whole of created reality. These two considerations make clear why the gift of God in Jesus Christ employs the different relational contexts of human beings in the concrete structures of the economy of salvation. One example, especially relevant to the theme of this book, is the insight that relational ontology provides concerning the role of material components of the symbolic activity of Christian liturgy.

Christian symbolic activity only has meaning in the interpersonal sphere of the life of faith. But this does not mean that the material components, belonging to the essence of certain symbolic actions, are to be relegated to a purely "thingly," impersonal level. Rather, the whole tradition of the Church explains that they are constitutive of certain sacraments, such as baptism and the sacrament of the body and blood of Christ. Relational ontology explains the use of water, oil, bread and wine as a realization of the relational nature of the things of the cosmos. It supplies the reason why the integration of material components into the relation Christ—liturgical assembly enables them to serve as medium of interpersonal communication in the communication of the life of faith.

III.
I - Thou Relation in the Immanent Trinity

Thomas Aquinas speaks of the "mutual communication" between God and rational creatures, in the discussion of the love between God and humankind.[17] This mutual communication occurs in the lives of believers and in the life of Jesus of Nazareth. But many theologians, as we have seen, do not go so far as to say that the communication between Jesus and the Father exceeds the creaturely aspect. Karl Rahner, among others in the Thomist tradition, rejects the concept of a mutual I—Thou relation in the immanent Trinity and, consequently, finds no corresponding one between the Father and the Son of God in the flesh.

Rahner says that the Logos really suffers in his humanity. Presumably he could also say that the Logos prays in his humanity.[18] However, he often presents a view of Jesus as a "creaturely enclosed man vis-à-vis God," as Bernhard Wenisch has pointed out.[19] Rahner says that "Jesus as man can worship and worshipped the Logos," adding that, although the divine person is united to the humanity, he remains likewise over against this man.[20]

Rahner's reasons for this position can be quickly summarized. First, there is the dogma of the Council of Chalcedon, which confesses the unity, "unseparated," and the difference, "unconfused," between the Word and the humanity of Jesus. The difference means that the humanity of Jesus stands fully on the side of the human race in need of redemption. The Word assumed a humanity whose existence is determined by sin and death. Consequently, it can be said that the fate of Jesus is, in a true sense, the fate of God. But, according to Rahner, it would be incorrect to say that God himself was touched by this suffering and death in his own proper life. For "pure Chalcedonianism" will always say that the Word, inseparably united to the humanity of Jesus, remains united but "unconfused." Therefore, the death of Jesus is the cause why and how God gives us his blessedness. But this death is not in itself already, "formally, the redemption. Rather we are redeemed formally by God's blessedness.[21]

Rahner accepts the full implications of the dogma of Chalcedon, and opposes the "new Chalcedonianism" espoused by Hans Urs von Balthasar,[22] which seems to him to tends to overlook the "unconfused." Rahner's understanding of Chalcedon furnishes the context for thinking about the nature of Jesus' self-consciousness, in connection with the part of the traditional christology that teaches Jesus' human soul had a direct vision of God from the outset of his existence.

On philosophical grounds Rahner argues that Jesus knew who he was with the subjective knowledge of self-consciousness. If ordinary human beings have this self-awareness as a common property of the human reality, it would be metaphysically inconceivable that the highest ontological determination of created reality existed at a lower level of self-consciousness than lower ontological determinations. Rahner locates the source of Jesus' self-consciousness in the direct vision of God enjoyed by his humanity from the moment of conception.[23] From this Rahner concludes that Jesus' orientation, as man and through vision, is to the Word, along with his orientation to the Father.

The position of Rahner on Jesus' self-consciousness can be easily modified, as David Coffey has shown. In the first place, according to the Scriptures, the orientation of Jesus is exclusively to the Father. Moreover, the self-consciousness of Jesus as man, as "truly man," is not a purely a priori, fundamental given. Some objective content of consciousness is needed to mediate Jesus' human self-consciousness. The objective content of consciousness that performs this function can only be the communion of being and life that obtains between the Father and Son in the immanent Trinity, and which now exists and is experienced in the humanity of Jesus, "inseparably" united to the Word. "This is what Jesus knew with the subjective knowledge of self-consciousness."[24]

The foregoing explanation of Jesus' self-consciousness implies, or could imply, that Jesus' response to the Father, in his humanity, has inner-Trinitarian implications. It is open to the notion of an inner-Trinitarian dialogue. Rahner, however, along with others, excludes such a dialogue on the basis of primary data of knowledge of the inner divine life. Schoonenberg, as we have seen, postulates the existence of such a dialogue after the Christ-event, on the basis of the personalization of Word and Spirit. While the basis of his theory is difficult to reconcile with God's transcendence, his conclusion about the inner-Trinitarian consequences of the prayer of Jesus deserves attention.

The main objection of Rahner, as well as others such as Bernard Lonergan, to a mutual I - Thou relation in the immanent Trinity, can be answered on the grounds of Trinitarian ontology, and within the perspective of the procession model.[25] The argument, as developed by Oeing-Hanhoff, begins with the Thomist view that God's individual being is known to us through reflection on being itself. It can be quickly summarized as follows:

A. When we think of being, we think of subsisting being. In a further step, if we think of being, and likewise think that being is necessary and excludes any non-being, we have a perception of divine subsisting being. We know every other being in this common way, as subsisting being. Only God's individual being is known to us. This can lead to a one-sided negative theology, which is simply turned to the unknowable God.

B. But, if we are think of God as infinite, subsistent being and, because spiritual being, one who has full knowledge of self, we are brought to the threshold of the mystery of God. In his full knowledge, God forms the perfect image of self. His whole being is expressed in his eternal Word. The being of this Word consists in being said. God's Word has nothing from itself, but all that God possesses. Since God's self-expression is full self-communication, the Word has no additional Word to speak!

C. There is no essential difference between the life communicated and shared. The Source and the Word are identically the divine life. This essential identity of divine persons with the divine life is the ground of their being in-each-other; for the unity of God is not the result of *perichoresis* of divine persons.

D. But this full self-communication of God constitutes a difference. The one divine being is absolutely simple. Therefore there is identity of loving and willing. Yet the divine being is differentiated through the expressed Word. Hence there are two subjects, which accomplish the divine knowing and loving. This means that the willing is modified in the Word's self-affirmation and self-love. Moreover the divine will is modified to personal love between the Source and the Word, brought forth through the Source's self-expression.

E. This personal love is the bestowal of self on the other, a mutual love. It modifies the divine will to a second way of self-mediation of the divine persons to each other. Thereby the divine being, remaining identical, is brought forth in the mode of being gift. The way of existence of God that now obtains in the mode of gift is the Holy Spirit breathed forth in love. Thus is constituted the third divine person.

From this consideration of the self-constitution of God, the self-realization of his threefold personal life, the inner-Trinitarian concept of person can be defined as follows: "Person is a mode of existence of divine being that is communicable."26 Divine persons are not mere modes of a divine being, but the divine being in a determined mode of existence. Since divine persons are modes of existence of the common divine essence, they live in one another. This *perichoresis* explains why the Son does not speak. The personal forming knowledge is the Father in him.

In the essential knowledge, the Son knows all that the Father knows. Therefore he knows himself. This also holds for the Spirit. Hence, each divine person is conscious of their peculiar manner of being, or their individuality. Moreover no person, as subject of the divine life, can be denied their own proper will; for, through the constitution of the three divine ways of being, the one divine will is modified. The Father has the divine knowledge and will as the source of all; the Son, in the way of the Word expressed by the Father. Thus the one divine being, and the will identified with it, is also modified in the divine "production" of the Word and Spirit.

Looking to the economic Trinity, it can be said that the will of the Father to send the Son is modified to the will of the Son to send himself, and to empty himself. The notion that the divine persons are not subjects conscious of themselves, possess no proper self-consciousness and proper will corresponding to their mode of existence, has no support in the traditional Trinitarian concept of person.27

On the basis of the relationality of the divine modes of existence, modal distinction from the divine essence, and *perichoresis,* it may be said that person is "a mode of existence of a rational essence to the other and in the other."[28] It is constitutive of being person in God's being, to be being-for others and being-in-others. Therefore, divine persons are only analogous to finite persons. The latter are persons *in themselves,* and come to be persons for others in a linguistic community. They can also will *not to be for others.*

Conclusion

The yield of the procession model allows us to conclude that the prayer of Jesus and the prayer of the Spirit, in the just, have a correspondence in the immanent Trinity. The prayer of Jesus, directed to the Father, is the historical expression of the eternal eucharist of the Word; the Spirit's prayer in the just, for the coming of the Son in glory, corresponds to the Spirit's role in the Trinity as mutual love, the bond of unity. Further discussion of this theme is found in Chapter 11. For now it suffices to return to the problem associated with Balthasar's view of the identification of the economic and immanent Trinity.

According to Balthasar the divine *kenosis* makes the economic Trinity possible. In the incarnation, the self-emptying of the immanent Trinity is extended into the world. This self-emptying of the Son (Phil 2:7) is likewise that of the one will of God, and so that of the Father who sends the Son. This self-emptying means that in Jesus' human life and death, the Son himself lives and dies. The unity of divinity and humanity in Jesus Christ is such that the fate of Jesus is that of God himself. Instead of saying that God has suffered and died in his humanity, Balthasar affirms that God has suffered and died himself in his humanity, and so redeemed us.29 Rahner's objection to this outlook has been mentioned in this chapter.[30] The subject of the next chapter offers the opportunity for additional reflection on this Trinitarian aspect of Jesus' earthly life.

IV.
Divine Sonship and the Life of Faith

The final section of this chapter inquires about the two ways of God's self-communication to a human reality. What knowledge is gained by the application of the procession model, and its complementary descending christology, to the mystery of Jesus Christ, and the mystery of the sanctification of fully constituted human persons?

A. Uncreated Grace

This theology "from above" has enabled modern Catholic theologians to recognize more clearly that the real form of grace is uncreated grace, namely, God's self-communication in the missions of the Word and Spirit. This makes intelligible the traditional teaching that grace of the justified, here on earth, is a real anticipation of the fulfillment, which is called the "beatific vision." In other words, the fulfillment of God's self-communication is only the ultimate determination, in the field of operation, of what is given to believers here on earth. As a consequence of this insight, many Catholic theologians have recognized the limitations of the scholastic teaching about the beatific vision. We will return to this topic in Chapter 12. But a brief word of explanation of the significance of this turn in Catholic theology, which has important consequences for a theology of worship, is useful at this juncture.

Juan Alfaro[31] has the merit of calling attention to the need to modify the teaching of Pope Benedict XIII that the blessed in heaven enjoy the beatific vision without creaturely mediation.[32] This understanding of the essence of beatitude is judged by Alfaro to be too individualistic. It does not take into account the fact that the mediatorship role, exercised now by the risen Lord in the communication of grace to humanity on earth, continues to be exercised in heaven. Christ is not simply a companion of the blessed, according to his humanity, but remains the unique mediator between God and humanity (1 Tim 2:5), in the one Spirit.[33] In this way, the missions of the Word and Spirit reach their completion.[34]

B. Divine Sonship and the Life of Faith

When divine sonship is conceived "from above," one sees that the highest possibility of the actualization of a humanity results in the union with the Word, while lesser actualizations result in the union of fully constituted human beings with the Holy Spirit. From this vantage point, we can think about the implied ascending christology, that is, the openness of creatures to God's self communication.

1. Divine Sonship and Faith in Jesus

In virtue of the grace of union, Jesus was the Son of God from the outset of his existence. But, as a human being, he lived by faith. His divine sonship came to expression and was realized in his human history. When his humanity was fully realized, in relation to the Father and to the whole of humankind, through the offering of his life for the world's salvation, the grace of the incarnation was fully realized in him. Through the death of the cross, his divine sonship was fully realized to the limits of the possibility in this life.[35] As a consequence, he was glorified and became source of the outpouring of the Spirit.

What is unique about Jesus' life of faith is the fact that his faith flowed from his divine sonship already given from the beginning of his existence. Through the incarnation he is other than God only in his humanity. His divinity, possessed from the outset, realizes itself in his humanity through his human response.

2. Divine Sonship and the Life of Faith of Human Persons[36]

Fully constituted human persons, as adults, receive divine sonship through a response of faith. This response is made possible by the action of the Holy Spirit in them. Hence from the side of the human being, conversion precedes the acquisition of grace; from the side of God, the human being is moved by the gift of the Spirit to the act of conversion. Consequently, from the standpoint of the bestowal of grace, faith flows from the bestowed divine sonship. But the divine sonship is received through the free response in faith to the gift of the Spirit. Hence, from the standpoint of the acceptance of grace, faith brings about divine sonship.

In the communication of the Spirit to human persons, they remain other than God in their whole personhood, though possessed by the Spirit who gives them a new divine mode of being. This divine sonship, realized through acceptance in faith, is also maintained through the continued response to God's offer of personal communion.

Conclusion

When the subject of sanctification of humanity is discussed from the perspective of the procession model and descending christology, it can be shown how the highest possible actualization of a humanity results in the hypostatic union, and lesser actualizations in the union of fully constituted human persons with the Holy Spirit. This approach offers an explanation of the difference between the relation of divine sonship and life of faith in the case of Jesus and ordinary human persons. But it does not explain why the uniquely highest determination of man's openness to God is the union of the humanity of Jesus with the Word in unity of person, and lesser determinations the union of human persons with the Holy Spirit. If it can be demonstrated that the grace by which Christ's humanity is united to the Son is the same grace by which human beings are sanctified, then a response to the question is available.

The Holy Spirit is the Spirit of Sonship, communicated by the Father. If the Spirit can be shown to be the Spirit of sonship in the case of the incarnation, one can see why the highest form of the determination of humanity is that in which it becomes united to the Word in unity of person, and lesser actualizations union of human persons with the Spirit. At the same time, it is also made intelligible that the "grace of Christ," which he communicates to his members, is the same grace as that by which his own humanity was sanctified and united in person to the Word. This subject is treated in the next chapter.

Notes

1. The following exposition makes use of many of the valuable insights found in D. Coffey, GRACE, THE GIFT OF THE HOLY SPIRIT.

2. St III, q. 3, a. 6.

3. DER HEILIGER GEIST ALS PERSON IN DER TRINITÄT BEI DER INKARNATION UND IM GNADENBUND: Ich - Du - Wir (Munster: Aschendorff, 2nd rev.ed. 1969) 209-214.

4. "Zur Theologie der Menschenwerdung," SCHRIFTEN ZUR THEOLOGIE IV (Einsiedeln: Benziger, 5th printing, 1967) 147, n. 3 [Eng. trans.: "On the Theology of the Incarnation," THEOLOGICAL INVESTIGATIONS IV (Baltimore, 1966) 113-114, n. 3].

5. "Zur Trinitätslehre," 484.

6. THE THREE-PERSONED GOD, 182.

7. THE THREE-PERSONED GOD, 183.

8. THE THREE-PERSONED GOD, 182.

9. THE THREE-PERSONED GOD, 296.

10. GRUNDZÜGE DER CHRISTOLOGIE (Gütersloh: Gutersloher Verlagshaus, 1964) 331.

11. "Zur Theologie der Menschenwerdung," 147 ["On the Theology of the Incarnation," 113-114, n. 3].

12. Confer: Schoonenberg, "Zur Trinitätslehre, 70 484.

13. "Trinitarische Ontologie und Metaphysik der Person," in W. Breuning, ed., Trinität, 177.

14. A. Gerken, THEOLOGIE DER EUCHARISTIE (Munich-Kosel, 1973) 197-210.

15. The idea that person is relational, as such, from the outset of existence and, at the same time, incommunicable because person stands in relation to other persons and things, is at the heart of the Christian concept of person. The notion derives from the witness of Scripture to the relation between the Father and Jesus, and is ultimately grounded on the Trinity.

16. In an interesting exchange between C. de Vogel and A. Gerken, the former attributes relationality to persons on the basis of the sharing in a common nature, and objects to the claim of identity of person with what is called "event" in the human sphere of experience ("Die Eucharistielehre Heute," ZEITSCHRIFT FÜR KATHOLISCHE THEOLOGIE 97 (1975) 389-414). Gerken shows that event and person can be thought together in such a way that person does not lose its ontological character and trait of continuity with itself. He traces de Vogel's point of view back to a static concept of person, derived from Boethius' definition: PERSONA "is individual substance of a rational nature" [LIBER DE PERSONA ET DUABUS NATURIS 3 PG 64.1343] ("Kann sich der Eucharistielehre ändem?" IBID. 415-429).

17. ST I,II, q. 65, a. 5.

18. "Probleme der Christologie von Heute," SCHRIFTEN ZUR THEOLOGIE I (Einsiedeln: Benzinger, 1954) 197-200.

19. "Zur Theologie Karl Rahner," MÜNCHENER THEOLOGISCHE ZEITSCHRIFT 28 (1977) 392. This brief article calls attention to certain areas of Rahner's theology that need development. But it is not a satisfactory appraisal of Rahner's thought.

20. "Einige Thesen zur Theologie der Herz-Jesu-Verehrung," SCHRIFTEN ZUR THEOLOGIE III (Einsiedeln: Benziger, 1964) 408 and note 12.

21. "Jesus Christus—Sinn des Lebens," SCHRIFTEN ZUR THEOLOGIE XV (Einsiedeln: Benziger, 1983) 211-212.

22. The thesis of Balthasar was discussed in chapter eight.

23. "Dogmatic Reflections on the Knowledge and Self-Consciousness of Christ," THEOLOGICAL INVESTIGATIONS V (London: Darton, Longman and Todd, 1966) 206; K. Rahner, ed., ENCYCLOPEDIA OF THEOLOGY: The Concise SACRMEN-TUM MUNDI (New York: Seabury, 1975) art. "Jesus Christ," 769.

24. D. Coffey, "The Incarnation of the Holy Spirit in Christ," THEOLOGICAL STUDIES 45 (1984) 473-474.

25. L. Oeing-Hanhoff, "Trinitarische Ontologie,170 158-163.

26. L. Oeing-Hanhoff, "Trinitarische Ontologie,170 160.

27. L. Oeing-Hanhoff, "Trinitarische Ontologie,170 162.

28. L. Oeing-Hanhoff, "Trinitarische Ontologie,170 162: "Persona est modus existendi rationalis essentiae ad alium et in alio."

29. W. Löser, "Trinitätstheologie Heute: Ansätze und Entwürfe," in W. Breuning, ed., TRINITÄT, 26-27, summarizes a description of Balthasar's thesis, drawn from K. Rahner's "Jesus Christus—Sinn des Lebens," SCHRIFTEN ZUR THEOLOGIE XV (1983) 210-211. Rahner calls Balthasar's approach "New Chalcedonianism," a theory that gained some support after Chalcedon was introduced into the liturgy in the hymn ONLY-BEGOTTEN SON: "...you became4 man and, nailed to the cross, 'O Christ our God...'" (H.-J. Schulz, THE BYZANTINE LITURGY (Pueblo: New York, 1986) 29; 213, note 7).

30. Rahner's objection to the "New Chalcedonianism" represents a serious challenge. However other theologians think that Rahner's "Pure Chalcedonianism" does not sufficiently integrate a biblical understanding of the event of the Cross. It is a theology of the incarnation, which needs to be modified by a theology of the Cross (W. Löser, "Trinitäts theologie Heute," 29).

31. "Cristo Glorioso, Revelador del Padre," GREGORIANUM 39 (1959) 222-270.

32. Dogmatic Constitution BENEDICTUS DEUS, Jan. 29, 1336 (DS 1000-1002).

33. D. Coffey, GRACE, THE GIFT OF THE HOLY SPIRIT, 257.

34. Vatican II's CONSTITUTION ON THE CHURCH follows the Council of Florence, which affirms that the beatific vision amounts to seeing "God three in one, as he is" (DECRETUM PRO GRAECIS [DS 1305]). But the constitution does not develop the idea of the mediatorship role of the risen Lord in this connection, although reference is made to 1 Tim 2:5 in relation to the prayer of the Church (LUMEN GENTIUM 49).

35. D. Coffey, GRACE, THE GIFT OF THE HOLY SPIRIT, 72-78.

36. D. Coffey, GRACE, THE GIFT OF THE HOLY SPIRIT, 78-82.

Chapter 11
The Yield of the Bestowal
Model: Incarnation, Grace,
Prayer

The subject of this chapter is the insights furnished by the use of the bestowal model to organize essential data of the economy of salvation. Chapter 9 pointed out the differences between the procession and bestowal models. But more needs to be said about the latter before analyzing its yield. What is its origin, and what support can it claim from the primary sources of theological reflection, including scripture, the Fathers of the Church, and liturgical sources?

I.
Origin of the Bestowal Model

We have used the word "model" several times without giving an explanation of its function in theology. Models are conceptual images, constructed with a view to highlighting essential elements, their relations, and the principles of the reality that is being studied. They have proved useful, especially in the social sciences, as a means of simplification of complex and amorphous social realities. Analytic models are the starting point for the development of a theory that can be used to explain real events or to predict future ones.[1] But their value depends on the extent to which they are grounded on correct knowledge of the social reality.

The value of a model in systematic theology depends on whether it derives from the data being studied or is imported from the outside. The former type is called an *endogenous model*, the latter *exogenous*. The process by which the theologian gets behind a particular theological explanation and identifies the model that determines the whole synthesis, can lead to some very interesting results.[2] For example, the dominant model of Church employed in official Catholic ecclesiology from the seventeenth to the twentieth century is that espoused by Robert Bellarmine. He described the Church as a juridically perfect society modelled on a constitutional monarchy. The limitations of this model are now recognized. Based on principles worked out through non-theological sciences, it fails to take account of the most essential aspects of the ecclesial reality.

Vatican II departs from this overly juridical image, to some extent, because the constitution on the Church supports the idea that the unique model of Church is that of Church-Mystery. In order to clarify the relationship between the social structures of the Church and the mystery of the Church, the model of the incarnation is introduced in *Lumen gentium* 8.1. The use of this model, drawn from the history of salvation, leads to new knowledge of all aspects of the life of the Church. Its value lies in its endogenous character.

The procession model of the immanent Trinity is likewise endogenous. That is why it has survived in both the Eastern and Western Trinitiarian theologies. The bestowal model can also claim this qualification. But it has not received the attention it deserves in the history of theological reflection on the Trinity.

A. Ascending Christology and the Immanent Trinity

The recovery of the bestowal model of the immanent Trinity, or the "remembering of a forgotten truth," is owed to the reflection on the consequences of an ascending christology. The process of thinking through a theology of grace, beginning "from below," poses the question about the implications of what is assumed in the framework of the procession model and descending christology, namely, the openness of humanity to God's self-communication. The question may be formulated in this way: What accounts for the fact that the highest actualization of humanity's potential for union with God is the incarnation of the Word, and the lower actualizations the communication of the Holy Spirit to fully constituted human persons?

Is there a correspondence between the grace of sanctification of the humanity of Jesus, and that of ordinary human persons? Is the realization of the supernatural potency of every human being always the work of the Holy Spirit? What are we to make out of the New Testament witness that the Spirit of God played a key role in the incarnation of the Word, and also a decisive role in the sanctification of ordinary human beings? Can it be said that the humanity of Jesus was sanctified by the sending of the Spirit from the Father, and so elevated to the highest potential of a humanity for union with the divine? This would imply that the "grace of Christ," the grace by which the humanity of Jesus was elevated to unity with the Word in a unity of person, is the same grace as that by which others are elevated to a unity with the Holy Spirit.

Much of the theological reflection of the Eastern and Western traditions, ordered by the procession model and its accompanying descending christology, views the incarnation simply as the assumption of a concrete humanity by the Word. The Spirit is often depicted as the one who anoints the humanity of Jesus that has already been assumed by the Word. Western scholastic theology explains that the Spirit is, by appropriation, the principle of the habitual sanctifying grace that was conferred on the fully constituted God-man. This explanation fits in nicely with the demands of the procession model, and the requirements of the correspondence between the economic and immanent Trinity. The Word proceeds from the Father, and the Spirit proceeds from the Father "through the Son," or "and the Son." Correspondingly, the Father sends the Son, who assumes the humanity of Jesus of Nazareth, and the Spirit is sent to sanctify this humanity in an activity that corresponds to the Spirit's role in the sanctification of ordinary people. However this explanation runs up against the problem of the reversal of the order of correspondence to the Trinitarian processions in the case of the sanctification of ordinary people. Here the order, according to the whole of traditional theology of the East and West, is the bestowal of the Spirit by which the justified person is brought into union with the Son and made son or daughter of the one Father. What is the basis *in the im-*

manent Trinity for the reversal of the procession model in the event of sanctification of ordinary people?

The nineteenth century German theologian Matthias Scheeben (1835-1888),[3] and Heribert Mühlen[4] have contributed much to the renewal of interest in pneumatology within Catholic theological circles. Both develop their Trinitarian theology exclusively on the basis of the procession model. Both argue that the Spirit anoints the humanity of Jesus already assumed by the Word. The essential difference between them lies in Scheeben's attachment to the scholastic position that the work of the Spirit in the sanctification of the humanity of Jesus can be attributed to the Spirit only by "appropriation." Mühlen understands that this activity is linked to a personal mission of the Spirit, and not proper to the Godhead as such.[5] Neither theologian has been successful in showing why the inversion of the Trinitarian order occurs in the instance of the sanctification of ordinary people. This inversion is simply accepted as a fact, without consequences at the level of primary data of Trinitarian theology.

It is evident that the theologies of Scheeben and Mühlen offer no easy solution to the traditional teaching that the just can be said to share in the "grace of Christ." The grace of union, that is, the grace that is the assumption of the humanity by the Word, is not communicable. Also the postulated habitual grace of Jesus, a result of the assumption of the humanity, is proper to himself. As his personal grace, it is not communicable. What, then, is the grace of Christ shared with those who are sanctified? Grace of Christ can be understood in the sense that *of Christ* represents an objective genitive; it is the grace merited by Christ's saving work and not, strictly speaking, Christ's own grace (subjective genitive). But can more be said than this? Is there a common grace shared by Christ and divinized human persons that accounts for the fact that believers are really united to the glorified Christ?

An ascending christology, just as a descending christology, views the humanity of Jesus as the unique, never to be surpassed instance of the highest possible realization of the supernatural potency of a humanity for union with the divine. However, when pneumatology is introduced into the process of the assumption of the humanity by the Word, a new insight is made available. The way is opened to understanding the Holy Spirit as the one who sanctifies the humanity of Jesus, created by the Godhead as such, elevating that humanity to union with the Word who assumes it. This same Spirit, sent by the risen Lord from the Father, unites ordinary persons with the Son and thus makes them sons and daughters of the Father in the unique Son. Here the grace of Christ, the grace he shares with the justified human persons, is identified as the one Holy Spirit.

The ascending christology described above differs from an ascending christology conceived on the basis of traditional scholastic pneumatology. For scholastic theology does not award a personal mission to the Spirit in the economy of salvation. Therefore the only divine person that can be singled out as having a personal role in the work of sanctification is the Word of God. The Word exercises this role in the incarnation by assuming the humanity of Jesus, from which results the "grace of union." According to many scholastic theologians, this grace suffices for the sanctification of the humanity of Jesus. Often they raised the question about the reality of an additional habitual grace, comparable to that received by ordinary people. In the instance of the sanctification of ordinary people, a work of the Godhead as such, the Word is given a personal role insofar as his glorified humanity exercises a mediatorship function, the role of "principal efficient instrumental cause."

This scholastic theology of sanctification is now more commonly recognized by Catholic theologians as too closely linked to a monotheistic theology of grace. If the real grace of sanctification, the grace by which human beings are divinized, corresponds to the way in which the Godhead exists in itself, it must be thought through in terms of the Father's self-communication in the missions of his Word and his Spirit. But the difficulty concerning the correspondence between the economic and immanent Trinity still remains, once the idea of the twofold personal mission of the Word and Spirit is integrated into a theology of grace. In fact it is exacerbated; for now there is an inversion of the Trinitarian procession both in the case of the incarnation and the sanctification of ordinary people.

This difficulty points to the need for a Trinitarian model that corresponds to ascending christology, and its implied theology of grace. If the economic Trinity corresponds to the immanent Trinity and the examples of God's self-communication indicate that there exists a priority of nature, not of time, of the mission of the Spirit in the event of the sanctification of a human reality, what does this reveal to us about the inner-Trinitarian procession of the Spirit? We have seen the solution that results from the use of the bestowal model. But what claim does it have for support from the primary sources of revelation?

B. The Bestowal Model and Tradition

The bestowal model finds some support in the New Testament theology of the anointing of Jesus, and more in the patristic reflection on this theme. But the more convincing grounds is derived from the implications of the unique love of Jesus for the Father.

1. The Theme of Anointment in the New Testament

The works of the New Testament speak in different ways about the uniqueness of Jesus. The two characteristic approaches can be called *Logos* and *Spirit christologies.*[6] They are presented side by side without any attempt to relate them explicitly to one another.

The prologue of the Fourth Gospel bases Jesus' relation to God on a Logos christology (Jn 1:1-2,14). Other writings of the New Testament speak of the uniqueness of Jesus in terms of his relation to the Spirit of God. The development of a Spirit christology was gradual. God's nearness, experienced in the apostolic preaching "of the word of the Cross" (1 Cor 1:18), is described in the Gospel according to Mark as the efficacious presence of the exalted Lord, or is based on a theology of the authority of the *Kyrios* in Matthew. Closely linked with this outlook is the association of the efficacy of the preaching of the death and resurrection of Jesus with the power of Spirit of God (Acts 2:33). From here it is but a short step to the relate the Spirit of God to the public ministry of Jesus (Lk 4:1,14; Mk 1:10-12).

In the New Testament writings that offer a developed Spirit christology, the Spirit of God is the source of the continuing mission of Jesus in the world, after his death. Luke connects the Spirit with the formation of the Christian community. John describes the Spirit as the power by which God's coming in Jesus continues to be realized in and through the community of believers. Through the Spirit, sent from the risen Lord, he remains the revealer. Paul uses *Pneuma* and *Kyrios* so interchangeably that he seems, at times, to identify the two. According to Paul, the Spirit has the function of structuring the Church of which Christ is the Head. In all these variations on Spirit christology, it is the Spirit through whom the Father approaches humankind, in the time of the Church, and the source of the return of the redeemed humanity through Christ to the Father.

The relation of Jesus to the Father is discussed in connection with the event of Jesus' baptism in the Jordan river. In the Synoptics' treatment, the anointing of Jesus by the Spirit at his baptism is interpreted as the revelation of the Jesus' identity. He is the unique Son of God, directed to his mission by the Father. In John 1:32-34, the divine sonship of Jesus is linked to the baptismal bestowal of the Spirit. John 3:34-35 associates the theme of the Father's love for his Son with the bestowal of the Spirit and divine sonship.

The bestowal of the Spirit is also introduced where the conception of Jesus is described. According to Matthew 1:18-23, God exercises the prerogative of Father in naming the child, while Joseph only announces the name (v.25). Jesus is conceived "of the Holy Spirit" (v.18), the life-giving power of God. Luke 1:35 states that Jesus was formed as "son of God" by the coming of the "Holy Spirit," "the power of the most high."

Peter's speech, in Acts 10:38, refers to the baptism of Jesus by John, and "of the way God anointed him with the Holy Spirit and power." Since the power to rule as Messiah is affirmed, it is but a logical step to describe the action of God at the baptism of Jesus as an anointing. But in recent literature the attempt has been made to associate the baptismal anointing of Jesus with the Spirit to the more original bestowal of the Spirit at the incarnation.

In the last century, M. J. Scheeben proposed that a distinction be made between a fundamental anointing of the humanity of Jesus by the Word, and an additional anointing of the assumed humanity by the Spirit.[7] H. Mühlen, on the contrary, distinguishes the anointing from the assumption of the humanity by the Word. Mühlen interprets the anointing of Jesus at his baptism as a revelation of the anointing of the Spirit that took place at his conception. Distinct from, and *logically posterior* to, the assumption of the humanity by the Word, this unction by the Spirit is viewed as the bestowal of sanctifying grace on Jesus' humanity, and likewise the manifestation of the gift of the Spirit to all humanity. It represents the birth of the Church, which is realized through the Pentecostal bestowal of the Spirit.[8]

However, Mühlen's argument goes beyond the available evidence. The claim that the New Testament texts allude to a distinction between the incarnation and anointing by the Spirit is, at the very least, questionable.[9] Mühlen seems to be influenced too much by the procession model of the inner-Trinitarian life. The unction of Jesus is a rich theme, but very rudimentary in the New Testament.

Regarding the New Testament grounding of the bestowal model, it can be said that the theology of the anointing of Jesus with the Spirit at his baptism, when associated with the role of the Spirit of God in Jesus' conception, provides the starting point for the development of a theology in which the Father is seen as sending the Spirit to sanctify and unite the humanity of Jesus, created by an activity of the Godhead as such, to the Word in the unity of person. This theology, which seems to exist in seminal form in the New Testament sources, was developed in the patristic period.

2. Patristic Witness

There is some evidence for the development of the theology of the anointing of Jesus with the Spirit into a theology of the incarnation, in the patristic period.

After the New Testament era, and in orthodox circles, the uniqueness of Jesus is explained by a Logos Christology or a Spirit christology. But the limits of the latter christology, at an earlier date, must be recognized. Justin Martyr speaks of the Logos effecting his own incarnation, identifying the Spirit of Luke 1:35 with the Logos.[10] From the middle of the second to the middle of the fourth century, the Logos is frequently described as providing the essential anointing of his humanity by the assumption itself. But in the latter part of the fourth century, in the wake of the controversies over the divinity of the Holy Spirit, more attention is paid to the role of the Spirit in the conception of Jesus.[11]

A good deal of information about this new understanding of the Spirit's role in the incarnation comes indirectly through the sources that witness to the developing theology of the transformation of the bread and wine of the Eucharistic celebration. For this transformation of the gifts of the Church was regarded as a process analogous to that of the incarnation.[12]

Up to the middle of the fourth century the Logos, generally viewed as accomplishing his own incarnation, was also understood as the one who effects the change of bread and wine into his body and blood. Afterwards, the Holy Spirit is assigned both the role of effecting the incarnation and the transformation of the Eucharistic gifts in Greek theology.[13] As a consequence a Logos epiclesis, asking for the sanctification of the Eucharistic bread and wine, is no longer found in the East from the end of the fourth century. Moreover the earlier Spirit epiclesis, understood as an invocation of the Logos, was now interpreted as the invoking of the coming of the Holy Spirit. This new view influenced a change in the content of the Eucharistic epiclesis. The earlier type called for the descent of the Spirit on the gifts in order to sanctify the participants of the Eucharist, and nothing was said about the transformation of the elements of bread and wine.[14] However the late fourth or early fifth century epiclesis of the Egyptian Liturgy of St. Basil petitions that the Holy Spirit "may come upon us and upon these gifts...and may sanctify them and make them holy of holies." The contemporary epiclesis of the Liturgy of St. John Chrysostom is even more developed in this direction: "Make...this bread, the precious body of your Christ, converting it by your Holy Spirit.... What...is in this cup, the precious blood of your Christ, converting it by Your holy Spirit."[15]

From the fifth century onward, numerous Greek theologians can be cited who describe the incarnation of the Word as a work of the Father, accomplished in the power of the Spirit.[16] Cyril of Alexandria's writings display a gradual evolution toward what is probably the best balanced synthesis of descending and ascending christologies among the Greek Fathers. The key texts have been collected and analyzed by David Coffey.[17] He shows clearly enough that,

> ...in his ascending christology Cyril took account of the fact that both the incarnation and grace were anointings of the man with the Holy Spirit, and was at pains to uphold the uniqueness of the anointing of Jesus in the incarnation.[18]

Augustine of Hippo also teaches that the unity of the humanity of Jesus with the divine Word is the work of the Holy Spirit.[19] But within his theological perspective that maintains the unity of the divine operation both in creation and the work of sanctification, the Spirit can only be described as having a special role by "appropriation."

3. The Nature of Jesus' Love of the Father

The most telling argument for the claim that the bestowal model pertains to the primary level of Trinitarian doctrine is derived from reflection on the nature of Jesus' love of the Father. The best presentation of this matter to date is that of David Coffey.[20] While a more ample critical analysis is needed, his orientation on the question and his conclusion are solidly based on the normative witness of Trinitarian doctrine, the New Testament. What we offer here is a paraphrase of the main lines of Coffey's exposition. Two steps are involved, which move from a consideration of Jesus' basic knowledge to his basic love.

a. Basic Knowledge of Jesus

The Council of Chalcedon, drawing on the confession of faith of previous generations of believers, affirmed that Jesus Christ is "truly man." We conclude from this that he did not lack self-consciousness, the self-awareness that is also enjoyed by all conscious human beings. He knew who he was, in his earthly state, with human knowledge. But since he is the God-man, his self-consciousness is not merely that which corresponds to the self-consciousness of fully constituted human persons. If he really knew who he is with the subjective knowledge of self--consciousness, then he knew the mystery of his being. This conclusion finds support in a philosophical consideration. It is metaphysically inconceivable that the one who, in his humanity, is the highest ontological determination of created being, exists at a lower level of self-consciousness than lower ontological determinations, namely, ordinary human persons. But there is also the Scriptural witness that Jesus knew, during his earthly life, who he was.

It is asking too much of Scripture to furnish the ground for the conclusion that Jesus enjoyed the beatific vision, as man, from the outset of his earthly existence. Rather, the New Testament seems to teach that Jesus lived by faith and not by vision. On the other hand, Scripture stresses that the all-consuming orientation of Jesus to the Father is his unique characteristic. It is this total attentiveness to the Father and the Father's will, the psychological relationship of unity with the Father, that mediates Jesus' subjective knowledge of self-consciousness.

This unique psychological relationship of unity with the Father led others to the explicit conclusion concerning Jesus' unique divine sonship. Consequently, there is no reason to reject the possibility that Jesus himself was led to the same conclusion *indirectly through his human experience*. But, in any case, we can conclude, on the basis of the full revelation of the mystery of Jesus, that the ontological ground of his psychological relation of unity with the Father is the hypostatic union. It is grounded on the communication of that subsistence from the Father to the humanity of Jesus, which constitutes Jesus of Nazareth the Son of God in his humanity. Briefly, the communion of life that obtains between the Father and the Word in the immanent Trinity, is experienced on the side of the Word in and through the assumed humanity. What Jesus knows with the subjective knowledge of self-consciousness, is what the Word knows in the immanent Trinity. But the Word knows this in his humanity through *an objective content of consciousness*, through the human experience of his psychological relationship to the Father.

b. Basic Love of Jesus

Jesus' psychological relationship with the Father is not only the foundation of his knowledge. It also provides the one, unique object of this love, namely, the Father. This love necessarily corresponds to his subjective consciousness and, like his consciousness, is a psychological dimension of the hypostatic union. Therefore the love of Jesus for the Father corresponds to the love of the Word for the Father in the immanent Trinity, in the same way that Jesus' human knowledge corresponds to the knowledge of the Word in the immanent Trinity.

Jesus' basic love of the Father, grounded on the hypostatic union, is not simply identifiable with his categorial acts of love of God, or the habit of love built up by these acts. How then does it relate to his human habit and acts of love of the Father? The new Testament attests in various ways that the believers are brought into ontological union with the Father through the work of the Spirit of God, and on this basis have psychological union with the Father. The Holy Spirit enables the response of love to the Father's love, a human love that is elicited and sustained by the Spirit in the believers. Something similar must also be said about Jesus, whose response to the Father is a human reality. But Jesus is the Son of God in a unique way. Hence his love of the Father must also be unique What, then, is the content of this love that Jesus returns to the Father?

(1) The Incarnation of the Holy Spirit in Christ

The divine sonship was received in a human way through the incarnation. Remaining in himself, the Son of God became man, and realized himself in his humanity up to the limits of the possibility of human nature during the course of his life on earth. This realization of the infinite divine sonship in a concrete humanity allows us to conclude that there was a human realization of the infinite love of the Son for the Father. Since the Holy Spirit is the identifiable source of the acceptable response of love of all ordinary human beings to the Father, it is but a short step to conclude that the Holy Spirit is received and returned in a human way, while remaining himself, by the divine Son in his humanity. This could explain the uniqueness of Jesus' basic love of the Father. According to this point of view, the Spirit is not simply the source of the supernatural love by which the acceptable fully human response is made to the Father. Rather the uniqueness of Jesus' love is the fact that it is the Holy Spirit himself who is returned to the Father.

The whole matter may be explained in this way. The divine sonship was fully realized in Jesus' humanity to the extent of the limits of the possibility of human nature. The agent of this changement by which the divine Son changed in the humanity of Jesus, was Jesus himself in his human freedom. This change came to expression in Jesus' categorical love, built up through repeated human acts. In this way the divine Son obtained the very concrete character of the human personality of Jesus of Nazareth. This progressive realization of the divine sonship included the progressive realization of Jesus' transcendental love of the Father, which can only be the Holy Spirit, who is also the source of the elicited acts of love of the Father accomplished by ordinary people. On the cross, this progressive incarnation of the Holy Spirit in Jesus' transcendental love of the Father attained the absolute limits of possibility in this life.

Through the glorification, Jesus apprehends the Father with full intellectual clarity. Because love follows knowledge, the Spirit became fully incarnated in his human love of the Father. No room is left for further elicited acts of love of the Father. In the vision of the Father is included all creation as known and loved by the Father. Knowing the Father's children with the knowledge with which the risen Lord knows the Father, he loves them with the love with which the Father loves them, namely, the Holy Spirit. The Spirit, incarnate in Jesus' human love, is the twofold love of God and humanity. Hence the sending of the Spirit at Pentecost by Jesus Christ is Jesus' love for his brethren, an essential dimension of his love of the Father.

Conclusion

Scripture, and the patristic theology of the anointing of Jesus by the Father, go part of the way toward establishing the bestowal model on the life of Jesus. Moreover, this model has been shown to be grounded on Jesus' love of the Father, expressed as a response to the Father's love for him. Jesus is brought into being as the divine Son in his humanity by the Father's bestowal of his love on him, namely, the Holy Spirit. The response of Jesus in his humanity is the return of this same love, the Holy Spirit. Given the correspondence between the economic and immanent Trinity, we conclude that the Spirit exists in the immanent Trinity as the mutual love of Father and Son.

The justification of the bestowal model comes from the person of Jesus himself, as presented in the New Testament. The demonstration shows how the theology of the incarnation harmonizes with it. Finally, it is shown that the incarnation of the Holy Spirit, in and through Jesus' human love, "is rightly seen only against *this* particular background of the immanent Trinity."[21] When the mission of the Spirit is explained exclusively from the background of the procession model, it is not possible to account for the fact that the Holy Spirit "took his 'shape' from the impress of Jesus' own relationship with God."[22]

II.
Bestowal Model: Incarnation and Grace

Beginning with the bestowal model, the data of the economic Trinity is organized in a way that differs from that of the procession model. The divine sonship of Jesus is acquired by the bestowal of the Spirit, who sanctifies and unites the humanity in unity of person to the Word. Here the order of the procession model is inverted. But it is not an inversion of the procession model. Rather, it corresponds to the manner of the bestowal of the Spirit by the Father on the Son in the immanent Trinity. The sending of the Spirit by the risen Lord to sanctify humanity and establish the Church is a theandric act. Its purpose is to make believers one with the Son, sons and daughters of the one Father. Insofar as it is an act of the Father, it relates to the manner of procession of the Spirit from the Father to the Son in the immanent Trinity.

The offer of the Spirit, made by the Father to human persons through the risen Lord, corresponds to the procession model. But the bestowal of the Spirit, conditioned by the acceptance in faith, makes the human person a son or daughter in the one Son. As transcendental act of the Father, it corresponds to the manner of the bestowal of the Spirit on the Son in the immanent Trinity. The sending of the Spirit by the risen Lord also has a correspondence in the immanent Trinity. Its purpose is to draw a person into union with the Son, and so to love the Father in the one Son. In other words, the sending of the Spirit by the risen Lord is a prolongation of the inner-Trinitarian answering love of the Son for the Father. In the risen Lord, it takes the form of a supreme act of love of the Father and all humanity in the Father; for it is ordered to enabling humankind to love the Father in, with, and through the one Son. It is the highest expression of the human love of Christ for the Father; for the explicit love of the neighbor is the primary act of human love of God.

The act by which the risen Lord sends the Spirit is a theandric act. As a divine act, flowing from the humanity of Christ, it can be called "sacramental." It is the sacrament of the transcendental act of the Father, which is a purely divine act. Through this mission of the Spirit, the Church is constituted and individual members sanctified. The once-for-all sending of the Spirit continues to be realized historically each time the word of God is preached and the sacraments celebrated.

As acts of Christ, word and sacrament correspond to the bestowal of the Spirit by the Son on the Father in the immanent Trinity; as acts of the Father, they correspond to the bestowal of the Spirit on the Son in the inner-divine life. As acts of the Father, word and sacrament have the purpose of drawing people into union with the one Son, making them children of the Father in the beloved Son. As acts of the risen Lord, word and sacrament have the purpose of drawing believers into divine sonship so that they will love the Father with a love of sons and daughters in the Son.

The theology of grace which emerges from the bestowal model makes clear that the grace of Christ, the grace that the Head and Bridegroom of the Church shares with believers, is the Holy Spirit. This Spirit, who sanctified and united the humanity of Jesus in the unity of person to the Word of God, in the time of the Church sanctifies all who accept the Father's offer of the Spirit, sent by the risen Lord.

III.
The Bestowal Model and Prayer

Many theologians, such as Karl Rahner, Bernard Lonergan, and Yves Congar, have difficulty with the notion that the prayer of Jesus has a correspondence in the inner-Trinitarian life. But the basis of the objection seems weak, namely, that it cannot be grounded on primary Trinitarian data. Ludger Oeing-Hofmann, as we have seen, demonstrates that the ground for interpersonal Trinitarian relations can be established from the analysis of Trinitarian ontology and the metaphysics of person. Ascending christology and the bestowal model of the Trinity also lead to the conclusion that the prayer of Jesus is the historical revelation of the Trinitarian dialogue. What this theology has to say about the prayer of Jesus, the prayer of the just, and the prayer of the Church as such can serve as a concluding section of this chapter.

A. The Prayer of Jesus

The prayer of Jesus, the exercise of his faith, is grounded on his divine sonship. His faith flows from this divine sonship, given from the first moment of his existence. In the free expression of his faith, the Spirit assumes the traits of his personal and individual love of God, that is, the concrete character of his unrepeatable human personality. Since the Spirit, as Jesus' transcendental love of the Father, becomes incarnate in Jesus' human love, his prayer is always the acceptable response to the Father. It corresponds to the bestowal of the love of the Son on the Father in the immanent Trinity, that love which is the Holy Spirit.

The response of Jesus' humanity to the Father reaches its highest expression in his glorified state. For the Spirit becomes fully incarnated in the human love of the risen Lord. The single act of love of the risen Lord for the Father issues in the sending of the Spirit as the Pentecostal event. This means that the "eternal intercession" of the High Priest before the Father for humankind is the full incarnation of the Spirit, by which the risen Lord loves all humanity, as an essential dimension of his love of the Father. Therefore, "in the Spirit" his eternal intercession, which is one single act of love—an act in which his whole being is concentrated—is always heard. As a consequence, the Father always responds by offering the Spirit to enable the response of faith, in and through which the Father bestows the Spirit of sonship by a purely divine act.

B. The Prayer of the Just

The reception of the Spirit makes the justified believers children of the one Father in the unique Son, and elicits from them a response of love of the Father. The unity with the Father is actualized fully by this response of love. The prayer of the just, as acceptable prayer, results from the mediation of Christ on the ground of his redemptive work. Christ both intercedes for the one who is praying and sends the Spirit in an activity that is sacrament of the bestowal of the Spirit by the Father.

As a result of this bestowal, there is the immediate union between the Father and the justified person. In Christ the just have ontological and psychological union with the Father, through the bestowal of the Spirit. The Spirit, given as the "earnest" or "first fruits" to the just on earth, is received in the state of blessedness in the fullness that corresponds to the holiness of their former life of faith. Thus the "light of glory" is truly Trinitarian. In heaven the vision of God is mediated through the One Mediator, who sends the Spirit from the Father. The blessed see the Father through Christ the One Mediator of the Spirit, in the power of the same Spirit.

The prayer of the just in heaven differs from that of the just on earth in that there is no room for elicited acts of love of humankind in the state of blessedness. Those who have entered the fulfilled kingdom have their being concentrated in a single act of love of the Father and of the Father's children. In both cases, that of the just on earth and in heaven, the prayer is efficacious because it is made in union with the prayer of Christ. But the unity is based on the active presence of the one Spirit who is, on the one hand, fully incarnated in the human love of the risen Lord and, on the other hand, enables the acceptable response of the fully human love of the just person.

C. The Prayer of the Liturgy of the Church

The prayer of the Church on earth is a prayer made with the confidence of faith that it will be heard. The ground for this confidence is the belief that it is made through, with, and in Christ, in the power of the Holy Spirit. When the Church prays for the coming of the Spirit, the issue is never in doubt. It is in the light of this conviction of faith that the efficacy of the "word" of sacramental celebrations becomes intelligible.

The verbal formulas that accompany the essential gestural actions of the sacramental celebrations should not be understood as simply announcing the offer of the grace that corresponds to the signification of the rite. It is incorrect to relegate the formulas merely to the function of signifying God's offer of grace. Rather, the sacramental word is, in the first place, a prayer—even when formulated in the indicative. Sacraments are a true offer of grace, and indeed *ex opere operato* (from the work worked), because the prayer of the Church is a sacramental manifestation of the union of the worshipping community with the one High Priest.

The certainty of a hearing before the Father is expressed in the use of such indicative active forms as "I absolve you from your sins;" "I baptize you in the name of the Father and of the Son and of the Holy Spirit." But the meaning of the sacramental word is always deprecative. It is a prayer of the Church made in union with Christ in the power of the Spirit, petitioning the Father to send the Spirit of sanctification. *It is this personalistic explanation of the efficacy of the sacraments, ex opere operato, that accounts for the dialogical structure of the liturgy and the essentially christological-Trinitarian dimension of Christian liturgy in all its forms.*

Summary and Conclusion

The main lines of the bestowal model, and its application to the theology of incarnation and grace, are represented by the following diagram.[23]

1. Through the missions of the Word and Spirit the humanity of Jesus is sanctified by the Spirit and united in unity of person to the Word.

2. The response of Jesus to the Father on behalf of humanity is realized fully in history through the Cross. In his human response, the transcendental love of the Father is incarnated, namely, the Spirit.

3. In the resurrection event, the Father responds to Jesus'love by sending the Spirit to make his body alive in glory.

4. The glorified Lord sends the Spirit by a theandric act, as the obverse of his love of the Father. Correspondingly, the Father bestows the Spirit in a purely transcendental act by which the Church is established and sanctified.

5. The risen Lord is Head of his Church, united to him as his earthly Body in the one Spirit. Thus a holy communion is founded between Christ and believers, of which the Spirit is the bond.

IMMANENT TRINITY

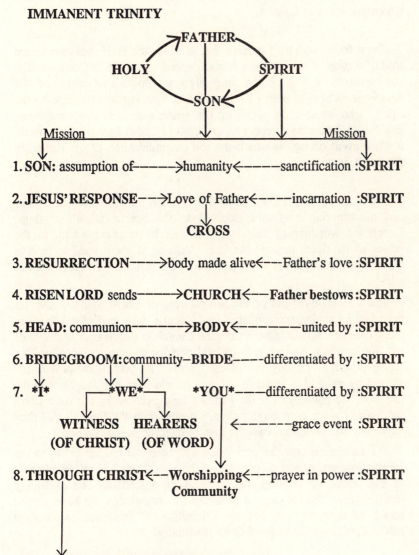

RETURN TO THE FATHER: GOD ALL IN ALL

6. But the risen Lord is Bridegroom, and the Church is his Bride. Hence a certain distance exists between them. This differentiation does not imply separation because the Church possesses the same Spirit whom Christ possesses in fullness.

7. Christ forms with his Church a *We,* in which the *YOU* is always united to, but distinguished from the *I,* and dependent on the *I.* Consequently, the members of the Church must always witness to Christ, and the hearers must always accept Christ as Lord. This is made possible by the Spirit, who anoints the word of the witness and, at the same time, enables the hearer to accept it as the word of Christ himself. As a result, a grace event occurs, in which the self-communication of the Father, in the Spirit, is realized.

8. The grace of God reaches its term only when it is accepted with praise and thanksgiving, and thus returned to the Source of all blessings. Hence the worshipping community fulfills its meaning when, in the power of the Spirit through the One Mediator, it opens itself to receive the love of the Father by a self-offering to the end that God may be all in all.

The Church lives out of the self-offering of Christ to the Father on behalf of humanity, accomplished in the Spirit. As vessel of the Spirit in the sphere of Christ's self-offering, the Church is the clearest visibility of the Spirit, whose essence it is to bind persons together personally. This is the power, the anonymity of the Spirit.[24] As such, the Spirit is bestowed by the Father to make ordinary people sons and daughters in the one Son, the one object of the Father's love. As sent by the risen Lord, the Spirit's work is to unite ordinary people with the Son, so that they may love the one Father with the love of children in the one Son.

We have seen how the procession and bestowal models relate to the incarnation, grace, and prayer. The yield of both models is considerable in the matter of ordering the material of descending and ascending christologies. Now it is time to apply the knowledge we have gained about the economic and immanent Trinity in a systematic presentation of the Trinitarian theology of Christian liturgy.

Notes

1. E. E. Hagen, "Analytic Models in the Study of Social Systems," American Sociological Review 68 (1981) 144.

2. A. Dulles, MODELS OF THE CHURCH (Garden City, N.J.: Doubleday, 1974).

3. HANDBUCH DER KATHOLISCHEN DOGMATIK. Gesammelte Schriften 6.1 (Freiburg im Br.: Herder 1954) 176-184; DIE MYSTERIEN DES CHRISTENTUMS. Gesammelte Schriften 6.2 (1958) [Engl. trans.: THE MYSTERIES OF CHRISTIANITY (St. Louis, Mo.: B. Herder, 1946)].

4. Reference has already been made to his DER HEILIGE GEIST ALS PERSON. Confer also Mühlen's Trinitarian grounded ecclesiology (UNA MYSTICA PERSONA). Die Kirche als das Mysterium der heilsgeschichtlichen Identität des heiligen Geist in Christus und den Christen: Eine Person in vielen Personen (Munich: Schöningh, 1967), and "Das Christusereignis als Tat des heiligen Geistes," MYSTERUIM SALUTIS III. 2, 513-544.

5. D. Coffey observes in a recent article that the efforts of Western theologians, especially H. Mühlen, to present a case for a proper mission of the Holy Spirit "have not proved conspicuously successful." This author himself provides a good summary exposition of the reasons why the proper mission of the Holy Spirit poses no threat to the traditional Western emphasis on the continuing mission of Christ ("The Proper Mission of the Holy Spirit," THEOLOGICAL STUDIES 47 [1986] 227-250).

6. E. J. Kilmartin, "A Modern Approach," 64ff; W. Kasper, JESUS THE CHRIST, 254-268; P. Schoonenberg, "Spirit Christology and Logos Christology," BIJDRAGEN 38 (1977) 350-375; P. J. Rosato, "Spirit Christology: Ambiguity and Promise," THEOLOGICAL STUDIES 38 (1972) 423-449.

7. THE MYSTERIES OF CHRISTIANITY, 331-334; HANDBUCH DER KATHOLISCHE DOGMATIK 6.1, 181-182.

8. DER HEILIGER GEIST ALS PERSON, 170-187.

9. J. Villalón, SACREMENTS DANS L'ESPRIT: Existence humaine et théologie existentielle. Théologie historique 43 (Paris: Beauchesne, 1977) 421-422.

10. Justin Martyr identifies the Spirit of Lk 1:35 with the "power of the Logos" (1 Apology 33). Confer J. Betz, DIE EUCHARISTIE IN DER ZIET DER GRIECHISCHEN VÄTER I.1 (Freiburg im Br.: Herder, 1955) 268.

11. Cyril of Jerusalem (313-386) teaches that the Holy Spirit belongs with the Father and Son to form a Trinity. But he is reluctant to inquire about the person and origin of the Spirit. (CATECHESES 16.24 [PG 33.952]). Around 359, Athanasius explicitly defends the consubstantiality of the Spirit with Father and Son in his struggle with the Pneumatomachians ("Spirit-fighters"): "He belongs to the Word and Father, and shares one and the same substance (HOMOOUSIOS) with them" (AD SERAPIONEM EPISTULAE 1.27 [PG 26.592]). Athanasius emphasizes that the incarnation is the work of the Holy Spirit: "When the Logos descended into the Holy Virgin, the Holy Spirit entered

with him, and in the Holy Spirit the Logos shaped and formed a body for himself..." (AD SERAPIONEM EPISTULAE 1.31 [PG 26.605A]).

12. For example, Ephraem of Syria (307-373) writes: "Fire and Spirit were in the womb, which bore you; fire and Spirit were in the river when you were baptized; fire and Spirit are in the bread and cup" (E. Beck, DES HEILIGEN EPHRAEM DES SYRERS HYMNEN DE FIDE 10.17 (CSCO 154) [Confer: P. Yousif, L'EUCHARISTIE CHEZ SAINT EPHRAEM DE NISIBE. Orientalia Christiana Analecta 224 (Rome: Pontifical Oriental Institute, 1984) 265-266]. Here the Spirit refers to the DIVINE NATURE OF THE LOGOS.

13. J. Betz, DIE EUCHARISTIE... I.1, 262-300, describes the evolution from the earlier consistent interpretation of Greek patristic writers to the new view concerning the source of the transformation of the Eucharistic elements. At the beginning of the post-apostolic period, and up through the first part of the fourth century, the change of the Eucharistic elements is seen as a kind of Eucharistic incarnation, and the Logos plays the key role. As the theology of the Holy Spirit developes, the accent gradually shifts to the role of the Spirit in the mediation of the incarnation. This goes a long way toward explaining the corresponding emphasis on the Spirit's activity in the transformation of the bread and wine of the Eucharist.

14. Examples of this form of epiclesis are found in the Eucharistic Prayer of the APOSTOLIC TRADITION of Hippolytus, which goes back to the first part of the third century, and in the East-Syrian anaphora of the Apostles Addai and Mari, which also reflects third century usage.

15. The change in the content of the epiclesis, with the emphasis placed on the Spirit's role in the conversion of the eucharistic elements, presumably occurred after 381, the year of the Council of Constantinople I, which defended the consubstantiality of the Spirit against the so-called Macedonians, or Pneumatomachians, "...those who resist the Holy Spirit" (Canon 1 [DS 151]).

16. For example, Peter Chrysologus (c. 406-c.450), SERMO 57 (PG 52.359); John of Damascus, who summarizes the Greek tradition (DE FIDE ORTHODOXA IV [PG 94.1160]).

17. GRACE, THE GIFT OF THE HOLY SPIRIT, 130-141.

18. GRACE, THE GIFT OF THE HOLY SPIRIT, 141.

19. J. Verhees, "Heiliger Geist und Inkarnation in der Theologie des Augustinus von Hippo. Unlöslicher Zusammenhang zwischen Theo-logie und Okumenie," REVUE DES ÉTUDES AUGUSTIENNES 22 (1976) 234-259.

20. "The Incarnation of the Holy Spirit in Christ," THEOLOGICAL STUDIES 45 (1984) 466-480.

21. IBID.

22. IBID.

23. A similar diagram is supplied by E. Salmann, "Trinität und Kirche," 372. But it is based on a procession model of the Western type, which includes the FILIOQUE. Here the Holy Spirit is simply seen as the overflow of the love of Father and Son.

24. In the immanent Trinity, the Spirit is not correctly described by a personal pronoun AT THE LEVEL OF PRIMARY TINITARIAN DATA. H. Mühlen suggests that the Spirit be called the "We in person" of which the source is the "We act" of the Father and Son. But, even in the Western version of the procession model, which Mühlen employs, the Spirit does not proceed from a common act of two subjects. The Father and Son do not relate to the Spirit as a We, which would imply two distinct principles. Rather the procession of the Spirit derives from the MUTUAL ACT of Father and Son, from Father and Son acting as one principle.

Chapter 12

The Mystery of the Liturgy
and Its Celebration

Systematic theology does not have the responsibility of attempting to prove from reason the truth of revelation of God. The task of theology is to contribute to some limited, but fruitful, understanding of what is known with certainty by faith.[1] We know by faith that the liturgy of the Church is ultimately the work of the Triune God. A theology of liturgy merely attempts to show how Christian worship, in all its forms, should be understood as the self-communication of the Triune God. The present chapter is directed to this end. Its purpose is to explain how the liturgy of the Church forms an integral part of the "secret plan of God...revealed by the Spirit to the holy apostles and prophets" (Eph 3:5).

The mystery of the liturgy is the mystery of the history of salvation, fully revealed in the special missions of the Father's one Word and one Spirit. It is, at its depth, the life and work of the Triune God in the economy of salvation. This fundamental Christian belief provides the clue to the proper, comprehensive approach to the theology of the liturgy. As yet, however, few modern Catholic theologians have taken up the challenge of working out a systematic Trinitarian theology of the liturgy. Jean Corbon, a priest of the Maronite rite residing in Beirut, is an exception. He has contributed an attractive schematic presentation of the theology of liturgy inspired by the witness of Scripture and patristic sources of the Syriac and Greek traditions.[2]

In this chapter, the path taken by Corbon is followed. Christian liturgy as a whole is explained as the place where the economic Trinity unfolds itself. At the same time, the economic Trinity is identified as the unique source, which binds together the variety of liturgical-sacramental celebrations. Frequently the exposition of this chapter merely paraphrases what Corbon writes. But there are major differences. Whereas he works with a procession model of the immanent Trinity and only incidentally introduces elements of an ascending christology, the following outline of a theology of worship incorporates the bestowal model and an ascending christology, and integrates the notion of the incarnation of the Spirit in Jesus' transcendental love of the Father.

I.
The Mystery of the Liturgy

There never was a time when the Trinitarian self-communication was not offered to humankind and bestowed on those who live according to the truth of their existence as they see it. But, at the outset of the history of the Triune God with humanity, the depth of God's love for his creatures remained hidden. This mystery was obscurely revealed in various ways to the people of Israel, especially with the promise of the new and definitive covenant (Jer 31:31ff). A further revelation occurred in the announcement to the Virgin Mary of her role in God's plan for the salvation of the world. But the full revelation took place in the incarnation of the Word, and the sending of the Spirit to establish the Church.

> Now, therefore, through the Church, God's manifold wisdom is made known...in accord with his age-old purpose, carried out in Christ Jesus our Lord. In Christ and through faith in him we can speak freely to God, drawing near him with confidence (Eph 3:10-12).

A. The Immanent Trinity

The mystery of the Triune God's self-communication to humankind is fully Trinitarian in its content and execution or accomplishment. In the inner-Trinitarian life the Father is the ultimate source of the Word and Spirit. From him issues his Word and his Spirit. But the Word is not spoken and the Spirit is not breathed forth into an eternal void. The Word is continually turned to the Father and gives self back to him in loving thanksgiving. The Spirit of the Father rests on the Word, as bestowal of his love, and the answering love of the Word to the Father is this same Spirit. The Father and the Son are "for one another" in their mutual love, the Holy Spirit.

Father and Son are identically the divine essence. This is the basis of their *perichoresis*, their being in one another. But they are really distinct from one another by an opposition of relation. The love between Father and Son, the Holy Spirit, as their mutual love, is the power of life of the living God. This love, this power of life, is shared with humanity. But the unfolding of this communication of the Holy Spirit in the world is carried out in a series of stages.

B. Economic Trinity: 1. Creation and Old Covenant

Initially the Father gives over his Word and his Spirit in an activity that pertains to the Godhead as such. In a work that can be described as analogous to the exercise of efficient causality, the world came into being. Although the world bears the marks of the Word and the Spirit, the Trinity of persons remains completely hidden. However, creation is a pure gift of God and has its meaning in acceptance. This comes through rational creatures who, though made like other creatures, are also created in the image and likeness of God (Gen 1:27). Created for fellowship with God, human beings fulfill their own meaning, and that of all creation, by accepting the love of God with thanksgiving and praise. As social beings who find their fulfillment in relation to the world, other beings, and, above all, God, rational creatures are already image of the mystery of the communion of life of the Father, Son, and Holy Spirit.

A major step in the revelation of the economic Trinity occurs in the personal promise of God's fidelity, and humanity's acceptance in word and deed. Through faith, humankind becomes responder to the personal God's word and deed, receiver and partner from Abraham to Mary the mother of Jesus. The gradual revelation that communion of life with God is the destiny of humanity reaches a new high in Mary's "Be it done unto me according to your word" (Lk 1:38). A human response is always associated with God's self-communication, made possible by God's own act. Mary's acceptance was the condition for the incarnation, in which the humanity, assumed by the Word, played no role.

Mary's word was neither the first word, nor the last word. God always has the first word and the last. The Father sends the Spirit, who sanctifies the "yes" of Mary by elevating and uniting the flesh of Mary's womb, the humanity of Jesus, to the Word in unity of person. But the "yes" of Mary was already the working of the Spirit of God. Eastern theology speaks of the action worked by the Spirit as "divine energy." When this energy is joined to the energy of a human being, there occurs a synergism: a co-action of conjoint energies. Through this synergism, by which the Spirit of God impregnates the energies of creatures, they are drawn into personal communion with God and do the works of God. The fruit of the action of the Spirit in Mary is the incarnation. Her "fiat," originating through the hidden action of the Spirit, issued in the response of God by which the humanity of Jesus, formed in the Virgin's womb, was sanctified by the Holy Spirit and elevated to unity in person with the Word.

2. Incarnation

As a consequence of Mary's response to God's word, a new stage of the unfolding of the economic Trinity is reached. Through the assumption of the flesh of Mary's womb, the *kenosis* of the Son of God in the economy of salvation begins: the self-emptying of the glory which the Son has in the Trinitarian life. Corresponding to the manner of the procession of the Spirit from the Father, that is, as bestowal of the Father's love on the Son, the sending of the Spirit by the Father on the humanity created to receive that love necessarily draws that being into union with the proper object of the Father's love, the Son. In this instance, the bestowal of the Spirit binds together the flesh of Mary's womb and the Son of God, effecting a new covenant between Word and flesh.

The incarnation displays the properly divine manner of loving. The Word empties himself of his glory, just as in the Trinity he completely gives self to the Father in perfect love. This *kenosis* of the Son reaches its fulfillment in the death of the cross. In the incarnation something absolutely new has occurred in the relation between God and creatures through the working of the Spirit. Jesus Christ is simply sacrament of salvation in the fullest sense. In him occurs the full self-communication of the Father through Word and Spirit. Therefore he is the holy presence of the loving Father in history. At the same time, he is the one who is able to make the perfect response to this communication of divine love, in and through which the divine plan for the world comes to full realization. In short, he is sacrament of the divine-human love of humankind (sanctification) and sacrament of the divine-human love of God (glorification).

3. Jesus' Public Ministry.

In the public ministry of Jesus, the new synergism of Word and flesh, effected by the Spirit, is revealed. It is shown forth in the baptism of Jesus, where the total self-gift of the Father and the total acceptance of the Son is revealed through the anointing with the Spirit. The new synergism is also displayed in the efficacy of Jesus' word and works.

In his ministry Jesus communicates the Spirit to others as the representative of his Father. His word and works signify the invisible offer of the Spirit of God to those who accept the Father's beloved Son. The bestowal of the Spirit by the Father corresponds to the manner of procession of the Spirit from Father to Son. Its purpose is to draw people into union with the Son, so that they may become truly the children of the one Father. Correspondingly, the sending of the Spirit by Christ aims at drawing others into union with the Father so that they will love his Father. But this sending of the Spirit by Christ, during his earthly life to individuals, does not have a merely juridical grounding based on Jesus' authority as unique messenger of God. It has an ontological basis in Jesus' transcendental love of the Father, namely, the Holy Spirit.

The expression of Jesus' love for the individual during his public life is a kind of incarnation of the Spirit, that is, the incarnation of Jesus' transcendental love. The love that Jesus displays toward others is, at its depth, the Spirit, who assumes the characteristics of Jesus' personal and individual human love of the Father. Consequently, the visible offer and sending of the Spirit, expressed in Jesus' theandric acts of love for the neighbor, corresponds to, and is ontologically grounded on, the answering bestowal of the Spirit by the Son on the Father in the immanent Trinity. Its purpose corresponds to Christ's love of the Father, that is, to enable human beings to respond to the Father as sons and daughters in the one Son.

4. Jesus' Death, Resurrection, and Ascension

The synergism of Jesus and the Father, in the Spirit, is especially revealed in the *kenosis* of the Cross. But this event is so intimately linked to the resurrection that we are inclined to think of two moments of the same event.

a. Death of the Cross

The Spirit who shared in the first *kenosis*, the incarnation itself, also plays a role in that of the Cross. The Spirit effects the synergism between the Word and the assumed humanity, by which the Son of God in the flesh delivers himself up fully to death in order to conquer it. This is the role of the Spirit as the principle of sanctification of the humanity of Jesus, by which it was bound in hypostatic union with the Word.

Only the Epistle to the Hebrews, among the New Testament texts, refers to the active presence of the Spirit of God in the event of the Cross. Heb 9:14 states that Jesus offered himself "through the eternal spirit." Exegetes dispute the meaning of this passage.[3] In the liturgical usage of the verse, evidence can be found for the identification of "eternal spirit" with the Holy Spirit. This probably holds true for the anaphora of Theodore of Mopsuestia,4 and certainly for the Gregorian Sacramentary[5] as well as the communion prayer of the old Roman Mass, which derives from a ninth century composition.[6] However the liturgical witness resists any precise theological interpretation.

Various theological interpretations are found in the Greek and Latin Fathers,[7] and the subject continues to be the object of study of systematic theologians.[8] In the christology previously developed in this book, it was argued that Jesus' life of faith, which flowed from his divine sonship already given, was lived in the power of the Spirit. It follows, from this consideration, that he offered himself on the cross in a fully human love to the Father "in the Spirit," source of his habitual, personal, individual, and incommunicable grace. But there is more. The Spirit's role at the cross corresponds to his unique personhood in the immanent Trinity. As the transcendental love of Jesus for the Father, the Spirit is fully incarnated in Jesus' love on the cross.

In the love of Jesus for the Father, unto the death of the cross, the Spirit took his shape from the impress of Jesus' own relation to the Father and attained the limits of the possibility, within history, of his incarnation in the human love of Jesus. This means that Jesus not only offered himself to the Father in the power of the Spirit, but also bestowed the Spirit on the Father, as his transcendental love of the Father. In the hour of Jesus, he gives himself completely to the Father in a love that is ultimately the Love shared by the Father and Son in the Trinity. The synergism between the humanity of Jesus and the divine Son, the conjoint energies of the Word and his humanity, reaches a depth which cannot be surpassed on earth.

The bestowal of Jesus' transcendental love on the Father, the Holy Spirit, is the response to the Father's love for the world. It is the anabatic, or upward, movement of the divine plan of salvation. Through it is revealed the katabatic, or downward, movement: the Father's giving of himself to the world in his only Son in order to redeem it. In short, the *kenosis* of the Father is revealed in the *kenosis* of the incarnate Son.

b. The Resurrection and Ascension of Jesus

The giving over of his Son totally in the flesh unto death, is the revelation of the Father's love for the world. But this love is not a demonstration of helpless benevolence. If the Son of God responds to the Father by a love that exceeds all imaginable limits, the Father has the last response. He totally receives back the Son, who gives himself freely to the Father in the obedience of love. The Father sends the Spirit of love, and the body of Christ is made alive in the Spirit. The body that rises from the grave is now and for always alive, and source of life for others. According to Paul, Jesus Christ has become the "vivifying Spirit" (1 Cor 15:45). Along with the Father, he has become the giver of life: "Indeed, just as the Father raises the dead and grants life, so the Son grants life to those to whom he wishes" (Jn:5:21).

The fully "spiritualized" resurrected body is described by Paul as a "spiritual body" and contrasted with a "physical body" (I Cor 15:44). Beyond that, he can only say that there is a link between the two, between the "perishable" and the "imperishable" (1 Cor 15:53), which remains a mystery: "Lo! I tell you a mystery...we shall all be changed" (v.51). Through the resurrection, Jesus has become the full realization of divinity in humanity, to the highest degree possible within the limits of human nature. Established at the right hand of the Father, he apprehends the Father with full intellectual clarity. Since the measure of love follows the intellectual perception of the object of love, this has consequences for what we call the incarnation of the Holy Spirit in the human love of the risen Lord. The full incarnation of the Spirit in Jesus' human love for the Father means that there is no room for elicited acts of love of the Father. Jesus' whole being is concentrated in a single act of love. The divinity of the Son has fully penetrated the human being of Jesus in its highest activity, which orders and subsumes all others, the love of the Father.

5. The Ascension of the Just

The ascension of the just who have died in the Lord is included in the ascension of Jesus, his exaltation at the right hand of the Father. They are the first fruits of the saving work of Jesus, the beginning of the return of all the justified, which will be completed when all the predestined are drawn into this same mystery. The traditional teaching of the churches of the East and West affirms that the blessed enjoy the vision of God before the resurrection of the body. According to Pope Benedict XII's constitution *Benedictus Deus*, those who have died and been purified

> ...also before the resurrection of their bodies and the general judgement, after the ascension of our Lord and Saviour Jesus Christ into heaven, were, are and will be in heaven...and after the passion and death of the Lord Jesus Christ saw and see the divine essence by intuitive vision.[9]

This return of the just to the Father is accomplished by the risen Lord, who sends the Spirit from the Father as an essential aspect of his love of the Father. It is this Spirit who bestows the knowledge and love by which the blessed love the Father through Christ in the beatific vision. According to Pope Leo XIII's encyclical letter *Divinum Illud*,[10] March 17, 1897, and Pope Pius XII's encyclical letter *Mystici corporis*,[11] June 29, 1943, the indwelling of the Holy Spirit in the just on earth differs from that of the blessed in heaven "only by reason of our condition or state." From this statement, one can conclude what seems to be more generally recognized today within Catholic theology, namely, that the mediatorship of Christ is not abolished but rather brought to fulfillment in the kingdom.

Those who are in Christ, the blessed, are in him "in the Spirit." They constitute the eschatological community, augmented by the death of the individual just person. The just on earth are already "justified" and "glorified" (Rom 8:30), on the basis of faith and divine sonship. But they are not yet at the definitive stage, which comes after physical death. Then they will be drawn fully into Christ through the full communication of the Spirit, who is given now as the "first fruits" (Rom 8:23; Col 1:22;

Eph 1:14). Then they will see the Father (1 Jn 3:2) through Christ in the Holy Spirit.

With the ascension of Jesus and the ascension of the blessed, the divine plan of salvation is fully realized for them. This means that the mystery of the inner-Trinitarian communion between Father, Son, and Spirit has now become a heavenly liturgy because it is *communicated and shared.*

6. Pentecost

As a consequence of his "vision" of the Father and the accompanying love, the risen Lord both knows the Father's children with the knowledge with which he knows the Father, and loves them with the love with which the Father loves them. Because of the profound unity between Jesus' love of the Father and his love of the Father's children, this love being ultimately the Holy Spirit incarnated in Jesus' human love, the sending of the Spirit at Pentecost follows.

Through the resurrection Jesus becomes cosender of the Spirit with the Father, because he becomes the full realization of divinity in his humanity. He becomes fully one, in his fully divinized humanity, with the coprinciple of the Spirit, namely, the Word. Therefore, as the Word bestows the Spirit on the Father in his eternal eucharist, so the risen Lord sends the Spirit, fully incarnated in his human love, to the end that all humanity may be enabled to love the Father fully "in spirit and truth" (Jn 4:24).

However the divinity of Christ, as divinity realized in humanity, cannot be equated with that of the Father, which is divinity simply given. This means that the sending of the Spirit by the risen Lord must be understood as related to, rather then simply identified with, the sending of the Spirit by the Father. In other words, Christ sends the Spirit at Pentecost, and in fullness once-for-all, by a *theandric act,* that is to say, by a divine act which flows from the glorified humanity. This act can be said to "signify" the sending of the Spirit by the Father, which is a purely *transcendental act.* Through the action, originating from the Father as a purely divine act and from the risen Lord as its "sacrament," to which corresponds the acceptance of the Holy Spirit by the "witnesses" (Acts 4:15) of the resurrection, the Church is constituted, and individuals are sanctified by faith.

The sending of the Spirit by the risen Lord is a kind of prolongation of the answering love of the Son for the Father in the immanent Trinity. It is ordered to enabling a corresponding response of love for the Father from all humanity. At the same time, it is the highest expression of the human love of the risen Lord for the Father; for the explicit love of the neighbor, ordered to the fulfillment of the neighbor's existence, communion with God, is the primary act of human love of God.

With the sending of the Spirit, "the river of the life-giving water" which flows "from the throne of God and of the Lamb" (Rev 22:1), the people of God on earth are made cosharers of the heavenly liturgy. But this happens in the measure that the *kenosis* of the faithful corresponds to the divine *kenosis*. The participants of the earthly liturgy become one with the Father, through Christ in the Spirit, to the extent that they fully give themselves in love to the Father *and* to the Father's other children.

7. Relationship Between the Heavenly and Earthly Liturgies

In the heavenly liturgy there is the Father who sends, the Son who is sent and who sends, and the Spirit who is sent to be the bond of unity. There are the angels and blessed who enjoy the incorruptible life. The divine energy that vivifies the blessed comes from the thrones of the Father *and* the Son. The risen Lord is with the Father, the source of all, to pour forth the "life-giving water," the Holy Spirit.

The celebration of this heavenly liturgy is depicted in tradition as beginning in the movement of the return to the Father. It is a celebration of the fulfillment of the economy of salvation. As a fulfillment, it never ceases. As fulfillment, it can be described with the one word: GLORY.

In and through the heavenly liturgy, the glory of the Triune God is realized; for the "secret plan" of God is that humankind may have life. There is also the glory of the blessed who freely give themselves, in praise and thanksgiving, to receive the meaning of their lives from God. The glory of God and the glory of the blessed is realized through the twofold movement: a back and forth play, in which the Father communicates self through Christ in the Spirit so that the "many" may be the glory of God, and in which the "many" freely receive God's gift in order to give glory to God.

The Father, from whom the energy of the gift of life proceeds eternally, reveals self as the source of that energy by which creatures are able to respond in love. In short, the eternal liturgy is the celebration of the sharing of life and love in which each participant is turned to the other as completely as possible. It is the true life of humanity lived at the heart of the inner-Trinitarian communion. There is the vision of God that includes personal communion with the Father, through Christ in the Spirit, and personal communion among all those who are in Christ.

The eternal liturgy is the mystery of the earthly liturgy. Through the ascension of Christ, the Body of Christ himself and ultimately the earthly body of Christ, the Church, are united to the heart of the Father. In the heavenly liturgy, the risen Lord is present as minister of his brothers and sisters and exercises the work of High Priest (Heb 2:13-17). He has become "source of 'eternal life' for all those who obey him" (Heb 5:9). Through his eternal intercession (Heb 7:25), the life-giving Spirit is sent in the final divine *kenosis*. The self-emptying of the Spirit began with the incarnation and continued when the Spirit took up the dead flesh of Jesus and bound it living to the Word. The *kenosis* of the Spirit is completed in the third Pentecost because now the Spirit binds believers to the dead and risen Lord.

Through the bestowal of the Spirit by the risen Lord from the Father, the heavenly liturgy is extended to earth. The Spirit, who grounds the heavenly liturgy as the transcendental love of the risen Lord for the Father and the source of the loving response of the blessed for the Father's gift, is the one who enables the return of the earthly assembly of believers to the Father through Christ.

The earthly liturgy is the sacramental accomplishment of the heavenly liturgy,[12] the foretaste of an anticipated reality. The earthly liturgy is the enactment of the desire and hope for something that already exists elsewhere. But it is also a real participation in the heavenly liturgy. In the earthly liturgy the Church makes its own self-offering to the Father as bride of Christ. At the same time, the Church is united to Christ as Body to Head, quickened by the one Spirit whom Christ possesses in fullness. This unity in the one Spirit enables a loving mutuality of self-offering in which the earthly liturgical assembly is united in its worship to the eternal worship of Christ.

The prayer of the earthly assembly of believers mounts to the throne of the Father and is always heard; for its mystery is the eternal worship of the one High Priest, *the sacrament of the divine human love of God* (glorification). The Church prays for the coming of the Holy Spirit; the Father responds by bestowing the Spirit on those who accept his offer in faith. At the same time, the epiclesis, the petition for the coming of the Spirit, made in the power of the Spirit, always implies a petition for the coming of the Lord himself. In the prayer of the Church, "the Spirit himself intercedes for us with sighs too deep for words" (Rom 8:26). The petition "Our Lord come" (1 Cor 16:22: *Marana tha*) bears fruit. Now the Lord comes as *the sacrament of the divine-human love of humanity,* as source of sanctification.

The liturgy of the earthly Church is always Christ's liturgy, because Christ is always actively present as the Head of the community assembled "in the name of Jesus." When the Church takes up corporeal elements and employs them in a symbolic action that signifies God's self-communication, it does so as the Body of Christ. The risen Lord relates himself to this activity as the sacrament of the divine-human love of humankind. As Lord of history and Head of his Church, Christ makes the symbolic actions of the Church realizing signs of his saving presence. This is especially manifested in the Eucharist.

From the outset of the Eucharistic celebration, Christ places all that the community does in the relation between himself and the believers. What the Church does is changed from the outset as a consequence of Christ being the host of the meal of the Church, the anticipated Messianic banquet. Since this meal is the meal of the people of God, gathered around the High Priest unto the glory of the Father, its mystery is the self-offering of Christ to the Father "on behalf of the many" and the self-offering of the Lord to the community under the form of sacrament of his Body and Blood.

Christ relates himself to the prayer of the bride, so that the liturgical community is included in his worship of the Father. He relates himself to the bread and wine which, symbolizing the self-offering of the Church, become realizing signs of Christ's offering of self to the Father and for personal communion with the children of the one Father. The change of the bread and wine is unique. It does not terminate simply in a change of meaning, but in a perfect correspondence of being and meaning. The bread and wine become "real symbols" of Christ's personal presence in the sense that there is unity of being between the symbol and the reality signified. Christ really gives himself sacramentally to the Father, and into the hands of the communicant in the sacrament of his Body and Blood.

The Eucharistic liturgy is the clearest witness of the faith of the Church that the co-working of the Spirit and Church, and Christ and Church, constitute the essence of the earthly liturgy. This "Divine Liturgy," as it is called in the East, demonstrates most vividly how the twofold aspect of the relationship of the Church to Christ is realized in liturgical practice. The Church is the Bride of Christ, and so cooperates with Christ in the work of its own upbuilding. Hence, in the epiklesis, the Church petitions that the Father send the Spirit to enable her to serve Christ effectively. The Church is the Body of Christ and so has the mission of radiating the glory of the risen Lord. Therefore the community petitions for the coming of the Spirit to sanctify the bread and wine. The faithful receive the sacrament of Christ's body and blood in order to bind themselves more consciously to their Head and explicitly commit themselves to his way of *kenosis*, of dying to self, in order to rise in glory.

II.
The Liturgy as Celebrated

The concrete forms of the earthly liturgy derive their shape from several sources. If one asks about the "formal reason" for a particular liturgical tradition, its exact and most immediate explanation, the answer is simply this: the global perception of the life of faith, which impregnates and structures the lives of the community in which the liturgy originates. But this life of faith, identified in its peculiarity with a particular community of Christians in a concrete historical and cultural situation, is grounded on the Holy Spirit. The Holy Spirit is the ultimate source of the historically and culturally conditioned liturgical expressions of faith.

The Spirit always refers the community, in its life and works, to the life and work of Jesus of Nazareth. This Spirit of Christ keeps alive the memory of Jesus and, at the same time, teaches the community how to celebrate the profound meaning of his life and work. In this sense, we must speak of the Spirit as the ultimate source of the authentic liturgical forms of expression of the Church's faith. The Spirit is the principal cause who organizes the specific elements of the liturgy into a unity of signification that corresponds to one or another dimension of the mystery of Christ.

Liturgy as a whole is grounded on the authority of Christ and the inspiration of the Holy Spirit. With regard to the chief rites of the Church, there are certain permanent, constitutive elements handed on within all of the authentic liturgical traditions. They are related either directly or indirectly to important events or activities of the public life of Jesus of Nazareth, or to his appearances after the resurrection. Above all, the Eucharistic celebration falls into this category, as memorial of the Last Supper and the totality of Christ's saving work.

These constitutive elements of the chief rites of the Church are understood in the traditional churches of East and West to be instituted by Christ, at least as far as their signification, even though the exact manner of the institution is open to debate. Accordingly, where these essential elements are maintained, the "sacramentality" of the chief rites is secured as long as they are celebrated in the context of the Church of Christ.

A. Liturgy of the Body and Bride of Christ

Liturgy is always the liturgy of the Church. It is the Church's self-expression, manifesting and realizing its nature. Hence what the participants of the liturgy experience is the sacramentality of the Church. Through faith the individual believer is placed in contact with this social sacrament as it actualizes itself.

All liturgical celebrations manifest, in the first place, the backward flow of doxological energy. This movement is already redeeming because it takes place through Christ in the Spirit. In this thanksgiving and praise, the Church expresses its openness to receive God's gift. Corresponding to this movement is that of the Father, through Christ in the Spirit; for the prayer of the Church is always heard.

The anabatic and katabatic movements of the liturgy are especially made clear in the chief rites of the Church. Here the liturgical assembly, the Church in action, shows itself as the community that loves God and loves God's children. The Church worships God, confessing that no work or word of God reaches its goal if it is not given back to God, and gives God praise. Then attention is turned to the needs of the community of believers and the world. More especially, an explicit petition is made for the bestowal of God's grace on those in whose favor the sacramental rite is celebrated. The desire of the Church, expressed on behalf of the individual, is acted out by appropriate symbolic gestures, which often include material elements (water, oil, bread and wine). At the same time, each sacrament announces, in its own way, that the Triune God is present in particular life situations of the community or individual, and how one is to respond so as to conform to God's will.

What the Church does, in all of its liturgical celebrations, manifests for the eyes of faith what Christ is doing. If the liturgical assembly worships the Father, it is *because* Christ himself is always before the Father as the chief liturgist of the communion of the blessed and of the believers on earth. If the liturgical assembly reaches out in its symbolic gestures of desire for the sanctification of the members of Christ's Body, it is *because* Christ is now, and always, reaching out as the sacrament of the divine-human love of humanity.

What the Church does, through Christ in the Spirit, as praise and petition before the Father, is the obverse of what the Father does through Christ in the Spirit, for those who turn to him in faith. "The river of the water of life" flows from the throne of God and the Lamb (Rev 22:1) when "The Spirit and the bride say, 'Come'" (Rev 22:17). Those who join in the petition, with open hearts, receive the life-giving Spirit: "And let him who hears say 'Come.' And let him who is thirsty come, let him who desires take the water of life without price70 (Rev 22:17).

B. Unity and Diversity of the Sacraments

The synergism of Spirit and Church, which is intended to be worked on the participants of the sacraments, is known from the signification which is grasped by faith. But in all cases there is a celebration of the economy of salvation, ordered to various life-situations of the community of faith. Each sacrament announces that the Triune God is to be found in some particular human and social situation, and how the participants are to respond so as to live a life faithful to the will of God in the concrete situation that is signified.

In each sacrament God is given glory, and the participants, who enter into this activity in faith, are glorified by the deepening of the sharing of the inner-Trinitarian life. Baptism is accomplished through the *epiklesis* of the Spirit for the new birth. In this rite the Spirit sanctifies the candidate, bringing him or her into union with the risen Lord and thus with the Father. Through the prayer for the healing of the sinner, or for the victory over sickness and death, the sacraments of reconciliation and of the sick are accomplished. In matrimony the *epiklesis* of the Spirit pleads for the grace that the partners exercise a priestly service toward one another in the family, which constitutes the primary cell of the local church. In ordination the *epiklesis* asks that the individual be bishop, presbyter of deacon for the community and, at least by implication, that the community be given the grace to accept the minister as a gift of the Spirit.[13]

The Eucharist is the sacrament of sacraments, to which all other sacraments are ordered in their own way. Baptism, for example, is the sacrament of entrance into the new people of God. It is ordered to the celebration of the Eucharist, the sacramental sharing in the Messianic banquet of the kingdom. As such the Eucharist is the place where the Church most fully manifests and realizes itself as the pilgrim people of God, united to the company of the blessed but living under the conditions of history. All is met in the Eucharistic celebration that is encountered in the other sacraments, but in an eminent way. There is the solemn Liturgy of the Word of God; the self-offering of the Bride in union with that of Christ, expressed in the Eucharistic Prayer; the personal communion of the members of Christ with their Head through participation in the sacrament of the body and blood of Christ; personal communion of the participants with one another through the exercise of differentiated ministries and common activity.

C. Ordained Ministry and the Liturgy

Through the Spirit the special ministry of leadership was established as one of the stable elements in the constitution of the Church. This belief is confessed by all authentic rites of Christian ordination, which petition for the coming of the Spirit to equip the candidate for the particular ministry. Traditionally ordained ministry, which serves leadership functions in the Church, is divided into the special ministry of episcopacy, presbyterate, and deaconate. Those who participate in these forms of ministry are understood to exercise an authority as representative of Christ, the Head of the Church. Instinctively, therefore, the Christian faith recognizes that bishops, presbyters, and deacons play a special role in the communication of the truth of revelation, through preaching of the gospel of Christ and assuring that the style of life of the community conforms to that gospel. This same instinct also awards to the ordained ministry the special role of representing Christ insofar as he is sacrament of the divine-human love of God. Therefore it assigns to the special ministry a special function in the worship of the Church, the Body of Christ.

The special ministry of the ordained participates in the authority of Christ, as representative of Christ's divine-human love of humanity *and* his divine-human love of God. But this should not lead us to conclude that the ordained ministry somehow is placed over against the liturgical community in an undifferentiated way. Rather, the ordained ministry is a ministry of, and in, the Church of God. It is best seen as a sacramental representation ononof the Trinitarian mystery of the Church. This ministry lives from both the synergism of the Spirit and Church and the synergism of Christ and Church. It is a ministry embedded in the relation Christ—Church, an embedding accomplished only by the Spirit.

Insofar as the ordained ministry officially represents the life of faith of the Church in the leadership of liturgical prayer, it also represents the Trinitarian self-communication under the aspect of enabling the response of the worshipping community to God's offer of love. Thereby it represents Christ as the primordial sacrament of the divine-human love of God. But this official ministry accomplishes this representation as a ministry embedded in the relation Christ—Church; for the liturgical ministry has nothing to say except the response of the Church, the Bride of Christ as differentiated from Christ. However, since the Church is the Body of Christ, united to its head, the presiding minister represents this unity by employing the prayer of the Church, which explicitly affirms the conviction that it is joined by Christ to his eternal intercession.

Conclusion

The process of bringing the liturgy back to the mystery of the economic Trinity can serve to clarify the intimate relation between the worship of the earthly Church and what is called the heavenly liturgy, or beatific vision. At the same time a better understanding of the inner-Trinitarian life is made available, and form is imparted to various aspects of the whole economy of salvation which would otherwise remain relatively unordered.

Having identified the fully realized economic Trinity as the heavenly liturgy, we have at the same time established the mystery of the earthly liturgy. The conclusion reached can be expressed as follows: There is only one liturgy, which has its earthly and heavenly realizations. The single difference between the two lies in the fact that the earthly liturgy has an earthly dimension. This corresponds to the nature of the Church on earth, its divine and human, visible and invisible structures.

The earthly liturgy is the worship of the pilgrim people of God on the way to the Kingdom. This people lives by faith in history and, more precisely, in the situation of the history of salvation. Although Jesus Christ, as the "man for others," has fully redeemed humankind by the Cross, there still remains the need to extend redemption to humanity, weighed down by sin and living under the laws of the history of sinful humanity. One of the chief ways in which this salvation is communicated is the situation of communal worship of the organized church.

Many questions can be raised about the peculiarity of the liturgy of the earthly Church. In particular, there is the subject of the chief rites of the new people of God. In the last part of this book, we turn to this theme. We ask about general principles that afford a better intellectual grasp of the seven sacraments of the Church. Since they are paradigms for all forms of Christian worship, the understanding of the various dimensions of the sacraments provides a deeper knowledge of the nature of the communal worship of the Church as a whole.

Notes

1. This whole matter is succinctly formulated in the First Vatican Council's DOG-MATIC CONSTITUTION ON THE CATHOLIC FAITH: Reason illumined by faith can attain some limited, but fruitful, understanding of the mysteries given by God when it inquires in a responsible way (DS 3016).

2. LITURGIE DU SOURCE (Paris: Cerf, 1980).

3. L. Sabourin, in his extensive study of the concept of Christ's priesthood, as found in the Epistle to the Hebrews, accepts the opinion of A. Vanhoye that "eternal spirit" is the Holy Spirit, who animates Christ in his sacrificial oblation and effects the sacrificial trans-formation of the humanity of the Son of God (PRIESTHOOD: A Comparative Study. Studies in History of Religions. Supplement to Numen XXV [Leiden: Brill, 1973] 202 & note 264). But the meaning of the passage is open to other interpretations. The recent encyclical letter of Pope John Paul II on the subject of the Holy Spirit, DOMINUM ET VIVIFICANTEM, chooses the option of Professor A. Vanhoye, while recognizing "other possible interpretations" (LITTERAE ENCYCLICAE DE SPIRITU SANCTO IN VITA ECCLESIAE ET MUNDI [Vatican City, 1986] 47, n. 40: "...'through the eternal spirit' ...means that the Holy Spirit acted in a special way in the absolute self-giving of the Son of Man, in order to transform this suffering into redemptive love").

4. In the anaphora of Theodore, it is said of Jesus that "He offered himself immaculate through the eternal Spirit to God" (A. Hänggi - I. Pahl, PREX EUCHARISTICA, 383).

5. The Gregorian Sacramentary paraphrases Heb 9:14 in this way: "He offered himself through the Holy Spirit" (L.A. MURATORI, LITURGIA ROMANA VETUS II [Venice, 1748] 277-278).

6. The first quasi-missal in the Gallican tradition, the SACRAMENTARIUM AM-BIANENSE, introduces a number of private prayers into the text of the ordinary of the Gregorian Mass. The prayer before the rite of communion reads: "Lord Jesus Christ...who by the will of the Father, with the cooperation of the Holy Spirit, vivified the world by your death" (E. Lodi, ENCHIRIDION EUCHOLOGIUM FONTIUM LITUGICARUM [Rome: Edizioni liturgiche, 1979] n. 3179, p. 1546). This prayer, inspired by Heb 9:14, identifies the eternal spirit with the Holy Spirit. The exact meaning of the original prayer cannot be established. This communion prayer is found in the Roman Missal of 1570, and is an optional prayer in the New Roman Missal of Paul VI.

7. John McGrath, "THROUGH THE ETERNAL SPIRIT: A HISTORICAL STUDY OF THE EXEGESIS OF HEBREWS 9:13-14. Dissertation (Rome: Gregorian University, 1961), offers a survey of the interpretaion given by Greek and Latin Fathers.

8. H. Mühlen's exegesis leads to the conclusion that "eternal spirit" refers to the continuance of the Spirit into the futhermost future. The Spirit, present at the cross as eternal spirit, is understood by Mühlen from the dogmatic point of view, as the one who makes the sacrifice of the Cross always present in the Church. The Spirit, who co-worked the redemption of humanity at the Cross, is the reason for the pneumatic inclusion of all the just in the sacrifice of the Cross, who will later be drawn into Jesus' self-offering "in the Spirit" (UNA MYSTICA PERSONA [Munich: Schöningh, 1967] nos. 8. 93-8.97).

9. DS 1000.

10. DS 3331.

11. DS 3815.

12. This relationship between the earthly and heavenly liturgy is a constant theme of the traditions of the East and West. In the liturgies themselves the theme is expressed in many ways. For the Byzantine tradition confer: R. Taft, THE GREAT ENTRANCE. Orientalia Christiana Analecta 200 (Rome: Pont. Inst. Orient., 2nd. ed., 1978). An excellent commentary on this relationship, as expressed in the Syro-Malabar liturgical tradition, linked to the East Syrian sources, is found in J. M. Pathrapankel, "Christian Life and the Heavenly Liturgy," in J. Vellian, ed., THE MALABAR CHURCH. Orientalia Christiana Analecta 186 (Rome: Pont. Inst. Orient. 1970) 55-71.

13. In the Syriac tradition, a prayer of petition of the rite of ordination explicitly asks that the community receive the grace to welcome the ordinand as a gift of the Spirit.

PART IV

Systematic Theology of the Sacraments: Perspectives and Principles

Part III dealt with the depth dimension of all liturgical activity of the Church. This last section introduces central themes found in the traditional Catholic systematic presentation of the concept of sacrament, and derived from reflection on the meaning and practice of the seven principal liturgical rites of the Church. The perspectives and principles of this sacramental theology are submitted to critical evaluation.

Chapter 13 situates the seven sacraments within a theology of creation and salvation history, with special attention given to christology, pneumatology, and ecclesiology. The subject of Chapter 14 is the external ritual activity associated with the sacraments. The Christian concept of symbol that underlies this type of celebration of the life of faith is identified, and the function of the elements that constitute the sacramental rite, as well as their relationship to one another is explicated. Also the peculiarity of the sacraments, as distinguished from the preaching of the word of God, is elucidated. This latter consideration supplies the basis for a theological explanation of the relative necessity of sacraments for the life of faith. The problem of the origin of the seven sacraments is the subject of Chapter 15. This subject entails a discussion of the roles of Jesus Christ and the Church in the institution of sacraments.

Chapter 16 provides further reflection on the theme "Word and Sacrament." It offers a short history of the theology of preaching and relates it to the history of reflection on the relation between preaching and the sacraments. The discussion of the two fundamentally interrelated ways of realization of the active presence of Christ in the activity of the Church, namely, word and sacrament, paves the way for a more extended exposition of the variety of differentiated modes of Christ's presence in the Church's liturgical-sacramental celebrations. This is the theme of Chapter 17. Associated with Christ, the assembled community is also active subject of the sacramental celebrations. Chapter 18 contains a brief exposition of the nature of the involvement of the faithful and the conditions for their fruitful participation in the liturgy of the sacraments. The final chapter proposes a solution to the classical theme of the specific efficacy of sacramental celebrations (Chapter 19).

Chapter 13

Basic Dimensions of

Sacramental Theology

The "secret plan of God" (Eph 3:3), "the mysterious design which was hidden in God" (Eph 3:9a), is the plan of "the Creator of all" (Eph 3:9a). The fulfillment of this plan comes through Christ: "It is in Christ and through his blood that we have been redeemed and our sins forgiven" (Eph 1:7). This is "the mystery, the plan he was pleased to decree in Christ, to be carried out in the fullness of time" (Eph 1:9-10a). But this plan includes creation and eschatological fulfillment, "namely, to bring all things in heaven and in earth into one under Christ's headship" (Eph 1:10b).

The sacramental celebrations of the earthly Church pertain to the divine design, the renewal of all creation. Therefore a systematic theology of sacraments cannot be properly constructed without introducing a theology of creation. At the same time, sacraments relate specifically to the "fullness of time," in which believers have been "sealed with the Holy Spirit...the pledge of our inheritance" (Eph 1:13) and are called by the "Father of glory" to share in "the wealth of his glorious heritage to be distributed among the members of the Church" (Eph 1:17-18) through Christ, whom the Father has made "Head of the Church" (Eph 1:22).

Consequently sacraments are only understandable within the scope of the redeeming work of Jesus Christ and the mission of the Spirit by which the Church of Christ was established and sanctified. These considerations determine the structure of this chapter, which outlines basic dimensions of a systematic theology of the sacraments.[1]

I.
Theology of Creation and Salvation History

From the outset of creation God's mysterious plan for the world was underway. It is this creation, and the history of humankind within it, that comes under the plan of God. God the creator and God the redeemer are one and the same. Consequently, the events of redemption do not bring forth an absolutely new creation. The mystery of salvation is effected in a special way through the incarnation, life, death, and glorification of Jesus Christ. But God's action takes place in and through the creation deformed by sin. The Word himself assumed a humanity of this creation and effected redemption through it.

Likewise, one does not find in the Church, its preaching of the word or sacramental celebrations, an absolutely new creation. Sinful human beings encounter the Father through the works of faith of the sinfully disposed Church. The Spirit uses sinful members, and the material things of the yet not fully renewed world, as the medium of communication of sanctification. This consideration makes clear that any attempt to establish a radical distinction between the realm of ordinary daily life of faith and the realm of the liturgy of the sacraments should be avoided. Sacramental celebrations have a special place in the economy of salvation, but this economy does not have a special place in a world which is, so to speak, otherwise "outside the temple.170 Sacramental celebrations should not be described as purely supernatural events in comparison with the normal daily life of Christians. Rather, they are special moments of that life, in a yet not fully redeemed world.

Through the word and symbolic actions of the liturgy, drawn from the word and symbolic actions of daily life, saving communication takes place between God and his people. The various forms of sacramental ritual communication correspond to the way in which God communicates with humanity in and through history. However, the mystery of salvation is effected in a special way through the Cross of Christ. It belongs to the event of the Cross, as mystery of God, to be further realized in the historical life of the Church—something that is not alloted to each event of the earthly life of Jesus except in relation to the Cross. This mystery of the Triune God can be represented, applied, and lived by the Church of every age. The sacraments, which derive ultimately from the historical event of the Cross, manifest and realize different ways in which Christians are integrated into the mystery of Christ in a variety of situations of the history of individuals and community.

The different sacraments are graceful supporters of Christians on the journey toward the kingdom. Through them, the participants are integrated into the paschal mystery of Christ in the way that is peculiar to a *celebration of the faith of the Church by a liturgical assembly of the Church*. Baptism is incorporation. It signifies participation in the death and resurrection of Christ (Rom 6:4-5). The community of the baptized, as a whole, is integrated continually into this mystery through the rite, originating at the Last Supper, which announces Christ's self-offering to the Father on behalf of the many (1 Cor 10:16-17; 11:23-26).

All the sacraments are related to fundamental situations of the lives of individuals (baptism, confirmation, reconciliation of sinners, anointing of the sick), of individuals together (matrimony), of individuals in relation to the service of the community as such (orders), and of the whole community (Eucharist). Sacraments are intended to sanctify typically basic situations of the lives of Christians, in the individual and social spheres. Through participation in these celebrations of faith, each one is made conscious of moving from one stage of human life to the next, supported by the community of faith on the way to the completion that comes from God alone.

Sacramental celebrations play out the promised fulfillment, and anticipate it here and now. In the patristic period the two movements within the history of salvation, the descent of the divine and the ascent of the human, are expressed in the language of a mystery play: God became man in order that humankind might become divine. This understanding of the economy of salvation determines the patristic theology of worship. The risen Lord and his saving work are confessed to be really present in and through Christian liturgy. He is the source and guide of the ascent of the faithful to the Father. The participation in the liturgy, according to this theology, generates the experience that one's personal way to God is a participation in the way of the whole people of God.

In this outlook, the Eucharist was naturally valued as the summit of all liturgical celebrations. The Church Fathers recognized that all forms of Christian worship have a meaning in themselves. Liturgy was not reckoned simply as a means to an end, a place for gaining spiritual nourishment for the work of faith in the world. Patristic theology reflects the instinctive grasp of the fact that all forms of liturgy manifest and realize the Church, are a real anticipation of the final gathering in Christ. Consequently, all the other activity of the Church was understood as ordered to the liturgical expression of the communal life of faith, deriving orientation, inspiration, spiritual power, and fulfillment from that source.

But the various forms of liturgy were viewed as ordered to the Eucharist. Under the conditions of history, that to which all liturgy refers, the unity of the people of God in Christ, is manifested and realized in the most profound way in the Eucharist. Here the community of faith gathers around Christ, the true host of the meal of the Church, to share in the anticipated Messianic banquet of the Kingdom in the power of the Spirit, and unto the glory of the Father.

A. Sacramental Nature of the Cosmos

The teaching about a hierarchy of liturgical rites, and a hierarchy of ritual activity within particular rites, is found everywhere in the patristic writings. It is the implicit presupposition of the mystagogical catecheses on the rites of initiation and of the church orders, such as that of the *Apostolic Tradition* of Hippolytus. The same kind of teaching is explicitly formulated in the scholastic theology of the twelfth and thirteenth centuries.

For example, the liturgical rites surrounding the Eucharistic Prayer, and communion of the body and blood of Christ, and those linked to the baptismal bath, Trinitarian formulas of consecration of the neophyte, and the post-baptismal laying on of hands and anointing, were placed at a lower level of importance by patristic commentators. But these ritual activities were not considered to be "merely ecclesiastical rites," without deeper sacramental meaning. On the contrary, their origin was traced to the faith of the Church. Therefore they were valued as mediating the saving work of Christ in the Spirit who inspires their use.

This understanding corresponds to a more general comprehension of the meaning of created reality and its relation to the history of salvation, which prevailed into the high Middle Ages. In this world view, salvation history begins with creation. The Father creates all things through his Word. Creation bears the mark of God's Word; it is a word that speaks of God's glory. But also creation takes place "in the Spirit of God," the life-giving breath by which the creative word of God goes forth. This creation is made for humankind, who are the crown of the handiwork of God and called to a life of personal intimacy with God. Creation is the sign of God's love for humanity, the sphere in which human life is maintained and developed and through which human beings actually encounter God's saving presence. Even down to the lowest level, creation manifests God's presence, calling for a response of praise and thanksgiving on the part of the creature.

Quite naturally, patristic theology placed the chief rites of the Church at the summit of the pyramid of values of the whole cosmos. These rites were considered to be the highest representations tionsof God's loving presence in the whole of created reality. The sacraments were cherished for their pedagogical function, that is to say, as providing a correct understanding of the manifold signs in the world which reflect God's glory. Above all, of course, sacraments were treasured as the most intense forms of God's self-communication after, and grounded on, the incarnation of God's Word.

We cannot enter into a detailed discussion of this subject. It suffices to note how the writings of Origen of Alexandria and Augustine of Hippo continually return to a theme often celebrated in Christian poetry. These two, who must be numbered among the most profound Christian thinkers of all time, teach that all creation bears the mark of truth through the Word of God; the mark of goodness, through the Spirit of God. As a consequence, they both recall the pedagogical function of the cosmos. All reality mirrors the divine and thereby attracts human beings toward the divine. This happens in different degrees, for the mystery of God is revealed in Word and Spirit at differentiated levels. At the summit is the incarnation of the Word; and, in the time of the Church, it is above all the sacraments that speak of God's truth and goodness.

The systematic theologians of the twelfth and thirteenth centuries were not strangers to this way of thinking. They also teach that the incarnate Word, through whom the Father created the world, bequeathed to the Church sacraments to provide a divine pedagogy. Associated with this understanding of sacraments was the notion that the material elements attain their full meaning when employed in the sacramental symbolic gestures. In other words, the material world not only serves to manifest God's love, but also can become the medium of communication of saving grace.

Thomas Aquinas, for example, transcends the pedagogical orientation of Origen and Augustine in his sacramental theology. He stresses that the justification of sinners, a consequence of the redeeming work of Jesus Christ, is the "greatest work of God" (*maximum opus Dei*).[2] Through the entrance of the Word into the sinfully disposed and sinful world, God's divinity is fully revealed, in his overflowing goodness. Aquinas associates the continuation of the manifestation of this goodness in the material world and its history stamped by sin, especially with the sacraments. The materiality into which the Word of God entered, and through which he effected redemption of humanity, continues to serve the risen Lord as an instrument through which the grace of God is manifested and communicated.[3] In brief, the created reality of the world, despite being deformed because of the sinful tendencies of humankind, is capable of serving as medium of God's self-communication on the ground of the goodness of God. The sacraments are the most important way of mutual exchange between God and believers, a *sacrum commercium.*

1. Modern Difficulty With the Category of Sacrament

In contemporary society, the concept "sacrament" remains very abstract for many people. To the extent that consciousness of a personal God wanes, the idea of personal encounter with the divine in and through creation, through human word and symbolic gestures which often include the use of material things, loses meaning. But even with a lively consciousness of a personal God, many experience him as a distant God: the God of Deism, who is spiritually attainable in the rarified atmosphere of subjective consciousness, but not really and personally met in and through human forms of communication.

Also many Christians find difficulty with the idea that the sacraments are really acts of the sinfully disposed Church, interpersonal, ecclesial actions through which a saving communication takes place with the Triune God. They rest more easily with the idea that sacraments are activities that take place *in the Church,* in the context of the liturgical assembly, but remain somehow separated from the world and its history, purely supernatural instruments employed by the Church. This kind of thinking has led, in the past, to an infra-personal understanding of sacramental grace. When sacraments are conceived as impersonal supernatural instruments of communication of grace, an impersonal view of grace almost inevitably follows. However, when sacraments are seen as the personal expression of the faith of the Church of which Christ, in the Spirit, is the living source, a personalistic understanding of sacramental grace is more likely to be the result.

According to the old patristic view, sacraments are acts of the Church, realizing its mission to carry on the saving work of Christ in history. Consequently, sacramental celebrations are identified as interpersonal ecclesiastical events in which the communication of the faith of the Church takes place through human word and symbolic gestures. In other words, the faith of the Church, ritually objectified, becomes personally significant for the life of the assembly as a whole and for the individual in whose favor the celebration takes place. In this human way, the opportunity is given to the concrete liturgical community to express communally the inner conviction of its faith, which is identified with the faith expressed in the rite.

Personal communication between the participants of the sacramental celebration involves some form of physical contact, which frequently includes the use of material things. Physical contact of some sort is always necessary for human communication in history. But this exercise of simple efficient causality is only the condition for what we have called "personal causality." The personal communication, in faith, between the participants of a sacramental celebration signifies for the eyes of faith a deeper reality: the activity of Christ who is, in the power of the Holy Spirit, the source of the communication in faith, the one who communicates the Spirit of sanctification from the Father.

The modern difficulty with the concept of sacrament has its historical roots, and is not simply the product of the twentieth century cultural revolution. In the West, a profound change took place in the understanding of the real world, which had its origin in the late Middle Ages and blossomed in the seventeenth and eighteenth centuries. This change is intimately linked to a new vision of the human person and the power of human reason.[4] The effects are already noticeable in the sixteenth century sacramental theology.

The post-Reformation secular sphere of philosophy stressed the power of human reason to reconstruct reality. This new rationalistic approach certainly contains a grain of truth. But the particular way in which it conceives the ability of human reason to manipulate and change reality includes a characteristic understanding of the transcendent ground of all being. It is the God of Deism. This new theology and philosophy is opposed to the old Biblical and Christian understanding of a God who works in and through history. The old view refuses to accept the notion that all reality comes under the power of impersonal "fate" or of human reason. It is not the rational creature that gives meaning to reality by manipulating it to serve the needs of humanity, according to the principle of reason.

Christian tradition teaches that the deepest meaning of creation is already given by God in the act of creation. In line with the old patristic doctrine of the hierarchy of beings reaching up to the mystery of God, graduated manifestations of the divine, scholastic theologians valued sacraments as a logical consequence and high point of the symbolic dimension of all creation. Hugo of St. Victor, for example, taught that sacramental signs, on the ground of creation, are forms of expression of grace established by the Creator. Hence he had some difficulty attempting to explain precisely how Christ could be said to have instituted sacraments. [5]

The post-Reformation understanding of the relation of human reason to reality seems to have taken hold already, in an imperceptible way, in the sixteenth century reflection on the institution of sacraments by Christ. Reformers held as fundamental the immediate, positive institution of sacraments by Christ. Since the New Testament seems to record only an explicit word of Jesus of Nazareth concerning baptism and Eucharist, they quite generally settled for two sacraments and relegated the other five traditional chief rites to the class of "merely ecclesiastical rites." Catholic theologians of the Counter-Reformation also, in great part, placed the accent on the immediate, positive institution of sacraments by Christ, while disputing over what Christ himself determined concerning the essential external rites of some sacraments. They, too, sought to discover an action, or word, of Jesus of Nazareth which could be construed as an act of institution of the five disputed sacraments. This led to a variety of theories in which the distinction between implicit and explicit institution played a key role.

The attempt to establish the institution of sacraments by a positive divine decree, without reference to the sacramental nature of all reality, does not correspond to the way of thinking of early, or high, scholasticism. The efforts, which were without notable success, point to a lack of ability to maintain an integrated view of the whole of reality. This inability probably accounts, in no small measure, for the insensitivity of the fathers of the Council of Trent toward the objection of a minority of the conciliar theologians concerning the formulation of the first canon of the Decree on the Sacraments. They suggested that the canon be rephrased so that it did not simply condemn the opinion that the sacraments of the new law are "more or less than seven."[6] These theologians agreed that the chief rites of the Church are seven. They also rejected the implications of Luther's intention in using the phrase "more or less than seven." However, they seemed to want to avoid limiting the concept of sacrament merely to the seven principal rites of the Church.

The narrow perception of the sacramental economy of salvation also accounts for the failure of post-Reformation Catholic theology to recognize explicitly that sacraments are acts of the Church itself and the corollary of this, namely, that the Church could be called a kind of "basic or comprehensive sacrament." Vatican II, as we have seen, provides a more integrated view of the real world. It describes the sacraments as acts of the Church, realizing itself as a "kind of sacrament" in all its basic activities. However, as Peter Hünermann observes in the article cited above, this council did not attempt to show how the understanding of Church and its sacraments might contribute to correcting a modern experience of reality.

By their very nature sacramental celebrations witness to a particular view of the world, one opposed to what seems to be characteristic of the modern industrial world view. In the latter outlook hope rests on human ingenuity. Here the past is not very important, and the future is defined as the product of present planning and activity. The only hope that can be named is the capacity of human reason. Sacramental celebrations, however, announce that the present achievement in human development is not merely the result of human work. Rather it is ultimately grounded on what God has done and is doing now.

The experience of God's saving activity in the sacraments generates a hope based on the ever new possibilities of the working of the Spirit through human activity. The sacraments offer a new orientation for human existence which breaks through the seemingly fixed, but really relative, ordering of daily life and reveals it as multi-dimensional. The sacramental structure of all reality is thereby discovered through the sacramental celebrations themselves. As co-accomplishment of the divine movement in and through history, sacraments have the potential to broaden the Christian experience of the sacramental universe. But this potential is only realizable on the condition of the existence of stable, mature Christian communities that witness by their daily lives, and in their liturgies, that this stability is based on Jesus Christ in the power of the Spirit.

2. Preparation for Sacramental Celebrations

The experience of the divine depth of sacramental celebrations has the potential to foster the Christian experience of the sacramental dimension of the routine daily life of faith. On the other hand, the daily experience of the symbolic character of human intercourse furnishes the grounds for a deeper understanding ngof the category of sacramental celebration. This latter subject was discussed in Chapter 2. The reader is referred especially to what was said about the dependence of human growth on contact with the world of things and persons, the anthropological basis of the unity of word and symbolic gesture, and the ways of fostering symbolic perception. Here we only call attention to how the phenomenon of gift-giving can be employed in the catechesis of the sacraments. It is a useful analogy, provided that the limitations are clearly recognized.

The bestowal of a gift on another, some material object of value, signifies the openness of the donor to allow the receiver access to the sphere of one's life. The reception of the gift, as gift, signifies the willingness of the recipient to enter into the sphere of the donor's personal existence and, simultaneously, the same kind of access to the donor. The gift is an instrument of personal communication. This gesture of giving and receiving mediates something of the intentional order: the desire for personal communication. Psychological unity is deepened by the word that accompanies the exchange. And both parties grow in a unity, in which the otherness of each gains in depth in the measure of their unity in love.

Sacramental celebrations are analogous to this phenomenon. In the human activity of gift-giving the distance between the signifying gesture and the signified reality, i.e., the giving of self, is not closed. The effect of the ontological order, the giving of new meaning to the material object, does not involve an ontic change of the material itself. The same thing may be said about the elements of water and oil employed in certain sacraments. The symbolic gestures of the sacraments signify the offer of saving grace in their special ways. But there is no ontic change in the water of baptism or oil used in confirmation or the anointing of the sick. These elements form part of the symbolic action, which signifies the purely transcendental act by which God's self-communication takes place, in the Spirit, immediately and directly. No ontic change takes place in the material elements, that enables them to serve as means through which God's self-communication is filtered.

In the case of the transformation of the elements of bread and wine employed in the Eucharist, something absolutely unique takes place. Here the gifts of bread and wine, which signify Christ's self-offering to the Father and to the believers, become real symbols of Christ's body and blood. Through the power of the Holy Spirit the bread and wine become united in unity of being with the risen Lord. This unity, achieved though the Eucharistic celebration in the power of the Spirit, is analogous to the unity that exists between the human body and human spirit. The human body is a real symbol of the human spirit. However the unity between body and spirit is given from the outset of human existence. In the case of the Eucharistic elements, the unity is achieved through the action of the Spirit.

The Eucharistic elements are, therefore, the highest instance of the sacramental presence of Christ. They signify not only the action of Christ offering himself to the Father and to the communicants, but also are forms of the personal presence of Christ in themselves. However, even in the case of the Eucharistic elements, it must be said that the same relationship to saving grace obtains as in the case of the other sacraments. In other words, the Eucharistic presence of Christ is sacrament of the self-communication of the Father in the Spirit. Hence communication with Christ in Holy Communion signifies the offer of saving grace, a purely divine act, which is not somehow filtered through the glorified humanity of the risen Lord in the act of participation of the Eucharistic elements.

B. The Seven Principal Rites of the Church

Within the sacramental perception of created reality, the seven sacraments appear as seven ways in which the Church actualizes itself as minister of Christ in the unfolding of the mission of salvation. These sacraments announce, especially through the symbolic actions and accompanying word of faith which form the heart of each type of celebration (the so-called "essential rites"), that God's saving presence is to be found in the human and social situation signified, and how the subject is to respond.

However, the "sacramental word" of the "essential rites" has a function that is only analogous to the word of Christian tradition which interprets the meaning of, and gives direction for, the acceptable response to particular situations of the human and social life. The sacramental word, even when expressed in the indicative form, is not merely, and not even mainly, a word of instruction. It is also incorrect to explain this word as simply a word from God, announcing what God is offering to the believer who participates in faith. Rather the sacramental word is a form of prayer of the Church for the grace signified by the whole sacramental celebration. This aspect of the sacrament distinguishes it from a catechesis, which gives instruction about the meaning of the variety of common and fundamental situations of the life of faith celebrated in the seven sacraments.

Sacraments have something in common with the symbolic actions and words employed by social groups to integrate new members into their ranks or to renew social relations. The difference lies in the depth reached by the integration. The sacramental incorporation into the Church, or the deepening of this incorporation, has a "we" character that goes beyond the level of the limited human solidarity of a particular group. It penetrates to the heart of the mystery of human existence, to the unity of the human race. For it is a sharing in the Spirit whom Christ possesses in fullness, and whom he sends from the Father to gather the "many" unto himself.

The sacramental forms of expression of the grace event, linked to the different situations of the life of the Church, were formulated under the influence of the memory of the life, death, and glorification of Jesus by Christian communities. The life of faith of the Church, guided by the Spirit, is the proper point of departure for the explanation of the origin of the concrete sacramental rites. While certain ritual activities were adopted by the early Judeo-Christian communities from Judaism, these rites were made to function in accord with the *memoryD of the Church. The decisive thing is the signification which the memory of the Christ-event bestows on them. Ultimately sacramental celebrations aim at being the event of a sharing, through Jesus Christ, in the Spirit bestowed by the Father, and the acceptance, in the power of the Spirit, of this gift of eternal life.*

The number "7" is not intended to exclude the possibility that a word of faith can be directed to another person in variety of situations of life, effectively announcing God's saving presence and providing a clue to the fitting response. There are limitless possibilities for sacramental events of this kind in the daily life of faith. Whenever the word of God is preached, and the hearer responds in faith, the life of union with God is deepened.

C. The One Mystery and the Sacraments

In the economy of salvation a saving event always has the same traits. It is a participation in the redemptive work realized by the Father through Christ in the one Spirit. According to the Pauline and Deuteropauline writings, Christ is the mystery of God made visible and expressive in the "word of the Cross" (1 Cor 1:18; confer 1 Cor 1-2). This mystery "hidden from ages in God" (Eph 3:9) is now a revealed mystery. Revealed and realized, it is to be further revealed and realized until the fulfillment of history.

Within this one comprehensive mystery, the Church is the realized mystery effected by Christ. In dependence on Christ, the Church also participates in the work of extension of this saving mystery in the world (Eph 3:10). The word mystery is not used of the liturgical activity of the Church in New Testament writings. Still communal worship is an essential aspect of the whole work of the Father, through Christ in the Spirit, in the time of the earthly Church. Moreover, as we have already seen, the heavenly liturgy, of which the earthly liturgy is "sacrament," is the economic Trinity in its definitive fulfillment. Consequently, the word mystery can be used of the Church's sacramental celebrations. However, in the concept of "mystery," as used in the New Testament, the activity of the Father, willing and working salvation through Christ in the Spirit, remains thematic.

In the patristic period, baptism and Eucharist are called mysteries. This means that, in a way peculiar to each of them, the one mystery is realized for the benefit of the believing participants. This one mystery was identified as the one Christ-event, which culminates in the Cross and resurrection. Various events of Christ's life, leading to the Cross, were called mysteries in the early Church and viewed as having significance for salvation, but only as related to the whole Christ-event. Correspondingly, the liturgical celebrations, which announce the whole Christ-event, did not focus on individual events of the life of Christ. Initially, apart from the annual Paschal Feast,[7] there did not exist particular liturgical feasts in which special events of Christ's earthly life were singled out for remembrance. Rather, at the outset there existed only the liturgical remembrance of the one mystery culminating in the death and glorification of Christ. Later on, in the Church of the Empire, feasts commemorating other events of Christ's life were established, such as Ascension of the Lord, Pentecost, Christmas, and Epiphany. But they were always enriched by the celebration of the Eucharist and so integrated within the celebration of the whole Christ-event.

II.
Christology

We have already discussed the implications of Logos and Spirit christology. It suffices here to offer some further comments on the concept of *primordial sacrament* as applied to Jesus Christ.

Jesus Christ is, on the one hand, the Son of God: the eternal image of the Father. As second person of the Trinity, he is the prototype of the Father. On the other hand, Jesus Christ is the Son of God in the flesh: the visible image of the Father. As incarnate Word, Jesus is the human image of the Father in a unique way: "He who has seen me has seen the Father; how can you say,'Show us the Father'?" (Jn 14:9). Whoever believes in him and accepts him obtains salvation: the sharing in the divine life in the communion of the Father, Son, and Spirit.

As the primordial sacrament of salvation, Jesus revealed the divine plan of God through his earthly word and work. Through the ministry of his public life he offered salvation to others. Just as the Spirit was sent by the Father to sanctify and unite a created humanity in person to the Word of God, so also the Spirit worked in the public ministry of Jesus to draw humankind into union with Jesus and so into communion with the Father of all.

The activity of Jesus' public life is a visible offering of the Spirit. The theandric activity of Jesus is the sacrament of the offer of the Spirit by the Father. Insofar as received in faith, the Spirit is bestowed by the Father. It is this same Spirit who awakens the faith of the hearers, enabling them to respond to the offer of salvation. When the offer of God's self-communication is accepted, the activity of Jesus becomes sacrament of the bestowal of the Spirit by the Father. Otherwise, without the acceptance by faith, there is no sacramental event in the full sense; for the existence of such an event is conditioned by the free response of the potential adult recipient, or, in the case of infant baptism, according to the traditional theology of the Church, by the response of the community of faith.

The activity of Jesus' public life is the activity of the person of the Word, flowing from his humanity. As such it is a theandric activity, a sacramental activity which cannot be compared to that of ordinary human beings. Others may serve as God's instruments in the communication of the Spirit. But the incarnate Word mirrors forth the offer of the Father's self-communication in a measure that transcends qualitatively that which might be possible for others. Jesus' ability to attract others to his Father must be measured by his mystery. On the ground of the hypostatic union, his power to elicit the free response from others to the love of the Father is without parallel. In this sense we can speak of Jesus as primordial sacrament of God's self-communication to ordinary people. However, the notion of primordial sacrament, as applied to Jesus of Nazareth's saving work, also has a pneumatological dimension. Jesus' human expression of his love of the Father and of the Father's children is the incarnation of the Holy Spirit, who is Jesus' transcendental love of the Father. From this point of view, Jesus' activity of love on behalf of the Father's children is the sacramental offer of the Holy Spirit and the sending of the same Spirit to those who hear and accept his message. The concept "primordial sacrament," as applied to Jesus, includes the idea of the "incarnation of the Spirit" in Jesus' human love of the Father and the Father's children.

Through the resurrection, Jesus becomes the full realization of divinity in humanity. Hence the Holy Spirit becomes fully incarnated in his human love. This means that the risen Lord becomes fully the primordial sacrament. Consequently, as we have already seen in Chapter 11, he sends the Spirit in fullness to the world in an act that is the sacrament of the bestowal of the Spirit by the Father. Thereby the Church is constituted through those who accept the Spirit in faith.

Both in his earthly state and as risen Lord, Jesus Christ is primordial sacrament of the loving nearness of the Father to the world. As such, he turns to humanity in mercy and love. This is what is meant by saying that Jesus is primordial sacrament, according to many recent writers.[8] But, in fact, this is not all that must be included in the concept. Primarily Jesus is turned to the Father. He prays to the Father (Lk 6:12), loves the Father (Jn 14:31), glorifies the Father up to the death of the cross (Jn 4:34; 17:4; 19:30; Phil 2:8; Heb 10:5-7). He does all this "for the many" (Mk 14:24).

The Fourth Gospel refers to the mysterious unity of Jesus with the Father (14:18; 17:11), a theme echoed in other New Testament writings. The Council of Chalcedon confesses the unity of humanity and divinity in the incarnate Son of God: a unity in which the humanity and divinity are unconfused and unseparated. This unity points to the fact that the humanity of Jesus is the unique source of mediation of the saving revelation of God to humankind. Encounter with Jesus is encounter with the Son of God, and so encounter with the primordial sacrament of the Father's love of all humanity. However, encounter with Jesus is also the encounter with the divine-human love of the incarnate Son for the Father, realized in and through the unique, personal, and free human love of Jesus. When one speaks of Jesus as "primordial sacrament of salvation," the dimension of Jesus' self-offering to the Father must be introduced, especially since Christ's self-offering to the Father is the incarnation of the transcendental love of Jesus, the Holy Spirit.

What can be said about Jesus of Nazareth in this regard, is also applicable to the risen Lord. In his glorified state, the risen Lord is the primordial sacrament of encounter with the Father: "God is one; one also is the Mediator between God and man, the man Jesus Christ, who gave himself as a ransom for all" (1 Tim 2:5). The encounter with the risen Lord involves the mediation of divine life. He is "the bread of life" (Jn 6:35). "Being therefore exalted at the right hand of God, and having received from the Father the promise of the Holy Spirit, he has poured out this which you see and hear" (Acts 2:33). On the other hand, the high priestly intercession of Jesus is the source of salvation for those who come to God though him:

> But he holds his priesthood permanently.... Consequently he is able for all time to save those who draw near to God through him, since he always lives to make intercession for them (Heb 7:24-25).

The aspects of the going forth from God and the going back to God are involved in the mystery of the self-emptying of the Son in the incarnation, death, and resurrection-glorification. Both aspects are expressed in the New Testament. Jesus is the way to the Father (Jn 14:6) as incarnate Word; his work (Jn 17:4) is the doing of the will of the Father (Jn 4:34). God's glory goes forth into the world through his obedience: "The Father who dwells in me accomplishes his works" (Jn 14:10). The Cross is the final historical revelation of God's loving plan of salvation for the world (Jn 3:11-16; 19:34; 1 Jn 5:6-8). Thus Jesus is the embodiment of the divine-human love of the world. But Jesus is also the embodiment of the divine-human love of God: "But I do as the Father commands me, so that the world may know that I love the Father" (Jn 14:31). "Therefore he is Mediator of the new covenant" (Heb 9:15); "...being made perfect he became the source of eternal salvation...High Priest after the order of Melchizedek" (Heb 5:9-10). Hence the Epistle to the Hebrews concludes: "Through him then let us continually offer up a sacrifice of praise to God" (13:15). Jesus Christ is the primordial sacrament in the comprehensive sense, that is, as embodiment of the divine-human love of God (glorification of God) and of the divine-human love of humanity (sanctification of humankind).[9] The implications of this theological outlook for the understanding of the dynamics of sacramental celebrations is treated in Chapter 14.

III.
Ecclesiology

Modern Catholic theology describes the Church as sacrament of salvation. This means that the social organism is an embodiment of the mystery of communion between the Trinity and humanity, as well as the real society by which the Triune God draws humanity into the communion of divine life. But the Church is a kind of sacrament only in dependence on Christ. It is not a new social sacrament that substitutes for the primordial sacrament, Jesus Christ. Rather the Church has a role to play in the economy of salvation, which is analogous to that which Christ exercised during his earthly life. The dependence of the Church on Christ is expressed by the Pauline imagery of head and body.

But if Christ is the Head and the Church is his Body, it does not follow that the Church can be described simply as the "continuation of the incarnation." The Church is not adequately conceived as a kind of sacramental representation of the risen Lord. The nineteenth century Tübingen theologian Johann Adam Möhler introduced the notion of the Church as continuation of the incarnation in reaction to a contemporary ecclesiology that focused too exclusively on the idea that the Church is a perfect society established by God in virtue of the merits of Christ, endowed with all the means necessary to obtain its supernatural end. Thereby he brought to light the weakness of an ecclesiology that neglects the fact of Christ's permanent, active presence in the Church. Möhler's viewpoint contains an element of truth, but it does not express the whole of the truth. Overstress on the christological aspect of the mystery of the Church entails the danger of a monophysitic ecclesiology, that is to say, a mystification of the identity and formal difference between Christ and the Church.[10]

Another Pauline image helps to correct this tendency. It is the description of the Church as the *Bride of Christ*. While the image of body underscores the unity between Christ and Church, the image of bride expresses the distance between the two. Traditional Catholic ecclesiology was not able to offer a satisfactory explanation of this unity and distance because it inherited a theology of the economic Trinity which either neglected, severely limited, or excluded the concept of a personal mission of the Holy Spirit. The personal mission of the Spirit explains why the Church is united to Christ and, at the same time, is not identified with Christ. In other words, the Spirit, whom Christ possesses in fullness, is shared with the Church. The Spirit is the bond of union between Christ and the Church and, simultaneously, the source of the distance between the Head and Body.

As yet Catholic theology has not sufficiently integrated the pneumatological dimension into its ecclesiology. A part of the traditional Catholic theology assigns the work of the Trinity, both in creation and sanctification, to the Godhead as such. Only the Logos is awarded a personal mission. M. J. Scheeben, who contributed significantly to the renewal of pneumatology in Catholic theology, did not transcend this outlook. According to him the Holy Spirit has a mission in the work of sanctification only by appropriation.[11] But he argues that the Spirit is personally present in the just by an indwelling that is proper to him, and not appropriated. This latter aspect of pneumatology is commonly accepted by Catholic theologians today. But the possible implications for a theology of the personal mission of the Spirit still remains unfinished business.

Pope Leo XIII's encyclical letter *Divinum Illud munus* teaches that the activity of the three persons of the Trinity in the world is one and the same, but fittingly ascribed to one or other person by appropriation.[12] On the other hand, Pope Pius XII's encyclical letter *Mystici corporis* observes that this teaching refers to the Trinity insofar as "supreme efficient cause."[13] It does not affect the truth that the Logos alone became man, or the theory that each person of the Trinity has his own personal relation to the justified.[14] However, as yet the Roman magisterium has devoted little attention to the problem of the personal mission of the Spirit in the economy of salvation and its consequences.[15]

Strictly speaking, the Church is not a continuation of the incarnation. There is a world of difference between the assumption of a humanity by the Logos and the gathering of a new people of God into Christ in the power of the Holy Spirit. The modern insight into the pneumatological character of the Church has brought with it a better appreciation of the nature of the Church. Living in union with Christ through the personal mission of the Spirit, the Church appears to be the continuation of the unction of Christ by the Spirit. We have seen that the Spirit had a personal mission in the sanctification of the humanity of Jesus, whereby it was united in unity of person to the Word. This unction of the Spirit can be understood, as Mühlen explains, as the anticipation of the birth of the Church.

Through the mission of the Spirit, the Church was established as the Body of Christ and its members united to Christ. The Church is a continuation of the historical movement of that phase of salvation history which was inaugurated by the anointing of Jesus' humanity in the incarnation; for at Pentecost the Spirit established the Church, which logically precedes the gathering of members, by uniting individual believers with Christ, and so with one another.

The Church can be called sacrament of the man Jesus Christ. Vatican II's *Sacrosanctum concilium* speaks of the Church as sacrament derived from Christ. Here the word "sacrament" seems to express the more general idea of the Church as a realization of the eternal plan of salvation. Sacrament takes on the meaning of the biblical concept of mystery.[16] In *Lumen gentium*, the council goes a step further by describing the Church as "in Christ, a kind of sacrament, i.e., sign and instrument of intimate union with God and of the unity of the whole human race."[17] As sacrament of Christ, the Church is Christ's sacrament (subjective genitive) and sacrament of his saving work (objective genitive). It is sacrament of the man Jesus, who is sanctifier and the Holy One. "In Christ," the Church is both communion of the saved (sign) and organ of salvation (instrument). "In Christ," the Church is effective sign of the vertical union of humanity with God and of the lateral union of human beings on earth.

The description of the Church as sacrament requires further explanation. If we are not to remain at the level of abstract concepts, it must be shown how the Church's activity signifies and effects communion of humanity with God and the unity of people among themselves. Here it is useful to introduce the notion of *encounter*, a central anthropological category.[18] It must be shown how we can speak of encounter in this context, and account must be taken of the social dimension of this encounter. For it is not only a question of an encounter with God and the individual believer, but also, and simultaneously, of one between the individual believers among themselves. But, while the concept of encounter helps us to understand that, and how, the Church is sacrament, it should be recalled that the Church is in Christ "in the Spirit." The theme of pneumatology needs to be introduced into the fuller explanation of the sacramental character of the Church. Both these topics deserve some elaboration here.

A. The Church as Place of Encounter

The English word "encounter" refers, more generally, to a meeting between opponents. It suggests a defensive, closed posture. In recent years the word has taken on a more positive meaning in theological discourse. Encounter is used to express the idea of meeting another in openness from which positive results may be expected. This meaning derives from its use as a translation of the German *Begegnung*, employed in the dialogue philosophy of Martin Buber.

While *Begegnung* normally has the neutral meaning of "meeting," Buber uses it in the context of a distinction between two types of knowledge: the one derived from the study of being as *it;* the other from the contemplation of a person as a *thou:* a center of a world that cannot be defined as an *it* but only as a *thou.Begegnung* describes the situation of immediate contact with a thou. From the encounter a special awareness arises. This knowledge can never be fully defined because a thou cannot be defined in terms of my utility, or classified among other objects.

Encounter, employed as a translation of Buber's *Begegnung,* includes the notion of engagement: a commitment of one person to another in the act of the encounter. Depending on what transpires in the meeting, the engagement can result in a commitment of both parties to a common action. As we have already seen in Chapter 5, some encounters lead to engagements that touch the very core of human and humanizing existence.

The essential Christian engagement is: Christ for us! We with Christ![19] It takes place in the ecclesiastical community. The various ways in which the community actualizes itself as the Body of Christ, through the exercise of its life of faith, entail instruction for the members which binds them to the way of life of Jesus, with the promise of eternal life. Correspondingly, the members are challenged to accept the instruction and to commit themselves to the exigencies of the new covenant, with a confidence of final victory based on the experience of encounter with Christ in his body, the Church.

The paradigm of the essential Christian engagement is the Lord's Supper. This celebration of the faith is the occasion for a specially intensive form of encounter of the believers among themselves. Ideally, the participants express their innermost being, their deepest intentions and feelings, and their love for one another. All of this takes place through ritual activity, symbolic action and word. Without this ritual incarnation the full self-expression of the life of the faith of the community would not be real, actual; for their exists no pure inwardness of the human being that can bring itself to full expression independently of the bodily activity.

At the level of the personal signs of the eucharist, there is the real, active presence of the risen Lord, which reaches its visible, corporeal limit in the transformed gifts of the bread and wine. The evidence for the encounter with the Lord in the communion of the sacrament of the body and blood is the experience of faith, which confirms the doctrinal claims of the Church. If a true encounter takes place between Christ and the communicant, it issues in a new action, which necessarily has a social dimension. This new activity is the test of the quality of the participation in the Lord's Supper, as can be gathered from the Pauline exhortation of 1 Cor 10:14-33; 11:17-34.

B. The Church of the Holy Spirit

When we speak of the Church as the place of encounter of God and believers and of believers among themselves, it is a question of encountering God in and through the members of the Church, who are Christ's Body. This is manifested most clearly in the celebration of the Eucharist. Here, in the most expressive way, the participants are united together in their self-offering in, with, and through the self-offering of Christ, and with Christ and one another in the communion of his body and blood.[20] But believers are in Christ's Body "in the Spirit." Hence the sacramental character of the individual, and the community as a whole, has to been seen in the light of pneumatology.

Vatican II's *Lumen gentium* explains that the Holy Spirit is a constitutive factor of the sacramentality of the Church: "Christ...rising from the dead...sent his life-giving Spirit upon his disciples, and through them set up his Body the Church as the universal sacrament of salvation."[21] *Gaudium et spes* refers to the sign quality of the Church, its power to manifest Christ's salvation to the world. This power is attributed to the Spirit, who keeps the Church as a "faithful Spouse of Christ" and so maintains the "sign of Christ on the face of the Church."[22] By virtue of the Spirit energizing the Church, the nature of the Church as sacrament is fully realized.

Through the activity of the Church "in the Spirit," Christ and his saving work are rendered present and operative. The sacramentality of the Church originates from the two missions emanating from the risen Lord, that of the apostles and that of the Holy Spirit. Both the apostles and the Holy Spirit are sent conjointly to gather the world into the Church, the Body of Christ. Christ is actively present in the apostolic mission "in the Spirit," who is co-missioned to work interiorly in and with the Church, and with divine freedom. The apostolic Church serves Christ ministerially in the obedience of faith; the Spirit sent from the Father, through the risen Lord, serves the work of Christ with divine sovereignty. On the other hand, the Church is the fruit of Christ's work and so manifests the presence of the Spirit of Christ, who is the great messianic gift of the Father.

The foregoing considerations lead to the conclusion that the Church is, in some sense, sacrament of the Holy Spirit. But in what sense? The Spirit's mission derives from that of the mission of the Word and has a completely Christ-ward reference. In and through the Church, the Spirit witnesses to Christ (Jn 15:26-27; 16:13-14) and not to himself. Consequently the Church itself witnesses to Christ. As Christ's Body, the Church radiates the glory of the Head, who possesses the Spirit in fullness. But to the extent that the Church, at any given period of history, is "in Christ," it manifests its spiritual nature, its fullness of the possession of the Spirit. From this point of view, the Church is more properly called sacrament of Christ in the Spirit. In and through the Church it is Christ that is encountered, while the Spirit works in a hidden way.

Walter Kasper identifies the Church as "sacrament of the Spirit." In accord with the teaching of Vatican II, he describes the Church as a complex reality made up of sinners and saints, a community that exists through the sharing of the one Spirit and his gifts. It is a visible, human structure, the effective presence and historical form of existence of the Spirit of Christ. In a word, the Church is the "temple of the Spirit" (1 Cor 3:16ff).[23]

Kasper employs this description of the Church, at least in part, to support an inclusive ecclesiology. Pius XII's encyclical letter *Mystici corporis* calls the Spirit the "soul" of the Church, within the context of what has been called an "exclusive ecclesiology," that is to say, one which simply identifies Church of Christ with the Roman Catholic Church. Encouraged by Vatican II's tentative approach to an inclusive ecclesiology, Kasper argues that the Spirit must be understood to be present and active in and through all communities that possess the essential elements of Church. From this viewpoint the Roman Catholic Church, in which the body of Christ subsists, does not exhaust the reality of Church in the world.

The expression "sacrament of the Spirit" means, for Kasper, that the Church is only sacrament; it is the proleptic sign of the lordship of God. No historical church can be simply identified with the Body of Christ because each and every one is precisely sacrament of the Body of Christ.[24] Since structural elements of the Church exist in other Christian communities, although not in the fullness possessed by the Roman Catholic

Church, and since the elements are grounded on the Spirit, these communities are "sacrament of the Spirit." In other words, they manifest and realize the presence and activity of the Holy Spirit.[25]

Kasper also argues that the Church can be called sacrament of the Spirit because it is "improvisation of the Spirit," led by the Spirit (Rom 8:14) in ever new ways.[26] Finally, he refers to Vatican II's teaching on the subject of communion ecclesiology, which was placed alongside juridical ecclesiology but not integrated with it. In his opinion, a solution to this tension can be found in the understanding of the Church as an open system, sacrament of the Spirit, who works with divine freedom.[27]

The introduction of the concept "sacrament of the Spirit" is a gain for ecclesiology. It accords with Pauline theology, which pictures the Spirit as the living link between the Church and the risen Lord. Through the presence of the Spirit, the Church becomes intimately related to the primordial sacrament, Christ. This means that just as the assumed humanity of Jesus of Nazareth served as organ of the Word, so the social structures of the Church serve the Spirit of Christ. The Church has a structure analogous to that of the hypostatic union and so a peculiar role to play in the economic function of the Spirit.

On this subject Vatican II's *Lumen gentium* teaches that the hierarchical society of the earthly Church and the Mystical Body of Christ form a "one complex reality." Composed of human and divine elements, the Church has a structure like that of the incarnate Word: "For just as the nature (humanity is meant!) assumed by the Word, indissolubly united to him, serves as living organism of salvation, in an not unlike way the social structure of the Church serves the Spirit of Christ vivifying it, for the growth of the body (cf. Eph 4:16)."[28] In this analogy the unity of the divine and human elements is the *tertium comparationis*. The basis of the analogy is "organ of salvation," which determines the mutual relation between the divine and human components.

From this point of view, the Church can be called sacrament in a sense that is analogous to the application of the concept to Christ. The humanity of Christ is instrument of the Word; for this humanity is assumed by the Logos himself in hypostatic union. This means that the Logos is the personal source of all human activity of Jesus. When the humanity of Jesus exercises its proper activity, it necessarily acts as instrument of the principal cause. In other words, the instrumental power of the humanity of Jesus is its proper power. To be instrument is constitutive for this humanity. All Jesus' acts are theandric acts, acts of the divine person flowing from his humanity. The humanity of Jesus is no autonomous, ontological subject.

Analogously, the Church can be understood as the instrument of the Spirit of Christ, the Spirit whom Christ possesses in fullness and whom he shares with his Church. The Church is a real society, made up of individual members who possess their own personalities. The life of the Church is expressed in the organized activity of the members. This organized activity, the social structure of the Church, enables the members to realize a unity of activity, in which each one has a role to play. The members of the Church, united in the social organism, contribute to the maintenance and growth of this society by the employment of their special gifts. However, the social structure of the Church is fashioned ultimately by the Spirit who works through it, or, more precisely, through the activity of the members. Those who form the social organism are ontically united to the Spirit and serve as instruments of the Spirit. Hence the activity of the Spirit depends on them.

The Holy Spirit works through the social structures of the Church, or, rather, through the members united in the social organism. Through the activity of the members, the Spirit gains a certain visibility by reason of the variety of personal charisms which he bestows for the good of all. For this reason the Church can be called "sacrament of the Spirit."

C. Trinitarian Ecclesiology

When the Church is considered in the light of the personal missions of the Word *and* the Holy Spirit, a Trinitarian ecclesiology comes to the foreground. A juridical ecclesiology conceives the Church as a perfect society equipped by divine right with all the means to achieve its supernatural goal, and in which an essential distinction is made between the governed and the governors. This theology stresses what Jesus did during his earthly life, and as risen Lord, to found the Church. The weakness of this approach was partially remedied by Pope Pius XII's encyclical letter *Mystici corporis*. But, while the Pope introduced the concept of Christ's active presence in the Church, his theology remains within the scope of the older juridical model.

A partial corrective to this one-sided ecclesiology was introduced by Vatican II's communion ecclesiology, placed alongside elements of a juridical ecclesiology. *Lumen gentium* refers to the older patristic idea that the Church is, in the first place, a community of baptized persons who have a common life in Christ and their measure of spiritual gifts to share with one another. However this communion ecclesiology of Vatican II shows signs, at times, of christomonistic tendency along the lines of the teaching of Paul, insofar as his writings identify the risen Lord as the ground of believers' union with God and one another, and so identify the *Pneuma* with the *Kyrios*. *Lumen gentium* 40-42 offers a good example of this tendency. The marginal references to the Holy Spirit do not offset the description of the present economy of grace, which takes the form: Christ, Church—People of God. However other passages of this constitution present a different point of view.

A pneumatological ecclesiology identifies the Holy Spirit as the principle of unity and source of all activity between Christ and the Church. The first chapter of the *Lumen gentium* outlines the traditional belief in the Spirit's personal mission to the Church and activity in all aspects of the life of the Church. It makes its own the Trinitarian vision of St. Irenaeus of Lyons, who speaks of the Church as "a people brought into unity from the unity of the Father, Son and Holy Spirit."[29] In addition, this constitution teaches that full incorporation into the Church implies possession of the Holy Spirit.[30] The Church is also described as fully constituted "sacrament of salvation" through the mission of the Spirit.[31] This latter pericope suggests that the Spirit is not merely a conserver of what Christ did for the Church, but functions as a kind of co-institutor of the Church. In the overall view of this constitution, the Spirit's role is not confined to the original Pentecostal event. We read, for example, that "the social structure of the Church serves the Spirit of Christ vivifying it, for the building up of the Body."[32] As was already noted regarding this last quotation, the comparison is made between the "nature assumed by the Word...serving him as living organ of salvation" and the social structure of the Church, animated by the Spirit.

Vatican II's pneumatology opens the way to a Trinitarian ecclesiology. In a very pregnant passage, the Decree on Ecumenism (*Unitatis redintegratio*) shows the way: "The supreme model and principle of this mystery (i.e., the unity of the Church) is the unity of the one God, of the Father and Son in the Holy Spirit."[33] This statement seems to mean that the new people of God is called to live a style of life like that of the Trinity, in which unity and multiplicity are bound together in a dynamic union of divine life. This communion, or dynamic personal union, is realized by the Spirit, who fashions the Church's life after that of the Trinity by the gifts he bestows on particular churches and individuals.

Because this is the nature of the Church, the Body of Christ is being built up to the extent that it displays the traits of unity and multiplicity in all dimensions of its life, including its most basic social structures. Thereby the Church also fulfills its essential mission. In the measure that the Church strives to be more perfectly the image of the Trinity, it reveals the mystery of the economic Trinity, the source of its life, to itself and to the world.

This Trinitarian ecclesiology has many important applications in the concrete life of the Church; for example, the relationship between episcopal churches, the relationship between the authority of those who hold office and that of others based solely on their personal charisms, and the personal responsibility of all members of the Church for the mission of the Church.

In regard to the liturgical life of the Church, this Trinitarian ecclesiology affords a broad horizon in which to think about the significance of the rich liturgical traditions of particular churches for the communion of churches as a whole. *Lumen gentium* recognizes that each church has special charisms that can contribute to the building up of the whole communion of churches:

> In virtue of this catholicity each part contributes its gifts to the other parts and to the whole Church, so that the whole and each of its parts are strengthened by the common sharing of all things and by the common effort to attain fullness of unity.[34]

This statement implies that the liturgical traditions of the various churches include values for one another in the matter of theology and practice of worship. Of course, this can only be known by personal acquaintance.

Likewise a Trinitarian ecclesiology supplies the reason why those who are responsible for the organization of the liturgy of a community should pay attention to the "communal nature" of Christian worship, in which

> each person, minister or lay, who has an office to perform, should carry out all and only those parts which pertain to his office by the nature of the rite and the norms of liturgy.[35]

In the liturgical life of the Church especially, the assembled community should make every effort to show itself as image of the Trinitarian life. It is a Trinitarian ecclesiology that ultimately grounds the need for the development of a liturgical theology that explains the sacramental activity in the concrete categories of interaction between charismatically endowed believers, who have their special gifts given for the common good.

IV.
Word and Sacrament in the Spirit

The word of God preached in the Church and the sacraments of Christ are also an ecclesial word, and an ecclesial celebration of the faith. This twofold identity obtains because the preaching of the word of God and the celebration of the sacraments of Christ are expressions of the life of faith, of which Christ "in the Spirit" is the living source.

At the most accessible level, the Word of God is an ecclesial word, and the sacraments of Christ are an ecclesial celebration of the faith. Through these exercises of the life of faith, members of the Church mediate the Spirit to one another and to those outside the baptized community who are disposed to hear the word of faith of the Church. This happens because the Spirit is the source of these exercises of faith, not because the community has the Spirit at its disposal. The mediation of the Church, aimed at bringing individuals into immediate union with God, is effective because of the personal mission of the Spirit. The Spirit works through the social structures of the Church, that is, through persons belonging to the social organism, and so the structured ecclesial work and sacrament can be said to serve as medium of the communication of saving grace.

The relationship of word of God and sacraments of Christ, to the faith of the Church is discussed more extensively in Chapters 16 and 17. For now attention is called to this theme insofar as it allows us to define more exactly the role of the Spirit in the preaching of God's word and the celebration of Christ's sacraments.

The Holy Spirit is the "quasi-formal cause" of what is communicated through the medium of word and sacrament. The term quasi-formal cause can be applied to the Spirit in the event of the communication of saving grace because here the Spirit exercises a function that is analogous to that of a formal cause. A substantial form determines the essence of a created being. It is not distinguished from the being as existent. Rather it is the ultimate determination of that being in its existence. The soul, for example, is described in scholastic philosophy as the essential form of the human person. However, the Holy Spirit is not a form imparted to creaturely reality, whereby it is determined in its individual, personal reality; the human being remains as such in the event of the communication of the Holy Spirit. The Spirit is not, in the strict sense, the formal cause of. the Father's self-communication. Rather, the Spirit, as communicated by the Father through Christ, elevates the integral human being to the highest possibility of human existence, namely, personal communion with the Triune God. This highest determination of human existence is described in the New Testament as configuration to Christ, and filial adoption. Briefly, the Spirit can be called the quasi-formal cause of saving grace because the communicated Spirit determines the essence of what is communicated.

The Spirit is also the principal efficient cause of the communication of salvation through word and sacrament. In other words, the Spirit is the ultimate cause of why and how the word and sacraments of the Church serve as medium of the offer of saving grace and, at the same time, the cause of why and how human beings can perceive and accept the offer of saving grace in historical forms of human personal communication. This consideration calls for special comment, since it provides a corrective to the traditional scholastic theological explanation of the relation of saving grace to the sacramental rites of the Church.

Traditional scholastic theology bases the relationship between grace and sacraments on an institutional act of Christ. He determined, in the case of all sacraments, at least "the specific signification and efficacy." When the minister, acting as representative of the Church, employs those symbolic actions and verbal formulas which express the signification and efficacy intended by the institutional will of Christ, the offer of the saving grace, signified by the rite, is always made.

Further speculation on the precise nature of the causal efficacy of the sacramental rites has led in various directions. A more recent Thomistic explanation provides the best approach within the traditional scholastic sacramental theology. Here it is argued that since the signification of the sacraments is directed by divine ordination, the effects are not limited to the intentional order, as is the case with the causality exercised by ordinary human signs. Sacraments "cause by signifying" in the sense that the symbolic activity modifies the action of the principal cause, and the effect, by manifesting the divine ordering.[36] Others develop this presentation by observing that a real relation exists between the sacramental rite and the person being graced because God's power extends to all being and to the relations among all beings. This real relation between the sacramental rite and the grace signified is a real relation only by extrinsic denomination, because grace is in the recipient and not in the sacramental sign.[37] This theory corresponds to the requirements of a relational ontology. However, it neglects to call the personal source of the divine order by its name: the Holy Spirit.

As source of the essential social structures of the Church, the Spirit ultimately structures word and sacrament into intelligible units, giving them unity of signification. The word of faith and the sacraments of the community of faith derive from the Spirit, who is the source of the faith. The word preached in the Church is truly God's word because, and insofar as, what is said derives from the inspiration of the Spirit working in the exercise of the faith of the witness. One can say that the word of faith is "anointed by the Holy Spirit" or, more prosaically, that the Spirit works through the word of faith.

When Christ is preached, the gift of faith is offered: "So faith comes from what is heard, and what is heard comes from the preaching of Christ" (Rom 10:17). Christ himself preaches through the preacher, according to Paul. This preaching of Christ, however, does not take place apart from the activity of the Holy Spirit, and it is only heard by those who have the Spirit: "And we impart this in words not taught by human wisdom but taught by the Spirit, interpreting spiritual truths to those who possess the Spirit" (1 Cor 2:13). Whatever may be said about Paul's understanding of the Spirit in relation to the risen Lord, that is to say, whether or not Paul identifies *Pneuma* with the risen Lord exercising his spiritual power, in the light of developed Trinitarian theology the role assigned to the Pauline *Pneuma* should be awarded to the Holy Spirit.

The truth of the word of faith is known and accepted only through the gift of faith: a permanent form of life on earth in which Christ and the believer are united in the one Spirit. This life includes the active presence of the Spirit, working in the believer, and so the spiritual presence of Christ who possesses the same Spirit in fullness. In this form of life, the believer lays hold of the hidden Christ in such a way that

Christ becomes principle of his or her life (Gal 2:19-20). The believers have the mind of Christ (1 Cor 2:16). In the Spirit, believers are enabled to understand the thought of the Spirit because thought belongs to the spirit who is able to conceive it.

> For what person knows a man's thought except the spirit of the man which is in him. So also no one knows the thought of God except the Spirit of God. Now, we have received not the spirit of the world, but the Spirit which is from God, that we might understand the gifts bestowed on us by God (1 Cor 2:11-12).

Exposed to the word of faith, a person develops, in the normal case, a capacity to understand it through the gift of faith. However, this capacity should not be understood as derived from an activity of the Spirit which is unrelated to the preaching of the word of God itself. If the preaching is received as word of God, it is because this preaching is itself "anointed" by the Spirit. The Spirit directs the whole process of signification and thereby transforms the human word into word of God. At the same time, the Spirit enables the hearer to recognize that this word is the word of God.

The Spirit also structures the sacramental word and gestures into a unity of signification. A sacrament exists because of this unity. Hence the action of the Spirit and the action of the sacramental celebration are not distinct. This means also that the effects of the sacramental celebrations are not distinct from the effects of the Spirit's activity in the believers, which take place in the course of the participation in the liturgical celebration. It is this pneumatological dimension of sacramental celebrations that provides the theological basis for a more satisfactory explanation of the traditional teaching that the sacraments confer grace, *ex opere operato*, on properly disposed subjects.[38]

In the Spirit, the sacramental word and symbolic actions form a sacrament and are efficacious. By the exercise of the intellect and will, illumined by faith which is granted by the Spirit, the believer is enabled to perceive and accept the gift the Spirit offered through the liturgical rite. Since the Spirit is *both the giver and the gift*, a positive refusal to recognize the Spirit's active presence in the external sacramental celebration renders the participation meaningless from the standpoint of salvation. On the one hand, the Spirit alone makes the exterior sacrament an efficacious sign of salvation; and on the other hand, the Spirit does not touch the heart without the collaboration of the adult participants and without faith having prepared them for the sharing in the sacraments of faith.

The role of the Spirit as sanctifier is made particularly clear in those sacramental rites which include an explicit invocation for the coming of the Spirit, for example, the Eucharistic Prayer and the central prayer of ordination rites. But the verbal form of all sacramental celebrations is, by its very nature, a prayer for the coming of the Spirit, made in union with the eternal intercession of the risen Lord. All the sacramental verbal formulas are essentially prayers which manifest a confidence based on the faith of which the Holy Spirit is the living source. Briefly, the sacramental word can be described as a prayer in which the cry of the Spirit is heard. The Spirit structures this prayer as intercession for his own bestowal by the Father in view of the specific purpose of each sacrament.

A. "Sacraments of the Spirit"

The Spirit, who founded and structures the Church, established the sacraments as constitutive elements of the life of faith. Therefore the sacraments are Spirit-endowed realities of the Church. When the Church actualizes itself in its liturgical celebrations, its sacramental character is most clearly manifested. Here the Church appears as sacrament of the activity of the Spirit and so, in this sense, sacrament of the Spirit. But this activity of the Spirit is an instance of the Spirit working through the participants of the sacramental celebration, in which all of the assembly have their special roles to play.

The more concretely the ecclesial community is understood as the sacrament of the Spirit, in the sense that all the members have their measure of gifts of the Spirit to share with one another, a clearer vision of the basically sacramental character of all the activity of the Church is achievable. In regard to the sacramental celebrations themselves, in which all are enjoined to play an active role in accord with their charisms and particular vocations in the life of the Church, this pneumatological perspective opens the way to a new approach to sacramental theology. It provides the starting point for a description of the dynamics of sacramental celebrations in categories of symbolic interaction of the participants, and for the identification of the specific symbolic activities as realities that are ultimately determined by the creative work of the Holy Spirit.[39]

Notes

1. An extensive treatment of this subject is found in R. Schulte, "Die Einzelsakramente als Ausgliederung des Wurzelsakramentes," 46-155.

2. ST I.II, q. 113, a.9.

3. ST III, q. 60ff.

4. P. Hünermann, "Die sacramentale Struktur der Wirklichkeit," HERDER KORRESPONDENZ 35 (1982) 340-345, provides a brief but illuminating outline of the changing view of reality which, since the sixteenth century, has had a profound effect on the understanding of sacrament.

5. W. Knoch, DIE EINSETZUNG DER SAKRAMENTE DURCH CHRISTUS: Eine Untersuchung zur Sakramententheologie der Frühscholastik von Anselm von Laon bis zu Wilhelm von Auxerre. Beiträge zur Geschichte der Philosophie und Theologie des Mittelalters. Neue Folge, Bd. 24 (Munster: Aschendorff, 1983) 73-145; J. Finkenzeller, DIE LEHRE VON DEN SAKRAMENTEN IM ALLGEMEINEN VON DER SCHRIFT BIS ZUR SCHOLASTIK. Handbuch der Dogmengeschichte IV. Fasc. 1a (Freiburg im Br.: Herder, 1980) 93-97.

6. M. Seybold, "Die Siebenzahl der Sakramente,"70 MÜNCHENER THEOLOGISCHE ZEITSCHRIFT 27 (1976) 113-138.

7. Data concerning the origin and practice of the annual Paschal Feast, as well as the implications of the second century controversy over the date of Easter, are difficult to interpret. This annual celebration of the feast of the resurrection of the Lord has roots in the New Testament communities, but there is insufficient evidence regarding the ordering of the celebration. Easter was celebrated very early in Asia Minor, and may have been introduced in other places after A.D. 135. THE EPISTULA APOSTOLORUM, A.D. 130/140, provides the first textual witness to its existence (W. Schneemelcher, ed., NEW TESTAMENT APOCRYPHA I [Philadelphia: Westminster, 1959] no. 15, p. 199).

8. For example, T. Schneider, ZEICHEN DER NÄHE GOTTES, 30-41.

9. W. Averbeck, "Sakramente—neu Verstanden?170 MÜNCHENER THEOLOGISCHE ZEITSCHRIFT 32 (1982) 49-51, calls attention to the one-sided presentation of Christ as primordial sacrament found in Schneider's book (cf. note 7 above) and offers a more balanced view, which incorporates the vertical aspect of the sacramentality of Christ.

10. H. Mühlen, UNA MYSTICA PERSONA, nos. 1.15-1.20.

11. THE MYSTERIES OF CHRISTIANITY, "The Appropriations of the Holy Spirit," 190-197.

12. DS 3326.

13. DS 3814.

14. S. Tromp, (Pius Papa XII) DE MYSTICO IESU CHRISTI CORPORE DEQUE NOSTRA IN EO CUM CHRISTO CONIUNCTIONE (Rome: Gregorian, 1948) 132.

15. The recent encyclical letter of Pope John Paul II, DOMINUM ET VIVIFICANTEM, on the subject of the Holy Spirit in the life of the Church and the world, is a rich source of theology of the Holy Spirit. However, he explicitly states that this document has

no intention of favoring "any particular solution of questions which are still open" (Ioannis Pauli PP. II. Litterae Encyclicae DE SPIRITU SANCTO IN VITA ECCLESIAE ET MUNDI [Vatican, 1986] I.2, p. 6.

16. SACROSANCTUM CONCILIUM, 5; 26.

17. LUMEN GENTIUM, 1; 9.

18. H. Wagner, "Begegnung als theologische Kategorie," 25-26.

19. L. Hödl, "Kirchliche Sakrament-Christiliche Engagement," ZEITSCHRIFT FÜR KATHOLISCHE THEOLOGIE 95 (1973) 1-19.

20. LUMEN GENTIUM, 3; 7.

21. LUMEN GENTIUM, 34.

22. GAUDIUM ET SPES, 43.

23. "Kirche - Ort des Geistes," in W. Kasper and G. Sauter, KIRCHE - ORT DES GEISTES. Kleine ökumenische Schriften (Freiburg im Br.: Herder, 1976) 41.

24. "Kirche - Ort des Geistes," 42-44.

25. "Kirche - Ort des Geistes," 47.

26. "Kirche - Ort des Geistes," 50.

27. "Kirche - Ort des Geistes," 52.

28 LUMEN GENTIUM, 8.1.

29. LUMEN GENTIUM, 4.

30. LUMEN GENTIUM, 14.

31. LUMEN GENTIUM, 48.

32. LUMEN GENTIUM, 8.1.

33. UNITATIS REDINTEGRATIO, 2.

34. LUMEN GENTIUM, 13.

35. SACROSANCTUM CONCILIUM, 28.

36. W. Van Roo, DE SACRAMENTIS IN GENERE (Rome: Gregorian, 2nd, rev, ed. 1960) 121.

37. P. McShane, "On the Causality of the Sacraments," THEOLOGICAL STUDIES 24 (1963) 423-436.

38. J. Villalón, SACREMENTS DANS L'ESPRIT, 395-397.

39. A. Schilson, "Katholische Sakramententheologie," 576.

Chapter 14

The Concept and
Constitution of the
Christian Sacrament

This chapter begins with the establishment of the grounds of the Christian concept of sacrament, namely, Jesus Christ. Then the nature and function of the elements that go to make up the external rites of Christian sacraments are discussed. The results of the foregoing analysis furnish the basis for the explanation of the distinction between "word and sacrament," that is, the preaching of the word of God and the sacraments of the Church. The identification of the special character of sacramental celebrations supplies the basis for a more precise theological explanation of a traditional theme of sacramental theology, namely the "necessity" of the sacraments. Scholastic theology traditionally reduces this necessity to the requirement of employing divinely instituted sacraments and the individual's need for a sacramental grace. The final section of this chapter shows why and how this approach needs to be broadened in view of the multidimensional character and peculiar nature of the sacraments of the Church.

I.
The Christian Concept of Sacrament.

The Holy Spirit is the living source of the life of faith. The Spirit is also the source of the global perception of the life of faith that impregnates and structures the lives of believers, and of the witness of this perception expressed in the basic activities of the Church, namely, preaching, service, and liturgy. What is witnessed by word and work, as well as corporate forms of worship, is the Christ-event and its chief consequences for humanity.

The Spirit keeps this mystery of salvation, witnessed by the Church, alive and fresh in her memory. The Spirit always refers Christians back to the historical source of the Church and its activity, Jesus Christ. That is why a Christian systematic development of the teaching about word and sacrament and their relationships always includes a consideration of their relationship to Jesus of Nazareth. However the formulation of this latter relationship is frequently not sufficiently carried through because of a failure to establish the christological foundation of the authentic Christian understanding of symbol.[1]

The Christian concept of symbol cannot be based on a synthesis of Platonic, or Neoplatonic, understandings of symbol with biblical information about believers' experience of God acting in and through historical events and persons. Nor can it be properly approached through a Thomistic theory of sacramental sign, according to which the intentional causality proper to sign is transformed into "physical causality" through a divine intervention, guaranteed because the sacraments are divinely instituted.[2] Karl Rahner's explanation of the symbolic causality proper to the "real symbol" also needs amplification.[3] The contributions of human sciences to the concept of symbol should be integrated into this theological theme; for they shed light on the peculiarly Christian view of symbol.

But the point of departure for a discussion of the connection between symbolic action and the word of God, through which faith comes by hearing (Rom 10:17) and seeing, must be Jesus Christ, the one Mediator between God and humanity (1 Tim 4:2; 1 Cor 12:3).

A. The One Mediator and the Many Mediations

Communication between persons exists at many levels. The most intense form consists in the communication of self to another, insofar as this is possible. This highest form is experienced as the awareness of the other being present and extending an invitation to enter into the unique sphere of his or her personal existence. In this encounter the other is experienced as a thou. Through such interpersonal communication the experience of the Other, the source of all otherness, can and does occur. God's self-communication takes place in and through this interpersonal communication between human beings.

1. Jesus the Mediator

Jesus Christ mediates "as man" (1 Tim 2:5). His mediation of God's self-communication is, nevertheless, unique. Since his humanity is united in person to the Word of God, his person cannot be separated from his message.[4] Therefore he is Mediator of the ultimate depth of human intercommunication, that is, God's self-communication.[5] What Jesus mediates as man is God's movement toward human beings. Through the response of faith to this mediation, the individual is drawn into communion with God. The effect of the direct contact with God, mediated through Jesus' activity, is described by the Greek Fathers as "deification."[6]

God's self-communication always takes place through historical events and human beings. The content of this experience is revealed, in its fullness, only in Jesus Christ. Likewise, the experience itself is mediated by Jesus of Nazareth to others in a unique way. In the activity of Jesus, God's living and loving presence is always fully mediated. According to Karl Barth, Jesus Christ mediates the "humanity of God," that is, God's loving presence reaching to the core of human existence. No human person as such, and from oneself, can do this.[7] Human beings as such are not the source of grace for another. On their side they are only the source of, and bear sole responsibility for, obscuring the light of God's abiding presence in and through history.

Since Jesus mediates through his human freedom, his words and signs have their basis and content in his obedient life. In Jesus, the human situation is clearly shown to be the place of God's presence and the sign of his presence for those enlightened by faith. God's glory is revealed for others in Jesus' words and signs, by which he expresses his loving obedience to the Father and his service of the Father's children.

2. The Many Mediations of God's Self Communication

The death and resurrection of Jesus and the sending of the Spirit by the risen Lord from the Father, create the situation in which God's abiding presence can be promised and shared, in and through the word and holy symbols of the Church. The unique mediation of Jesus does not exclude other mediations. His mediation constitutes the immediacy of the presence of God in the most radical sense possible in history. But it can be exercised through believers in their communication with one another and with those outside the community of faith.8 Paul takes for granted mediations of this sort (2 Cor 5:19-20). In fact, they are the precondition for the possibility of Christ's continued mediation from God to humanity in history. However, these mediations are made possible only by the Spirit of Christ, who awakens the obedience of faith by which believers are enabled to accept Christ as Savior and witness to him, and by which others can discern Christ's saving presence in this witness.

When this word of God is preached in faith, God reveals self through the obedience of faith. The preaching of the disciples of Christ is a word that mediates salvation. The human word of faith is a "demonstration of the Spirit and (his) power" (1 Cor 2:4). This word brings peace, new life, reconciliation. It issues in self-forgetful love and hopeful courage.

According to the New Testament writings, the disciples mediate the word of the Cross through their obedient lives, words, and actions. Not only Jesus of Nazareth, but also his disciples, through their persons, words, and actions, are the means by which God discloses, in and through history, his saving presence and its claims. In short, the human situation, insofar as accepted in obedience and devotion to the following of the way of Jesus Christ, becomes the sign of God's presence in the world calling for the decision of faith from all who are given the gift of the Spirit "to see and hear."

Two observations are relevant here. First of all, the earthly spheres of the holy and profane cannot be defined in terms of places or situations in which God is present or absent. God is always present to human beings in all situations of their lives, with his offer of self-communication. Second, in the event of God's saving activity and the response of believers, "grace" describes the active orientation of the creature to

God himself, grounded on God's self-communication and corresponding to humankind's native openness in the areas of freedom, hope and love.

Through hearing the word of God and receiving it in faith, the hearer gains a new horizon of understanding, which unlocks the meaning of the human experience of being an open question, supplying the answer to the mystery of human existence. Through hearing and accepting the word of God, believers are freed from anxiety about sin and the world, from the impulse to self-seeking and self-justification. They receive from the word of God the knowledge of who they are, and they are enabled to discern what direction they must take to move along in order to make progress in human growth.

The concept "salvation history," as applied to the individual person, refers to the history of the free acceptance of this graceful word of God. It is the history of human beings' growth in personhood, growth in the awareness of the divine ground of human existence and in the deepening of the commitment to the claims that God's saving presence makes on them. Accordingly, a saving event takes place when a person assumes a position with respect to one's true human situation, because he or she has one's orientation to God only in relation to something in this world.

These saving events take place more generally in special moments of human existence, in which the meaning and non-meaning of life comes into play, where human existence is condensed and symbolically referred beyond itself. Such events reach a high point when one responds to the human situation in accord with the interpretation given to it by the word of God in Jesus Christ.

The foregoing consideration provides the clue to the authentic Christian concept of symbol, located at the center of salvation history, Jesus Christ. This concept relates to the more original meaning of symbol, rediscovered and developed in modern anthropology. We have already treated the question of the relationship between the word of tradition and the "boundary situations" that word evokes or transforms. In Christ, these boundary situations, which are given and cannot be manipulated, which reveal the human being as an open question, are changed into situations of salvation.

Jesus Christ, true God and true man, entered into the human context fully. He took up all that belongs to it, and qualified it anew. He interpreted the ambiguity of boundary situations by announcing the new situation of humanity realized through his person, words, and actions. He proclaimed that the human situation is filled with God's loving presence and taught his hearers how they should respond to this presence. Through the preaching of the Cross, these boundary situations continue to be the time of God's grace for humanity.

II.
Elements of the Christian Sacrament: Word and Symbolic Action

The relation between boundary situations and the word of interpretation has been analyzed in detail by Gerhard Ebeling. Briefly, he points out that word provokes a situation, creates it. The word may enlighten a "neutral situation" or change an existing situation in one direction or another.[9] This relation to situation inherent in the original function of word is exemplified very dramatically in the celebrations of the sacraments.[10] Sacramental celebrations symbolically represent human situations and make them, through the word of God, into situations of salvation, times of grace and signs of God's grace for the subjects.

In sacramental celebrations particular boundary situations are related no longer to an undefined transcendent reality, but concretely to God's loving presence and fidelity, confronting and calling believers to a decision of faith. Sacraments, as activities of the community of faith, symbolize the transcendent presence of God in particular situations of life. They consist in the celebration of human and social situations, symbolically represented and proclaimed to be filled with the saving presence of God, who makes concrete claims on the participants.

However, the sacramental word has a function that is only *analogous* to the word of tradition that affords instruction about the meaning of human situations and the appropriate response to them. Moreover the sacramental word is only analogous to the word of Christian tradition that serves to provide information about the mystery dimension of the human situation, for example, catechetical instruction.

The external aspect of the sacramental celebrations consists in verbal formulas and symbolical actions, which sometimes include the use of material elements such as oil, water, bread and wine. The persons involved in the celebration are the Triune God, Father, risen Lord, and

Holy Spirit, along with the assembled community of faith. The Father is the ultimate source of the celebration; Christ acts as Head of the community, as the chief celebrant; the Holy Spirit vivifies the community so that it may engage itself in this dialogue of love. The assembled faithful have different roles to play. There is the ordained minister who presides, the subject in whose favor the celebration takes place, and the community as a whole. All of these persons have functions that contribute to the realization of the sacramental celebration.

Without the involvement of the Triune God, and the risen Lord in his humanity, the activity would be essentially meaningless. The *ideal* realization of the sacramental celebration occurs only when all the believers who are present actively engage their faith; for all forms of the earthly liturgy are *sacramental realizations* of the heavenly liturgy, and only reach their full stature when each of the participants is turned to all the others, as far as this is possible, in the openness of love. But in any case, sacramental celebrations are not realizable, as saving events, without the personal involvement, in faith, of some representatives or representative of the Church, lay person or ordained minister. The reason for this should be obvious. Sacramental celebrations are, in the first place, acts of worship of God. It is the aspect of formal worship that differentiates sacramental celebrations from the variety of forms of Christian preaching that furnish instruction about the fact of God's presence in all situations of life, calling for the decision of faith.

A. Scholastic Doctrine Concerning the Composition of Sacraments

The Fathers of the Church were concerned more with the mystery aspect of the sacraments, the synergism of the human and divine activity, than with the composition of the external rites. Still, they did not neglect this latter subject, as is shown in the debate about the validity of baptism administered "in the name of Jesus," rather than by the Trinitarian formula, and the practice of conferring baptism with a single immersion, rather than with a triple immersion.[11]

The subject of the composition of the external rites of the sacraments became a prominent theme in Western scholastic theology during the twelfth century. Probably the earliest exponent of a general theory about the composition of sacramental rites was Gerhoh of Ratisbon (d. 1169). Inspired by the writings of Augustine of Hippo, he describes sacramental rites as composed of element and word (*ex elemento et verbo*).[12] During the thirteenth century the so-called hylomorphic theory was applied to the composition of the sacraments. It is not established, as yet, who took the first step in this direction, but the theory was fully evolved by the time of Thomas Aquinas.[13]

The philosophical theory that conceives created realities as composed of prime matter (completely undetermined) and substantial form, offered an analogy for explanation of the relation between the symbolical action and verbal formulas of the sacraments. The symbolical gesture, at the heart of the sacramental celebrations, was called proximate matter (*materia proxima*) to distinguish it from the material elements employed in some sacraments, which were called remote matter (*materia remota*) insofar as apt for use in the rite. The verbal formulas, which determine the otherwise ambiguous meaning conveyed by the symbolic gesture, were given the name form of the sacrament (*forma sacramenti*). This terminology was taken over in the official documents of the magisterium of the Catholic Church.[14]

According to Aquinas, the *forma sacramenti* is the expression of the interior word of faith of the Church: "Sacraments are protestations of the faith."[15] The meaning of these forms is the meaning that the faith of the Church gives to them.[16] The faith of the Church is always the source of the sacramental formulas. However, the formulas, when recited, do not necessarily bring to expression the living faith of the Church, that is to say, actualize it here and now. In themselves the formulas are a dead letter. They must be given life. This happens when the intention of the Church, expressed in the exterior word,[17] is incarnated in the concrete celebration. In order for this to occur, the competent minister must have the intention to "do what the Church does" (*faciendi quod facit ecclesia*).[18]

The nature of the intention to do what the Church does was disputed among the scholastics of the high Middle Ages. Opinions run from the one extreme of external conformity of the minister to the proper ritual comportment approved by the Church, to the other of interior conformity of the minister's will to what the Church intends by the rite. In the post-Reformation period, scholastic theology more commonly held that an "internal intention," that is, a hidden intention not to do what the Church does, invalidates the sacrament.

The frequent appeal to the Council of Trent's teaching to support the theory of "internal intention" cannot be sustained.[19] Furthermore, the real basis of this theory is a theology of the role of the presiding minister, which makes him the sole active agent in the realization of a sacrament. This latter theological opinion has been discarded by modern Catholic theology, as well as the official magisterium. Vatican II's *Sacrosanctum concilium* formulates, in an unequivocal way, the neglected truth that the community assembled for any liturgical celebration is, as a whole, the active subject of the liturgical act. On the ground that the whole assembly is the active subject of any liturgical act, it seems to be highly improbable that the liturgical leader could negate the sacramental dimension of this activity by his interior refusal to act as minister of the Church and, consequently, of Christ.

An exterior intention of the minister to celebrate the sacrament, displayed by the proper comportment, is not sufficient, by itself, for the realization of a sacramental event. Some part of the assembly, or at least some participant, must have a living faith that corresponds to the meaning of the celebration. The constant tradition of the Church, since the patristic period, explicitly affirms that lack of faith or holiness does not render an ordained minister incapable of accomplishing a valid sacrament. The reason is clear: The sacramental celebration has, as its chief celebrant, the High Priest, Jesus Christ. The minister is only the servant of Christ. But one may not draw the conclusion from this argument that the exterior performance of a sacramental rite by an assembly in which all the baptized participants lack faith, is the accomplishment of an authentic sacramental celebration.[20] Of course, in practice, it may be doubted whether activities of this type ever occur in the context of a community that merits the name "church."

Regarding the realization of a true "sacramental event" for the subjects in whose favor the sacramental celebration takes place, two observations may be noted in passing. First, the reception of the offer of the grace, signified by the sacrament, depends entirely on the openness in faith of adult subjects. Second, the requirement of subjective faith in the adult subject, for the realization of the permanent relational connection to the Church effected by baptism or by the ordination to permanent ministerial office, needs further investigation. Part of the traditional teaching of the West maintains that the "sacramental character" of baptism is received as long as the subject, wishing to be enrolled in the Christian community for social reasons, does not implicitly or explicitly exclude this effect. Here we approach the borderline. For example, the leader of a village decides to become a Christian "in name only, simply because the rest of the community is Christian. It may be seriously questioned whether, in this case, the subject is really baptized.

An important pastoral problem, analogous to the example mentioned above, concerns the status of the marriage of partners baptized in infancy, who have been raised completely outside the context of the Christian life of faith. Part of the Western tradition holds that when these partners contract marriage, they are joined in a "sacramental marriage," as distinguished from a marriage of the non-baptized. In fact, the pastoral practice of the Catholic Church assumes that these partners have received the sacrament of matrimony solely on the basis of being baptized. Again, as in the analogous case of the leader of a village cited above, it may be questioned whether this opinion pays enough attention to the importance of the marriage partners' acceptance of the human and social situation in accord with the meaning symbolized by the sacrament of matrimony.[21]

A saying of Hugo of St. Victor that intimately links sacraments to faith is repeated by later scholastics. Thomas Aquinas paraphrases it in this way: "All sacraments have their efficacy from faith" (*omnia sacramenta ex fide efficaciam habent*).[22] In the past this saying, as related to the realization of a sacrament, was explained in the following way. Living faith is always found in some members of the universal Church. For this reason, a sacrament is realized when a minister has the proper intention (exterior; interior) to do what the Church does. This theory must be disregarded, since there is no ground for the assertion that the faith of the universal Church is immediately and directly involved in the concrete liturgical celebrations of a local assembly. But, if the realization of a sacrament depends on the existence of living faith in some members, or member, of the concrete liturgical assembly, there still remains a further question. How does the faith of the Church, expressed in the particular liturgical assembly, relate to the realization of a sacrament? In order to respond to this question, one needs to reflect on the nature of the sacramental formula associated with the essential symbolical activity of the sacramental celebration.

B. Sacramental Word and Symbolical Action

The sacramental formula has a function that must be differentiated from that of the symbolical gesture accompanying it, although together they form a unity of signification.

1. Symbolical Action

It belongs to the nature of the human person to be active. Activity is constitutive of human existence in the world. Human beings are only really there when they act, when they realize themselves as being-in-the-world. Through activity (action and reaction) personal beings are the ones they desire to be. There is no need to expand further on this axiom: Action is an inner aspect in the basic constitution of the rational creature.

Humankind experiences the need to act, to relate oneself, to dispose oneself, especially in significant situations of life that call for decision. When situations of this type are related to the life of faith, it becomes clear why a response of faith, made within the context of corporate worship, should include forms of activity by which believers express themselves in ordinary daily life. Symbolical actions such as washing, laying on of hands, the sharing of a meal, have their own dynamism. The gesture of reaching out to the other, and the corresponding gesture of response, allow both of the parties involved to recognize their own desires in the gestures. In both cases there is a linguistic setting, expressed or presumed, in which the gestures move and which ultimately determines their meaning. But neither in daily life nor in the liturgy is the symbolical gesture a redundant duplication of a verbal component.[23] Through the symbolical gestures, in the case of the liturgy, both the community as a whole and the individual in whose favor the celebration takes place, act out their response to a particular human situation which is signified.

2. Sacramental Word

Scholastic theology speaks of the analogy between the incarnation of the Word and the composition of a sacrament. It is fitting, so the argument goes, that sacraments should be composed of verbal and gestural elements; for they manifest and realize the saving work of the Word made flesh. According to this analogy, the sacramental word is the form that determines the meaning of the symbolical action, just as the Word of God assumed the humanity of Jesus of Nazareth and became man.

This explanation is completely focused on the formation of the external sign. Here the word is decisive. In modern theological language one might say: It is primarily the word that makes the basic situations of human existence, symbolically represented by the sacramental actions, clearly situations of salvation which call for the response of faith. In the old scholastic view it is argued that when, in the celebration of the sacraments of the Church, the competent minister supplies the sacramental gesture and adds the sacramental word, the sacrament is accomplished. There is realized a true and efficacious sign of grace, of a grace being offered by Christ through the minister to the potential "recipient." If the subject of the sacrament is properly disposed, the sacramental grace is conferred in and through the ritual activity (*ex opere operato*). The "essential rites" of the sacraments are distinguished from the surrounding ritual actions and prayers, activities of the Church whereby the community prepares itself for the communication of the sacramental grace.

Contemporary Catholic theologians often speak of the word of the sacrament as a "performative word." This means that the sacramental formula, constitutive of the sacrament, *does what it says*. However, this explanation of the sacramental word is insufficient, as the witness of Scripture and liturgy itself show.

In the last two decades, more attention has been given to the dialogue character of the whole economy of salvation. Unfortunately systematic theologians have not, as a general rule, drawn out the implications of this characteristic that penetrates the economy of salvation under all its aspects. One still finds examples where sacraments are described in ways that recall the outlook of the old school theology. One instance of this is Karl Rahner's frequently repeated description of sacraments as "the most radical example of the word of God to believers.70 No doubt this statement contains a truth, but it is too one-sided.

A few systematic theologians, and more especially some liturgists, have begun to draw out the consequences of the dialogue structure of liturgy for all aspects of sacramental theology. Among the leaders of this approach must be named Emil Lengeling.[24] From this point of view, the liturgy is not conceived as the exercise of the virtue of religion, in which the movement is exclusively from the faithful to God. Rather, as Vatican II's *Sacrosanctum Concilium* explains, the liturgy is both God's word to the community and the community's response to God. However this way of depicting the twofold movement of the liturgy is open to a misunderstanding. It can give the impression that the external liturgy contains elements that represent exclusively either the movement from God to the community or vice versa. In particular, it leaves the way open to a description of the sacramental word, at the heart of the celebration of a sacrament, as simply a word of God addressed to those sharing in the liturgy.

The proper approach to the dialogical structure of the liturgy, and this includes the so-called essential sacramental rites, is the very ancient one. According to this understanding, the whole of the verbal dimension of the liturgical-sacramental celebrations, including the formulas that decisively determine the meaning of the essential sacramental gestures, is identifiable as the response of faith of the worshipping community: a response, grounded on the risen Lord who dwells in the believers by faith (Eph 3:17). This theological outlook is based on the mystery of the mediation of the God-man, Jesus Christ, before the Father on behalf of the world. In this christological context, the whole verbal dimension of the communal worship of the Church, including the formulas of the essential sacramental rites, are defined as *prayer*: a response of the faith of the Church made in, with, and through the High Priest, Jesus Christ, in the power of the Holy Spirit.

New Testament sources support this understanding of the verbal aspect of liturgy. The bestowal of the gift of the Spirit (Acts 8:15-17) and the anointing of the sick (Jas 5:14-15), take place in conjunction with the prayer of church leaders. Baptism happens through the invocation of the Father, Son, and Holy Spirit (Mtt 28:19). The Lord's Supper is celebrated in conformity with the command of Jesus: "Do this in my *anamnesis*" (Lk 22:19). Consequently, it includes, as an essential ingredient, "blessing" of God (Mk 14:22) or "thanksgiving" (1 Cor 11:23).

In the writings of the Fathers of the Church, the so-called "forms of the sacraments" are generally described as prayer for the obvious reason that they have the traits of prayer. The form of baptism in the patristic period is that of a confession of faith in the Triune God, elicited through questions addressed by the one baptizing: "Do you believe in the Father?....Do you believe in his only Son?...in the Holy Spirit..."[25] The Eucharistic Prayer, in some Eastern churches, originally had its high point in a prayer for the coming of the Logos, or for the coming of the Spirit understood as the Logos, to the end that he might come upon the eucharistic gifts for the purpose of sanctifying the participants of the Lord's Supper. After the latter part of the fourth century, more commonly the Father was petitioned to send the Holy Spirit to sanctify the gifts of the Church and the assembly. In the West, the Eucharistic Prayer as a whole was conceived, initially, as the form of the sacrament. [26] The sacramental word of the rites of ordination, both in the East and West, have always had a petitionary form.

While the central verbal formulas of sacramental rites were originally epicletic, subsequent liturgical and theological developments in the West resulted in the use of an indicative formula for some sacraments. This contributed to the twelfth- and thirteenth-century view that the essential forms of the sacraments represent an exclusively katabatic movement, that is, from God to the "recipients" of the sacraments. While the ancient petitionary forms were retained in the Eucharist, anointing of the sick, and ordination rites, a distinction was made between the essential sacramental word and the surrounding prayers. The latter was awarded the function of expanding on the meaning of the essential rite and of integrating the prayer of the Church with the descending word of God, viz. Christ, expressed in the "form of the sacrament."

The epicletic formulas highlight the divine origin of the efficacy of the sacraments. The indicative active form of the sacraments announces the presence of the saving event here and now. For example: "I baptize you...; I absolve you...." The eastern indicative, passive formula of baptism:" May the servant be baptized...," represents a kind of middle position between the two. In the case of the epicletic forms, it is clear that the sacramental word is a word of faith of the community, petitioning for God's sanctifying activity, based on God's fidelity to institutions established by him. A certain analogy exists between this form of the sacrament and the prayer associated with the solemn feasts of the old covenant, in which a petition is made for God to work the blessings associated with the institutions established by him.

The indicative form of the sacraments is analogous to the prophetic oracle announcing that Yahweh will do this or that, depending on the response of his people in obedience to his will. These oracles, which often begin with the formula: "Thus says the Lord God...," are a word of God in the form of the expression of the prophet's conviction of faith. They reach their goal, issue in a saving event, to the extent that the people respond in the obedience of faith. But here the analogy ends. The prophetic oracle, addressed to the community as such, is based on the prophet's personal charism, and is a new disclosure of God's intention for his people. The sacramental word, in the indicative, active form, is not a new disclosure in this sense. Moreover, it is the expression of the Church's faith in response to the revelation of God in Jesus Christ.

The sacraments combine the community's self-offering to the Father, through Christ in the Spirit, with a prayer for the sanctification of the subject in whose favor the celebration takes place (six sacraments) or for the assembled faithful (Eucharist). Since the faith of the Church is expressed in the celebration of the "sacraments of faith,"[27] the leader of the celebration must have the "intention to do what the Church does," that is, carry out the rite in accord with the prescriptions of the Church. In the word of the sacrament, the Church prays through Jesus Christ for the coming of the Spirit in order that the grace signified by the sacramental rite may be bestowed. Ultimately, the sacramental word is a confession of the synergism between the Spirit and Church, and between the risen Lord and Church, which alone can ground the sacramental event of sanctification.

The gradual dominance of the indicative, active form of some sacraments, in the West, reflects the Church's confidence that grace is really being offered in and through the rite. But its usage was influenced, in no small measure, by the loss of insight concerning the community's active role in the liturgy. When the essential rites of sacraments are conceived as performed *in the Church* by the minister of Christ, who represents Christ for the Church, the epicletic nature of the forms of the sacraments tends to be placed in the background of theological reflection or even neglected. However, when the sacraments are understood more precisely as *sacraments of the Church,* in which the one presiding acts as representative of the Church of which Christ is the Head, the anabatic trait of the sacraments almost necessarily comes to the foreground.

An analogy between the preaching of the word of God and the sacrament can help to make understandable the nature of the sacramental word. The preaching of the word of God is a preaching of the faith in response to the obedience of faith. The act of preaching has a *dialogical character,* since it is a response to the word of God working inwardly in the preacher. The preaching of the preacher is a word about Christ. Nevertheless, because it is the response to the Word of God who, in the

Spirit, is the living source of this preaching, the activity is a preaching of Christ himself. As such it awakens in the hearer a response of faith, which is ultimately a response to the Word of God working inwardly in the hearer.

Sacramental celebrations also have an essentially dialogical character. The formulas of the sacraments are a response to the Word of God working inwardly in the Church in the power of the Spirit. They are, therefore, necessarily inserted into the prayer of Christ, his eternal intercession. On the ground of the prayer of Christ, together with the epiclesis of the Church and the promise given through the institution of the sacraments, the ritual action represents infallibly the offer of saving grace by the Father through the risen Lord in the Spirit.

Briefly, sacramental celebrations are symbolical actions animated by the prayer of the Church, which is inserted into the prayer of the High Priest, Jesus Christ. Because the intercession of the Church, made in union with Christ, is always heard by the Father, sacraments are always an offer of the Spirit, made by the Father through the theandric act of the risen Lord, in accord with the signification of the symbolical action and epiclesis.

Sacraments are the effective signs of Jesus Christ's divine-human love of the Father (glorification) and of his divine-human love of humanity (sanctification). All the sacraments have the aspect of worship of the Father, the worship of the Church made in union with the one High Priest. At the same time, within this anabatic dimension, all the sacraments include intercession before the Father on behalf of the subjects in whose favor the celebrations take place. This intercession is made by the Church in union with the "eternal intercession" of Christ. Consequently, sacraments are the expression of Jesus Christ's love of the Father under the aspect of love of the children of the Father. This intercession of Christ is aimed at bringing the subject of the sacraments into union with himself so that they will love the Father with the love of son or daughter in the one Son.

The sacramental word is the expression of the Church's confidence in faith that its intercession is united by Christ to his own. Hence it serves as transparency for Christ's eternal intercession. However, at the same time, the sacraments are signs of the *efficacy* of Christ's eternal intercession, which elicited the response of the Father in the once-for-all Pentecostal event: the sending of the Spirit to establish the Church and sanctify those who accept the gift of God in faith. Therefore sacraments are effective signs of the mystery of the sending of the Spirit by the risen Lord from the Father in a theandric act, sacrament of the transcendental act of the Father. From this point of view, we speak of the sacraments as efficacious signs of Christ's divine-human love of the Father, under the aspect of his divine-human love of the Father's children, and describe Christ as the sanctifier. Since the mystery of the sacraments includes Christ's active role as High Priest and sanctifier, both aspects must be included in a theological explanation of the efficacy of the sacraments.

III.
Relation Between Preaching and Sacraments

The previous remarks on the nature of the sacramental word offer a clue to the proper approach to the question of the difference between the preaching of the word of God and the sacraments. This subject, which is also discussed in Chapter 16, has attracted some attention in the past few decades, and has roots in Western Reformation theology.

During the sixteenth-century debate about the relative value of the preaching of the word of God, and the celebration of the sacraments, the typical Reformation stress fell on the acquisition of salvation through hearing the word of God in faith (*sola praedicatione*). This starting point severely limits the concept of salvation through the "Word alone" (*Verbo solo*) and tends to relegate sacraments to the rank of appendage to preaching. On the other hand, the traditional scholastic description of sacraments as "efficacious signs of grace instituted by Christ," when used as a gauge for evaluating the sacramental quality of preaching, often results in reducing preaching of the word to a deficient form of sacrament.

Karl Rahner suggested that sacraments should be conceived as the word of God in the highest degree.[28] This proposal has some merit. Through sacramental celebrations the Church actualizes itself, as sacrament of Christ, in existentially basic situations of the lives of individuals (four sacraments), of individuals in relation to one another (matrimony), of an individual in relation to the community (orders), of the community as such (Eucharist). Preaching in the Church, on the other hand, is exercised by an individual who announces the saving presence of God and gives instruction as to how one is to respond in specific situations of life or, more generally, in all situations of the life of faith. Because individuals, including the ordained minister, cannot claim that their preaching is an act of the Church in the fullest sense, they cannot place it at the level of the sacraments. No individual can make a sacrament for others simply out of the exercise of his or her own life of faith, just as no individual, as such, can make a sacrament for himself or herself.

Both sacraments and the preaching of the word are forms of expression of the life of faith. In short, they are indirectly word of God. But they differ in the intensity of the incarnation of the faith of the Church and in the intensity of the response that they can be expected to elicit, in the normal case, from those who engage themselves. Moreover, sacraments cannot be reduced simply to "word of God," insofar as this phrase implies a reduction of the sacramental word to a katabatic function or the identification of the gestural element with a deficient form of word. We have already discussed the anabatic aspect of the sacramental word and the special contribution made by the gestural element. However, in the interest of establishing a clearer distinction between preaching and sacraments, one further observation is useful concerning the complex structure of the sacraments.

The equating of the gestural and verbal elements of sacraments would be an impoverishment of the concept of sacrament. If one looks at the matter more closely, it becomes evident that, in various ways, sacramental celebrations correspond to the complex reality of human personal being, to the human being's condition as being-in-the world.

In human personal development, freedom and decision are decisive as integrating aspects. But human beings exist as embedded in the world, and from this situation one's possibilities and limits are set. Human personal beings develop by realizing their relational connections with the world of things and persons. Corporeality and historicity are essential aspects of human personal being.

Sacraments, in one way or another, incorporate societal and relevant substructures. In these celebrations of faith there is a playing out of the relations between the community and individual, and individuals among themselves. Attention is given to the dependencies of human beings on the world of things. Communication takes place through the drawing out of the relational possibilities of material elements such as water, oil, bread, and wine. Also, as noted previously, the symbolic gestures incarnate desire, enabling the community and individual to recognize their desires in the gestures. Consequently, sacramental celebrations afford a more complete celebrative realization of personal being. They furnish the ground for the deeper insight that humankind should not limit their relationality to one or another of their possible relations and, above all, view this relationality in terms of the most fundamental relation of creature to Creator.[29]

The distinction between preaching and sacraments can also be discussed from the standpoint of their primary orientation. Some years ago, Leo Scheffczyk explained the relation between preaching and sacraments by building on a theory proposed by Otto Semmelroth.[30] According to Scheffczyk, the peculiarity of sacrament lies in the aspect of worship. Both preaching and sacrament involve a twofold dimension: bestowal of God's grace and the response of believers. Preaching is both a proclamation of the faith of the preacher and a response of the preacher himself to God in obedience of faith. At the same time, preaching is calculated to evoke the response of worship from the hearer. However the "ascending movement" is more fully actualized in the sacrament. The believer enters more fully into the movement of the word and responds to God more completely.

Scheffczyk explicitly dissociated himself from the position of Karl Rahner, who had described the sacraments as another form of preaching.[31] Sacraments are not another form of preaching, not even the highest realization of the word of God in the sense described by Rahner. Scheffczyk considered this view too anthropocentric. He argued that Rahner's approach can explain the ordering of word and sacrament, and the necessity of sacrament, solely in terms of the human subject. But, says Scheffczyk, "man and the fulfillment of his being cannot be the ultimate goal of the divine action."[32] Rather the divine activity reaches its term when it leads rational creatures to praise God and to recognize him as the alpha and omega. The anthropocentric aspect must be understood as a movement in the overlapping theocentric dimension of both word and sacrament.

Scheffczyk finds Semmelroth's presentation of the relationship of word and sacrament close to his own. The latter interprets word and sacrament in terms of two phases of the Christ-event: incarnation (word) and Cross (sacrament). Semmelroth explains that sacraments are relatively necessary in order that the subjective appropriation of salvation might correspond better to the twofold movement of the bestowal of grace and the response of the creature. Scheffczyk, however, does not think that this explanation suffices to establish the distinction between word and sacrament. According to him the specific form of the sacrament, as distinguished from preaching, is the human cooperation with God, a movement "upward."[33]

This explanation seems to imply that the sacrament has a twofold goal: to enable the human cooperation in the grace event by a response of acceptance of God's love *and* to afford the opportunity for believers to offer acceptable worship of praise and thanksgiving. In other words, the *and* seems to be disjunctive. However, in a very radical sense, the creature praises God for his goodness by accepting God's self-communication. If the ultimate goal of creation is identified with God himself, then it cannot be the praise offered by human beings to God. It must be the self-communication of God in creation.[34] This communication reaches its highest fulfillment when rational creatures praise God, that is, make their own intention that for which God created them. This means recognizing the offer of personal communion with God and accepting it.

The response of the creature is praise of God, and one can speak of a "change" in God occurring through it, at least in the sense that God changes in intentionality with respect to the worshipper. However this glory given to God does not add new perfection to God. The praise of God benefits only the creature. It amounts to letting God be God in one's life. Hence in a very real sense, the goal of worship, as of all creation, is anthropocentric.

However, Scheffczyk's distinction between preaching and sacrament, based on the aspect of worship, must be taken seriously. The problem with his explanation seems to be traceable to the acceptance, at least implicit, of a traditional scholastic distinction between the liturgical and sacramental dimensions of the sacramental celebrations. If the essential sacramental rites, the so-called essential symbolic actions and formulas, are understood to represent the movement from God in Christ to us, and the liturgical rites and prayers surrounding the essential rites the movement of the liturgical assembly to God, then worship appears to precede and follow the accomplishment of the sacrament. From this perspective, the sacrament itself, while it cannot be fully subsumed under the reality of "word," differs from the word of preaching only to the extent that it integrates the encounter with God into the fuller relational dimensions of human, personal existence. It accidentally differs from the event of preaching because the element of response, of that worship which is essential for preaching to reach its intended goal,[35] is given an ecclesial expression in the liturgical prayer enclosing the essential sacramental rite.

We have already seen, in this chapter, that the essential sacramental word of the seven sacraments has an anabatic, or ascending, dimension. Thereby the old scholastic distinction between the liturgy, as the prayer of the Church, and the sacraments, as acts of God in Christ offering grace, was shown to be inadequate. The real reason why sacramental celebrations differ from the preaching of the word of God, from the standpoint of the katabatic and anabatic movements, lies in the epicletic nature of the essential sacramental rites themselves, as we have described it above.

IV.
Necessity of the Sacraments

The necessity of the sacraments can be discussed from the standpoint of the nature of the Church. There is a traditional liturgical-sacramental principle that can be formulated in this way: The basic activities of the Church, those that manifest and realize its given sacramental structure, should be clearly and credibly represented. This means that the building up of the Church should be made visible through sacramental celebrations of ecclesial life. The devaluation of any of the sacramental celebrations, which mirror the mystery of the Church, leads to a misunderstanding of the *sacramental character* of the Church itself. If, for example, the commissioning to office in the Church took place by a merely juridical act, the relation of special ministry to the sacramental structure of the Church would be obscured, and the understanding of the nature of the Church, of which permanent forms of ministry of leadership are an essential structure, would be placed in jeopardy.[36] If entrance into the Church involved only an agreement between the community and candidate, the self-understanding of the Church expressed in the contract would scarcely mediate the experience of the reality of incorporation into Christ "in the Spirit." If one is accepted as member of the Church only on the basis of church leaders' juridical decision, an understanding of the Church as a merely human society alongside other societies would inevitably result.

It also seems evident that sacraments must exist because of the constitution of the human person and its relational nature. Personal beings are relational; they relate themselves as far as possible to all created being and, in this way, are enabled to relate to the author of all creation. This explains why the gift of God in Christ uses a variety of relational contexts in the concrete structures of the economy of salvation, a subject discussed in Chapter 10.

The particular necessity for participation in the ecclesial form of penance, after one has sinned seriously against the known will of God, is based on the Christian conviction that the sin of a member of the Church is a sin of a member of Christ's Body. As such reconciliation with God through Christ should have an ecclesial dimension, because Christ works through his Church.

All sacraments have a christological and ecclesiological dimension. Readmission to the full life of the Church takes place through sacramental readmission, in which Christ's forgiveness is proclaimed by the representative of the Church "in the name of Jesus." In this way the penitent becomes qualified to participate in the Eucharist, of which Christ himself is the true host. One may not short-circuit the relation Church-Christ and approach the Eucharistic Christ, who invites his members to his table, without first encountering Christ as the merciful judge through a form of reconciliation with his Church. This condition obtains because the risen Lord works through the structures of his Church and, at the same time, must await the free acceptance of his gift in accord with the specific meaning of each sacrament.

The question of the necessity of active participation in the celebration of sacraments can be treated under the aspect of the social obligation of members of the Church. There is a responsibility to participate in sacramental celebrations for the benefit of the community as a whole, which may not be neglected; for this participation is a important way of preaching one's faith to others as a means of contributing to the building up of the whole community.

It should also be clear, as numerous recent writings have pointed out, that sacraments must exist to focus attention on the fact that God's saving presence is found in all situations of the lives of believers, calling for the decision of faith, and to serve as paradigms for the way in which believers should respond. Preaching in generalities does not sufficiently relate God's word to specific situations in which the claim of a response is found. Even when preaching is directed to concrete common situations of the hearers, it provides only instruction about the necessary and adequate response. However, sacramental celebrations provide the opportunity for believers to make the response itself to the human and social situations of the life of faith that are signified. Consequently they enable the subject to play out a response here and now, to make a commitment that can be expected to carry through in daily life. This consideration allows us to speak of the relative necessity of sacraments.[37] However the idea needs to be deepened.

Whether they are available to all Christians, as the opportunity presents itself (five sacraments), or to a large number (matrimony), or to some called to special ministry in the Church (orders), the sacramental celebrations supply the need of the subjects to hear the confident prayer of faith of the Church made on their behalf. At the same time, the subjects of the sacraments are granted the opportunity to make this prayer their own and so respond most appropriately to God's claims on them in the human and social situation that is represented. In this way, sacraments serve as concrete examples of how believers should prayerfully respond to God's will in any and all of the variety of individual and social situations of the daily life of faith. In this sense, it can be said that sacraments "must" exist.

Notes

1. Kasper, "Wort und Sakrament," 270-273; A. Skowronek, SAKRAMENT IN DER EVANGELISCHEN THEOLOGIE DER GEGENWART (Munich: Schöningh, 1970) 254-257.

2. Van Roo, DE SACRAMENTIS IN GENERE, 306-343.

3. Rahner understands "real symbol" as the spatial-temporal appearance and perceptibility in which a thing appearing makes itself known, and making itself known makes itself present insofar as it forms, or more precisely by forming, this appearance really distinct from itself (THE CHURCH AND THE SACRAMENTS, 37). The limitations of Rahner's concept of real symbol, as applied to sacraments, is worked out partially by X. J. Seibert, HUMANITY—PLACE OF SACRAMENT: A Contemporary Theological Specification of an Ecclesial Self-Understanding. Dissertation, Albert-Ludwigs-Universität (Freiburg im Br., 1979) 408-417. According to the author, Rahner establishes how a sacramental symbol comes to be such, but he does not follow through concerning the structure of the return to the other, that is, the being present to the other in love.

4. K. Rahner, "The Position of Christology in the Church between Exegesis and Dogmatics," THEOLOGICAL INVESTIGATIONS XI (New York: Herder, 1974) 202-203.

5. K. Rahner, "One Mediator and Many Mediations," THEOLOGICAL INVESTIGATIONS IX (New York: Herder, 1972) 176-180.

6. The Greek Fathers are careful to point out the distance which remains between the sanctified human being as image, and the divine archetype (P. Evdokimov, L'ORTHODOXIE [Paris: Delachaux & Niestlé, 1959], 93-95). The sanctified believer is described as the "human face of God," and the face of God is seen as expressed in human traits (IBID., 79).

7. E. Jüngel, "Ein Sakrament - Was ist Das?" in E. Jüngel & K. Rahner, WAS IST EIN SAKRAMENT? (Freiburg im Br.: Herder, 1971) 55-59.

8. Rahner, "One Mediator and Many Mediations, 0 183.

9. "Erwägungen zum evangelischen Sakramentsverstandnis," in WORT GOTTES UND TRADITION (Gottingen: Vandenhoeck & Ruprecht, 1964) 223; GOD AND WORD (Philadelphia: Fortress, 1967) 18.

10. Kasper, "Wort und Sakrament," 277.

11. The Fathers of the Church, appealing to Mt 28:19, generally reject the practice that obtained in some heretical sects of baptizing "in the name of Jesus" with one immersion. For example, Origen (IN ROMANOS COMMENTARII 5.8 [PG14.1039]): Basil the Great (DE SPIRITU SANCTO 12.28 [PG 32.116]); Ambrose of Milan (DE SPIRITU SANCTO 1.3,42 [PG 16.714]); Pelagius I (EP. "ADMONEMUS UT" to Bishop Gaudentius [DS 445]). However, in a letter to Archbishop Leander of Seville, Pope Gregory the Great conceded that the practice of one immersion was legitimate for the Spanish Church so as not to lend support to the Arian view that the triple immersion symbolized three distinct natures in the Trinity (Ep.1.43 [PG 77.497]). Also Pope Nicolaus, in a response to the Bulgarians, seems to judge that baptism administered in the "name of Jesus" is valid ("AD CONSULTA VESTRA," Nov. 13, 866 [DS 646]).

12. "De simoniacis," in LIBELLI DE LITE III. 255 (cited by J. Finkenzeller, DIE LEHRER VON DEN SAKRAMENTEN, 81).

13. ST III. q.60, a.4-8.

14. Council of Constance: INTERROG. HUSSITARUM (DS 1262); Council of Florence: DECRETUM PRO ARMENIS (DS 1310); Council of Trent: DECRETUM DE S. PAENITENTIA (DS 1671).

15. IV Sent. d.17, q.3, a.1, sol.2.

16. ST III. q.60, a.7, ad 1.

17. ST q. 64, a.8, ad 2.

18. ST III. q.60, a.7, ad 3.

19. The ACTA of the Council of Trent provide the evidence that the fathers did not wish to enter into the scholastic dispute about the nature of the ministerial intention. While the council affirms the need of an intention on the part of the minister (DS 1611), it leaves the way open for the theory of "external intention" (G. Rambaldi. L'OGGETTO DELL'INTENZIONE SACRAMENTALE NEI TEOLOGI DEI SECOLI XVII [Rome: Gregorian, 1944] 51).

20. The traditional Catholic teaching that an unbeliever could validly, and in the case of necessity licitly, administer baptism to an infant does not represent an exception to the rule. The unbeliever is understood to act as minister of the Church, and by his or her serious intention "to do what the Church does" serves as proxy for the community of

faith. —However the presuppositions behind this position need further investigation. It has never been convincingly demonstrated that a non-believer can serve as minister of the Church.

21. E. Kilmartin, "When is Marriage a Sacrament?" THEOLOGICAL STUDIES 34 (1973) 275-286.

22. IV Sent. d.1, q.2, a.6, sol.2, ad 3.

23. G. Barden has contributed a brief, insightful article on the subject of the linguistic aspect of gesture, and applies it to the liturgy ("The Speaking of Sacraments: Some Reflections on Ritual and Language," IRISH THEOLOGICAL QUARTERLY 40 [1973] 38-49).

24. LITURGIE - DIALOG ZWISCHEN GOTT UND MENSCH. Herausgegeben und bearbeitet von Klemens Richter (Freiburg im Br.: Herder, 1981); Theodor Maas-Ewerd, "Liturgie-Dialog zwischen Gott und Mensch: zum heutigen Liturtgieverständnis," HEILIGER DIENST 35 (1981) 181-184.

25. In the region around Antioch, at the beginning of the sixth century, there appeared the indicative passive formula: "May the servant be baptized..." The Western indicative baptismal formula, in its active form: "I baptize you..., 0 is found definitively in the eighth century. Before that time the baptismal formula was an interrogation in the faith. The minister put the threefold confession of belief in the Father, Son, and Holy Spirit to the candidate, who answered thrice: "I believe."

26. However, some patristic writers, such as Ambrose of Milan, emphasize that the words spoken by Christ at the Last Supper continue to have their consecratory power when spoken by the priest in the liturgy. Ambrose himself may have been influenced, directly or indirectly, by John Chrysostom's Homily on the Betrayal of Judas which stresses the enduring power of the words of Christ spoken at the Last Supper. For a commentary on John Chrysostom's teaching on this subject, confer E. J. Kilmartin, "John Chrysostom's Influence on Gabriel Qatraya'a Theology of Eucharistic Consecration," THEOLOGICAL STUDIES 42 (1982) 444-457.

27. SACROSANCTUM CONCILIUM, 59.

28. "Was ist ein Sakrament?" STIMMEN DER ZEIT 188 (1971) 22 (Eng. trans.: "What is a Sacrament?" WORSHIP 47 [1973] 281). This article is expanded in Rahner's contribution to E. Jüngel & K. Rahner, WAS IST EIN SAKRAMENT?

29. A. Gerken, THEOLOGIE DER EUCHARISTIE, 196-197.

30. VON DER HEILSMACHT DES WORTES. Grundzüge einer Theologie des Wortes (Munich: Max Hueber, 1966) 264-286. O. Semmelroth, "Theologische Deutung der Verkündigung des Wortes Gottes," CATHOLICA 14 (1960) 270-291; CHURCH AND SACRAMENTS (Notre Dame: Fides, 1965) 38-48.

31. VON DER HEILSMACHT DES WORTES, 280-282.

32. VON DER HEILSMACHT DES WORTES, 182.

33. VON DER HEILSMACHT DES WORTES, 286.

34. P. A. Donnelly, "St. Thomas and the Ultimate Purpose of Creation," THEOLOGICAL STUDIES 2 (1941) 53-83.

35. In his latest contribution to the theology of the sacraments, Scheffczyk rightly stresses that no work or word of God reaches its goal if it is not "given back to God," and gives God praise ("Jesus Christus—Ursakrament der Erlösung," 51ff).

36 H.-J. Schulz, "Der Grundstruktur des kirchlichen Amtes im Spiegel der Eucharistiefeier und der Ordinationsliturgie des römischen und des byzantinsichen Ritus," CATHOLICA 29 (1975) 340.

37. O. H. Pesch, "Besinnung auf die Sakramente: Historische und systematische Überlegungen und ihre pastoralen Konsequenzen," FREIBURGER ZEITSCHRIFT FÜR PHILOSOPHIE UND THEOLOGIE 18 (1971) 315.

Chapter 15

The Seven Sacraments of the Church

Sacraments belong to a category of liturgical activity in which the Church's role in the mediation of the saving grace of Christ is expressed in an explicit way. They pertain to a class of liturgical blessings tradition- ally employed by the churches of the East and West to petition God's grace in favor of individuals in special circumstances. The subjects of the blessings experience the support of the prayer of the Church, are made vividly aware of God's saving presence for them, and are en- couraged to respond fully to the claims God makes on them in the par- ticular situation in which they find themselves. One thinks, for example, of the ancient liturgical rite of coronation of a king, or the ritual incor- poration of a candidate into a religious order.[1]

Sacraments have a unique place within this type of liturgical activity. But the difference is not reducible to the fact that the sacraments are ef- ficacious signs of the offer of saving grace. All forms of liturgical bless- ing, by their very nature, have this sacramental dimension. The privileged place awarded to the traditional sacraments is based on the conviction of faith that they constitute the essence of the Church's litur- gical-sacramental activity. While other liturgical forms of celebration of the faith of the Church may come and go, sacraments are *permanent, constitutive elements of the institutional Church.* As chief rites, they originate from the same divine initiative by which the Church itself came into being, and they are the authentic, indispensable ways by which the Church expresses its nature. Since God alone, author of the Church, is also author of the sacraments of the Church, the Church makes the special claim that the mystery of salvation is always mediated in and through the sacraments. Because God wills that the sacraments be constitutive elements of the institutional Church, the Church is not at liberty to neglect to use them, much less disregard their role in the corporate life of the community of faith.

God alone, being the author of the Church, is also the author of the constitutive elements of the Church, including the sacraments. This fact of the divine institution grounds the special claim of the Church that the mystery of salvation is always mediated in and through the sacraments to properly disposed subjects. It also accounts for the Church's consciousness of the responsibility to preserve intact the essentials of the traditional forms of the sacraments, as well as for the Christian instinct that leads the faithful to participate in these celebrations of faith when they find themselves in the particular situations for which a corresponding sacrament exists.

But if the Holy Spirit inspired the Church to celebrate its faith in these special ways in times past, the same Holy Spirit continues to inspire the Church to make changes in its liturgical-sacramental practice in accord with the demands of new historical and cultural contexts. The response of the Church to this prompting of the Spirit allows us to describe the Church as collaborator, or even "coauthor," in the formulation of the traditional liturgical-sacramental rites. The idea of coauthorship does not imply that any of the sacraments, or the ritual activity employed in the celebration, are "merely ecclesiastical rites," in the sense that the Church created them solely on its own authority. What the Church does in this matter originates from the inspiration of the Holy Spirit.

The history of the corporate worship of the Church does not provide hard evidence that the celebration of all of the sacraments coincided simultaneously with the establishment of the Church, or earliest period of its existence.[2] Only after a relatively long period of time is evidence found for the employment of all the traditional seven sacraments in the communion of churches of the patristic age. Moreover, the forms of celebration of the sacraments in the traditional churches of the East and West were never completely identical. The differences were clearly determined by the influence of the variety of historical and cultural contexts of the communities of Christians.

It has always been the conviction of faith of the Eastern and Western traditions that the Church played a subordinate role in the origin of the sacraments, and in the development and changes of ritual expression. But a variety of approaches have been taken by theologians to the problem of a more precise explanation of the complementary activity of God and the Church in this aspect of the corporate life of faith. This theological question is the subject of this chapter. First the question of the initiative of God in Christ is discussed, and then the role of the Church.

I.
The Initiative of Christ

New Testament sources assign to Jesus Christ the decisive role in the institution of baptism and the Eucharist, as well as in the determination of the normative ritual forms of their celebration. The description of what Jesus did at the Last Supper is accompanied, in the Lukan version, by his command: "Do this in my memorial" (22:19). The Gospel according to Matthew closes with the instruction of the risen Lord to baptize in the name of the Trinity (28:19). At the same time the meaning and efficacy of these sacraments are grounded on the mystery of the Christ-event: the death and resurrection-glorification of Jesus. This twofold relation of Christ to baptism and Eucharist is a theme that constantly recurs in the homilies, theological treatises, and liturgical sources of the first millennium.

With the birth of systematic thelogy of the sacraments in the first part of the twelfth century, new perspectives begin to be introduced. Subsequently a more differentiated analysis was attempted that built on the gains of the previous contributions. In recent times a new approach has been taken to the theological explanation of the initiative of Christ in the matter of the origin of the sacraments, and in the various traditional liturgical forms by which they are accomplished.

A. Early Scholasticism[3]

The early scholastic theologians do not display a uniform treatment of the question of the role of Christ in the institution and liturgical forms of the sacraments. At the outset, Hugo of St. Victor worked out an admirable presentation of this theme in his salvation-history systematics. He integrated three levels of theological reflection. Contemporary theologians, on the other hand, employed one or other of these perspectives, and their teaching was repeated by their followers down through the remainder of the twelfth century. In short, reflection on the institution and formation of the rites of the sacraments in early Scholasticism was carried on at several levels that do not occur in continuous succession. Only at the term of the age of early Scholasticism, or at the threshold of the high scholastic period, do we find evidence of a return to a more comprehensive systematic exposition. This is found in the work of William of Auxerre, written between 1215 and 1229. He received, and developed, the heritage of Hugo of St. Victor, thus paving the way for the elaborations of the high scholastics.

The characteristics of these three levels of reflection can be quickly summarized.[4] At the first level, theologians do not work with a catalog of seven sacraments. This fixed enumeration had not yet become normative for all theological schools. Rather, the traditional patristic list of two major sacraments, namely, baptism and Eucharist, is the main object of theological analysis. The treatment of the theme of institution is inspired by the witness of Scripture, as well as the teaching of the Fathers. Especially the mystical piety of the early Eastern tradition exercised considerable influence. In this view, the origin of baptism and Eucharist are associated with both the word and saving work of Jesus. The testimony of Scripture concerning verbal institution was linked with the other Scriptural teaching about the grounding of sacraments on the death and resurrection of Jesus. For example, John 19:30, which states that blood and water flowed from the pierced side of Jesus on the cross, was interpreted as signifying the giving over of baptism and Eucharist to the Church. In other words, verbal institution and institution based on the personal redemptive activity of Jesus were fused into a conceptual unity. Early scholastic theologians, who followed this outlook, speak of the verbal and personal aspects as complimentary dimensions of the institution of sacraments.

At this level of theological reflection, the scriptural and patristic witness to the dignity of baptism and Eucharist was stressed. Instituted by a word of Jesus, and brought into being through the event of the Cross, they constituted the primary criteria for the understanding of the sacraments of the new covenant. Within this frame of reference the problem of the institution of orders, penance, and confirmation did not attract the attention of theologians. However, the sacrament of the sick, called "extreme unction" (*extrema unctio*), was treated marginally.

At the second level, concurrent with the first level described above, sacraments are linked more exclusively with the mystery of the person and saving work of Christ. The aspect of the verbal institution is relegated to the background. Little or no attention is given to the verbal institution of the sacraments, even in the case of baptism and Eucharist. Probably the best formulation of the central insight at this stage of reflection comes from Gilbert of Poitiers, who died as bishop of Poitiers in 1154, and his school. Here the origin (*origo*) of the major sacraments (*sacramenta maiora*)[5] is Jesus Christ himself and his saving work. In other words, sacraments derive from "the mysteries of the life of Christ" (*sacramenta [vitae] Christi*), that is to say, the stages of the saving work of Christ from the incarnation to his exaltation and his sending of the Holy Spirit from the Father. Moreover the efficacy of the sacraments is attributed to the activity of their author. Christ himself acts when the priest dispenses the major sacraments, for they communicate "the mysteries of the person of Christ the Savior" (*sacramenta [personae] Christi [salvatoris]*).

The third level of reflection coincides with the development of the ecclesiological insight that the Church is organ of salvation, an integral part of the continuing history of salvation. In this perspective the sacraments are regarded as means of salvation consigned to the Church by Christ himself. The sacraments, authoritatively dispensed by the Church on the ground of the divine commission, are explained as different ways in which the one divine plan of salvation continues to be manifested and realized. As the holy signs of the new covenant, sacraments point to the one universal Savior and, at the same time, reveal the mystery of the Church. In these celebrations of the faith, the one Church of Christ recognizes itself as the earthly body of Christ, instrument of the economy of salvation that extends from creation beyond the old covenant to Jesus Christ and his Church.

When various sectarian communities of Christians denied the divine origin or severely criticized the traditional practice of administration of some sacraments, they also brought into question the Church's understanding of itself as divinely appointed organ of salvation. Consequently, theologians were challenged to investigate the Scriptural sources that could furnish proof of the divine institution of the sacraments, as well as of the correctness of the pastoral practice by which they were administered. As a result the theme of verbal institution of the sacraments came more and more to the forefront as a proper theological question.

In the era of early scholasticism, and contemporaneous with these three levels of theological reflection, the list of seven sacraments was formulated and soon accepted by the majority of theological schools. Generally speaking, school theology divided these "major sacraments" into four groups. The division was determined by the more commonly accepted and scripturally based explanation of their origins. The sacrament of God the Creator is matrimony, and the sacraments of God the legislator are orders and penance. The sacraments of Christ are baptism and Eucharist. Confirmation and "extreme unction" are described as the sacraments of the apostles, who first employed them. However, the variety of sacraments, originating at different stages of the history of salvation, were understood to be unified in Jesus Christ, the universal Savior. In other words, they were explained as deriving their ultimate meaning from their relation to Christ, the Lord and Head of the Church.

Despite the subsequent numerous developments in the theological reflection on the meaning and efficacy of the seven sacraments, the basic insight concerning the christological aspect endured down to the sixteenth century. It furnished the grounds for the theological statement of the Council of Trent concerning the origin of the sacrament.

Trent defined the depth dimension of the Church's understanding of the sacraments as "institution by Christ, the Lord" (*institutio a Christo domino*). This confession about the origin of the seven sacraments, dispensed by the Church, points in two directions. First, it is a confession of faith that saving grace is offered in and through the administration of the sacraments. Second, and conversely, this confession is intended to bind the subjective faith of the members of the Church in the matter of the participation in the sacraments of the Church which, on her side, is grounded on the redemptive work of Christ. More precisely, the faithful are bound to participate in the sacramental celebrations of the Church, which correspond to special situations of the life of faith in which they find themselves. As members of the Body of Christ, the faithful are bound to share in the Eucharist, the sacramental source of the unity of the Church; after having sinned in such a way as to seriously rupture their relationship with the Church and so with God, they are bound to engage themselves in the celebration of the sacrament of reconciliation. Similar observations can be made about the other sacraments.

B. Modern Approaches

The definition of Trent, concerning the "institution of the sacraments by Christ the Lord" left open the question about the verbal institution by Jesus, at least in the case of some sacraments.[6] After the council, in the post-Reformation period, this latter question attracted considerable interest. The subject of the freedom of the Church to create and change elements of the "essential rites" of sacraments was hotly debated. Some theologians held that the essential rites used by the Catholic Church were instituted by Christ. Others favored a more nuanced theory, at least in the case of some sacraments, based on the history of development of the liturgies of the sacraments as well as contemporary differences between Eastern and Western forms of celebration.

Historical research has made obsolete the more rigid view concerning Christ's institution of the essential elements of all the sacramental rites. Also the opinion that the original apostolic community established the essential sacramental gestures and formulas of certain sacraments, for which Christ supplied only the signification, has been shown to lack solid historical foundation.[7] At present there is not even unanimity among Catholic scholars regarding the institution of baptism and the Lord's Supper by an explicit mandate of Jesus. The command to baptize, attributed to the risen Lord in Matt 28:19, is widely considered to be an interpretation of the will of the Lord made by the early Church.[8] The origin of the command: "Do this in my memorial," found only in the Lukan and Pauline versions of the narrative of the institution of the Eucharist, is likewise disputed.

The search for a reasonable explanation of the origin and variety of sacraments has led in two directions. Some theologians theorize that Jesus must have spoken some word, however vague, which influenced the Church, under the inspiration of the Holy Spirit, to celebrate seven sacraments.[9] Karl Rahner finds no need for such a word. The fact that

Christ instituted the Church as "basic sacrament of salvation" is, for him, sufficient ground for speaking about the institution of seven sacraments by Christ. When the Church fully actualizes itself for the sake of an individual or the community as a whole (eucharist), in fundamental situations of the life of faith, a sacrament is realized.[10]

In the last chapter, it was implied that the one necessary and sufficient basis for the christological origin of the sacraments is the Christian understanding of the role of symbol and word in the economy of salvation.[11] Sacraments are related to boundary situations, revealed by Jesus as the place of God's saving presence calling for a decision of faith. Through the sacraments the Church witnesses to what Jesus witnessed, namely, that God is to be found in the human situation and that one who knows this in faith must proclaim it. The Church therefore preaches this in the name of Jesus. It does so in a solemn way for situations that pertain to the essential structures of the institutional life of the Church, because of the instinctive awareness that the Church itself has a sacramental structure which must be continually affirmed. Thus there are the sacraments of initiation (baptism-confirmation), ordination to the permanent ministry of the Church, and the Lord's Supper. In the same way, the Church consecrates individuals entering into marriage, which is the fundamental cell of the Christian community. The Church also speaks a special word to God in favor of individuals in need of hearing the gospel message of forgiveness or undergoing the crisis of physical sickness.

On christological grounds, the central place given to the seven sacraments in the life of the Church cannot be faulted. The refusal of a traditional Reformation theology to recognize five sacraments as instituted by Christ is conditioned by a narrow theological outlook that took shape in the form of biblical literalism, neglect of ecclesiology, and a lack of sensitivity toward the sacramental nature of the whole cosmos. Gerhard Ebeling, one of a few systematic theologians of the Evangelical tradition who have attempted a new approach to the problem of the institution of sacraments by Christ, breaks with the opinion that grounds the existence of sacraments on an explicit word of Jesus. Ebeling does not think that such a word is decisive for the question of the number of sacraments.

1. Gerhard Ebeling on the Institution of Sacraments

Ebeling's theology of sacraments is developed from his understanding of the early Reformation stress on "Word alone" (*Verbo solo*), with the help of the notion of *situation*. He distinguishes a sacrament from any other form of preaching because the Word is proclaimed more emphatically by word and symbolical gesture. This happens in baptism and the Lord's Supper, which respectively symbolize Jesus' baptism at the beginning of his public ministry and the Cross where he made his total offering of life to God. The soteriological meaning of these sacraments derives from this christological source. The sacraments of baptism and Eucharist relate to the more basic situations of human existence: the being determined through birth to death, but in such a way that the coming to life is the beginning of death, and death the entrance into the true life. According to Ebeling, among the traditional sacraments only baptism and Eucharist directly represent the mystery of Christ's death and resurrection and, consequently, speak to the most basic situations of humanity. Therefore they alone deserve to be called sacraments in the strict sense.[12]

Ebeling's understanding of the concept of sacrament corresponds to some degree with what Catholic theologians sometimes call "major" sacraments. The distinction between major and minor sacraments is often made on the basis of the relative importance of sacraments for the life of the Church and the assumption that the seven sacraments are only *analogously* related to one another.[13] Also his formulation of the notion of sacrament provides a way for conservative Reformation theologians to continue to retain baptism and the Lord's Supper as authentic sacraments, despite the doubt cast on the institution of sacraments by the historical Jesus by the critical work of Reformation biblical exegetes.

There is no need to discuss further Ebeling's attempt to limit the number of sacraments to two, on the basis of significant events of Jesus' life. His thesis resonates partially with the outlook of the mystical piety of the early Eastern tradition that fuses verbal institution with that based on Jesus' personal redemptive activity. However he is obviously influenced by a traditional Reformation dogma that confesses only two sacraments. Nevertheless, it is worth noting that Ebeling implicitly recognizes at least the possibility of the initiative of the Church in the institution of baptism and Eucharist. When this is coupled with his teaching about the relation of the word of God to situation, it is difficult to understand why he would not be open to the possibility of affirming the full "sacramentality" of the other five traditional sacraments. However, an openness of this sort is conditioned by a systematic development of the full implications of the relationship between Church and sacraments, a task that Ebeling has not carried through.

II.
The Initiative of the Church

The initiative of the Church in the constitution and forms of celebration of the sacraments is displayed in two ways. The Church both singles out particular boundary situations and develops elaborate rites to announce their depth dimension. Two things can be mentioned in this connection. First, despite cultural and theological differences in the mode of celebrations of the sacraments within the several traditions of the East and West, common characteristics are found that allow for the recognition that the different rites are a proper expression of the same Christian sacraments. Second, the various Eastern and Western traditions generally recognize seven sacraments as the chief rites of the Church. Both these observations call for further comment.

On the one hand a structural analysis of the traditional sacramental rites shows that the initiative of the Church conforms to a christologically grounded concept of symbol, and not precisely to influences from other sources. However, the history of interpretation of the structure of Christian sacraments, at least in the West, demonstrates how theologians and the official magisterium overlooked the original insight that gave birth to the consistent structure. On the other hand, the almost universal affirmation of the number of the sacraments, by the traditional churches of the East and West, shows that the christologically based concept of symbol was deeply impressed in the consciousness of the Church. But, at the same time, if we again confine ourselves to the West, the history of the explanation of the catalog of *seven* sacraments provides evidence of a gradual loss of appreciation of the deeper significance of this catalog in relation to the whole economy of salvation.

We begin with the structural analysis of the sacramental rites and the interpretation of the structure in traditional Catholic theology. Afterward, the subject of the history of the origin and interpretation of the catalog of the sacraments is discussed.

A. Structural Analysis of the Sacramental Rites[14]

In general, all forms of Christian liturgy, including the sacraments, relate to that class of ritual re-enactment of social groups in which their origins are recalled and identity confirmed. Ritual activity of this type belongs to the order of practice. This means that it is not simply the expression of a desire for some possible good, but rather the affirmation of a reality that is already given. However, this reality must be continually expressed if it is to exist. But what is symbolically represented is realized only to the extent that it is already present in the relational connections between the members of the social group.

Christian sacraments belong to this order of practice. But what is realized pertains to an order that corresponds only partially to the celebrations of social groups based on limited human goals, and correspondingly limited personal relations. Christian sacraments signify a human and social reality *and* also a depth dimension that transcends the merely anthropological level. They are not intended to be the manifestation and realization of merely human relations and limited human aims. However, the twofold signification is not actualized by two ritual activities distinct from one another. The one and the same sacramental celebration signifies a human and social reality and, simultaneously, the deeper spiritual reality that is the ultimate ground of the existence of the Christian community. Consequently, we speak of two levels of signification of the one sacramental rite.

Sacraments are complex realities in which the divine and human components are intimately linked. The ritual expression of the human reality is identically the ritual expression of a divine-human reality. But there is a formal difference in the ritual expression that must be recognized. This can be described with the help of the concept of levels of signification that are intrinsically related to one another, in a relationship of mutual dependence. In other words the meaning directly signified, the denotation, connotes something else that is not perceived or known independently of the meaning that is denoted.

In the instance of Christian sacraments, when one knows what is denoted one can conclude to what is connoted, if one knows the nature of the Christian community, that is, the Body and Bride of Christ that lives through Christ in the Spirit. It is obvious that a Christian sacrament signifies some human and social reality and provides instruction as to how that reality is to be lived in the social Body of the Church. But the eyes of faith penetrate to a deeper level, perceive what is connoted. This deeper meaning is expressed by the word of faith that penetrates the whole of the liturgy of a sacrament, assuring the community's recognition of the real relation of the rite to the mystery of Christ. Moreover the very kernel of the celebration, containing an implied or explicit prayer of intercession of the Church, assures the faithful of the efficacy of the sacrament; for they know that this prayer is always joined to the eternal intercession of Christ, the High Priest.

It is extremely important, especially from the pastoral point of view, that the structure of sacramental rites be recognized. Otherwise there is a danger that they will be conceived as merely the ritual expressions of a desire for a divine gift, without immediate consequences for the practice of the life of faith. The analysis of each of the sacramental rites shows that the elements, constitutive of their framework, have a meaning found in rites of non-Christian religious societies. Taken together in the sacraments, these elements express one meaning, something social and interpersonal, located at the level of human experience. The symbolic action and word at the heart of each sacrament, as well as the surrounding liturgical rites and prayers, are chosen to afford understanding of, and prayerful commitment to, the deeper dimension of the human situation which cannot be denoted. The spiritual reality of the divine saving presence, which makes claims on the subjects of the sacraments and assures support in the living out of the human situation symbolized, is not experienced independently of the gift of the faith. Hence, it can only be connoted.

The rite of baptism, already analyzed in Chapter II, can serve as an example. It denotes incorporation into the Church, with rights and duties corresponding to the nature of the Church. It denotes entrance into the community, something that is sensibly experienced and can be lived on the human and social level. This denotation, in turn, connotes, for the eyes of faith, incorporation into the Church, the Body and Bride of Christ animated by the Spirit. While this connotation is explicitly expressed in the rite of baptism, it should not lead one to conclude that baptism first incorporates the candidate into Christ in the power of the Spirit and then, in a separate and distinct movement, into the Church, the social Body and Bride of Christ.

1. Traditional Scholastic Explanation of Levels of Signification

The history of interpretation of the levels of signification of Christian sacraments shows that Western theology eventually lost vital contact with the structure described above.[15] Nevertheless, this structure of signification was retained in the liturgical rites themselves, and in recent years has received more attention.[16]

For example, scholastic tracts on the sacrament of penance correctly emphasized the aspect of reconciliation with God. But the idea of reconciliation with the Church through the celebration of the sacrament was only marginally discussed or, at times, ignored. Moreover, when the concept of reconciliation with the Church was introduced, it was frequently explained as the effect of sacramental reconciliation with God. This understanding of the signification of the sacrament of reconciliation had the effect of fostering objections against the canonical requirement of reception of sacramental absolution from a priest after the commission of serious sin. If one is sincerely sorry for offending God, and resolved to sin no more, so the argument goes, why is it necessary to submit to absolution in the sacrament of penance? Conversely, this outlook could produce only unsatisfactory solutions in defense of the Church's requirement of the sacrament of penance after serious sin.

More recently, especially as a consequence of a debate carried on shortly after World War II, Catholic theologians are more inclined to consider penance as the sacrament which, denoting reconciliation with the Church, connotes the full reconciliation with God. Undoubtedly this understanding is correct. In the event of the celebration of the sacrament of penance, it makes no sense to speak of two reconciliations completely distinct from one another and transpiring in temporal succession. Rather full reconciliation with God comes in the form of an activity that is lived here and now at the human and social level, that is, reconciliation with the community, which implies entering more deeply into the common life of faith. However, there still exists a tendency in Catholic circles to confuse the order of sacramental signification, to the detriment of the christological and anthropological grounding of the sacrament of penance and other sacraments.

The playing off of one level of sacramental signification against the other is a weakness of the generally excellent introductions to the revised rites of the Roman liturgy. The twofold signification of the sacrament of reconciliation is explained, but not according to the relationship based on the structure of the personal communication between God and humanity in salvation history. Rather, what is ultimately signified by the sacrament of penance, reconciliation with God, is said to entail reconciliation with the Church.[17] The introduction to the rite of confirmation provides another example of the neglect of the order of the levels of signification. Here the sacrament is said to be conferred by chrismation and the formula, "Be sealed with the gift of the Holy Spirit." The prayer that precedes this kernel of the liturgy of confirmation, "All powerful God...," accompanied by a laying on of hands, is described as an "integrating rite." It is explained that this rite does not pertain to the "valid giving of the sacrament" but nevertheless is to be awarded a prominent place: "...it is to be strongly emphasized for the integrity of the rite and the fuller understanding of the sacrament."[18] Pope Paul VI's apostolic constitution, *Divinae consortium naturae*, August 15, 1971, discusses more fully the function of this latter rite, explaining that it contributes to the integrity but not to the valid administration of the sacrament.[19]

The teaching of the apostolic constitution, and instruction on the rite of confirmation, are obviously set in the context of the traditional scholastic preoccupation with a minimal, essential ritual gesture and formula that can serve to announce, and mediate, the mystery dimension of the bestowal of the Holy Spirit. However, it is noteworthy that Paul VI does not explicitly exclude the possibility that the magisterium of the Catholic Church could determine that the so-called integrating rite is sufficient for the administration of the sacrament of confirmation in the Roman liturgy.[20]

The phrase "integrating rite" is sometimes used by modern Catholic theologians to award a special importance to certain rites that contribute to the signification of the sacraments, without implying that they exercise so-called "sacramental causality." However this implication can scarcely be maintained. It makes no sense to speak of rites of the Church that contribute to the signification of a sacrament but do not effectively signify the offer of saving grace. Even in the case of the so-called essential rites of the sacraments, part of the scholastic tradition affirms that "they cause by signifying" (*sacramenta significando causant*).

Scholastic sacramental theology cannot be faulted in its teaching that the brief formula and chrismation, designated as the essential rite of confirmation, can carry the whole weight of signification when the sacrament of confirmation is conferred in cases of urgent necessity, where the possibility of completing the whole of the liturgy is excluded. However, when this essential rite is placed in the normal celebration, it does not exhaust the sacramental dimension.

The longer prayer of the rite of confirmation, accompanying the gesture of laying on of hands, is made in union with the eternal intercession of Christ for the grace of the sacrament, the gift of the Spirit. Moreover this prayer explicitly refers to the concrete human and social situation into which the candidate is being integrated. It witnesses eloquently to the levels of signification of sacramental rites and their interdependence. Finally, the gesture of laying on of the hands of the minister is a traditional sacramental gesture, symbolizing the acquisition of a new relation to the Church and participation in its deepest mystery. Looked at from the standpoint of the structural analysis of sacramental rites and the theology of liturgical prayer, this so-called integrating rite must be awarded a truly sacramental character. The Eastern Byzantine liturgy of confirmation contains this rite, employing a long prayer that is substantially identical with the one found in the Roman liturgy. It has always been considered by that liturgical tradition to be the high point of the rite that follows the water bath as the completion of Christian initiation.[21]

B. The Origin and History of the Catalog of Seven Sacraments

The initiative exercised by the Church, in the matter of celebrating specific boundary situations of the life of faith, has a christological basis. It also corresponds to the nature of the Church as sign and instrument of Christ's saving work. The Church remains true to itself only if it preaches the good news of God's saving presence in all situations, and his readiness to sustain believers in carrying out their obedience of faith.

Sacraments clearly relate to the nature of the Church. But has the Church actually made an irreversible decision to express itself only in sacramental rites included in the catalog of seven sacraments? Does this liturgical way of expression of the nature of the Church correspond to a divine decision concerning the number of the "chief rites" of the Church? What evidence do we have for excluding the possibility of the expansion of this catalog, apart from the fact that the Church has recognized only these sacraments as "instituted by Christ the Lord"?

The only possible dogmatic support for the claim that the sacraments are limited by divine law to those listed in the traditional catalog is found in the Council of Trent's solemn rejection of the proposition that "the sacraments of the new law...are more or less than seven."[22] However this condemnation cannot be interpreted to read that *only* seven sacraments pertain by divine law to the divinely ordained essence of the Church.[23] There is simply no evidence which demonstrates that this council intended to formulate an irreversible decision that would bind the Church until the end of time. It is not outside the realm of theoretical possibility that the Church could establish other sacraments for particular situations in which Christians more commonly have need of a special word of God in the form of solemn prayer and accompanying symbolic gestures.

We need not pursue this speculative question further.[24] What is more important, concerning Trent's definition, is the claim that the "chief rites" of the Church are, in fact, those included in the catalog of seven. When was this teaching formulated in an explicit manner? And what does the history of the formation and explanation of the catalog of seven sacraments tell us about the Church's understanding of these sacraments in relation to the whole economy of salvation?

1. Origin of the Catalog of Seven Sacraments

An early catalog of seven sacraments is found in the tract *De sacramentis* of Master Simon.[25] It is almost identical with that of the contemporary, anonymous *Sententiae divinitatis* (c. 1145), which is partially dependent on the work of Master Simon.[26] Shortly thereafter a variety of such catalogs appear, arranged in accord with different criteria for identifying groups. In the thirteenth century, the Catholic Church officially recognized the catalog of seven. Eastern churches also, for the most part, found little difficulty with this teaching, especially where their liturgical practice continued to correspond to their traditional liturgical books.

The arrangement of the catalog, commonly accepted by the end of the twelfth century, took this shape: baptism, confirmation, Eucharist, penance, extreme unction, orders, and matrimony. This ordering displays a certain sensitivity toward the inner-connection between the first five sacraments, ordered to the support of individual believers, and to the more "social nature" of the last two. In the first group of three, confirmation has a special connection with the rite of the water bath. The Eucharist is the completion of the whole ritual of initiation. In the celebration of the Eucharist the new member of the Church participates fully in the life of worship of the community. Penance is linked to baptism as the sacrament of the continuing manifestation of the mercy of God toward Christians who have fallen back from their commitment to the life of the Gospel and seek reconciliation. The sacrament of the sick is the last one ordered to the spiritual welfare of the individual. Orders incorporates the individual into special ministries of the Church. Matrimony is the sacrament through which the partners are supported in their lives of faith with one another, and thereby become more effective in their ministry of faith to their children and the community at large. However, the ordering of the sacraments in this final form was explained differently by theologians.

While no consensus was reached regarding the explanation of the ordering of the catalog of seven sacraments even in the thirteenth century, the catalog itself was commonly accepted during the latter part of the twelfth century. From his study of twelfth century sources, Eduard Dhanis concluded that the consensus about the number of sacraments was based on the prominence of these rites in the life of the Church.[27] While this conclusion seems reasonable, his long and detailed essay does not offer a satisfactory explanation why the sacraments are listed as seven. The list could have included more sacraments if, for example, the ministries included under order (*ordo*) were listed separately.

Augustine's description of sacrament as "sign of a sacred thing" (*sacrae rei signum*), commented on frequently at this time, does not explain the list. Also the narrower contemporary description of sacrament, that included the concept of efficacious sign of grace being offered, does not account for the limited list of holy signs.[28] The numerous theologians who did not regard the rite of matrimony or penance as efficacious sign of grace, nevertheless included them in the list of sacraments. Catalogs of rites of the Church formulated before the middle of the twelfth century do not account for the sevenfold enumeration. They were either too short or too long, with a prominence, comparable to that awarded to the list of seven, assigned only to baptism and Eucharist. Regarding the remainder of the "holy signs," apart from baptism and Eucharist, many possibilities of schematization are conceivable, none of which logically lead to the number seven.

The twelfth century formulation of the catalog of seven sacraments is probably best explained from the qualitative property attributed to the number seven, *and* the special place that the enumerated rites have in the common life of the Church. The qualitative concept of numbers, inherited from the Fathers of the Church, was a popular theme in the mystical speculation characteristic of medieval intellectual circles. It was taken for granted that the number seven is the symbol of perfection. Theologians considered this number to represent the divine unity (three persons in one God) and the unity of creation (four elements). The divine and cosmic perfection symbolized by the number seven led to its employment in the differentiated description of aspects of the life of faith, such as the seven gifts of the Holy Spirit and the seven moral virtues.[29]

Certain ecclesiastical rites, such as baptism and Eucharist, would naturally be considered to stand in a more intimate and immediate relation to the number seven, understood as symbol of perfection, as well as to the concept of sacrament, understood not only as a sign of something holy but also as sign of grace being bestowed. The choice of other rites, such as matrimony and penance, represents a problem insofar as many theologians did not consider them to be sacraments in the full sense. Probably they were chosen to fill out the sevenfold list because of their prominent place in the common life of the Church. The decision to include order (*ordo*) as such, without differentiating various orders,[30] is best explained by the limitations imposed by the number seven. The omission of other rites, such as the anointing of a king or the taking of the religious habit, may have been influenced by the requirement of the number seven as well as their less than central role in the common life of the Church.

We have no direct evidence from the scholastic writings of the twelfth century confirming the theory that the sevenfold list was influenced by the qualitative excellence of the number seven. It may be significant, in this regard, that the writings of theologians which provide the earliest lists of the sacraments do not mention the number seven itself. However, it seems probable that the list was drawn up in such a way that it might serve as a symbol for the perfection, and sacramental nature, of the whole economy of salvation.

2. The Council of Trent and the Second Vatican Council

A consideration of the qualitative concept of the number seven was not completely absent from the deliberations of the Council of Trent on the subject of the number of sacraments. The *Acta* of the council show that the theologians and fathers were concerned with the arithmetical enumeration of the sacraments. Nevertheless some theologians wished that a symbolical understanding dingdingof the number seven should be taken into account. They judged that a qualitative understanding of the number seven could be maintained while, at the same time, allowing for the arithmetical-numerical fixing of the number of sacraments at seven. Consequently, this minority group petitioned that the phrase "more or less than seven" be stricken from the proposed canon concerning the number of sacraments. It is also noteworthy that those theologians who were not opposed to the retention of "more or less" in the condemned proposition, did not exclude the qualitative understanding of the number seven.[31]

In the general congregation of the council leading up to the formulation of the canons on the sacraments, the qualitative dimension of the number seven, as applied to the sacraments, gradually faded into the background. The fathers did not accept the petition of the minority group of theologians that "more or less" be omitted from the first canon. Thus it read in part: "If anyone says that all the sacraments of the new law were not instituted by Jesus Christ, our Lord, or are more or less than seven...*anathema sit.*"[32]

However, just as "instituted by Jesus Christ, our Lord" was not intended by the council to mean that Jesus Christ instituted all the sacraments in species and number by an explicit word during his earthly life, so also the inclusion of "more or less" does not exclude the qualitative dimension of the number seven. The council did not intend to teach that Christ instituted all the sacraments during the course of his earthly ministry. This was a matter of legitimate discussion among Catholic theologians. Likewise the council did not explicitly, or implicitly, intend to eliminate the symbolical dimension of the catalog of seven sacraments. This had been shown in the conciliar debates to be also a matter of legitimate debate. At the most one can say that the catalog of seven provided a response to the Reformers' abbreviated list of sacraments, as well as a defence of the sacramental principle: The grace of God is conferred in and through the seven chief rites of the Church. In this way the canon opposed the Reformers' one-sided interpretation of the biblical principle of justification by faith, that is, justification *by fiducial faith alone.*

In the post-Tridentine period the teaching of the council about seven sacraments was narrowly interpreted in Catholic theological circles, with few exceptions. Consequently, a restricted understanding of the sacramental dimension of the economy of salvation resulted. Commentaries on the sacramental liturgies frequently related the divine saving presence exclusively, or mainly, to the "essential rites" of the sacraments, and the personal presence of Christ was discussed quite generally only with reference to the eucharist.

In this century the renewed understanding of the sacramental nature of the whole breadth of the economy of salvation has changed this way of thinking. What was known implicitly, but scarcely reflected on in depth by theologians and the magisterium of the Church, came to the forefront at Vatican II. This council affirmed the sacramental dimension of the whole economy of salvation and, as we have already seen, describes the Church itself as a "kind of sacrament." As a result of this teaching, the seven sacraments are now understood more commonly as representative of the deepest concentration of the sacramentality latent in all church activity, including preaching and other forms of liturgical celebration. Also Vatican II paid special attention to the subject of the various modes of Christ's active presence in the Church, the ground for the sacramental dimension of the activity of Church, sacrament of Christ. This important subject is treated in Chapter 17.

Notes

1. Lists of the chief rites, or "sacraments," of the Church formulated by the early Western scholastics, frequently included these two forms of liturgical blessings.

2. The sacrament of confirmation is one example. The complicated history of confirmation, as yet not completely clarified, indicates that in the third century a complete baptismal rite had developed in the West. It included a post-baptismal rite of laying on of hands by the bishops, accompanied by an anointing, and sign of the cross (APOSTOLIC TRADITION of Hippolytus 21 [B. Botte, LA TRADITION APOSTOLIQUE 44-59]). But in the ancient Syrian practice the anointing preceded the water bath (G. Winkler, "The Original Meaning and Implications of the Prebaptismal Anointing," WORSHIP 51 [1978]24-45).

3. The latest critical investigation of the teaching of early Scholasticism on the subject of institution of the sacraments by Christ is found in W. Knoch, DIE EINSETZUNG DER SAKRAMENTE DURCH CHRISTUS.

4. Knoch, DIE EINSETZUNG DER SAKRAMENTE DURCH CHRISTUS, 411-416.

5. Knoch, DIE EINSETZUNG DER SAKRAMENTE DURCH CHRISTUS, 412.

6. DECRETUM DE SACRAMENTIS, Cn 1 (DS 1601). Trent neither defined immediate institution of sacraments by Christ before his ascension, nor closed the question about the institution of some sacraments under the inspiration of the Holy Spirit. The latter theory, for example, was applied by Alexander of Hales and Bonaventure, as well as the early scholastics Hugo of St. Victor and Peter Lombard, to explain the origin of confirmation.

On the subject of the intention of the Council of Trent's definition of the institution of sacraments, confer: M. de Baets, "Quelle question le concile de Trent a éntendu trancher touchant l'institution des sacrements par le Christ, 0 REVIUE THOMISTE 14 (1906) 31-47.

7. At the time of the Council of Trent, the apostolic origin of the Roman liturgical tradition as a whole was affirmed by many. For example, the appeal was made to the authority of the early apostolic community at Rome even to defend the apostolic character of the main lines of the sixteenth century Roman liturgy of the Mass (R. Theisen, MASS LITURGY AND THE COUNCIL OF TRENT [Collegeville: St. John's University, 1965] 37-40).

8. R. Brown and others, eds., THE JEROME BIBLICAL COMMENTARY II (New Jersey: Prentice-Hall, 1968) 113-114.

9. W. Van Roo, "Reflection on Karl Rahner's 'Kirche und Sakramente'," GREGORIANUM 44 (1963) 495-498; Schillebeeckx, CHRIST, THE SACRAMENT OF THE ENCOUNTER WITH GOD, 116-118.

10. "What is a Sacrament?" 282-283; THE CHURCH AND THE SACRAMENTS, 41-74.

11. The fact that the Church uses these sacraments is not explained ONLY on this christological grounds. There must also be the NEW DIVINE INITIATIVE, the work of the Holy Spirit. The Spirit, the source of the memory of the Church, enables the community of faith to recall the life, death, and glorification of Jesus as the high point of the mystery of God's plan of salvation, and also inspires the Church to choose these ritual expressions which conform to the mystery of Christ and the mystery of the Church, Body of which Christ is Head and Bride of which Christ is the bridegroom.

12. "Erwägungen zur evangelischen Sakramentenverständnis," 225; Jüngel, "Ein Sakrament—Was ist Das?" 38-39; 59-61, also favors this position.

13. Y. Congar, "The Notion of 'Major' or 'Principle' Sacraments," CONCILIUM 31 (New York: Paulist, 1968) 21-32; Rahner, "What is a Sacrament?" 284.

14. M. Amaladoss, "Semiologie et sacrement," LA MAISON DIEU 97 (1973) 17-35, has contributed a useful analysis of the application of semiology to Christian sacraments. Semiology attempts to explain what a symbol is, how it is structured, and how it communi-

cates or symbolizes. Confer Chapter 2 for further remarks on the application of the methods of semiotics to Christian sacraments.

15. The same criticism can also be leveled at Eastern Orthodox theologians.

16. Thomas Aquinas suggested the analogy between the spiritual and natural life in order to explain the fittingness of the sacraments. He grounded the analogy on the New Testament description of baptism as birth, and Eucharist as nourishment. This approach, which supplies at least a weak relational connection between significant aspects and phases of ordinary daily life and the life of faith, eventually came to be favored by Catholic theologians. More recently, however, the ecclesiological dimension of sacramental symbolism has received more attention. E. H. Schillebeeckx, for example, discusses the psychological value of the variety of sacraments, but his basic theological explantion for the existence of seven sacraments is grounded on the nature of the Church as historical manifestation of Christ's saving work (CHRIST, THE SACRAMENT OF THE ENCOUNTER WITH GOD, 176-179).

17. THE RITE OF PENANCE (Collegeville: Liturgical Press, 1975) 5-6.

18. THE RITE OF CONFIRMATION (Washington, D.C.: USCC, 1975) 11.

19. THE RITE OF CONFIRMATION, 8.

20. L. Ligier, LA CONFIRMATION: Sens et conjonction oecuménique hier et aujourd'hui. Théologie historique 23 (Paris: Beauchesne, 1973) 29.

21. Ligier, LA CONFIRMATION, passim.

22. DS 1601.

23. Rahner, THE CHURCH AND THE SACRAMENTS, 68-71; Schillebeeckx, CHRIST, THE SACRAMENT OF THE ENCOUNTER WITH GOD, 118; 176-179.

24. As yet no convincing argument has been made for additions to the traditional catalog of seven sacraments. The attempts to interpret confirmation as a sacrament of puberty is sometimes met in the writings of so-called conservative theologians and bishops. These writers are seemingly unaware that a step in this direction would make confirmation not the completion of the rite of initiation, but an eighth sacrament.

25. Knoch, DIE EINSETZUNG DER SAKRAMENTE DURCH CHRISTUS, 177-193.

26. IBID., 294-295.

27. "Quelques anciennes formules septénaires des sacrements," REVUE D'HISTOIRE ECCLESIASTIQUE 27 (1931) 17-26.

28. Dhanis, "Quelques anciennes formules," 18; Knoch, DIE EINSETZUNG DER SAKRAMENTE DURCH CHRISTUS, passim.

29. Schupp, GLAUBE-KULTUR-SYMBOL, 154-162; Seybold, "Die Siebenzahl der Sakramente," 115.

30. It should not be assumed that the theologians commonly agreed on the variety of official ministries that merited the status of sacrament and, consequently, inclusion under ORDO in the catalog of sacraments. Many theologians were not inclined to view episcopal consecration as a sacrament in the full sense that was accorded to presbyteral ordination. On the other hand, ordination to the subdiaconate was frequently understood to be a sacrament in the strict sense. In modern times, the magisterium of the Catholic Church recognizes only the ordination rites of episcopacy, presbyterate and diaconate as sacraments.

31. Seybold, "Die Siebenzahl der Sakramente," 137.

32. DS 1601.

Chapter 16
A Short History of the Theology of Word and Sacrament

The last part of this book has focused on a central theme of the theology of worship, the chief rites of the Church. But there is another subject that merits special attention within a comprehensive, systematic exposition of Christian worship. It is a theology of preaching, of that basic activity of the Church which, while exercised in various ways within the broad scope of the life of faith, serves an indispensable function within the liturgical celebrations worthy of the name Christian.

A "liturgy of the word of God" traditionally accompanies the "liturgy of the sacraments." It includes a proclamation of Scripture; for it is inconceivable that the normative witness of Christian faith would be omitted from the solemn celebration of the faith of the Church. But the proclamation of Scripture by reading is not sufficient to meet the needs of the community of faith. In new historical and cultural situations, with their new questions and answers, the Scripture needs interpretation in order that it might provide guidance. A bridge must be built between the biblical questions and answers, and the new problems evoked in each new age. Here the authentic preaching of the word of God comes into play. Not only the reading of Scripture, but also the exposition of the written word of God is a constitutive element of the liturgy of the Church.

Chapter 14 dealt with the subject of the relationship between preaching and sacraments. There the emphasis was placed on the difference between the two basic activities of the Church. The present chapter provides the opportunity to offer a short history of theology of preaching of the word of God, and to relate it to the history of reflection on the relationship between preaching and sacraments.

The exposition begins with an outline of some basic aspects of the theology of preaching found in the New Testament. This is followed by observations on the patristic contribution to this theme. The third part recalls certain factors that,in no small measure, account for the relatively undeveloped systematic theology of the word of God in twelfth and thirteenth century scholasticism. The fourth part treats the question of the difference between the traditional Reformation and Catholic theologies of word and sacrament. The chapter concludes with an evaluation of modern theological approaches to the subject of word and sacrament, and the contribution of Vatican II.

I.
New Testament Perspectives on Theology of Preaching[1]

Because God is the ground of all reality, everything depends on him. There is no word that does not depend on the intervention of God. In this sense, it can be said that every spoken word is a word of God. But the word of God is always spoken by human beings. For example, even a word that expresses a mystical experience of God is a word about God. No matter how genuine the religious experience may be, it is the expression of the experience of creaturehood in the encounter with the transcendent ground of all being,

The people of Israel equated the Law of Moses with the word of God. But in what sense can the Law be so described? The claim made on the individual to conduct oneself humanly exists before it was formulated in the written law. It was already given with human existence. Since God is the ultimate source of human existence, the claim is God's claim.

Because it addresses human being in conscience, the claim can be formulated in a word, the Decalogue. This written law appeals to insight. Through it one experiences the unconditional demands to live true to one's own proper creaturehood. At the same time, however, this law becomes a source of added anxiety. It contributes to the deepening of that anxiety which is the root of all inhuman behavior: the anxiety to secure oneself at any price, based on the experience of human weakness.

The gospel is different from the Law. It is the self-mediation of God in a human word. Its goal is to mediate a certainty that overcomes all anxiety. According to Paul, the gospel is a word of God in the deepest sense, although it is also a human word (1 Thess 2:13). But how can the gospel, namely, Christian preaching of the Good News, be construed as word of God? The authentic gospel proclaims: Believe that you have a share in Jesus Christ's relation to the Father. The word that awakens the faith to respond to this message is the word of God: a word that God himself addresses to the hearer in such a way that the hearer is enabled to say "Thou," and really reach God in the response.

Jesus Christ is the Word of God in person. But it is through the human words and actions of Jesus that God reveals himself and draws forth the response of faith from the hearers. In brief, this activity of Jesus has its source in his obedient life. God comes near to humanity in the exercise of Jesus' obedience of faith.

Jesus' obedience unto the death of the cross is his final historical response to the God of love and, conversely, the decisive revelation of God's love for the world. The death and glorification of Jesus create the situation in which God's final word must be expressed and shared in the world though the words and signs of faith. As "word of the Cross" (1 Cor 1:18), Jesus' obedience unto death is the abiding sign that draws out the decision of faith to follow his way. It is the key to the knowledge that the way of the law, of seeking salvation through the works of the law, is folly (Gal 3:1). When the lordship of God, revealed in Jesus' obedience, is proclaimed in faith, God creates space for his coming, precisely in and through this obedience of faith. The word of faith brings what it says: "It is the power of God for salvation to everyone who has faith" (Rom 1:16). It is not merely a word about life, it is a word of Life. It frees from anxiety, self-seeking, and self-justification, and issues in self-forgetful love.

The "chosen witnesses" of the resurrection of Jesus are such on the basis of their faith, which Christ effects through his resurrection appearances. These manifestations contain the aspect of a real historical encounter with the risen Lord and, at the same time, are a saving event because of the transempirical activity of the risen Lord, present to the witnesses "in the power of the Spirit," as source of their act of faith in the abiding presence of Christ the Savior.

The content of the "office" of the chosen witnesses of the resurrection of Jesus is their obedient exercise of faith, by which they proclaim Christ's abiding, saving presence in their words and actions (Acts 3:4-16). Sent in full power, on the ground of their faith these witnesses drew others into the community of the new covenant. In the churches that succeeded the original apostolic community of Jerusalem, the stable office of leadership was held by Christians who were not "eye-witnesses" of the resurrection. As official preachers of the Christian communities they mediated the faith of the Church, derived from the apostolic witness, as their successors have done. In short, the efficacious presence of Christ, in the Spirit, in the exercise of preaching of church leaders, is a special mode of the fundamental presence of Christ, in the Spirit, by faith.[2]

The word of God, read and preached in the Church, is a word of Christ and the Church, that is, *the word of faith of the Church of which Christ, in the Spirit, is the living source.* In brief, no word of God exists in the Church that is a word of Christ and not also a word of faith of the Church. Christ does not make himself present in the Church through a word that is only his word, spoken through another. The apostles themselves understood that they were servants of the word of God. But their service consists in their obedience of faith, to which they were enabled by the risen Lord. Especially the apostle Paul makes clear that the word of God is spoken when he witnesses to his faith. In short, the word of God, that engenders faith, exists in this world in the form of a believing response to God.

This principle holds not only for preaching but also for the sacraments. The word of the sacramental rites, the "essential sacramental formula," is a confident prayer of the Church. This is the concrete way in which God announces the offer of the grace signified by the sacraments. Therefore the essential difference between the preached word and the sacramental formula lies not at the level of an essential distinction between two types of word of God, one more directly word of God than the other. Preaching is the response of faith of the preacher to his or her mission of witness to the faith of the Church. The sacramental word is the response of the faith of the community, in the form of prayer, in obedience to its responsibility as social organism of salvation with respect to the subject of the sacramental celebration.

II.
Patristic Theology of Preaching

This is not the place to offer an extended exposition of the patristic contribution to the theology of preaching or the relation of preaching to sacraments. Numerous studies are available that deal with this subject in detail. The sources of the catechetical and homiletic practice provide much valuable information for a theology of preaching. Above all, the writings of the Fathers of the East, such as Origen and John Chrysostom, and the West, among whom must be mentioned Ambrose, Augustine, Jerome, and Pope Leo I, supply many valuable insights.[3]

In general, it can be confidently stated that the Fathers of the Church commonly teach that God is actively present in the reading of Scripture and the preaching of the word of God. This conviction was supported by the experience of the effect of preaching on the hearers. But it had its basis also in the theology of preaching of the New Testament, as well as in the understanding of the consequences of the reception of the Spirit in ordination rites. Missioned through ordination for the ministry of preaching the apostolic word, the authorized preacher could count on the support of the Holy Spirit to give guidance in this task.

The relationship between preaching and sacraments was not worked out systematically by patristic writers, apart from Origen.[4] A typical Origenist saying is: "bread (drink) of the word; bread (drink) of the Eucharist." This signals a systematic approach to the modes of communication of the soul with the divine Logos. The great Alexandrian theologian uses the imagery of food and drink to argue for the relatively superior value of the word of God, spoken in the Church, in comparison to communion of the eucharistic species. His typical argument is exemplified by the following quotation:

> You who customarily are present at the divine mysteries, know how, when receiving the body of the Lord, you guard it with great care and respect, lest any particle should fall.... But if you

use such great caution...in preserving his body, how can you think it less guilty to have neglected the word of God than his body.[5]

According to Origen the verbal word is a more efficacious means of communication with the Logos than the sacrament of Christ's body and blood. This spiritualizing tendency of Origen's Eucharistic theology shows itself in two ways. First, he transfers traditional sacramental concepts to verbal realities both within and outside the ritual Eucharist. In the former case this move leads to a depreciation of the material-earthly sacramental reality, and the highlighting of the verbal presence of the Logos in the Eucharistic Prayer. In the latter instance, a "Eucharistizing" of preaching and reading of Scripture results in the enlarging of the scope of means of saving encounter with the Word of God. Second, the spiritualizing tendency consists in the internalizing of the saving encounter with Christ. In other words, preaching and Eucharistic communion first attain their fruition in the soul of the believer, led by these means to the spiritual ascent that results in union with the divine Logos.

The spiritualizing tendency of Origen, influenced by Platonic metaphysics of knowledge, an Old Testament theology of word, and the unsettled state of christological questions, does not offer a suitable starting point for a modern discussion of the relationship between word and sacrament. Nevertheless Origen's manner of theologizing supplies a model for a new systematic approach that breaks away from the narrow interests of a traditional Catholic sacramental theology, or a traditional Reformation theology of word of God.

What is clearly needed at the present time, as exemplified in the theological problem posed by the bread and drink of the word and the Eucharistic species, is a comprehensive systematic reflection on everything that Christian tradition can identify as means of encounter with the risen Lord. The vision of a theology of "communication in general" (*communicatio in genere*) that supplants the scholastic treatise on "Principles of Sacramental Theology" (*De sacramentis in genere*) presents a unique challenge to Catholic and Reformation theologians. Success in such a venture could be expected to have very positive effects not only on the liturgical life of the Catholic and Reformation churches, but also on the ecumenical relations between them.

It is worthwhile observing here that twentieth-century attempts to develop a systematic theology of word and sacrament have received support through the use of the image of the two tables in official documents of the Catholic Church. Vatican II employs the expression "table of the word" and "table of the bread" to emphasize the dignity of the word of God,[6] the two ministries of the priest,[7] and the relationship between the two parts of the Mass.[8] The imagery of two tables, already found in the fourth century,[9] is also employed by Pope John Paul II in his Holy Thursday letter of 1980, *Dominicae cenae*.[10] However, these official documents are content to accentuate the relatively greater importance of the "table of the bread of the Lord.70

III.
The Orientation of Medieval Scholasticism

While Scripture has a developed theology of the word of God, only a rudimentary theology of the sacraments is achieved. In the patristic period interest shifted to some extent in the opposite direction. Due to a number of factors attention was focused on the theology of the sacraments. Nevertheless, only in the second half of the twelfth century does a systematic theology of the sacraments appear, in an age in which the Western branch of Christianity was beginning to formulate a more explicit concept of the place of the institutional Church in society.

The movement to free the local churches from the domination of secular rulers, made possible because of the initiative of the bishop of Rome, helped to foster a clearer perception of the nature of the Church as an independent juridical entity within the broader social, political states. One byproduct of this development was a theoretical distinction between the Church conceived as institution of salvation and the Church regarded as the holy people of God united to Christ by faith and grace. This ecclesiology, never fully worked out in a systematic way, reinforced an implicit presupposition that has roots in the early Middle Ages, namely, the conviction, taken more or less for granted, that the institutional Church is the hierarchy.

This is not the place to describe all the factors that contributed to this equating of institutional Church with the hierarchy. We can only single out the theological heritage, received from the early Middle Ages, concerning the central role of the priest in the Mass, as well as the gradual reduction of the laity, in theory and practice, to the state of passive bystanders. This theology and practice certainly contributed to what later became a more clearly articulated view of the distinction between Church as institution and as the Mystical Body of Christ.

One good example of the way this emerging understanding of the social reality of the Church influenced early scholastic theology is the contribution it made to the reception of the patristic teaching about the relationship between Church and Eucharist. The authentic Augustinian tradition explained that this relationship is *reciprocal,* that is, the Eucharist makes the Church and the Church makes the Eucharist. However, early scholastics received this heritage of eucharistic ecclesiology at a time when a profound cleavage had emerged between the conception of Church as a juridical institution and as the Mystical Body of Christ. Especially in the latter half of the twelfth century, only a part of the Eucharistic ecclesiology of Augustine was retained. The role of the Eucharist in the building up of the Church loomed large in theological reflection on the meaning of participation in Holy Communion. The "reality ultimately signified and effected" by the sacrament of the body and blood of Christ, the *res et non sacramentum,* was described as the unity of the spiritual body of Christ.[11]

This one-sided view of the relationship of Eucharist to Church, in its turn, lent support to the distinction between the visible, social reality of Church, and the spiritual reality of the Church conceived as Body of Christ. The baptized, who belonged to various "states" of the Christian society, had one thing in common when they gathered in the church building for Mass: the viewing and/or receiving the consecrated host—a twofold form of integration into the spiritual Body of Christ.

Another result of the distinction between the juridical and spiritual Church was the explanation of the relation of the presiding minister and assembly of the faithful to the liturgy of the sacraments. We have alluded to the beginning of this distinction in the example of the earlier developing theology of the priest's role in the Mass. Early scholasticism supplied the explicit, and new, formulation of this relationship. Prescinding from the rudimentary beginnings of reflection on the proper ministers of the sacrament of matrimony, the presiding ordained minister was considered to be the only active subject of the other six sacraments.[12] This liturgical leader was recognized as the representative of the whole Church and, consequently, of the concrete liturgical assembly, in the ritual activity that led up to, and followed, the "essential rite" of the sacraments. The essential rite itself was conceived as the work of the presiding minister, acting as representative of Christ, the sanctifier, for the benefit of the recipients of a sacrament. Theological speculation was concerned exclusively with the descending movement of God's sanctifying activity in the accomplishment of this essential rite, except in the case of the Eucharist.

Regarding the Eucharistic celebration, early scholastics commonly taught that the priest, as representative of Christ, offers the sacrifice of Christ in the memorial of the Last Supper and serves as minister of Christ in the consecration of the bread and wine through the recitation of the account of the Last Supper. As representative of the Church, the priest offers sacrificial worship in the name of the whole Church. The universal Church was conceived as offerer of the Mass through the representative action of the priest. The gathered community is generally described as participating in the Mass through its devotion. The subject of the ritual involvement of the faithful is not commonly considered.[13]

While a systematic theology of the sacraments was formulated and richly embellished during the twelfth and thirteenth centuries, the close link between the hierarchy and the sacraments continued to develop in the way described above. As a result the sacraments were regarded as activities of Christ in the Church, but not precisely activities of the Church, except insofar as the minister who represents Christ must also be an ordained minister of the Church of Christ and have the intention "to do what the Church does" in the celebration of the sacraments.

Entrusted to the hierarchy by Christ, the sacraments were considered to be the means by which Christ himself *always* acts as sanctifier in and through his ministers. Hence they were treasured as means of sanctification without parallel, in no way dependent on the faith of the minister or of the gathered community, in so far as they are means of the offer of saving grace. The activity of the faithful in the liturgy of the sacraments had its place in the reception of the sacraments; for fruitful reception of the grace of the sacraments was considered to be dependent on the recipient's openness in faith.

Conceived as acts of Christ the sanctifier, as infallible means of the offer of saving grace from above, the sacraments could scarcely be compared to the preaching of the word of God. Nevertheless, scholastic theology did not consider that preaching was unimportant. Theologians themselves thought that their teaching was a preaching of the word of God. And their lectures were, in great part, taken up with the exegesis of Scripture. Moreover preaching to the common folk had a high priority in the consciousness of the official Church. It was encouraged as an valuable contribution to the renewal of Christian communities, as the early history of the activity of the Order of Preachers (Dominicans) and Franciscans shows. However, although preaching was recognized, in theory and practice, as a basic activity of the Church, no effort similar to that expended on the sacraments was made by twelfth and thirteenth century theologians toward the formulation of a systematic theology of preaching of the word of God. Only rudimentary theologies of preaching existed.

The problem of the relation between preaching and sacraments was not a central theme in early and high scholastic systematic theology. More generally, this topic was implied in the description of the relatively higher dignity and efficacy of the sacraments. Scholastic theology took for granted that preaching of the word of God is a means of communication and strengthening of the life of faith, a means ordained by God. However, its efficacy was rightly seen as conditioned by the content of preaching. To the extent that the preacher announces the word of God, that is, witnesses to the faith of the Church, the preaching was reckoned to be an offer of saving grace to the hearers. Nevertheless, since it could not be presumed that preaching in the Church always represents the authentic faith of the Church, this activity lacked the qualification of infallible offer of God's grace.

No such weakness could be predicated of the sacraments, dispensed by the Church through her authorized ministers. The traditional dogma of the Western Church, explicitly formulated by Augustine of Hippo and always supported by the magisterium, affirmed that the efficacy of sacraments does not depend on the personal faith, or holiness, of the individual who acts as administrator. This doctrine grounded the scholastic position that sacraments are always an authentic means of communication of the grace they signify, when administered in accord with the prescriptions of the Church; for, as such, they do not express the faith of the minister. Rather they express the faith of the Church, which is always conformed to the will of the author, namely, Christ who instituted the sacraments as a means of grace.

As regards the occurrence of a *saving event*, scholastic theology applied the same condition to the preaching of the word of God and the celebration of sacraments. The offer of grace of God results in the bestowal of that grace to the extent that the hearer of the word, or the adult recipient of the sacrament, accepts God's gift, and the consequences that flow from it, in the freedom of faith.

The scholastic manner of distinguishing the efficacy of the sacraments from that of the preaching of the word is based on a distinction between the work of the minister of Christ in the preaching of the faith of the Church, and the work of the minister of Christ in the administration of the sacraments of Christ's Church. Both activities were ordained by God. But only the sacrament, rightly administered according to the official directives of the Church, warranted the claim to be infallible sign of grace. This approach treats the relation between preaching and sacraments from the standpoint of the model of guaranteed offer of grace. It deals with the question only under the aspect of the certainty of the movement of God the sanctifier toward the hearer of the word or the recipient of the sacrament.

IV.
Traditional Reformation and Catholic Theologies of Word and Sacrament

From the thirteenth to the sixteenth century Western scholastic theology continued to maintain the orientation of high scholasticism. But with the advent of the Reformation upheaval, the problem of "word and sacrament" became a lively issue. Within Reformation churches a theology of the word of God, based on Scripture, was developed. However, it was played off against a theology of sacraments as formulated in the scholastic systematic sacramental theology of the sixteenth century.

This new theology of the word of God represents a justifiable reaction against the tendency of contemporary school theology to exaggerate the efficacy of the sacraments as objective means of grace by failing to apply rigidly the principle that the conditions for a saving event remain the same both within and outside sacramental celebrations. This is exemplified, for instance, in the thesis that the grace of a sacrament is bestowed on the unconscious subject who has the habitual disposition to receive the sacrament. But while it may be said that there were good grounds for the Reformation reaction against the popular idea, often supported unwittingly by theologians, that the sacraments are a "cheap means of grace," the Reformation alternative was frequently weakened by a reduction of the theology of the Word of God to a theology of preaching.

This option did not do justice to a theology of communication between God and humankind based on the variety of modes of communication of the faith. As a result the gestural, symbolical dimension of the sacrament received marginal treatment. This devaluation of the symbolical activity of the liturgical-sacramental rites has always been severely criticized by Catholic theologians, and rightly so. At present a number of Reformation theologians also recognize the limitations of a sacramental theology that overemphasizes the verbal dimension.

A typical traditional Reformation approach to the sacraments has the living word as the center of gravity, with the symbolical aspects on the periphery. Sacraments are conceived as constituted by the word of promise to which is added a ceremony, one instituted by Christ. The sacramental sign, in the case of baptism, is viewed as an extrinsic complement to Christ's active presence through the word. The Lord's Supper is interpreted in an analogous way. Even in the traditional high Lutheran theology of the Lord's Supper, one that stresses the objective presence of the risen Lord under the forms of bread and wine, the accent is placed on Christ's presenting his body and blood through the word to be received in a corporeal way.

Catholic theology, on the other hand, has always displayed the highest regard for the symbolical, gestural element of the sacraments. This is expressed in many ways in the manuals of scholastic sacramental theology. The lengthy discussion about what constitutes the valid remote and proximate matter of the sacramental celebrations, what water is appropriate for baptism, what oil for confirmation and the sacrament of the sick, what bread and winefor the Eucharist, etc., were considered matters of vital importance. The correct gestural action, and its proximity to the sacramental word, were not subjects to be taken lightly.

The theological point of view that grounds this preoccupation with details was based on the conviction that the ritual activity, constitutive of the sacraments, is in some sense of divine institution. Consequently, conformity to the practice of the Church is required by divine law. But there is more. This ritual activity was never brought under the category of a ceremony added to the sacramental formulas as a means to support the subjective faith of the recipients. Rather the essential ritual activity was considered to be constitutive of the sacrament itself.

According to this theology, what God in Christ announces through the sacramental word, he completes by the sacramental gesture. Both the word and gesture form a unity of signification in which God in Christ is represented as speaking and acting, or rather is speaking and acting. In short, the symbolical action constitutes the most palpable representation of what is proclaimed by the word. It completes the word by fixing the term of the word in the celebration, and conferring on the word its fullness of meaning and efficacy.

This difference between a traditional Reformation and Catholic theology of sacraments does not, however, necessarily imply a radical difference at the level of the ritual activity surrounding the essential sacramental rites or, indeed, a basically different understanding of the nature of the essential verbal formulas of the sacraments.

Some Catholic writers have explained the difference between a Reformation and Catholic theology of worship in terms of the distinction between theurgy and liturgy. Robert Bonnert, to mention one example, describes the Lutheran theology of worship as focused almost exclusively on the action of God in word and sacrament, to which corresponds the community's acceptance of the gift of grace without adding its own contribution. Catholic theology, on the other hand, is said to favor the notion of the conjoint action of God and the liturgical assembly.[14]

This way of differentiating traditional Lutheran and Catholic theologies of worship is open to question. It is not clear whether a really deep difference exists between them concerning the community's engagement in the expression of its faith during the ritual activity surrounding the essential sacramental rites. Both theologies award to the community the role of really worshipping God "in spirit and truth," made possible by the gift of faith. Only in the case of the Eucharistic Liturgy is the anabatic movement interpreted differently; for Catholic theology insists on the traditional belief of a sacramental, real offering of the sacrifice of the Cross by the community in, with, and through Christ.

As regards the so-called essential sacramental rites, both Lutheran and Catholic traditions have favored an exclusively katabatic orientation. In both theologies, for example, the sacramental word of baptism is interpreted as a word from God to the candidate. The narrative of the institution of the Eucharist is explained as a word of Christ spoken through the priest or minister, in virtue of which the bread and wine "become" (Catholic), or simply "are" (Lutheran), the sacrament of the body and blood of Jesus Christ.[15]

V.
Modern Approaches to Word and Sacrament

In the twentieth century numerous theologians have attempted to deepen the understanding of the distinction, and relation, between word and sacrament. A typical recent proposal, clearly reminiscent of the old scholastic approach, employs the model of sacrament, conceived as guaranteed offer of saving grace. This suggestion has the merit of underscoring the difference between preaching and sacraments, insofar as fallible or infallible offer of grace. But it labors under the disadvantage of seeming to imply that the authentic preaching of the word is a deficient mode of sacrament.

Dissatisfied with this solution, other theologians have introduced the model of word of God. Karl Rahner, as was already mentioned, defines the sacraments as the most condensed and expressive form of the word of God, spoken by the Church itself in favor of believers in particular boundary situations of the common life of faith.[16] This explanation has the advantage of showing that word and sacrament, the preaching of the word and the chief rites of the Church, are not two completely different ways of the divine mediation of salvation, but rather complimentary ways of actualizing the faith of the Church. It has become the preferred explanation of many Catholic theologians.[17] Nevertheless, it is far from satisfactory.

The weakness of the above attempt to differentiate and relate word and sacrament, beginning from a theology of word, derives from two sources. First, "sacramental word" is discussed exclusively under the katabatic aspect. Second, while some sacraments have only a verbal dimension, namely, penance and matrimony, other sacraments include a symbolic gesture such as laying on of hands (ordination) or a gesture that includes the use of material elements (water, oil, bread and wine). This aspect of sacramental rites is not adequately treated.

We have already discussed the peculiar nature of the sacramental word in Chapter 14. Here it was shown that this word has an epicletic, or petitionary prayer, character. Karl Rahner's explanation does not reckon with the implications of this trait. Furthermore, the verbal dimension, in the identification of the formal difference between preaching and sacraments, is emphasized to the detriment of the gestural element that is an essential ingredient of some sacramental rites. In other words, there is a tendency toward encouraging the imbalance that is characteristic of a traditional Reformation theology of sacraments.

VI.
Vatican II on Word and Sacrament

Vatican II's most important teaching on the theology of the word is found in the Sacrosanctum concilium and the Dogmatic Constitution on Divine Revelation (*Dei Verbum*). It can be summarized as follows: The content of the service of the word is the history of salvation; the proper actor in the preaching of the word of God is God himself; God is present in his word, and in the minister of his word; the word of God has the power to communicate salvation. This teaching of the council underscores the sacramental quality of the word of God. However the emphasis of the council falls on the sacraments as the fullest expression of the divine activity in salvation history after the incarnation.

Vatican II's constitutions on the liturgy and revelation explain the relationship between word and sacrament as follows. First of all, the frame of reference is God's way of acting in the history of the chosen people of the old covenant. God's deeds are given a certain priority. They manifest and confirm God's word, while his word proclaims his deeds and clarifies their mystery.[18] Jesus Christ conforms to this structure, completing his mission by his "words and deeds...especially by his death and...resurrection...sending of the Spirit."[19] Second, the presentation of word and sacrament is orientated by this view of salvation history. Christ's presence in the Eucharist and other sacraments is given priority over his presence in the liturgical reading of Scripture.[20] The preaching of the Gospel is said to prepare the faithful for the sacraments.[21] What the word announces is made present in and through the sacramental, symbolic actions.[22]

The teaching of the council concerning the Catholic understanding of word and sacrament can be formulated in two propositions. First, word and action are complimentary aspects of the one unique activity of God in salvation history. Second, the structure of God's action in salvation history is maintained in the verbal and gestural elements of the sacramental celebrations.

According to this viewpoint, what God announces by his word in salvation history is completed by what he does in and through events of history. In the present situation of salvation history, the word and action of God are mediated by the Church, the special organ of salvation. This mediation happens in the most expressive way in the sacraments. These ritual celebrations of the faith both announce God's saving action and represent it by symbolic gestures.

Vatican II's explicit teaching on the subject of the relationship between word and sacrament scarcely transcends the traditional point of view that differentiates the two on the basis of the quality and expressiveness of the katabatic movement. However, when one introduces the implications of the dialogical character of the liturgy of the sacraments, espoused by *Sacrosanctum concilium*, a new dimension is added. In this constitutions's description of the liturgy a distinction is avoided between liturgy and theurgy, between the katabatic and anabatic movements, at the level of the ritual, visible celebrations of the faith. The liturgy, as described in this constitution, is essentially a dialogue between God and community in which the ritual celebration appears as the response of faith to the hidden word of God experienced at the depth of the life of faith. This opens the way to the understanding of the sacramental word of the essential rites of the sacrament as epicletic, a prayer of the Church, and the inclusion of the sacramental gesture into this upward movement.

Conclusion

I. From the foregoing considerations, we can formulate the difference and relation between preaching and sacraments in this way: Sacraments are distinguished from preaching the word by reason of the epicletic nature; by the complimentary aspects of word and symbolic gesture in the case of five sacraments, which corresponds more fully to the way God acts in salvation history; and, finally, by what they announce, on the ground of divine institution, in favor of individuals in specific situations of the common life of faith.

II. Having established the distinction between preaching and sacraments, between preaching and the sacramental word, that formulates the meaning of each sacrament, there still remains the task of developing a comprehensive, systematic theology of the preaching of the word of God.

In the event of preaching, which takes place in numberless ways, there is a personal encounter with God who claims the hearer in one's concrete historical situation. The word-event presupposes that someone is present who can hear and respond, and a real-life situation in which the word can be heard and answered. God is the speaker, addressing the hearer in such a way that he can be heard and his message received. This address and response is made possible because God's word comes in the form of the expression of the faith of the Church.

In the foreground of this theological concept of word of God is the theme of the *personal, active presence* of God in the event of the preaching of the word of God. Believers, sharing in the faith of the Church, are drawn into the sphere of this saving presence, share in a saving event. Consequently, the theme of mediation of salvation is included in this theology of the word of God. But it is a secondary consideration; for everywhere, in all situations in which God mediates self, salvation is mediated.

As a consequence of the teaching of Vatican II on the subject of word of God, Catholic theology has been given a special mission to communicate an awareness of the profound nature of the preaching of the word and its indispensable role in the whole of the life of faith. Therefore the task of working out a comprehensive theology of the saving presence of God in the Church includes the unfolding of a theology of the event of preaching in all its manifold possibilities. Post-conciliar Roman documents have also shown the way to such a theology by listing the presence of God in Christ in preaching among the modes of the presence of Christ in the basic activity of the Church.

III. Vatican II contributed a more balanced approach to preaching and sacramental celebrations, two basic ways in which the common life of the faith is expressed and realized. However the council has certainly not said the last word on this subject.

Notes

1. A brief article by P. Knauer furnishes the structure of this exposition ("Was heisst Wort Gottes," GEIST UND LEBEN 48 [1975] 6-17.

2. The faith of the Church is also mediated by the witness of all believers. No special efficacy can be attributed, a priori, to the preaching of church leaders. One can only affirm that they have received the Spirit in ordination as the pledge of support in their ministry of preaching, to the extent they are open to his inspirations.

3. F. Schnitzler, "Theologie des Wortes Gottes,170 TRIERER THEOLOGISCHE ZEITSCHRIFT 88 (1979) 157-160, has contributed a valuable list of studies dealing with the teaching of these Fathers on the subject of preaching the word of God.

4. L. Lies has shown how Origen's systematic theology of word and Eucharist can contribute significantly to a modern theology, both to stimulate reflection and to provide criticism (WORT UND EUCHARISTIE BEI ORIGENES: Zur Spiritualisierungstendenz des Eucharistieverständnis. Innsbrucker Theologische Studien I [Innsbruck: Tyrolia, 1978].

5. Hom. in Exod 13.3 (GCS 29.264).

6. DEI VERBUM, 21.

7. PRESBYTERORUM ORDINIS, 18.

8. SACROSANCTUM CONCILIUM, 48 and 51.

9. Hilary of Poitier, TRACTATUS IN PS 127.10 (CSEL XXII, 635): "Mensa enim domini...mensa lectionum dominicarum."

10. "The Mystery and Worship of the Most Holy Eucharist," nos. 10-11. Confer E.J. Kilmartin, CHURCH, EUCHARIST AND PRIESTHOOD (New York: Paulist, 1981) 43-47 (commentary); 84-90 (text).

11. G. Macy supplies representative texts of early scholastics who underscore the "ecclesiastical" or corporate aspect of sacramental communion (THE THEOLOGIES OF THE EUCHARIST IN THE EARLY SCHOLASTIC PERIOD: A STUDY OF THE SALVIFIC FUNCTION OF THE SACRAMENT ACCORDING TO THE THEOLOGIANS 1080-1220 [Oxford: Clarendon/Oxford University, 1984]).

12. The one exception was emergency baptism. According to traditional teaching and practice, anyone can serve as minister of this sacrament in cases of extreme necessity.

13. Among the early scholastics who do not limit the ritual involvement to the official representatives of the Church can be listed Odo of Cambrai (d.1113), EXPOSITIO IN CANONEM MISSAE; Rupert of Deutz (d.1129), DE DIVINIS OFFICIIS; Stephen of Autun (d.1189), TRACTATUS DE SACRAMENTO ALTARIS. Confer: M. Schaefer, TWELFTH CENTURY LATIN COMMENTARIES ON THE MASS: Christological and Ecclesiological Dimensions. Dissertation, University of Notre Dame (Notre Dame, Indiana, 1983), 32-71 (Odo of Cambrai), 72-120 (Rupert of Deutz), 334-359 (Stephen of Autun).

14. "Parole et sacrement en perspective luthérienne et catholique," IRENIKON 45 (1972) 22-50.

15. Lutheran theology has always had difficulty with the notion of the "conversion" of the bread and wine into the body and blood of Christ. But while the theological concept of consubstantiation, or the coexistence of the bread and wine with the risen Lord, has been employed against radical Reformation theologies that reduce the Lord's Supper to a mere memorial, generally Lutheran theologians have avoided such speculation.

16. "What is a Sacrament?"

17. F. Schnitzler, "Theologie des Wortes Gottes," reviews current literature on the theology of word of God. He concludes, with W. Kasper and others, that sacraments are best described as the most concentrated form of the word of God, spoken by the Church in favor of individuals in concrete situations of the life of faith (154).

18. DEI VERBUM, 2.

19. DEI VERBUM, 4.

20. SACROSANCTUM CONCILIUM, 7.

21. SACROSANCTUM CONCILIUM 9.

22. SACROSANCTUM CONCILIUM, 7.

Chapter 17

The Modes of Christ's

Presence in the Liturgy

New Testament sources locate the risen Lord at the right hand of God. A solemn confession of this aspect of the implications of the glorification of Jesus is found in Revelation and the Epistle to the Hebrews. The former source describes the heavenly liturgy already in progress; the latter speaks of Jesus' investiture as High Priest of the new covenant, associated with his entrance into the heavenly sanctuary. The expression "God's right hand" is also used to convey the idea that the risen Lord rules all history, that he is present to the world in power (Acts 2:33-36; Col 1:15-20). Alongside the affirmation of Christ's cosmic presence and nearness to all the affairs of humanity, the New Testament also singles out a special presence with, and even in, believers. The apostle Paul offers profound observations on the "mystery of Christ in you" (Col 1:27), which he associates with the personal presence of Christ in the community of believers as such, and their various activities.

The personal presence of Christ in all the basic activities of the Church, carried out by individual members and the community as such, is a fundamental belief of all Christian traditions. But the christological dimension of the preaching of the word of God by the official ministry of leadership, and the liturgical celebrations of the faith of the Church, have always been given special consideration.

In Chapter 16, it was observed that scholastic theology did not work out a systematic treatment of word and sacrament. Consequently, this school theology provides no ordered presentation of the relationship between Christ's presence in preaching and sacraments that could merit the qualification "systematic." In fact, during the period of the emergence of systematic theology in the West, and in the centuries following down to modern times, Catholic school theology concentrated on the mystery of Christ's Eucharistic presence. This aspect of the active presence of Christ, offering his once-for-all sacrifice to the Father in and through the Eucharistic celebration of the Church, was discussed from a variety of viewpoints. On the other hand, the somatic presence of Christ, under the forms of Eucharistic bread and wine, was explained in a more uniform way, with the help of the concept of change of the "substance" of bread and wine into the body and blood of Christ.

The scholastic doctrine of "transubstantiation" that finally took hold and was appropriated by the magisterium in the thirteenth century, is the product of over a century of theological reflection, occasioned by the teaching of Berengarius of Tours. This eleventh century theologian seemed to reduce the visible sacrament of the body and blood of Christ to the level of an external sign that points to the invisible, spiritual union of the recipient with Christ. At any rate, this was the judgment of contemporaries. The controversy occasioned by his writings initiated a long process of profound theological analysis. A similar crisis arose in the sixteenth century, when some Reformation theologians challenged the scriptural basis of the Catholic belief that a substantial real presence of the risen Lord, under the forms of bread and wine, is brought about by the change of the substance of the material elements. The Catholic reaction to this denial of a cardinal aspect of traditional Eucharistic faith resulted in a renewed effort to deepen the understanding of this mode of Christ's real presence in the liturgy.

Under the influence of modern biblical exegesis, systematic theology, and, above all, liturgical studies, Catholic theology has broadened its treatment of the subject of Christ's presence in the Church. During the last fifty years, stimulated by earlier contributions of Odo Casel, and the lively exchanges provoked by them, Catholic theologians have begun to rethink the neglected theme of the manifold modes of Christ's presence in the whole scope of the life of faith. In the post-Vatican II period, this has led to the search for a key to the systematic ordering of the modes of Christ's presence in the Church's liturgy.

The theme of this chapter is the systematic ordering of the modes of Christ's presence in the liturgy. A convenient starting point is provided by the official Catholic teaching on the subject, as it developed from the time of Pope Pius XII, through Vatican II, to the modern post-conciliar period. From the background of a critical assessment of this teaching, a systematic approach to the problem is suggested.

I.
Official Catholic Teaching on the Modes of Christ's Liturgical Presence

Pope Pius XII's encyclical letter, *Mystici corporis,* alluded briefly to the mystery of Christ's activity in the liturgy: "It is he who baptizes, offers, sacrifices through the Church."[1] Four years later, his encyclical letter *Mediator Dei* provided the occasion for a further comment on the subject.

A. Mediator Dei

Pius XII's major contribution to the theology and practice of the liturgy begins with a reference to 1 Tim 2:5, a text traditionally employed to express the twofold direction of priestly, prophetic, and kingly work of Christ, namely, that of sanctifier of humanity and High Priest of the worship acceptable to God. The one Mediator between God and humankind

> undertook the mission which was to endow humankind with the rich blessings of supernatural grace...and...gave himself...in prayer and sacrifice to the task of saving souls, even to the point of offering himself...a victim unspotted unto God....[2]

In a second step, the Church's ministerial role in the twofold mediation of Christ is introduced, and it is especially related to the liturgy:

> ...the Church prolongs the priestly mission of Jesus Christ mainly by means of the sacred liturgy. She does this, in the first place, at the altar, where the sacrifice of the Cross is represented....She does it next by means of the sacraments...through which men are made partakers of supernatural life.[3]

This efficacy of this activity of the Church derives from the abiding presence of Christ in the whole scope of the liturgical activity: "Together with the Church the divine Founder is present in every liturgical action."[4]

Building on these premises, the encyclical formulates a kind of definition of the essence of liturgy:

> The sacred liturgy is, consequently (*igitur*), the public worship which our Redeemer as Head of the Church renders to the Father, as well as the worship which the community of the faithful renders to its Founder, and through him to the heavenly Father. [5]

Contrary to the premises previous established, the encyclical defines the liturgy only in terms of the anabatic aspect. However, this narrow outlook corresponds to the more general explanation of the role of worship in human life, based on the relation of creature to Creator. At the outset of the first part of the body of the encyclical that deals with the nature, source, and development of the liturgy, liturgy is situated under the category of the exercise of the virtue of religion:

> But man turns properly to God when he acknowledges his supreme majesty and supreme authority...when he accords, in short, due worship to the one true God by practicing the virtue of religion.

This idea is prolonged later on:

> The worship rendered by the Church to God must be, in its entirety, interior as well as exterior. It is exterior because the nature of man as a composite of body and soul requires it to be so....But the chief element of divine worship must be interior. For one must always live in Christ,...so that in him, with him and through him the heavenly Father may be daily glorified.[6]

In this perspective the liturgical prayers and rites, surrounding the essential sacramental formulas and symbolical actions, represent the upward movement of worship of God. The kernel of the Eucharistic celebration represents both the ascending and descending movements of liturgical sacramental rites: the offering of the sacrifice of Christ to God through the ministry of the priest, and the consecration of the bread and wine by which the earthly elements are changed into the body and blood of Christ. Otherwise, the essential sacramental rites are conceived as the katabatic component of sacramental celebrations: "...the sacraments...through which men are made partakers of supernatural life."

Also following the lead of scholastic theology, Pius XII identifies the direct, active subject of the liturgy with those who are officially designated for this ministry. For example, he explains that the people offer the sacrifice of the Mass "through the hands of the priest," through the official minister of the Church who presides at the celebration.[7] Also the proper subjects of the divine office are identified as those who have been officially authorized for this service:

> The divine office is the prayer of the Mystical Body of Jesus Christ, offered to God in the name and on behalf of all Christians, when recited by priests and other ministers of the Church, and by religious who are deputed by the Church for this.[8]

However an excessively clerical view of the active subject of liturgy is overcome to some extent, because the idea of the laity's active sharing in the liturgical rites is included: By reason of baptism, "they are appointed to give worship to God. Thus they participate, according to their condition, in the priesthood of Christ."[9]

Where Christ's liturgical presence is discussed, it is associated with all liturgical activity: "Together with the Church, her divine Founder is present in all liturgical activity." The principal modes of this presence are listed as follows:

> Christ is present in the august sacrifice of the altar, both in the person of his minister and above all under the Eucharistic species; he is present in the sacraments by his power, which he infuses in them as ready instruments of sanctification; he is present, finally, in the prayer of praise and petition directed to God, according to that saying: "For, where there are two or three gathered in my name, there I am in the midst of them" (Mt 18:20).[10]

B. Vatican II's Constitution on the Sacred Liturgy

Sacrosanctum concilium (7.1) integrates the teaching of *Mediator Dei* into its presentation of the modes of Christ's liturgical presence. But the approved text is the result of much debate and differs considerably from the initial project of the Preparatory Commission charged with the development of a schema on the liturgy.

1. Project I

The initial project of April 1961 begins with the christological foundation of liturgy. Like *Mediator Dei*, the mystery of the liturgy is identified with the twofold priestly role of Christ, Mediator between God and humankind. But the activity of Christ, both as sanctifier and High Priest, determines the concept of liturgy that guided the commission's deliberations. As a result, the project describes the liturgy as a dialogue between God and the community, one initiated by God's sanctifying action in Christ that grounds the response of praise and thanksgiving of the community in, with, and through Christ. While the dialogical aspect of liturgy is not absent from the encyclical, it is only marginally treated. As we have already seen, it does not influence the definition of liturgy.

The first project omits a detailed list of modes of Christ's presence in the various components of liturgical rites. Rather it offers this more general statement:

> Hence in all liturgical action Christ is present who speaks to us, carries on this same work of salvation that he accomplished during his earthly life, and continually offers praise to God the Father. [11]

This description places the katabatic aspect (sanctification) before the anabatic (glorification). It corresponds to the dialogue structure of liturgy in which the action of God precedes the response of the faithful. From the standpoint of Reformation theology, one could say that the cardinal doctrine of justification by faith determines the presentation of the modes of Christ's liturgical presence. In other words, corresponding to the genetic process, the sanctifying action of God is given first place before the primarily intentional, anabatic movement of the worshipping community's response. Consequently the anabatic aspect of the liturgy is seen in a new light. It cannot be correctly described as act of the virtue of religion, because the gift of piety and the divine virtues codetermine this movement from the believers to God. [12]

2. Project II

The second project of August 1961, formulated as a result of numerous suggestions made to improve the first one, also works with the dialogical concept of liturgy. But the presentation of the modes of Christ's presence is more detailed, and closely parallels that of *Mediator Dei*. Following the affirmation of the personal presence of Christ "in the Church," this list of liturgical modes of his presence follows:[13]

> For he, he himself, is in the Church "in the all holy sacrifice of the altar,"[14] "the same one now offering the sacrifice through the ministry of the priest, who offered himself then on the cross,"[15] and offers together with himself the Church,[16] and unites her to himself as associate in his priesthood. "He is in the sacraments by his power...."[17] Finally, he is "in the praise and supplication directed to God."[18]

Here the list of modes of presence of Christ moves from the anabatic to the katabatic, and back to the anabatic. It is not determined by the dialogical, genetic structure of the liturgy in which God's initiative comes before the response of the community. Neither does the list correspond to the sequence of the ritual activities of the liturgy. Rather it is determined by the relative dignity of the various modes of Christ's presence, namely, Eucharist, sacraments, divine office.

3. Projects III & IV; Schemas I & II

The third and fourth projects (October 1961; November 1961) and the first and second schemas (January 1962; July 1962) state the fact of Christ's presence in the liturgy in different ways: "Christ...is present in the sacred liturgy" (Project III);[19] "Christ always stands with his Church...in liturgical actions" (Project IV);[20] "Christ is always present to his Church...in the liturgical actions" (Schemas I & II).[21] Immediately after these introductions to the theme of Christ's liturgical presence, Mt 18: 20 is cited as a scriptural basis.

The list of modes of Christ's active presence is the same in all four documents: reading of Scripture (Schema II adds: and explanation of scriptural text); prayer of praise of the Father; sacraments; sacrifice of the Mass. This ordering reflects even more clearly than Project I the genetic process (sanctification-glorification) and dialogical structure of liturgy.

No reference is made in any of these four documents to the somatic presence of Christ in the Eucharistic elements. This exclusion seems to have been motivated by the fact that they deal exclusively with Christ's liturgical activity. However, the idea that Christ gives himself to us and we receive Christ's body and blood in our hands from his hands, is part of the old Western, as well as Eastern, patristic tradition. This early Eucharistic theology requires that Christ's activity in the distribution of the bread and cup be singled out, and emphasized, in a formal discussion of the modes of Christ's active liturgical presence.[22]

4. Sacrosanctum Concilium 7.1

The approved text of the *Constitution on the Sacred Liturgy* dealing with the modes of Christ's liturgical presence is an adaptation of Project II. Consequently, it resembles the presentation of *Mediator Dei*. *Sacrosanctum concilium* 7.1 differs from both these sources, apart from minor changes, by the insertion of a reference to Christ's presence in the reading of Scripture before that of his presence in the official prayer of the Divine Office.

By adopting *Mediator Dei*'s ordering of the list of modes of Christ's liturgical presence, *Sacrosanctum concilium* 7.1 acknowledges the relatively higher dignity of the eucharistic presence, and avoids the arrangement that reflects the genetic process and dialogical structure of liturgy. It is also noteworthy in this regard that *Sacrosanctum concilium* 7.2 maintains the orientation of *Mediator Dei*'s definition of liturgy. Here it is said that in the liturgy "by which God...is glorified, and men sanctified, Christ always associates the Church, his Spouse, who invokes her Lord and through him offers worship to the eternal Father." In this pericope, the genetic process, in which *sanctification comes before glorification*, is not described. But this is not characteristic of the constitution. The dialogical structure of liturgy is overlooked in *Sacrosanctum concilium* 47 and 112. Otherwise, the ordering of the divine and human components of liturgy places God's initiative (sanctification) before the community's response (glorification).[23]

Conclusion

a. Projects I, III, IV and Schemas I, II follow the structure of the sequence of the rites of liturgical-sacramental celebrations: The reading of Scripture, and celebration of the sacraments, are set in the context of the Church's response of worship. Project I refers to more general components of liturgy, insofar as they affirm the dialogical structure of Christ's activity as *sanctifier and glorifier*. Projects III/IV and Schemas I/II distinguish more clearly between the predominantly katabatic and anabatic elements of liturgy and, consequently, between Christ's work of sanctification and glorification.

b. *Mediator Dei*, Project II, and *Sacrosanctum concilium* 7.1 list Christ's modes of presence in accord with the relative dignity of the various elements of the liturgy. The Eucharistic presence is mentioned first, and the order of the two essential dimensions of the Eucharist is determined by the dependence of the permanent sacrament of the body and blood of Christ on the representation of the sacrifice of Christ. Project II omits mention of the somatic presence of Christ in the Eucharistic elements, for it is concerned exclusively with Christ's modes of active presence. The lists of *Mediator Dei and Sacrosanctum concilium* 7.1 are intended to include all the most important modes of Christ's personal liturgical presence. Consequently, they mention the somatic real presence in the Eucharistic bread and wine. The order of dignity of the modes of Christ's presence accounts for the placing of sacraments and Divine Office after the Eucharist. For the same reason, the constitution lists the reading of Scripture before the Divine Office.

The sequence of modes of Christ's presence in *Mediator Dei*, Project II, and *Sacrosanctum concilium* 7.1 corresponds partially to the ritual structure of sacramental celebrations in which the prayer of the Church surrounds the essential sacramental action. This ordering also corresponds to the scholastic outlook in which the essential sacramental rites are understood to represent the descending movement from God to the recipient.

c. All the descriptions of the modes of Christ's liturgical presence which we have considered, labor under the difficulty of attempting to distinguish the katabatic and anabatic dimensions of liturgy by associating one or other aspect with specific ritual activity. While it is perfectly correct to say that the different elements of liturgical-sacramental celebrations have either a predominantly anabatic or katabatic orientation, all such activity always involves both aspects.

Looked at from the viewpoint of the genetic process or the dialogical structure of worship, God's sanctifying activity, through Christ in the Spirit, grounds the response of the worshipping community. The response, expressed liturgically, is the corporeal expression of the interior acceptance of the offer of grace. The aspects of sanctification and glorification pertain to all liturgical activity and must be thought through together in their mutual relationship of dependence when the attempt is made to deepen the understanding of the modes of Christ's liturgical presence. Even the "substantial" presence of Christ in the Eucharistic elements cannot be discussed only from perspective of the katabatic dimension of the economy of salvation. Christ's presence "for us as the food and drink of eternal life" cannot be adequately understood without introducing the notion of the self-offering of Jesus to the Father, represented through the solemn Eucharistic Prayer in which the community expresses its own worship. Christ's offering of himself to believers in Holy Communion is also an act of worship of the Father; for this movement toward the communicants is intended to draw them into spiritual union with himself, in the power of the Spirit, so that they will love the Father with the love of daughters and sons in the one Son.

d. The basic differences in the ordering of the modes of Christ's liturgical presence in Roman documents from *Mediator Dei* to *Sacrosanctum concilium* are determined by either a theological understanding of the nature of liturgy, or by the relatively higher dignity awarded in tradition to the Eucharist and other chief rites of the Church over the merely verbal elements of liturgical prayer and reading or explanation of the Scripture. The predominantly katabatic or anabatic components of liturgy are listed in Projects I, III, IV and Schemas I, II in such a way that they call attention to the nature of the liturgical act, its genetic-dialogical structure. The list of components of the liturgy found in *Mediator Dei*, Project II, and *Sacrosanctum concilium* 7.1, is determined by the traditional order of dignity. The arrangement is not influenced by a theological understanding of the nature of liturgy. But the arrangement corresponds to a theological conception in which liturgy as such is viewed as having an anabatic orientation, while essential sacramental rites a more or less exclusively katabatic one.

C. The Post-Conciliar Documents

The most important post-conciliar Roman documents that take up the theme of Christ's modes of liturgical presence generally supply modified versions of the presentation of *Sacrosanctum concilium* 7.1, and sometimes include additions. The longest contribution to the topic of Christ's presence in the Church is found in Pope Paul VI's encyclical letter *Mysterium fidei*, September 3, 1965. His list begins with an enumeration of various modes of Christ's active presence. They include the liturgical prayer of the Church, which the encyclical supports by introducing Mt 18:20, and the works of witness of faith and the service of love—all basic activities of the Church. In addition, Paul VI enumerates a list of modes of presence of Christ that correspond to fundamental tasks of the hierarchy, namely, preaching, governing, and the priestly functions: offering the sacrifice of the Mass and administration of the sacraments. Special attention is given to Christ's real presence under the forms of the Eucharistic bread and wine, the main theme of this encyclical letter.[24]

The Instruction on Worship of the Eucharistic Mystery, May 25, 1967,[25] The General Instruction of the Roman Mass of Pope Paul VI,[26] and the instruction of the Roman Ritual "Concerning Communion and the Worship of the Eucharistic Mystery"[27] are mainly concerned with Christ's eucharistic presence. The General Instruction on the Liturgy of the Hours also provides a brief catalog of Christ's modes of liturgical presence. [28]

All these documents begin their lists with the active presence of Christ in the community as such. The General Instruction on the Liturgy of the Hours, art. 13, is the only one that refers to the pneumatological dimension of Christ's presence. Here we read that Christ exercises his work of redemption "in the Holy Spirit through the Church." After this statement, there follows a modified list of modes of Christ's presence that corresponds to that of *Mediator Dei*: Eucharist, sacraments, Divine Office. In the latter connection, Christ is said to be present when the community gathers, when the word is proclaimed, and when the Church prays and sings.

The next few pages of this chapter offer schematic outlines that summarize and compare, in parallel columns, the different approaches of Roman documents to the modes of Christ's liturgical presence. The first schema deals with documents from *Mediator Dei* to *Sacrosanctum concilium*; the second outlines the presentation of the first three postconciliar documents, mentioned above. In this latter regard two variations are especially noteworthy. The Instruction on the Eucharistic Mystery (Euch.Myst.), nos. 9 and 55, and the instruction of the Roman Ritual on Holy Communion and Worship of the Eucharistic Mystery (RR.Ins.), no.6, list Christ's presence in the presiding minister of the Mass after his presence in the word of Scripture. The General Instruc-

SCHEMA I:
MODES OF CHRIST'S PRESENCE: MEDIATOR DEI TO SACROSANCTUM CONCILIUM

Katabatic and Anabatic Modes of Christ's Liturgical Presence

Project I	Projects III/IV; Schemas I/II	*Med. Dei*	Project II	*Sac.conc*
SPEAKING [katabatic]	READING SCRIPTURE (explan. of text: Sch. II) [katabatic]	SACRIFICE Person of Priest at Altar [anabatic]	SACRIFICE Person of Priest at Altar [anabatic]	SACRIFICE Person of Priest at Altar [anabatic]
CONTINUA-TION OF SAVING WORK [katabatic/anabatic]	PRAISE OF FATHER [anabatic]	EUCHARIS-TIC SPECIES [katabatic]		EUCHARIS-TIC SPECIES [katabatic]
	SACRAMENTS [katabatic]	SACRAMENTS [katabatic]	SACRAMENTS [katabatic]	SACRA-MENTS [katabatic]
				READING OF SCRIPTURE [katabatic]
PRAISE OF FATHER [anabatic]	SACRIFICE Person of Priest at Altar [anabatic]	DIVINE OFFICE [anabatic]	DIVINE OFFICE [anabatic]	DIVINE OFFICE [anabatic]

SCHEMA II.
MODES OF CHRIST'S PRESENCE: POST-CONCILIAR DOCUMENTS

Katabatic and Anabatic Modes of Christ's Liturgical Presence

Euch. Myst. 9	Euch. Myst. 55	GIRM 7	RR. Ins. 6
PRESENCE IN COMMUNITY (Mt 18:20)	PRESENCE IN COMMUNITY	1) PRESENCE IN COMMUNITY GATHERED TO CELEBRATE THE SACRIFICE OF CHRIST, WITH PRIEST PRESIDING AND ACTING IN PERSONA CHRISTI [anabatic]	PRESENCE IN ASSEMBLED COMMUNITY
READING OF SCRIPTURE [katabatic]	READING AND EXPLANATION OF SCRIPTURE [katabatic]		READING AND EXPLANATION OF SCRIPTURE [katabatic]
EUCHARIST SACRIFICE:		2) IN MASS:	
		IN ASSEMBLED COMMUNITY;	
IN PERSON OF MINISTER [anabatic]	IN PERSON OF MINISTER [katabatic/ anabatic]	IN PERSON OF MINISTER; [katabatic/ anabatic]	IN PERSON OF MINISTER [katabatic/ anabatic]
		IN "HIS WORD" [katabatic]	
	EUCHARISTIC SPECIES (SUBSTAN- TIALLY) [katabatic]	EUCHARISTIC SPECIES (SUBSTAN- TIALLY) [katabatic]	EUCHARISTIC SPECIES (SUBSTAN- TIALLY) [katabatic]

tion of the Roman Mass of Pope Paul VI (GIRM), no.7, situates Christ's presence in the presiding minister of the Eucharistic Liturgy before his presence in the word of Scripture.

D. Ordering of Modes of Christ's Liturgical Presence, Based on Official Documents from Mediator Dei to Post-conciliar Period

The Roman documents previously considered provide the basis for the ordering of the modes of Christ's liturgical presence that can be arranged in one of two ways. The starting point for the first is the dialogical structure of liturgy: action of God and response of the faithful. There is the action of the Father, through Christ in the Spirit, creating and maintaining the community of faith. The members of the Church, recognizing in the ritual language and symbolic actions of the liturgy their own faith, are enabled to express themselves in response to God's gift with praise and thanksgiving. In this activity the worshipping assembly experiences and recognizes itself as the Body And Bride of Christ who himself works in and through the exercise of the faith that is expressed liturgically. This way of viewing the matter is preferred by Emil J. Lengeling.[29] The second way of ordering the modes of presence works with the specific elements of the liturgy. Armando Cuva has chosen this method.[30]

1. Presentation of Armando Cuva.

Cuva's monograph begins with citations of the more important official documents from *Mediator Dei* to the General Instruction on the Liturgy of the Hours on the subject of the modes of Christ's liturgical presence. In this connection he points out how the more original understanding of the sacramentality of the history of salvation was recaptured by Vatican II. The council encouraged the application of the concept "mysterium-sacramentum" to Christ, Church, and liturgy. These three great realities of the history of salvation are viewed as signs that contain, manifest, and communicate supernatural gifts.[31]

The author then recalls the traditional conviction concerning Christ's presence in the liturgical assembly, the basis for the elaboration of the modes of Christ's presence in the official documents. The New Testament writings witness to this belief in a variety of ways. Patristic sources take for granted this ecclesial aspect of Christ's presence. But while the Fathers of the Church affirm that Christ is present in a group of the faithful that is organized hierarchically and legitimately assembled for worship, they do not submit this theme to systematic theological analysis.[32]

a. Commentary on Official Documents

Following this introduction, Cuva summarizes the teaching of the twentieth century magisterium on the modes of Christ's presence in the liturgy. The teaching of the official documents is, to a great extent, based on traditional Catholic scholastic systematic theology. Hence in his commentary, Cuva employs this theology in order to explain the meaning intended by the rather brief presentations of the official texts. In his opinion the lists of modes of presence of Christ found in the documents, despite minor variations, reflect a consistent orientation. According to Cuva, the general series that best corresponds to these lists is the following: liturgical assembly, minister, proclamation of Scripture, prayer, constitutive elements of the sacraments, sacramentals.

What follows is a brief description of the main lines of Cuva's long commentary.

(1) *Liturgical Assembly.*[33] Liturgy affords the opportunity for an intensification of Christ's presence in virtue of the assembly's expression of its common faith and love. The basis of this presence of Christ is fourfold: the gathering in his name, the community endowed with grace, the baptismal character that qualifies the members to participate in the priestly worship of Christ, and the animating presence of the Holy Spirit.

(2) *Presiding Minister.*[34] In the midst of the liturgical assembly the presiding minister represents the invisible and principal minister, Christ in his humanity. "All ministers are sacrament of the presence of Christ and, in a certain sense, Christ himself sacramentally present."[35] But the more noble the office that is exercised by the minister, the more profoundly the minister is sign of Christ. The dignity is measured by the extent to which the office relates to Christ, who is the great sacrament. Therefore the more noble offices are those instituted by Christ himself.

Ordained ministry generally exercises liturgical offices of divine institution, the exceptions being the ministers of matrimony and the extraordinary minister of baptism. Also liturgical offices of ecclesiastical institution are ordinarily assigned to the ordained ministry. The requirement of hierarchical ministry for the liturgical celebrations derives from the hierarchical constitution of the Church, an essential structure that must be displayed in the liturgy of the Church.

In his liturgical role the minister shares in the instrumental causality of Christ's humanity. Through the presiding minister, the invisible instrumentality of the humanity of Christ is made visible and prolonged in the liturgical action. Hence the minister is a vicar of Christ. But he is also, in the more profound sense, image of Christ. Personally distinct from Christ, the minister is personally united to Christ by the Holy Spirit when he acts in Christ's name. By reason of this "representative identity" the minister and Christ form one mystical person. There is no question of merely juridical representation of Christ in the administration of sacraments. Rather, since Christ is existentially personified in the minister of the liturgical-sacramental celebrations, the activity of the minister in the sacraments is a salvific act of Christ himself in a visible form.

(3) *Proclamation of the Scripture.*[36] When the written word of God is proclaimed, Christ is operationally present. This means that the proclamation of the word of God is sacramental. It is an ecclesiastical act that works the salvation which is proclaimed, provided the hearers are open to receive this word of God.

Authentic preaching, or fruitful reflection on the word of God, ordinarily takes place with the divine assistance. Therefore Christ is also operationally present in it. According to Cuva, *Sacrosanctum concilium* 7 omits this form of presence of Christ so as not to give the impression that it has the same rank as the proclamation of Scripture. But he observes that *Lumen gentium* 21 and *Mysterium Fidei* refer to Christ's presence in the preaching of the hierarchy.

(4) *Prayer.*[37] As witnessed by Matthew 18:20, all forms of common prayer are a special mode of Christ's operative presence. The prayer of the Church, liturgical prayer, represents an intensification of Christ's presence. The recitation of the divine office admits of different levels of Christ's presence, depending on the extent to which the Church itself is officially involved in the activity. Hence the highest level of intensity of Christ's presence occurs when the bishop presides at the Liturgy of the Hours. A lower level of intensity is realized in groups deputed officially for this service. The lowest level takes place in groups without official appointment.

(5) *Sacraments.*[38] The constitutive elements of the sacraments were instituted by Christ, and are an offer of the grace of Christ. In the administration of these sacraments Christ is operationally present, acting by means of his minister. According to *Sacrosanctum concilium* 7, Christ is present in the sacraments "by his power." This means that sacraments share in the power by which the humanity of Christ works instrumentally to effect the sanctification of the recipients. This active, dynamic presence of Christ in the sacraments is distinguished from his substantial presence in the eucharistic species.

(6) *Sacramentals*[39] Sacramentals differ from sacraments on two counts. They are of ecclesiastical institution, and their efficacy pertains to the order of actual graces. The value of the sacramentals comes from the impetration of the Church and is dependent on the merits of the Church. However, they can be described as acts of Christ. Christ, united to the Church in the Spirit, gives to the Church the authority to institute sacramentals. In this qualified sense, sacramentals are both the act of the Church and of Christ. But Christ is present in the sacramentals in a way that is inferior to his presence in the sacraments, for the efficacy of the sacramentals depends on the action of the Church and the value of its mediation.

b. Theological Synthesis[40]

The last part of Cuva's study develops a systematic exposition of the subject, always within the framework of classical scholastic theology. This material may be quickly summarized in nine steps.

(1) The starting point is the real presence of the risen Lord in heaven. This unique real presence is the basis for the possibility of his presence in the liturgy of the earthly Church.

(2) The presence of Christ as God-man in heaven is prolonged in the liturgy of the Church. The risen Lord is one subject with two principles of operation, namely, the divine and human. Therefore the nature of Christ's presence should be thought through in accord with the distinction between Christ's presence as God, and his presence as man.

(3) The elements of the liturgy are either of divine or ecclesiastical institution. This distinction must be borne in mind when reflecting on the nature and implications of the modes of Christ's real presence in these elements. Elements of divine institution are: Eucharistic sacrifice,

sacraments, hierarchical proclamation of Scripture, special ministry of the ordained. Elements of ecclesiastical institution include sacramentals, official prayer, non-hierarchical proclamation of the word, the aspects of the ordering of the liturgical assembly.

(4) The real presence of Christ in the liturgy is dependent on a real basis of proximity. Here a distinction should be made between a "substantial presence," the presence of the whole Christ himself, and his operational presence. The former is the condition for the latter. The operational presence is realized through principal and instrumental causality.

As God, Christ is substantially present to, and operationally present in, all creation. This is a natural presence. Likewise he is substantially present as God to the justified by inhabitation through grace. In virtue of the hypostatic union, Christ is present as God to his own humanity and, consequently, present as God in the sacrament of Christ's body and blood. As God, Christ is operationally present in the liturgical structures of divine and ecclesiastical institution.

As man, Christ is substantially present as the condition for his operational presence in all liturgical activity; for every operational presence presupposes the substantial presence of the agent. In liturgical structures of divine institution, the humanity of Christ is present as instrumental efficient cause, as instrument conjoined to the Word of God in hypostatic union (*instrumentum coniunctum*). On this operational presence depends the efficacy of the activity of the human minister and the sacramental rites; for both are instruments of Christ (*instrumenta separata*). In liturgical structures of ecclesiastical institution, Christ as man is the principal efficient cause of the acceptable worship of the Church.

As man, Christ is substantially present *in the Eucharistic species*. All the operational presences of his humanity, which presuppose his substantial presence as man, are transitory; the substantial presence in the Eucharistic species remains after the consecration and after the liturgical celebration. This Eucharistic presence of Christ, being a permanent substantial presence, is superior to the various forms of Christ's operational presence in the liturgy. It is also superior to his substantial supernatural presence as the Word of God through inhabitation in the just; for it is a substantial presence of the whole Christ, God-man. However, the goal of the communication of the body and blood of Christ is the deepening of the divine presence of the Word of God by grace in the believing communicants. Hence, from this standpoint, the presence of Christ in the justified is superior to his sacramental presence in the Eucharistic species.

(5) There is a consensus among Catholic theologians that Christ is operationally present in liturgical structures of divine institution. They also agree that Christ is present as the principal instrumental efficient cause, employing sacraments as his earthly instruments. The various classical approaches to the understanding of this instrumental causality of the humanity of Christ provide partial, but valuable, insights: The humanity of Christ, rich in merits (*moral causality*), communicates immediately from Christ-God the grace (*physical causality*) which is signified (*significative or instrumental symbolic causality*) and effectively claimed by his humanity (*intentional causality*).

(6) The mystery of Christ's redeeming work is present in the liturgy; for, by its very nature, this mystery is present to all times. However Catholic theologians differ in their approaches to an explanation of the relationship between the contemporary liturgical activity of the Church and the past saving acts of Christ.

(7) The Holy Spirit is the ontological condition for the operational presence of Christ in the liturgy. Only in the Spirit can the truth of Christ be taught and heard, the Church pray and accomplish the liturgical-sacramental celebrations. Only the Spirit of God, insofar as uncreated grace, can enable the human activity to really attain God as he is in himself, to adore and possess him.

The subjective principle of worship is the Holy Spirit. In the sphere of the Spirit, the operational presence of Christ in the liturgy intensifies the habitual presence of Christ within the holy members of the assembly. In the power of the Spirit, Christ incorporates more deeply into himself the faithful whom he finds open to his saving presence.

(8) There is also the matter of the presence of the community to Christ in the liturgy. In the liturgical activity the various modes of participation of the faithful, corresponding to the modes of Christ's presence, are rich in actual graces. Through the sacraments, sacramental grace is bestowed by which faith, hope, and sanctifying grace are increased. This intensification of the life of faith corresponds to the inten-

sification of Christ's real and operational presence in the believers, and their presence to Christ in the Spirit.

(9) The modes of Christ's presence in the liturgy are determined by the various elements by which the liturgy is constituted. The principal signs that represent Christ's presence are the assembly, minister, proclamation of Scripture, prayers, constitutive elements of the sacraments, and sacramentals. The most basic liturgical sign by which Christ's presence is realized is the assembly itself. The assembly constitutes the living context for the proclamation of Scripture, prayer, and sacraments. The prayer of the Liturgy of the Hours is a special application of Matthew 18:20.

c. Observations

Cuva's explanation of the modes of Christ's presence in the liturgy is formulated within the context of classical scholastic theology and terminology. It is a useful summary of the mind-set that undoubtedly influenced the presentation of the official documents we have discussed.

The ordering of the common elements of the liturgy that represent the different modes of Christ's presence follows the sequence of occurrence in the liturgical-sacramental celebrations. Cuva's series corresponds best to what is found in the official documents. If one wishes to insert the Eucharist into this series in a way that reflects the ordering of the official documents, Eucharistic sacrifice should be placed before prayer as the most intensive mode of Christ's operative presence, and the sacrament of the Eucharist before the other sacraments for the same reason.

The inclusion of sacramentals after the common elements of liturgical-sacramental celebrations is correct on the basis of official documents. According to the Roman Ritual, *De benedictionibus*, "the ministry of blessing is linked to a peculiar exercise of the priesthood of Christ."[41] Furthermore, these sacramentals are a kind of imitation of a sacrament. They include prayer, reading of Scripture, often a homily, and the ecclesiastical minimum of "official administrator of a blessing" and "recipient." When the divine office is included in the list, it should come after the sacramentals, both because of the order of the official documents and its structure, which is not so closely related to the liturgical-sacramental celebrations.

2. Ordering According to Dialogical Structure of the Liturgy

In the dialogical structure of the liturgy, the sequence of modes of Christ's presence begins with the assembly of believers in which Christ is present as the sharing source of the life of faith. Christ is personally present in the believers. This is a pneumatic presence, that is to say, a presence realized through the personal presence of the Holy Spirit. Since the one Spirit is in the believers, and is fully "incarnated" in the glorified humanity of the risen Lord, the Spirit is the bond by which Christ is personally present to them.

But Christ is personally present to the believers not only in a one to one relationship. He is also present to them insofar as they constitute a corporate body which is capable of a collective, collegial act. The presupposition for such an act is the social structure, enabling a communication between the members of the social body, which is expressive of a common understanding and will. The social structure enables the integration of the acts of individuals, which issues in a new reality. This social act cannot be simply identified with the acts of individual members of the assembly. Rather, it is really distinguished from the contributions of the individuals through which it comes into existence, and yet identified with their contributions. In other words we have to speak of an identity of a social act with the activity of the individuals, and of a formal difference between the social act and the acts of individuals. When individuals express a common understanding and will, their individual activity is raised to the higher level of *personal social activity*.

For example, a regional church, made up of local episcopal churches, is capable of a collegial act. When the bishops, as representatives of the local churches come together in a synod, they are capable of reaching a common decision. In this case the wills of the members of the episcopal college are integrated into the collegial will. This collegial act cannot be simply described as the sum total of acts of individual bishops. It is a new reality, which constitutes an instance of mediation between the regional church as a whole and the individual bishops and their local episcopal churches.

In the case of the liturgy, the social act constitutes an instance of mediation between the community as a whole and the individual participant. The risen Lord in the Spirit works through the social structures of the Church; or rather, through the persons within the social structures. The structures are the instruments through which the members of the community work and which enable unity of activity. The participants retain their personalities but work precisely as members of the Church through the social structures. These structures are established ultimately by the Holy Spirit, and correspond to the mystery of Christ. Therefore the Spirit works through them, and Christ himself also works through the same structures. But in both cases they work through persons united in the one social organism, each of whom has his or her special gifts and vocation.

Through the liturgy the Church manifests and realizes itself in the fullest way possible. Consequently, the ministry of leadership in the Church assumes the leadership of the liturgical forms of expression of the faith of the Church. This essential structure of the institutional Church was established by the Holy Spirit, with the mission to support and foster the unity of the members in faith and love. Having been placed in a permanent relationship to the Church as leaders by sacramental ordination, the ministers exercise their proper role through fidelity to the apostolic faith in word and practice. Only in this way do they represent the apostolic Church and, consequently, Christ who works in their ministry in the power of the Holy Spirit.

The presiding minister of liturgical celebrations represents the apostolic Church and Christ. By expressing the faith of the Church, as formulated in the symbolical language and actions of the liturgy, the minister represents the Church, speaks in the name of the believing Bride of Christ. But the minister also represents Christ in two ways. First, ordained ministers represent Christ in the sense that Christ employs them in his Church to exercise a ministry of leadership by which the community of believers is built up. Second, they represent Christ in the liturgy because they lead the community in worship in the name of Christ. It is the invisible Head of the Church who unites the activity of the liturgical community to his acceptable worship of the Father. The visible minister, who speaks in the name of the Church, also speaks in the name of Christ, who has missioned the minister to serve as transparency for his operational presence as High Priest of the worshipping community.

In the series of modes of presence of Christ, organized according to the dialogical concept of liturgy, the person of the presiding minister is situated after the liturgical assembly as a whole. But this ordering does not imply that the liturgical activity of the minister is a special mode of Christ's operational presence that can be realized independently of the minister's ecclesiastical relationship. Rather, this ordering implies that the minister's activity as representative of Christ is conditioned by the ecclesial context. Only by the exercise of the ministry of the Church can the minister be said to represent Christ, the Head of the Church. The ordained minister is relational to both the assembly and to Christ. Therefore in the series of modes of presence of Christ, it is more accurate to place the minister after the liturgical assembly in parenthesis: liturgical assembly (minister). This is meant to indicate that the minister is embedded in the relation Christ--Church. In other words, the relationship of the liturgical leader to Christ and to the Church must be conceived as one of mutual dependence. The minister represents Christ because he represents the Church of Christ, and he represents the Church of Christ because he represents Christ. When the minister is conceived as representing Christ and the Church, where the *and* is understood as disjunctive, a false theology of liturgical ministry is fostered. For Christ is not operationally present in the liturgy apart from the operational activity of his Church.

After the corporate body of the assembly and the person of the presiding minister, the proclamation of the word of God by reading and exposition of Scripture follows in the dialogical concept of liturgy. The proclamation of Scripture, the normative witness to the faith of the Church, as well as its authentic interpretation by the presiding minister, have a predominantly katabatic trait: the handing on of the faith of the Church to the assembly, to which corresponds the assembly's hearing and receptive "amen."

In the series based on elements of the liturgical-sacramental celebrations, sacraments are correctly listed next. The purpose of the sacraments, the reason for their institution, is the sanctification of the subjects in whose favor they are celebrated. Sacramental celebrations contain an offer of saving grace. But they are an activity in which the anabatic and katabatic movements come together in a profound unity. The sacraments represent a kind of bridge between the proclamation of Scripture and the common prayer of the Church. Emil Lengeling situates sacraments after the reading and interpretation of Scripture because of their "prevailing katabatic content."[42] This explanation is acceptable as long as one does not overlook the implications of the qualification "prevailing."

The essential rites of the sacraments have a katabatic content because of their profound anabatic content. The katabatic movement is a consequence of the anabatic. The essential sacramental formula is epicletic by its very nature. The essential symbolic gesture, as accepted by the subject of the sacrament, is the expression of the desire for the reception of the grace petitioned by the Church. On the other hand, the symbolic gesture expresses the reaching out of the community to the subject in whose favor the celebration is accomplished. It is the expression of the desire of the Church that the individual be sanctified. This ecclesial gesture, made by the presiding minister, serves as transparency for the saving act of Christ himself, the desire of Christ to draw the subject into more intimate union with himself and so with the Father. From this point of view the symbolic gesture expresses indirectly what is more directly represented by the verbal formula of the sacrament. For the obverse of Christ's reaching out to the subject of the sacrament is his efficacious prayer before the Father, which is sacramentally represented by the sacramental word.

The sacrament of Christ's body and blood belongs with the prevailing katabatic elements of the liturgical-sacramental celebrations. It is placed after the sacraments as the most intensive form of Christ's presence, in accord with its katabatic content. The common prayer of the liturgy comes at the end of the series by reason of its prevailing anabatic orientation. The sacrificial prayer of the Eucharist is listed after common prayer, for it is the high point of the prayer of the Church made in union with Christ.

The series: assembly (minister), word, sacraments (Eucharistic species), common prayer (Eucharistic sacrifice) is favored by Lengeling. A somewhat similar ordering is adopted by Pope John Paul II in his address to the bishops of Switzerland, July 9, 1982, although he omits a reference to common prayer.

All that takes place in the liturgy concerns the Lord himself who is present in the assembled community, in the presiding priest, in the word, in the sacraments, in the sacrifice of the Mass under the Eucharistic species.[43]

II.
Theological Approach to the Liturgical Presence of Christ

Vatican II's *Sacrosanctum concilium* and subsequent documents set forth the positive doctrine of the Church on the subject of the liturgical presence of Christ. After the council a number of contributions were made toward the development of a systematic explanation of this traditional teaching. Representative contributions are outlined by Franciskus Eisenbach, [44] who also furnishes a useful summary of the main results of this investigation.[45]

The following systematic presentation takes into account this literature, which explores the conditions of the possibility of a liturgical presence of Christ, and attempts to order the different modes of Christ's liturgical presence in relation to one another. Since it is a question of the personal presence of Christ in the liturgical celebrations of the Church, one can begin with ecclesiology, or with christology; for a personal presence of Christ in the liturgy of the Church implies a personal presence of the worshipping community to Christ. Ultimately it is a question of mutual personal presence of Christ and community of believers in the liturgy. Another useful starting point is a working definition of liturgy, such as the one found in *Sacrosanctum concilium* 7. Guided by the concept of liturgy contained in this description, the individual elements of the liturgical-sacramental celebrations can be related to one another and ordered systematically.[46]

The way chosen here is a salvation history approach. Initially the implications of the glorification of Christ, and the sending of the Spirit to establish the Church, are drawn out. Having identified the conditions of the possibility of the personal presence of Christ in the liturgy, the relationship between the modes of his presence is explained. However these two themes do not exhaust the subject of the personal presence of Christ in the liturgy. There is also the matter of the relationship of the historical redemptive work of Jesus of Nazareth to the liturgy.

If the liturgy is a means of participation in Christ's redemptive work, then we must speak of a presence of that work in, and through, liturgical celebrations. But in what sense can it be said that the past redemptive acts of Jesus are present in the liturgy, and how does this presence relate to the event of the sanctification of the liturgical assembly? Finally, to complete the discussion of Christ's liturgical presence, some brief comments are made on the subject of the relationship between the two phases of the "liturgy of Jesus Christ," the earthly and heavenly.

A. Christ's Personal Presence in the Liturgy

This systematic explanation of Christ's personal presence in the liturgy begins from the biblical perspective in which salvation history is grasped as a process, the progressive realization of the divine plan of salvation from creation to eschatological fulfillment. When the divine plan is viewed from the experiential perspective, from the standpoint of the experiential measurement of historical succession, the understanding inginginvolved is that of a process as a process. Here Jesus Christ is recognized as one who has suffered and died, and entered into his glory. Hence it is the glorified Christ who is present to his Church, who bears the marks of his passion as his glory. He himself is at the term of history, and no longer lives under the conditions of space and time. If he is present in the liturgy of the Church, he is not present under the conditions of the full personal presence of human beings to one another in history.

From this biblical perspective we begin by asking about the conditions for the possibility of a personal presence of the *Kyrios* in history. The response to this question provides the basis for a systematic theology of the presence of Christ in the liturgy. For the liturgy, in all its forms, brings to the surface of the life of faith what the Church already possesses in Christ, in the Spirit. This presence of the *Kyrios* in the community of faith is the ultimate ground of the various modes of his liturgical presence.

The biblical perspective suffices for the present task of explaining the conditions for the possibility of the presence of Christ in the Church, the modes of his presence in the different elements of the liturgy, and the relationship between the liturgical modes of Christ's presence. However, as will be seen, the experiential, or biblical, perspective on the history of salvation is not adequate to make understandable the precise modality under which Christ is present in the liturgy of the earthly Church. In order to shed light on this question, there is need to introduce a different perspective which, to some degree, makes intelligible the notion of the actual presence of the past saving acts of Jesus of Nazareth in, and through, the liturgy of the Church.

1. Presence of Christ by Faith[47]

The personal presence of Christ in the Church is a kind of prolongation of the presence of the glorified Lord who sits at the right hand of the Father. As risen Lord he now has a new mode of existence beyond the confines of space and time. But because he is established as Lord of history, he is present to history for all time. This cosmic presence is distinguished from Christ's presence to the Church and its members.

Christ's personal presence as head and bridegroom of his Church, united to him as body and bride in the Holy Spirit, is not something that can be seen and known through merely human senses. He cannot be present to the world in the condition he was present as Jesus of Nazareth, that is to say, as if he were still far from the end of history. He can only be present as the one who comes from the future of the history of the world to draw humankind toward the fulfillment that he already enjoys.

The new personal presence of Christ to believers is grounded on the resurrection of Jesus. In his glorified state the possibility is opened for his abiding presence in the Church. But his personal presence is conditioned by Christ making himself accessible to human beings. This making himself accessible requires both some inner-worldly medium of communication, and the enabling of human beings to recognize the presence of the Lord as Savior in the medium. These conditions were fulfilled in the resurrection appearances.

The appearances of the risen Lord recounted in the New Testament have the aspect of a real encounter initiated by the Lord. He enables himself to be seen (1 Cor 15:5-8). Thereby he effects faith in his abiding presence in the "chosen witnesses" (Acts 1:8). The appearances, however they may be described phenomenologically, are the inner-worldly aspect of a purely divine act by which the Holy Spirit enabled the chosen witnesses to recognize the saving personal presence of the Lord.[48] The theandric act by which the risen Lord makes himself present to these witnesses is sacrament of the transcendental act by which the Spirit enables them to "see" the Lord (Jn 20:18; 1 Cor 15:5-8). The activity of Christ, together with the complementary work of the Spirit, creates faith in Christ's abiding presence in history (Mt 28:20). It is not because the witnesses "see the Lord" with their earthly eyes that they believe. This seeing is the condition for the seeing with the eyes of faith. Only through the gift of faith can the witnesses know that this is the Lord present to them as Savior and, consequently, permanently present to them in their earthly journey.

In the resurrection appearances the risen Lord is present to the witnesses as the object of their act of faith. At the same time, he is present in the witnesses as the sharing source, in the Spirit, of the act of faith by which the witnesses know and confess the Lord. This presence of the risen Lord in the witnesses is a new presence of a spiritual kind. It is a new presence in the Holy Spirit, who illumines the believers inwardly and forms them in such a way that they recognize the Lord's presence in the faith created and supported by the Spirit.

The resurrection appearances, which effected faith in the saving presence of the Lord, are unique. From this point onward the personal presence of Christ to the chosen witnesses and in their lives of faith, is maintained through their memory in the Spirit. Moreover, it is through the witness of their faith that the personal presence of Christ is mediated to others. The preaching of the witnesses can be described as anointed by the Spirit. It is the inner-worldly way by which the Spirit, working in, and through, the believing witnesses, elicits the response of faith of hearers of the Good News. When the first disciples preached their faith, Christ himself communicates his personal presence to the hearers in the Spirit: "Blessed are those who have not seen and yet believe" (Jn 20:29).

Through the response of the disciples, accepting in faith the abiding presence of the risen Lord, they constitute the new people of God sent in the power of the Holy Spirit to draw humanity to Christ. This human response of faith established the faith of the Church, which is indefectible. This apostolic faith is maintained in the faith of the Church as a whole. Through the witness to this faith, Christ is personally present to those who receive the gift of the Spirit, by which they are able to recognize his personal presence and confess him as their Savior.

2. Christ's Presence through the Exercise of the Faith of the Church[49]

Christ's presence in the Church differs from that of the full personal presence of one human being to another, conditioned by physical localized proximity. However Christ's presence in the members of the Church is more intimate and intense than the personal presence of one human being to another; for the Holy Spirit, whom Christ possesses in fullness, is given to believers whereby they are united to Christ in the one Spirit.

Through this union with Christ in the one Spirit, believers are mutually present to one another in a new way. They communicate with one another through the exercise of their faith at a depth that transcends all merely human possibilities. In this communication, they mediate the communication of Christ himself, who works through the exercise of faith in the power of the Spirit.

The various modes of Christ's personal presence in the Church are dependent on the exercise of the faith of the Church for their realizations. This means that the various ways in which the Church expresses her faith in the saving presence of Christ are the ways by which Christ himself represents and realizes his presence. When the chosen witnesses of the resurrection preached their faith, Christ was present in the preaching drawing the hearers to himself in the power of the Spirit. In this instance the word of God was preached in the form of a believing response of the witnesses to their experience of Christ's abiding presence, and to the mission they had received as a consequence of this experience.

What is said about the word of God preached by the chosen witnesses can be said about the word preached by their successors. When the faith of the Church is preached, Christ is present and active. Moreover no one comes to faith in Christ except through the word of faith of the Church.

The sacramental word, which expresses the meaning of the sacramental action, is an ecclesial word of faith which has an essentially epicletic character. The sacramental actions of the seven sacraments are gestures of the faith by which the community goes out to the individual, and the individual, in whose favor the celebration takes place, goes out to the community. Through this exercise of faith, of which Christ in the Spirit is the living source, Christ himself and his redemptive work are represented. Christ, united to his Church in the Spirit, is actively present in these sacramental celebrations for the benefit of the participants.

3. Special Presence of Christ in the Liturgical Events [50]

One can approach the question of Christ's special presence in liturgical events from a consideration of the concept of celebration. In celebrations of life, a characteristically humanizing activity, the forms of expression of daily life are stylized, and made to serve as transparency for permanent values, hidden, or less apparent, in routine living in the individual and social sphere. The liturgy falls into the category of celebration. The forms of liturgy follow the laws governing ordinary human and humanizing enactment of permanent realities and value relations, which undergird and support daily life. Also the purpose of liturgical celebrations is analogous to that of secular forms of celebration. They bring to the surface the ground of the Christian life of faith in order that this life may be lived more intensely in the celebration, and thereby nourish the daily practice of the faith.

However the special presence of Christ in liturgical events, from the standpoint of the whole of Christian tradition, derives from the special content of the celebration of faith: the mystery of Christ.[51] The liturgy is a commemorative representation of the saving work of Christ. Its celebrative character arises from this content. This mode of representation of the life of faith is what makes the presence of Christ in the liturgy preeminent. No other mode can match it in rank and intensity. Corresponding to the different forms of the Church's commemorative representation, Christ himself exercises his saving work in one or other modality. What the concrete liturgical rites signify is what Christ accomplishes by his operative presence.

4. Mutual Presence of Christ and the Church

The Lord represents himself and his saving work through the symbolic word and action of the liturgy. But the assembly of believers and its liturgical activity constitutes this symbolism. The mystery of Christ appears in its objective reality in the relative, temporal, and spatial conditions of the Church's liturgy. The mystery employs the worshipping community as the means of its expression, as the concrete representation of itself. Therefore in the liturgy there is the objective offer of salvation by Christ, and also the human, mediation of this offer, for the offer can only be realized in and by human communication.

a. The Possibility of Human Cooperation

Human cooperation is the essential condition for the possibility of the presence of the mystery of salvation in the liturgy of the Church. But what makes believers capable of an activity that represents and realizes the divine saving work?

The human being, as a thinking subject, is capable of making another person, or thing, intentionally present to oneself in memory. Furthermore, persons can make themselves mutually present to one another through words and "things," in which they express themselves, through which they become defined in relation to one another. This consideration raises the question about the essence of person and the conditions which this essence implies for the possibility of encounter with another person. Twentieth century studies have shown quite clearly that the possibility of mutual presence of persons to one another is based on the relationality given with human existence. Through the actualization of this essentially relational nature in openness to others, in dialogical self-realization, human beings become themselves, grow in personhood.

This philosophical conclusion, based on observation of human beings at work and play, is supported by the biblical concept of person. According to Scripture, the human being is a creature essentially related to the Creator, and determined by God to responsible relational activity toward the Creator and the whole of creation. The relationality to other persons pertains to the essence of personhood. It is ultimately grounded on the Trinity: the essential relationality of the divine persons to one another.

The concept of the relational nature of the human being has important application in the field of theology of the liturgy. The essential relationality of the Lord to the believing con-celebrating participants, and vice versa, makes intelligible the reciprocal presence of the Lord and community in the accomplishment of the liturgy of the Church.

b. The Bond of the Reciprocal Presence

Relationality explains the possibility of mutual presence of human beings to one another. But the possibility of full personal presence is conditioned by localized presence in space and time. Physical presence, and the communication by word and gesture are the conditions for the realization of reciprocal full personal presence. However, Jesus of Nazareth lived in the past and died. As the glorified Lord, he lives in the realm of God outside space and time. As *Kyrios* he can only be present to believers as the one who is to come when history is fulfilled. Therefore his coming now, from above as it were, cannot be a real coming to believers in history, under the conditions of historical space and time.

A real coming of the Lord, that entails a real coming of believers to the Lord, a mutual presence of Christ and the assembly of the faithful, requires that the latter enter into God's time while remaining under the temporal conditions of history. In other words, believers must become contemporaneous with the risen Lord who lives in the end-time. But how can a movement "from below" and a movement "from above," which belong to essentially different spheres of time, that is, the time of God and the time of humankind, mutually determine one another so that a mutual presence results?

According to the New Testament there is a historical time, which moves to a future end (Mt 24:14). But worldtime in no way determines its own end. God is the one who determines the "due time" (Gal 6:3). The eternal life which he promised in times past, "This he has now manifested in his own good time" (Titus 1:3). The mystery of Jesus Christ was "attested at the fitting time" (1 Tim 2:6).

The end of worldtime is the coming of the Kingdom of God, when "his kingdom will appear" (Lk 19:11). But this coming of the Kingdom in Jesus Christ is already the definitive endpoint of world time: "Behold the Kingdom of God is in your midst" (Lk 17:20). In Christ "the end of the ages has encountered us" (1 Cor 10:11); "Now is the day of salvation" (2 Cor 6:2).

God's time, which transcends all historical time and is contemporaneous with all such time, has definitively broken into history in Jesus Christ. It is the time of God's love, which fully appeared in Jesus Christ because he opened himself to the love of the Father. His love for the Father is the revelation of the Father's love for him and all humanity in him. It is the reciprocal presence of God's love for the world and the human being's definitive response to that love.[52]

The time of God's love enters the world in and through the full response of Jesus. After the ascension, the *Kyrios* is present to the world, opening humankind to God's time by the sending of the Holy Spirit. The power that makes God's time accessible is the Spirit, the "earnest," the "first fruits" of the time of God. By loving one enters into God's time and brings this time to others: "We know that we have crossed over from death to life, for we love our brothers" (1 Jn 3:14).

Our love for one another manifests that we stand in God's time, and effects our standing in God's time. Finally, if we live in God's love found in Jesus, we will enable others to experience the time of God present in that love. While hate locks all time within itself, and so has no real time, in love unending time begins.

The time of God reaches into our world in the love of Jesus, by the power of the Spirit who establishes the Church, the Body And Bride of Christ. For the Church is the concrete presence of God's time in its life of faith, hope, and love. Above all, the liturgy of the Church is a manifestation and realization of God's time. Here the mutual loving presence of the Lord and the assembly of believers, in the one Holy Spirit, is realized in the most intense way possible under the conditions of history.

The concrete form of expression of this mutual presence of Christ and the Church is by word and symbolic action borrowed from daily life. The saving encounter with the Lord is determined by this "speech" as a whole. This human form of expression, to which correspond seeing and hearing, is the way in which the risen Lord represents his saving work. Only in this way can Christ and his saving work be personally present to believers. But the one who enables the human forms of expression of faith, hope and love to enter into God's time, to be the self-representation of the person and saving work of Jesus Christ, is the Holy Spirit. On the one hand, the Spirit ultimately structures the liturgical forms of expression of the faith of the Church in conformity with the historical saving work of Jesus of Nazareth, and the will of the risen Lord. At the same time, the Spirit is the source of the faith which enables the worshipping community to recognize, and accept with thanksgiving, the salvation represented in the liturgical word and symbolic gestures of the faith.

5. Specific Modes of Liturgical Presence of Christ[53]

The elements of the liturgical expression of faith always represent the twofold dimension of a saving event: the self-communication of the Triune God through Christ in the Holy Spirit (movement "from above"), and the self-offering of the community through Christ in the Spirit to the Father (movement "from below"). The different elements of the liturgy always contain both the anabatic and katabatic movements.

The anabatic is immediately accessible, for it is externalized in the liturgical rite. The katabatic, by its very nature, cannot be directly externalized. The transcendent self-communication of the Father in the Spirit is a purely divine act, not filtered through any "means" of grace. The "sacrament of this self-communication," the risen Lord in his glorified humanity, cannot be rendered directly visible to the eye at the level of the external liturgical rites. In other words, there is no purely katabatic element of the liturgical rites that exclusively manifests and realizes the divine movement of sanctification.

The worship of God, and the sanctification of the worshippers, are aspects of the one event of grace offered, bestowed, and accepted. This event is historically accessible under the form of the worship of God. In the case of Jesus of Nazareth, his self-offering to the Father "for the many" is the anabatic movement of the grace event, revealing the self-communication of the Father that is realized through the missions of the Word and Spirit. In the time of the Church, it is the worship of the community, expressed in the word and symbolic gestures of the faith, that yields liturgical rites of sanctification. More precisely, one should say that the liturgical expression of the worship of the Church is the transparency of transcendence in immanence. Through the symbolic expression of the faith of the Church, Christ represents himself; for the exercise of the faith of the Church in the Spirit, is inwardly grasped by the Lord who is present to this faith.

The self-realization of the faith of the Church, through the liturgical assembly, is an actualizing of the personal presence of the risen Lord, given in this faith. This is possible because the Spirit, in the Head and members of the Church, is the principle of the reciprocal presence of the Lord and the Church. The initiative of the Father, through Christ in the Spirit, comes before the liturgical action of believers. But the responding act of believers, in the Spirit, belongs constitutively to the realization of the liturgy as work of Christ and the Church.

The liturgical assembly, as such, represents itself as a community of faith in the common ways of exercise of the faith of the Church. Thereby Christ represents himself as the source of this faith, created by the Spirit whom he sent from the Father. Since the liturgical assembly represents itself, it necessarily represents itself as the community called to worship the Father through Christ in the Spirit, and as the community called to further the mission of Christ its head by exercising the ministry of sanctification on behalf of one another and the whole of humanity.

All the forms of liturgical expression of faith are complementary modes of the one personal self-representation of the ecclesial commuity, as the people of God called to worship the Father in spirit and truth and, at the same time, to act as minister of the sanctifying activity of the Father in the world. Consequently, all the forms of liturgical expression of the faith necessarily represent Christ who is the sacrament of the divine-human love of the Father (glorification), and the sacrament of the divine-human love of humanity (sanctification).

The most important forms of liturgical expression are word and symbolic action. The word enables a person to makes oneself personally present to another in the relationship of speaker to hearer. Through physical appearance and symbolic gestures the person is, or remains, present. The word, together with the physical appearance and symbolic gestures, enables a person to be fully personally present to another.

In the liturgy the members of the assembly become fully present to one another through the word of faith and the symbolical actions of faith. Through the same word and activity Christ becomes fully present to the community in a personal way. Christ makes himself present to the community in the word of faith; in the symbolical gestures Christ is present as the one who shares the fruits of his redemptive work.

By means of the constitutive elements of the seven sacraments, Christ's active and abiding presence in the Church is manifested. They are symbolical representations of Christ's saving presence, instituted by him and established in the Church through the Spirit. They are not the product of human ingenuity, or a casuistic application of principles derived from theological reflection on the paschal mystery. However, the sacraments, divinely instituted according to their content, are accomplished only by the word and symbolical gestures of the faith of the Church.

The verbal and gestural activity, accomplished liturgically by the Church and Christ, in their mutual presence to one another, has its high point in the presence of Christ in the Eucharistic species. This highest possible instance includes the operational presence of the incarnate Word, and a special mode of his substantial presence which we call "somatic." The sacrament of the Eucharist represents and renders present Christ in his self-offering to the Father and to believers. In the acceptance of this presence, constituted in a twofold way, there is effected a mutual presence of Christ and Church that is unsurpassable in time. This acceptance represents and realizes Christ's earthly Body, the Church, created and now newly being built up by his sacrifice. Hence the Church finds here the fullest expression of her mystery. The somatic presence of Christ to his Body the Church is the guarantee for the real, personal, and operational presence of the Lord in the rest of the liturgical forms of expression of this presence, ordered to this center.[54]

6. The Eucharistic Presence of Christ[55]

The mystery of the Eucharist consists in the presence of Christ's self-offering to the Father, and his self-offering to the community in the sacrament of his body and blood. The condition for this twofold presence was the apostolic act of acceptance of the meaning of the Last Supper, as understood in the light of faith awakened through the experience of the resurrection of Christ. Therefore the Eucharistic presence of Christ is only possible in the realm of the faith of the Church. In other words, the establishment of the Eucharist, its meaning as meaning for believers, was the work of believers. For meaning depends not only on the person who gives it but also on the individual or community that accepts it. The establishment of the meaning of the Eucharist involved the activity of the disciples, cooperating with the risen Lord, and the action of the Spirit who anticipates and includes the action of the faithful disciples.

The Eucharistic presence of Christ in the Church was secured once for all by the apostolic acceptance. Since the faith of the Church is indefectible, the celebration of the Lord's Supper will continue until the fulfillment of history.

a. The Celebration of the Eucharistic Liturgy

The celebration of the Eucharist is an act of obedience in faith to the command of Christ: "Do this im memory of me." But the community does not simply directly copy the Last Supper. The Eucharist is not a dramatic representation of what Christ did at the Last Supper. Rather, it is the Eucharistic celebration of the Church, the Body and Bride of Christ. The Eucharist is the response of the Church to the command of Christ to do what he did in a way that corresponds to the nature of the Church.

In this liturgy, the Church imitates what Christ did by employing the ritual gestures and elements of food and drink that correspond to those used at the Last Supper. Moreover, the community does what Christ did spiritually by following him, that is to say, by offering itself to the Father in order to obtain the meaning of its life.

In the Eucharistic Prayer the Church *recalls.* Through this first fulfill-ment of the command of Christ, the Church offers praise and thanksgiv-ing to the Father for the gift of Christ. Conformed to this particular liturgical memorial celebration, the thankful proclamation of salvation history has its high point in the reference to the historical institution of the Eucharist by Christ. Immediately following this scriptural reference the Roman Rite, and many other liturgical traditions, introduce the rit-ual act of the offering of the gifts of bread and wine. This symbolical act has many dimensions. As product of human work, the elements signify the self-offering of the Church in imitation of Christ. As thank-offering it expresses the idea that the community rejoices because God as made it worthy to offer acceptable worship. As offering of material gifts back to God, it is the liturgical way of acknowledging that all we have is ul-timately God's gift. The material gifts symbolize, in the context of this liturgy, the greatest gift of God: Christ himself. They are, above all, sym-bols of Christ's sacrificed body and blood. This understanding is wit-nessed by the various liturgical traditions, which refer to the bread and wine as "figures" (Latin) or "antitypes" (Greek) of the body·and blood of Christ.

The *returning* of all God's gifts with thanksgiving, including Christ himself, to the Father, does not mean that we have no need of them. Rather, it signifies that we always have need of God's gifts, especially the gift of Christ. This outlook is confirmed by the epiclesis which peti-tions the Father to send the Spirit to sanctify the material gifts of bread and wine, in order that they may become the reality of the Lord's gift of himself to the community.

Looked at from the viewpoint of the ritual activity of the community, this liturgical celebration denotes the Church's self-offering to the Father expressed in prayer and the symbolical offering of the Eucharis-tic gifts of bread and wine. The confidence of the community that its of-fering is acceptable to the Father is grounded on the awareness that it is following the command of Christ. This confidence is explicitly formu-lated in the epiclesis. The petition is made, in the certainly of faith, that the Father always hears it and sends the Spirit to sanctify the gifts of the Church, to transform them into the sacrament of the body and blood of Christ.

b. The Mystery of the Eucharist

All the activity of the Church in the Eucharist serves as transparency for the active presence of Christ. It connotes Christ's operational presence, uniting the self-offering of the Church to his "eternal worship" of the Father (glorification). At the same time, the Church's self-offering to the Father includes her self-emptying in the ministry of Christ for the sanctification of the world. This connotes Christ's active presence enabling the believers to follow him in their mission of furthering his redemptive work (sanctification).

The anamnesis-offering of the bread and wine is complemented by the epiclesis, which petitions that the symbols of the Church's self-offering become the symbols of Christ's self-offering to the community. It connotes the presence of Christ, constituted in the twofold way of offering himself to the Father, and to the believers as the food and drink of eternal life. Above all, the epiclesis is the work of the Lord present in the Spirit to the faith of the Church.

If the Church relates its activity to the Last Supper, this connotes the risen Lord's active presence, relating the Last Supper to the liturgy of the Church. If the Church petitions for the coming of the Spirit to sanctify the gifts, this connotes the "eternal intercession" of the risen Lord before the Father for the sending of the Spirit to transform the gifts. The risen Lord, as the host of his meal, places the Eucharistic gifts in the relation between himself and the community. In this way he changes their meaning, an ontological change. It is the Spirit who seals the relationship between the Eucharistic gifts of the Church and the risen Lord. Thereby the bread and wine, symbols of the Church's self-offering. become "real symbols"[56] of Christ's self-offering to the Father and to the Church. The sanctified bread and wine always remain symbols of the Church's self-offering in relation to the liturgical exercise of the faith of the Church. But at the deeper level, seen only by the eyes of faith, they become sacrament of the sacrificed body and blood.

The Eucharistic assembly, through its presiding minister, bestows the meaning on the symbolic activity of the Eucharist by expressing its faith, which connotes Jesus Christ himself accomplishing his saving work. The specifically divine contribution is the sanctification of the gifts of bread and wine, accomplished by the Holy Spirit.

c. The Somatic Real Presence of Christ

The celebration of the Eucharist represents the Church as sharing in the eschatological meal of the Kingdom with Christ as High Priest, host, and nourishment. It is the sacramental real promise of the coming Kingdom of God from which the Church derives meaning and life. What the Church represents in the liturgy is fully realized through the abiding presence of Christ in the power of the Spirit.

The abiding presence of Christ in the Church obtains its most intensive expression in the sacrament of the body and blood. Here the personal presence of Christ is objectively fixed as a consequence of the celebration of the memorial of the Last Supper and the death of the Lord. Moreover, the unconsumed sacrament remains sacrament after the liturgical celebration. Once Christ gives himself as eschatological gift to the community in the sacramental meal of the Kingdom, he does not withdraw his presence.

This somatic real presence of Christ should not be conceived as a kind of static presence. The sanctified bread and wine are the crystallized form of Christ's self-offering to the Father and to the worshipping community. By placing the bread and wine in the relation between himself and the community, he makes them realizing signs of this self-offering. Since the somatic real presence is relational, a presence for someone, and the risen Lord relates himself through the sacrament of his body and blood to someone, the Church can say, according to the old tradition, that believers receive Christ in their hands from his hands. The somatic real presence does not exclude but rather includes the active presence of Christ, who is the true host of the Eucharistic banquet.

The somatic real presence of Christ is unique. It does not correspond to Christ's active presence in the exercise of the life of faith. There is an analogy between the Eucharistic presence and Christ's presence in the symbolical actions of the other sacraments. They represent Christ as present, sharing the fruits of his redemptive work. But the other sacraments are accomplished through symbolic actions in which the material elements sometimes employed are sacramental only in the scope of the action itself. The sanctified bread and wine remain sacramental after the Eucharistic Prayer, in and through which the elements become and remain sacrament.

Through the sacrament of the somatic presence, Christ is manifested as fully as possible in the realm of history, as the abiding Lord on whom the Church's life of faith depends. In the other sacraments, the activity of the faith of the Church comes to the foreground as the condition on which Christ depends for his personal presence in the Church.

B. Presence of the Redemptive Work of Jesus of Nazareth

We have seen that from the biblical perspective Christ is present in the Church as the one who comes from the future Kingdom of God. He is present as the risen Lord, in the Spirit, by faith. Consequently, there is a real relation between the earthly and the heavenly liturgy. However Christ is present in the earthly liturgy under the modality of the Savior who unites the worshipping community with himself in his passover from suffering to glory. Above all, the Eucharistic Liturgy expresses this truth. This modality differs from that of Christ's presence in the ongoing heavenly liturgy of the blessed, who have passed with Christ into the life of beatitude.

Christian insight has never been completely satisfied with theological theories that explain the presence of the historical saving acts of Christ in the liturgy as a presence by their effects. The analogy with the presence of significant past historical acts through their effects on the present human situation is a useful tool for catechetics. People are able to understand this type of presence because they find a correspondence in their experience of the causality exercised by past events on their present condition. But this "effectus" theory, a prominent one in the tradition of scholastic theology, is not adequate to express the Christian insight that grasps in the life of Christ, and in the liturgical celebrations, the single movement of the world to the Father. Consequently, the question of the profound relationship between the historical saving acts of Christ and the liturgy has remained a vital question of theological inquiry.

Several preliminary remarks are in order before a response is proposed to the question whether, and how, the saving acts of Christ are actually present in the liturgy.

First of all, it is incorrect to historicize the presence of Christ's saving acts in the liturgy, to conceive them as being repeated now, again, for the benefit of the liturgical community. Scripture rejects this possibility on the basis of the profound nature of the reciprocal love of Jesus and the Father expressed in the event of the Cross. Among other reasons, it may be noted that any activity of this type is impossible for Christ because he no longer lives by faith but by vision, beyond the conditions of space and time. Second, it is not sufficient to say that Christ is never separated from his saving work, or that the liturgy is a "prolongation of the mysteries of the life of Christ." Such statements merely present problems for further understanding. What do they mean? Third, it is futile to attempt to identify some "deepest reality" of the saving work of Christ, "an enduring element of his redemptive acts," which accounts for their continuing presence in the liturgy. From the 1930s up to the Second Vatican Council a number of theories were proposed in the attempt to uncover this profound reality. There was the idea that the ecstasy of the divine existence of Christ, in virtue of the hypostatic union, extends to the ecstasy of Christ's human acts. Hence the human acts could be said to participate in the "eternity" of the Word of God.[57] A not unrelated proposal of Victor Warnack explains that the metaphysical act by which Christ passed from suffering to glory elevated the historical act by which he entered into glory beyond time.[58] Many followers of the Thomistic school have sought a solution in the immobile act of beatific love, "the soul of the redemptive acts."[59] The idea that the human saving acts are personalized by the Word of God forms the basis of Eduard Schillebeeckx's approach. He concludes that these human acts of Christ participate in the duration proper to the hypostatic union, i.e., in the eternity of the Word.[60]

The appeal to the beatific love provides no solution to the problem, for what is at issue is the historical acts of love of Jesus of Nazareth. All the remaining theories labor under the difficulty of the failure to take account of the distinction between time and eternity.

The relation between time and eternity is the relation between the eternal divine action and its consequent term. The fact that God knows, wills, and effects time-conditioned events, does not imply a divine concurrence, in the sense that God and the world become parallel successions. Eternity, as predicated of God, means total simultaneity. There is no temporal succession in God. Consequently there is no happening in this world that can become timeless, not even the sacrifice of the Cross. The predication of timelessness to some postulated kernel of Christ's redemptive work, awarding to it a form of participation in God's eternity, is meaningless. Moreover approaches which move in this direction run the risk of bringing into question the constant belief of the Church that the Word of God redeemed the world by his subjection to the circumstances of place and time. Fourth, the question of the presence of the saving acts of Christ in the liturgy cannot be resolved adequately when the history of salvation is viewed from the experiential perspective alone. From this standpoint, as we have seen, past historical events are past. They can only be understood as present in their effects, and in subjective memory.

The Epistle to the Hebrews shares this outlook. Here the historical event of Christ's death is described as something that happened once for all (7:28). Through his self-offering, Christ entered once for all in the sanctuary of heaven (9:11), and "achieved eternal redemption" (9:12). "This is why he is Mediator of the new covenant" (9:15). "He was offered up once to take away the sins of many" (9:28).

From this standpoint Christian liturgy celebrates *objective redemption* accomplished through the historical life of Jesus. Accordingly, Christ himself is present in the liturgy as the one who has suffered, died and is glorified. He is present as the *Kyrios,* who dies no more, and who is able to make efficacious intercession for us in virtue of his historical sacrifice. But the historical mysteries themselves are not present, for they lie in the past. They are present in their effects, insofar as the salvation offered to us now is grounded on Christ's past, saving work.

Scholastic theology, from this vantage point, distinguishes between objective and subjective redemption. In virtue of Jesus' passing from this world to the Father, the redemption of the world is already realized in the Head of redeemed humanity. The passover to the Father is fully realized for Jesus, insofar as Beloved Son. Through the full realization of his divinity in his humanity, Christ has become fully relational to the Father in his humanity. This full realization concretely occurs through the bestowal of his transcendental love on the Father, fully incarnated in his human love.

In what happened through the exaltation of Jesus, we can speak of the fulfillment of the divine plan of salvation insofar as the ultimate meaning of the world consists in the one acceptable response to the gratuity of God made in the once for all self-offering of Jesus. This passover of Christ to the Father is the way by which the salvation of humanity is achieved in the Head of humanity, and, at the same time, the reason why individual persons have the possibility of achieving salvation. Therefore scholastic theology refers to the real relation between objective redemption accomplished by Christ, and the subjective redemption of ordinary human beings.

From the experiential perspective, the distinction between objective and subjective redemption must be maintained. This distinction is grounded on the fundamental conviction of faith that the salvation of the world took place through the history of the life and death of Jesus Christ. However the whole matter can, and indeed should, be considered from the divine perspective. And this results in different insights.[61]

The essence of the divine plan of salvation is God's self-communication to rational creatures. This communication, however, becomes gift only when it is accepted. Otherwise it remains an offer on God's part, without attaining its goal because of refusal of the gift by free human beings. But the essence of the divine plan is not frustrated because it includes the mission of the Word, who alone is able to respond fully to the gift of God in the name of creation. In Christ the response to the Father's offer of self-communication in his Word and Spirit completes the circle of the offer of the gift and its acceptance by the grateful recipient.

According to Scripture, the ultimate meaning of the world is the passover of the incarnate Son to the Father: the complete acceptance of the Father's love, expressed by the beloved Son's self-offering in openness to receive the meaning of his life from the Father. Since the beloved Son supplies the sole acceptable response of the world to God's graceful presence, God's self-communication to ordinary people comes through their incorporation into this response. In other words, from the divine perspective the distinction between objective and subjective redemption is not relevant to the ultimate intelligibility of the essential content of the divine plan.

Temporal succession and spatial duration are relevant to the event of the Cross, by which the passover of Christ took place. Such succession and duration is relevant to the saving events in which God's offer of grace is accepted by free human beings in concrete situations of life. In this sense, the distinction holds between objective redemption, attained in Christ, and subjective redemption to be realized by the response of faith of believers.

But the ultimate intelligibility is the identity between subjective and objective redemption. The Father saves humanity by drawing human beings into the single transitus of Jesus Christ. If we are saved "in, with, and through Christ," it makes sense to speak of the presence of Christ in the liturgy of the Church as the presence of the one who is in the process of his single *transitus* to the Father.

The notion that the saving acts of Christ are present in the celebrations of the sacraments is not a new idea in Catholic systematic theology. It was a firm tenet of Thomas Aquinas, which he attempted to clarify by the use of the notions of principal and efficient instrumental causes.

Aquinas teaches that God is the principal efficient cause, and the mysteries of Christ's life the instrumental cause, of our salvation.[62] He says that this instrumental cause is applied (*applicatur*) spiritually by faith, and corporeally in the sacraments.[63] On the subject of the relationship between the resurrection of Christ and the resurrection of others, Aquinas reasons that because the humanity of Christ is instrument of his divinity, *ex consequente* all actions and passions of Christ instrumentally work for human salvation *in virtute divinitatis*.[64] In other words, the effect follows from the instrumental cause according to the conditions of the principal cause. Since God is the principal cause, and the resurrection of Christ the instrumental cause of our resurrection, our resurrection "follows" (*sequitur*) the resurrection of Christ "according to the divine disposition at a certain time."[65]

Aquinas seems to have had no particular difficulty with the idea that the human living of Christ exercises efficient causality in our sanctification. On the one hand, in the realist metaphysics of the Angelic Doctor agent, instrument and effect are always coexistent. On the other hand, the idea that past events are present now offers no difficulty from the divine perspective in which he views the matter. Removes in space and time are not relevant to the ultimate intelligibility that is involved when God wills humanity to be sanctified through the instrumentality of the human living of Christ.

The effect of the God acting through the instrumentality of the mysteries of Christ's life is the real configuration of the believer to Christ, which takes the concrete form of psychological participation in the religious attitudes of Christ, expressed in the historical actions and passions of his earthly life. This occurs because Christ is present to the believer in his passage from suffering to glory. However this presence does not imply that the past saving acts of Christ are reproduced anew in the one being sanctified. The need for such a "reactualization" is ruled out from the divine perspective in which temporal succession and spacial duration lack intelligibility at the level of ultimate intelligibility.

The configuration to Christ, or rather the modification of the basic configuration to Christ already shared by believers, that is realized in the liturgy, pertains to the anabatic movement of the celebration. The liturgical celebration itself mediates this configuration, which takes the form of the response to the Father in praise and thanksgiving for the gift of salvation in Christ. However this anabatic movement is made possible because of the katabatic, divine action of communication of the Holy Spirit.

The mystery of the liturgy includes the self-communication of the Father in the Holy Spirit, which has the goal of uniting believers with the beloved Son, of making them daughters and sons of the one Father in the beloved Son. The sacrament of this purely transcendental act is the theandric act of the risen Lord, who sends the Spirit from the Father in order that human beings may be enabled to love the Father with the love of daughters and sons in the one beloved Son. Therefore we must speak of the efficient instrumental causality exercised by the *Kyrios* in the process of the sanctification of believers by which they are enabled to enter into the movement of the historical acts by which Jesus' passover to the Father was accomplished. This modality of Christ's presence in the liturgy pertains to the katabatic movement that grounds the anabatic.

In short, Christ is active in both movements of the liturgical dialogue. Christ is present as sanctifier in the liturgical-sacramental celebrations of the Church, and as the High Priest of the worship of the assembly. Through the gift of the Spirit, whom he sends from the Father, the community is made children of the Father, and participates in the "mind of Christ" (1 Cor 2:16b). Thereby they are enabled to offer acceptable worship with Christ in his single passover to the Father. Modifications of the configuration to Christ occur in the various forms of the liturgical-sacramental celebrations because of the modalities of the representation of the mysteries of Christ's life. But in all cases, historical realities of the life of Christ are present as the instrumental action on the worshipping community by which the believers are enabled to respond to the Father in accord with the meaning of the celebration.

C. The Earthly and the Heavenly Liturgy

Christian tradition customarily refers to two liturgies of the economy of salvation: the earthly and heavenly. These liturgies are not completely separate and distinct from one another. Rather they represent two phases of the history of salvation. The source of the two phases is the earthly worship of Jesus of Nazareth, by which he made his acceptable self-offering to the Father.

The first phase of the "liturgy of Jesus Christ" began with his ascension, which included the ascension of the just who had died in the Lord. The worship of Jesus became "liturgy" because the Kyrios united the blessed to his worship by sending the Spirit from the Father to them in fullness. In heaven the worship of Christ became a social reality in the which the blessed, in the power of the Spirit, are united with Christ in the worship of the Father by vision, and not by faith.

The second phase of the "liturgy of Jesus Christ" began with the sending of the Spirit by the risen Lord from the Father to form the Church. In virtue of the fact that the Church is the Body and Bride, united with Christ the Head and Bridegroom in the one Spirit, the earthly Church shares in the one liturgy of Jesus Christ, which is fully realized in heaven. Therefore the mystery of the liturgy of the earthly Church is the heavenly liturgy. But since the subjects of the earthly liturgy live by faith and not by vision, their liturgy can be described as the sacrament of the heavenly liturgy. This means that the earthly liturgy has its source in the heavenly liturgy, effectively signifies the union of the earthly Church with the heavenly Church, and is the anticipation of the fulfillment to be attained by the just. Likewise the earthly liturgy has, in common with the heavenly liturgy, the commemorative dimension. The glorified Lord, in the heavenly liturgy, is the crucified Lord. In the earthly liturgy, above all the death of the Lord is recalled.

Yet there is a sense in which the earthly liturgy cannot be identified as sacrament of the heavenly liturgy. Sacraments are correctly described by Thomas Aquinas as commemorative, demonstrative, and prognostic signs. As a commemorative signs, the liturgical-sacramental celebrations of the earthly Church are more accurately identified as the liturgy of the mystery of the earthly worship of Jesus Christ, become social through the establishment of the Church in the Spirit.

The difference between the earthly and heavenly liturgies arises from the situation of believers in history. In the first place, Christ can only be made accessible, personally present, through the exercise of the faith of the Church. Second, the believers themselves can only worship in, with, and through Christ by faith, and not by vision. Third, believers offer acceptable worship to God under the conditions of the worship of Jesus of Nazareth, who lived by faith. Hence the condition for the acceptable worship of the earthly believers is the commitment to the way of the Cross of Jesus Christ.

In the earthly liturgy, the recalling of the passover of Jesus from suffering to glory has the function of reminding the assembly of its task, namely, to commit itself to the only way in which the participants can be united to the worship of the Lord in historical time and space. But this recalling of the passover of Christ in faith is a work of the Spirit. Our memory in the Spirit allows us, as believers, to bring the historical event of Jesus' saving work to the center of our lives and history.[66] Theories about the way in which the past redemptive acts of Christ are rendered present in the liturgy have to be worked out with a eye to the concrete activity of the worshipping community. After all, the liturgy is a response to the saving action of God in Christ made possible because the Spirit, the personal source of the living memory of the Church, never fails to remind the Church that Christ is Savior.

The dialogical character of the liturgy is possible because the Spirit, possessed by Christ in fullness and sent by him to draw his members into communion with himself, enables the Church to participate in the memory of Christ. Therefore the Church responds to this remembrance by praise and thanksgiving to the "living Father" (Jn 6:57) and, at the same time, turns toward the risen Lord who, as high priest of the heavenly and earthly liturgies, is the source of redemption.

The proper approach to the explanation of the presence of the historical saving acts of Christ in the liturgy should begin with the witness of the liturgy itself, the concrete expression of the Christian conscience sustained by the Holy Spirit. Here it is made clear that the movement is not from the historical saving events to us through a trans-historical presence of the kernel of these historical acts. Rather, the Church goes back in memory to Christ's passion, death and glorification. This recalling of Christ as the "man for others" makes us realize that his passover is not completed until his relationality to all the just is fully realized by their passing from suffering to glory in his single transitus to the Father.

Christ's passover is not yet completed in the whole Christ, Head and Body. Therefore the Church knows that it is called to participate in the movement of Christ to the Father that carries it toward the fulfilled kingdom. This movement is made possible in virtue of his exaltation of

Jesus on the cross: "So must the Son of man be lifted up, that all who believe may have eternal life in him" (Jn 3:14b). It is realized in the power of the Spirit sent by the *Kyrios,* who configures believers to Jesus, communicating the human attitudes that enable those who are in Christ to participate in his self-offering to the Father.

Summary and Conclusion

According to *Sacrosanctum concilium* 7, the liturgy of the earthly Church is primarily the work of the High Priest, Jesus Christ. It is accomplished by him as Head of the Church, his Body, bound to him by faith, and as Bridegroom who acts together with the Church, his Bride, united to him in the one Spirit. In the liturgical celebration a mutual and real presence of the Lord and his Church occurs, enabled by the Holy Spirit. Hence, through the effective and expressive symbolic verbal and gestural elements of the liturgy, Christ continues his saving work for the salvation of humankind and the glorification of the Father.

This working definition of the liturgy affirms that the glorified Lord has bound the Church to himself in the Spirit. The personal presence of Christ in the Church results from the initiative of the risen Lord who effected faith in his abiding presence through the resurrection appearances.

This abiding presence is a new presence in the Spirit, who can be called the "medium" of this mutual presence of Christ and the Church. This means that the Spirit is distinguished from the other two who are present to one another and, at the same time, enables their mutual presence to one another. In other words, the Spirit is the same in the Head and members of the Church, and is the way of the efficacious presence of Christ for the salvation of humankind, as well as the condition for any liturgical celebration accomplished by the Church in union with Christ.

Consequently, all liturgical accomplishments have a dialogical character, in which the action of Christ and the action of the assembly in the same Spirit constitute together the full mutual presence of the Lord and the Church. This understanding of how the liturgical presence of the Lord is realized, provides access to the explanation of the unity and differentiation of the individual modes of Christ's liturgical presence.

The one unique personal presence of Christ, in the faith of the Church, includes the presence of his saving work which cannot be separated from his person. Christ brings himself and his saving work to appearance in the temporal-spatial conditions of the liturgy in order that the assembly might be incorporated into his *transitus* to the Father. This mystery presence is unfolded in different ways, which enable believers to encounter and accept him through a response of thanksgiving and commitment. As a result the unity of the members of Christ's Body with Christ, and among themselves, is realized, the anticipation of the fulfillment of the Kingdom.

The unity of Head and members is represented especially in the liturgical assembly constituted by the presiding minister and the community of believers. The personal encounter of the minister and community, in which the encounter of Christ and his members takes place, is achieved in various ways. There is the common prayer of the Church, the preaching of the word of God, the celebration of the sacraments. The Eucharist is the highest possible instance of the personal presence of Christ; for it includes his substantial and actual presence under the form of the permanent sacrament of his body and blood.

In the acceptance of the sacrament of the body and blood of Christ, the faithful encounter Christ in a fully active and corporeal way. The Lord, present in the exercise of the faith of the Church as incarnate Lord, substantially and operationally, unfolds this presence through the Church in its different forms of liturgical memorial celebration, of which the most comprehensive and intensive form is the eucharistic celebration.

Notes

1. AAS 35 (1943) 218 (DS 3806).

2. AAS 39 (1947) 521.

3. MEDIATOR DEI, 522.

4. MEDIATOR DEI, 528.

5. MEDIATOR DEI, 528 (DS 3840).

6. MEDIATOR DEI, 530-531 (DS 3842).

7. MEDIATOR DEI, 552-555.

8. MEDIATOR DEI, 573.

9. MEDIATOR DEI, 555.

10. MEDIATOR DEI, 528 (DS 3840). —The use of Mt 18:20 corresponds to a longstanding interpretation that associates the text with communal worship. But this exegesis is based on a questionable reading of vv. 18-20. J.D.M. Derret provides a rather convincing argument that the pericope should read as follows: "Again I tell you that if two individuals (literally, two of you [=Christians] arrive at an accord on earth concerning any (literally, any and every) claim that they may be pursuing, it shall be allowed, ratified (literally, it should succeed, 'come off') on the part of my heavenly Father. For where two or three are convened in my name, there I am among them" ("'Where two or three are convened in my name...'; A Sad Misunderstanding," EXPOSITORY TIMES 91 [1979] 84). Derret concludes that v. 20, in the context of the pericope, "has nothing to do with prayer. It means that unofficial disputes-settlers, peace makers, perform a divine function" (86). —However, other texts, such as Mt 9:29 or Jn 15:7, suffice to support the idea that the Lord is present in communal worship.

11. F. Eisenbach, DIE GEGENWART JESU CHRISTI IM GOTTESDIENST: Systematische Studien zur Liturgiekonstitution des II. Vaticanischen Konzils (Mainz: Matthias-Grünewald, 1982) 153, n. 97.

12. In the perspective of the first project of the Preparatory Commission, the depth of the anabatic aspect of liturgy is best described as GLORIFICATION OF GOD, GROUNDED ON THE DIVINE GIFT OF THE LIFE OF FAITH.

13. Eisenbach, DIE GEGENWART JESU CHRISTI, 155, n. 100.

14. MEDIATOR DEI, 528.

15. Council of Trent, DOCTRINA DE SS. MISSAE SACRIFICIO, DS 1743.

16. MYSTICI CORPORIS, 223.

17. MEDIATOR DEI, 528.

18. MEDIATOR DEI, 528.

19. Eisenbach, DIE GEGENWART JESU CHRISTI, 158, n. 108.

20. Eisenbach, DIE GEGENWART JESU CHRISTI, 159, n. 111.

21. Eisenbach, DIE GEGENWART JESU CHRISTI, 161, 171.

22. Traditional scholastic theology's doctrine of transubstantiation conveys an exclusively static concept of Christ's real presence under the forms of bread and wine. The philosophical basis of the speculative side of this teaching is an ontology of substance. At the time of Vatican II, Catholic theology had not worked out, and to this day has not completed the task of developing, some form of relational ontology that might afford a better grasp of the connection between Christ's active and somatic presence in the Eucharistic species. However, some effort is being made by modern Catholic theologians to integrate the patristic insight, based on the New Testament witness to the Eucharist, that the communication of Christ's body and blood, through the ministry of the Church, includes the activity of Christ himself.

23. SACROSANCTUM CONCILIUM, 5; 6; 9; 10; 33; 41; 48; 59; 61; 89.3; 92; 93; 102-104; 106; 109.

24. AAS 57 (1965) 562-564.

25. Nos. 9; 55 (AAS 59 [1967]) 547; 569-570).

26. MISSALE ROMANUM, art. 7 (ed. typica, 1970).

27. RITUALE ROMANUM, De communione et cultu myst. euch., art. 6 (ed. typica, 1973).

28. INSTRUCTIO GENERALIS DE LITURGIA HORARUM, art. 13 (ed. typica, 1971).

29. "Zur Aktualpräsenz Christi in der Liturgie," in MENS CONCORDAT VOCI. Pour Mgr. A.M. Martimort a l'occasion de ses 40 années d'enseignement et des 20 ans de la Constitution SACROSANCTUM CONCILIUM (Desclée: Paris, 1983) 518-531.

30. LA PRESENZA DI CRISTO NELLA LITURGIA (Rome: Edizioni liturgiche, 1973).

31. LA PRESENZA DI CRISTO, 9-28.

32. LA PRESENZA DI CRISTO, 31-49.

33. LA PRESENZA DI CRISTO, 50-57.

34. LA PRESENZA DI CRISTO, 58-71.

35. LA PRESENZA DI CRISTO, 60.

36. LA PRESENZA DI CRISTO, 72-96.

37. LA PRESENZA DI CRISTO, 97-112.

38. LA PRESENZA DI CRISTO, 113-133.

39. LA PRESENZA DI CRISTO, 133-140.

40. LA PRESENZA DI CRISTO, 143-198.

41. PRAEN. 17 (ed. typica, 1983).

42. "Zur Aktualpräsenz Christi," 522.

43. OSSERVATORE ROMANO, July 10, 1982, 5.

44. DIE GEGENWART JESU CHRISTI, 697-741.

45. DIE GEGENWART JESU CHRISTI, 741-744.

46. Eisenbach follows this method (DIE GEGENWART JESU CHRISTI, 766-777).

47. B. Langemeyer, "Die Weisen der Gegenwart Christi im liturgischen Geschehen," in O. Semmelroth, ed., MARTYRIA, LEITURGIA, DIAKONIA, 288-292; E.J. Kilmartin, "Apostolic Office: Sacrament of Christ," THEOLOGICAL STUDIES 36 (1975) 255.

48. An example of two typical modern Catholic interpretations of the reality of the Easter appearances is found in the exchange between A. Kolping ("Um den Realitäscharakter des Ostererscheinungen," THEOLOGISCHE REVUE 73 [1977] 441-449) and L. Scheffczyk ("Wissenschaft Nachschrift," IBID. 449-453). However, despite his more nuanced interpretation of the reality of the Easter appearances, Kolping makes his own a quotation from Scheffczyk's AUFERSTEHUNG. Prinzip des christilichen Glaubens (Einsiedeln: Johannes, 1976) 79: "It is...exegetically uncontestable that the biblical witness of the resurrection, 'expresses the fact of resuscitation,' likewise 'that the knowledge of the community and disciples concerning the resurrection is attained by a revelation and did not originate on the ground of human invention or reflection'..." (443).

49. Langemeyer, "Die Weisen der Gegenwart Christi," 292-295.

50. Langemeyer, "Die Weisen der Gegenwart Christi," 295-299.

51. Eisenbach draws attention to the weakness of Langemeyer's explanation of the special presence of Christ in liturgical events. The latter author remains at the level of the anthropological-phenomenological description which he himself had already judged to be insufficient in his introduction ("Die Weisen der Gegenwart Christi," 288). According to Eisenbach, "The 'genuine theological determination,' which Langemeyer requires, must be derived from the content of the liturgical celebration, namely from the Christus-Mysterium" (DIE GEGENWART JESU CHRISTI, 727).

52. H. Schlier, "Das Ende der Zeit," GEIST UND LEBEN 40 (1967) 203-217.

53. Langemeyer, "Die Weisen der Gegenwart Christi," 300-307.

54. Eisenbach, DIE GEGENWART JESU CHRISTI, 743-744; 761-762.

55. A. Gerken, THEOLOGIE DER EUCHARISTIE, 211-228.

56. A REAL SYMBOL, as previously stated, is one in which there is unity of being between the signifying and signified realities. This, for example, the human body is a real symbol of the human being as a whole.

57. This theory of D. Feuling is cited by G. Söhngen in "Le role aggissant des mystères du Christ dans la liturgie," LES QUESTIONS LITURGIQUES ET PAROISSIALES 24 (1938) 103-104.

58. DIE LIEBE ALS GRUNDMOTIF DES NEUTESTAMENTLICHEN THEOLOGIE (Düsseldorf: Patmos, 1951) 371-400.

59. J. Gaillard, "Bulletin de thélogie sacrementaire. Chronique de liturgie: théologie des mystères," REVUE THOMISTE 57 (1957) 540-541.

60. CHRIST, THE SACRAMENT OF THE ENCOUNTER WITH GOD, 59-61.

61. R. McNamara, "Christus Patiens in the Mass and Sacraments: Higher Perspectives," IRISH THEOLOGICAL QUARTERLY 42 (1975) 17-35. The development of

this section, on the subject of the presence of the redemptive acts of Christ in the liturgy, is dependent on this article.

62. ST III. 48,6.

63. DE VERITATE 27,4.

64. ST III. 48,6.

65. In 1 Cor 15, lect. 15.

66. E. J. Kilmartin, "Sacramental Theology: The Eucharist in Recent Literature," THEOLOGICAL STUDIES 32 (1971) 244-246, reviews literature which explores the subject of the mystery presence of Christ's redemptive acts within the broader context of the implications of the liturgical remembrance of the Church in the Spirit. The Spirit, as "soul of the Church," is particularly the source of the memory of the Church, by which she participates in the memory of Christ himself. The ecclesiological and pneumatological aspects of this problem are touched on by Eisenbach (DIE GEGENWART JESU CHRISTI, 766-777). Likewise, A. Schilson notes the need for the introduction of the pneumatological and ecclesiological grounding of the presence of the redemptive act of Christ in his critical analysis of the strengths and weaknesses of O. Casel's MYSTERIEN-LEHRE (THEOLOGIE ALS SAKRAMENTENTHEOLOGIE, PASSIM).

Chapter 18
Active Participation in
Sacramental Celebrations

All liturgical celebrations represent the being together of God, community, and individual believer in loving communion. Above all, the chief rites of the Church are an objectively high point of the expression of the life of faith in its essentially dialogical structure.[1] Here the event of communion with the Father through Christ in the Spirit is manifested in a fully human and social way. Here is found in a concentrated fashion all that constitutes the life of faith of the new people of God. In addition, the sacramental celebrations are aimed at concrete situations of life where God's presence claims the participants in a specific way.

Sacramental celebrations are "necessary" because the believer needs the assurance of the faith of the Church that God is present in these common ecclesial situations; that God gives the grace to enable the person to respond to the claims that he makes on them in these situations; and that one's prayer for the needed grace is heard. The latter assurance derives from the sacramental word: a prayer of the Church united to Christ's eternal intercession, with which the subject of the sacrament identifies.

The formulas that express the meaning of the chief rites of the Church are a word of God, spoken under the condition of history. All such words of God are announced in the Church in the form of a human word that is an expression of the faith of the Church. They are not a word of God, spoken by God to his creatures directly in the clothing of human words. Scripture itself is not the account of what God dictates to a chosen and willing secretary. In the inspired writings the personality of the author is reflected in the style of composition and culturally conditioned forms of expression. But the author's personality is also manifested in the uniquely personal grasp of the revelation of God that is set forth—an understanding that is conditioned by that of the community of faith in which the author lived. That is why we can and must, for example, distinguish the peculiar theological orientations of the synoptic Gospels.

The word of God is not something that exists merely in the form of Scripture, to become a living word through reflective reading and proclamation in the liturgical assembly. The word of God is spoken whenever the authentic faith of the Church is expressed. This word of God, in the form of witness of the faith, addresses hearers in their concrete situation of life and claims the response of faith. It meets the hearer as a word to be answered by the commitment of the whole of one's being. Essentially the word of God is a word of address that meets a person, affects him or her, and is accepted in faith or rejected.

Sacraments, above all, manifest the relationship between the word of God, in the form of the expression of the faith of the Church, and the response of faith that the word of God claims. But the word of God, in the sacramental celebrations of the Church, comes in the form of invocation of the Church for the grace that corresponds to the concrete situation of the individual in whose favor the sacrament is accomplished. This implies that the individual agrees with this prayer of the Church made on his or her behalf, and commits self to the consequences of the ecclesial calling upon God in the situations signified by the sacrament. Sacramental celebrations are potentially a subjective high point in the life of faith of the community and the individual subject. But they become so only in the measure of one's personal involvement in the celebration itself.

I.
Personal Engagement

Sacraments are forms of response of faith of the community and individual subject and, at the same time, are saving events which happen to the participants. In other words, the action placed by the participants and the divine action form an indissoluble unity. The sacramental celebration does not involve two separate and distinct actions, one accomplished by the minister serving as instrument of Christ, and the other by the subject who unlocks the mystery dimension by faith, freely accepting the offer of the grace signified by the rite. Rather, the sacramental celebration corresponds to the structure of all authentic human, and humanizing, activity.

As was explained in Chapter 2, in all true personal engagements there is an indissoluble unity between the action which a person places and the human and humanizing event that happens. Analogously, we can speak of sacramental celebrations as dependent on the human engagement for their salutary effects. This engagement is initiated by the gift of faith. However the measure in which the believer enters into this celebration of faith determines one's personal growth in the life of faith.

The importance of personal engagement in sacramental celebrations must be continually stressed. From the pastoral point of view that means that care must be taken to prepare the community and the individual for participation, and the celebration itself should be conducted in a way that is calculated to foster personal involvement.

There is no need to develop this theme further. It has been dealt with under a variety of perspectives in earlier sections of this book, However, the reader's attention is called to the following topics: the importance of fostering symbolic perception as a preparation for the liturgy; the identification of spheres of human life in which modern people experience transcendence, and the possibilities of their integration into the liturgy of the sacraments; the need for a better grasp of the original Christian understanding of symbol as an aid to active participation in sacramental celebrations; the requirement of a style of celebration calculated to evoke the proper response to what is signified by each sacrament; the value of healthy ritual behavior for stimulating mutual sharing in faith and for contributing to the deepening of the unity of the liturgical community.

II.

Fundamental Condition for Fruitful Participation in the Celebration of the Sacraments

Sacraments should not be considered foreign intrusions into the lives of Christians, who otherwise carry on in a fully human way through the works of faith and love in their routine living. Rather, sacraments meet a basic need of believers that corresponds to the very nature of humankind.

The anthropological ground of sacramental celebrations is clearly expressed in the teaching and practice of the apostolic Church and the early post-apostolic period. Baptism and the Lord's Supper were understood as ways of realizing the essential Christian engagement: Christ for us; we with Christ. These essential ways of realization of this engagement correspond to the basic condition of the human being: a being bound to instruction, in need of a word, and so fundamentally answerable to a word. In this original understanding of sacrament, the believer is presented as one who has neither the first nor the last word, but rather is answerable to the first word, and must await a response to his or her answer.

The understanding of the human being as instruction-bound can help to clarify the fundamental prerequisite for the encounter of Christians with Christ in the sacraments.[2] The whole of Christian tradition teaches us that it is especially through the sacraments of the Church that Christ, in the Spirit, instructs Christians and binds them to the new way of life. The subjects of the sacraments are touched in the measure that they recognize themselves as instruction-bound and respond in the obedience of faith under the movement of the Spirit.

In the response of faith the promise of fulfillment, announced by the sacramental celebrations, is made real. God's turning toward the subjects of the sacraments is experienced as self-communication, and this gives birth to unshakeable hope. This sacramental engagement with Christ in the Spirit, which transforms the historical present into the time of God's love, engenders confidence in the fidelity and love of God and a sure hope that at the end of historical time those who are faithful to the way of Christ will enter fully into God's time.

Notes

1. E. J. Kilmartin, "A Modern Approach," 93-96.

2. Kilmartin, "A Modern Approach," 96-101; L. Hödl, "Kirchliche Sakrament—christliche Engagement," ZIETSCHRIFT FÜR KATHOLISCHE THEOLOGIE 95 (1973) 1-19

Chapter 19

The Efficacy of the

Sacraments

Christian faith connects the celebration of the sacraments with the communication of the grace of God. But what is the relationship between what the community does and the effect of grace that is associated with the liturgy of the sacraments? How are we to approach the understanding of the role of the sacraments in the communication of divine life through Christ in the Spirit?

I.
The Explanation of Scholastic Theology

Traditional scholastic theology begins the discussion of the efficacy of sacraments with the divine activity, and then attempts to integrate the ecclesial activity into the sacramental grace event. This is done by situating the presiding minister on the side of God and Christ, and then on the side of the Church. The minister is described as acting in the place of Christ. More frequently now the term "in the person of Christ" (*in persona Christi*) is used in official Roman documents to stress that the minister represents Christ, is a kind of "real symbol" or sacrament of Christ's sanctifying activity. Correspondingly, the liturgy of the Church's sacraments is understood to contain a rite: the essential symbolic gesture and word, instituted by Christ at least as far as signification. When the minister performs this rite he represents Christ vis-à-vis the recipient of the sacrament.

The minister not only "administers" the sacrament as representative of Christ, he also acts as the representative of the Church. The latter role is carried out by reciting the liturgical prayers and performing the ritual activity that surrounds the essential sacramental rites, which are determined by the Church. In addition the Church enters into the realization of the essential sacramental rites by providing the correct forms that correspond to the will of Christ and by specifying their meaning. Therefore the minister must follow the lead of the tradition of the Church in order to administer a true sacrament; for sacraments have been entrusted to the Church as such and not to the minister independently of the Church. This condition is formulated in the traditional axiom that the minister must have the intention "to do what the Church does" (faciendi quod facit ecclesia).

This intention can simply mean that the minister must perform the ritual act according to the way deemed necessary by the Church. As was mentioned in Chapter 14, it is open to debate whether this minimum intention, that is to say, the proper execution of the rite, is sufficient for the realization of a valid sacrament in an ecclesial context. The need for the minister to perform the essential rite prescribed by the Church is based on the requirement to follow the will of Christ known to the Church in faith. So the formula "to do what the Church does" can be reduced to: "to do what Christ wills to be done" in the celebration of his sacraments. This would not be realized if the minister correctly performed the rite but, at the same time, publicly disavowed any intention to act as the leader of the liturgy. In this case the minister would be disassociating himself from the community and its liturgy in such a way that his sacramental role of representing Christ and the Church would be inconceivable.

The further condition, that the minister does not exclude the goal of the sacramental rite by a secret intention, can be formulated positively as "to intend, at least implicitly, to do what the Church intends to do through the celebration." Ultimately this means "to intend what Christ intends." This doctrine of intention, that is, the possibility of simulating a sacrament by a secret intention, establishes a very weak link between the worshipping community and the sacramental rite. It implies that the community can claim the essential sacramental rite as its own only in virtue of the fact that its official ministry has the power to represent Christ, the Head of the Church.

The new ecclesiological turn of sacramental theology has resulted in a more nuanced approach to the relation between the minister of the sacrament and both Christ and the Church. Sacraments are now more generally understood, in Catholic theology, to be acts of the Church as such, not merely acts of the minister of Christ in the Church, to whose hierarchy the sacraments have been entrusted. This means that the local assembly, which represents the Church in space and time, is the direct subject of the whole liturgical action under the leadership of the ordained ministry. Hence the presiding liturgical minister is seen more clearly as representative both of the Church and Christ in all aspects of the liturgical-sacramental celebrations. Consequently, it becomes less evident that the minister alone can invalidate a sacrament by a secret intention, while he is acting visibly as the representative of the Church.[1] Furthermore, the sharp distinction between what the minister does in the liturgy exclusively in the person of Christ, that is, the essential sacramental rite, and what he does in the person of the Church, that is, the remainder of the liturgical prayer and symbolical activity, becomes questionable. Rather, the minister appears to be, in all liturgical activity, the representative of Christ because he represents, in virtue of ordination, the community of which Christ is Head.

The correctness of this latter point of view becomes evident when one realizes that even the so-called essential matter and form of the sacraments are the expression of the faith of the Church which corresponds to the will of Christ who, in the Spirit, is the living source of that faith. It is supported even more decisively by the traditional conviction of the Church of the patristic period that the essential "word" of the sacraments is an invocation made by the presiding minister in the name of the community and in union with the eternal intercession of the one High Priest, Christ.

The local community as such is the real symbol of Christ in its sacramental activity, realized under the leadership of the minister who, according to tradition, must be ordained—except in certain cases such as matrimony and emergency baptism. Of course, the ordained minister represents Christ in a special way, as the one who presides over the liturgy. However, he represents Christ because he represents the Church of which Christ is the Head.

When the gathered community, under the leadership of the qualified minister, expresses itself in its essential acts, it necessarily expresses and mediates the ground of its being: Christ in the Spirit, notwithstanding any inward disavowal of the liturgical leader. The secret disavowal of the leader disqualifies him, as member of the Church, from participation in the grace of the celebration. But it does not disqualify him from acting as official representative of the Church and Christ.

As official act of the Church, the sacramental rite is the event of the offer of grace in favor of the participants. However the question is still left open: What concept of causality can be used to shed light on the mode of communication of the new sacramental grace that is offered in the celebration?

The more recent approach of Catholic theology, within the framework of the old scholastic theology, employs the model of transient efficient causality in a new way. It builds on the old principle that sacraments cause by signifying (*significando causant*). But the signifying and causal functions of the sacraments are brought together in such a way that they are not opposed to one another. In short, the model is that of the causality of sign.[2]

In this systematic approach, which corresponds in part to that of Thomas Aquinas, sacraments have an effect analogous to that of human signs. Both produce an effect of the intentional order. Sacraments cause knowledge by manifesting the divine will to sanctify the subject of the sacrament, and so elicit the proper response of faith. But the effect of the sacraments goes beyond that of the intentional order. Because God is the author of all being and all relations of being, a real relation is established by the divine will between the external rite and the sacramental grace bestowed on the believing recipient. The grace is not in the sacramental sign, except by "extrinsic denomination"; grace is in the person being justified, or more deeply sanctified. But there is always a real offer of grace through the sacramental sign. Since grace is linked to the sign through a real relation established by God, and the reception of the grace signified depends on the response of faith to the sacramental sign, the sign can be called an instrumental cause of grace.

A. Evaluation

This theological analysis of the causality of the sacraments recalls certain basic principles: A. Sacraments are paradigms of the sanctification of human beings that takes place in and through historical forms of communication; B. sacramental celebrations are new grace events; C. the essential sacramental rites are personal symbolic activities grounded on the action of the Father, through Christ in the Spirit; D. the offer of grace is a transcendental act, emanating from God's pure divinity, that is to say, the communication of the Spirit by the Father; E. this offer of grace has a christological dimension, in that it is offered by Christ in a theandric act that is "sacrament" of the transcendental act of the Father, that is, sacrament of the offer of the Spirit; F. the bestowal of grace depends on the response of faith of the "recipient," who can rupture the intended communication that is essentially *dialogical.*

All grace events are unique and historical. The historical forms of these events play a mediating role in the sense that they enable God to offer himself and the human being to accept in a personal way. The historical forms are not a "means" or "medium" of God's self-communication in the sense that grace is filtered through the historical forms of communication. God's self-communication is immediate by its very nature. What can be said in general about God's self-communication, holds also for the sacraments. It even holds for the sacrament of the Eucharist.

The difference between the Eucharist, as sacrament of Christ's body and blood, and other sacraments, lies in the fact that Christ offers himself in the Eucharist. In the Eucharistic meal, anticipation of the messianic banquet, Christ makes the elements, in the power of the Spirit, the permanent sacrament of his abiding presence in the Church. As offered by Christ through the ministry of the priest to the communicant, the sacrament of his body and blood represents Christ's theandric act of offering of the Spirit, an act that is sacrament of the transcendental act by which the Father offers the Spirit. Received in faith, the Eucharistic species become the sacrament of the bestowal of the Spirit by the Father.

The scholastic theology of the efficacy of the sacraments is orientated by a descending christology. It highlights the mystery content of the liturgy. However, it tends to neglect the ecclesiological dimension and the role of the faith of the Church in the accomplishment of the sacraments. When the sacramental event is viewed not only from the standpoint of descending christology but also from that of ascending christology, and the two viewpoints are integrated, another understanding of the causality of the sacraments emerges.

II.
A Modern Liturgical Approach to the Efficacy of Sacraments

From the viewpoint of the liturgical celebration itself, the symbolical activity that expresses the purpose of each sacrament is so intimately connected with the symbolized reality (God's self-communication) that the latter can only be approached as a reality through the rite as act of the believing community.[3]

A. The Liturgical Community

The liturgical community itself is the proper active subject of the sacramental celebrations. Its role in the efficacy of the sacraments must be thought through together with that of the presiding minister, and the person in whose favor the celebration takes place. As act of the concrete worshipping community, the liturgy is an instance of human and social communication. But it differs from other examples of the social, ritual activity of humanly constituted groups. The latter have a limited view of reality and narrow goals. The liturgy affords a comprehensive interpretation of humankind, world, and history and aims at the integration of the participants into the ground of all reality: the Triune God.

B. Sacraments and Faith of the Church

Through the liturgy the reality of the faith of the Church finds its objective articulation. The fixed forms of expression of this faith correspond to the gift of faith, which is a personal reality. Therefore these forms of expression of faith have the capacity to draw out the subjective response of believers. As expression of the faith of the Church, sacraments signify the belief that the grace of God is being offered and, at the same time, indicate the response expected from the participants. Insofar as the sacraments affirm the conviction of faith that grace is being offered, they realize what they signify; for their employment is inspired by the Spirit. Insofar as they signify the grateful response of the participants, they do not necessarily realize what they signify; for the participants do not always agree with the offer of grace in the form in which the agreement is expressed in the liturgy itself.

The dialogue structure of the sacraments indicates that the self-communication of God cannot be described after the model of physical instrumental causality, the model of instrument of art. In this instance the instrument is placed over against the object being acted on. Efficient causality must play a role in the process of communication of grace. There must be contact between the Triune God and those who are to respond to the offer of grace, a contact that conditions the latter to accept the grace being offered. This contact comes through the sacramental rite itself and an inner-working of the Spirit in faith that enables the respondent to know and accept the deeper meaning of the ritual activity.

However sacraments are a human activity in which the faith of the Church as a whole and the faith of the concrete assembly is expressed. Such rites cannot be conceived as situated vis-à-vis the worshipping community. Rather, they are the human language and symbolic actions by which the community expresses itself, and through which God's self-communication takes place and is received in a fruitful way.

More precisely, we should say that the whole of the liturgical action of the sacraments is a form of response of faith to the inner-word of God that works in the faith of the Church and the concrete participants of the celebration to the extent that they agree with the fixed forms of expression of the faith of the Church. As we have already noted, even the essential forms of the rites of the sacraments are a response of faith. They are fundamentally an invocation for the coming of the Spirit of sanctification, which corresponds to the meaning of the particular sacrament.

In the liturgy the creative activity of God is manifested through the explicit response of praise and thanksgiving made by the community for the gift of the Spirit bestowed by the Father through Christ. The whole purpose of the divine plan of redemption is the drawing of humankind back to the Father through the gift of the Son in the incarnation, and through the gift of the Spirit whereby we know that the incarnate Son is the way and whereby we love the way and the goal, the Father. This purpose finds its historical expression and realization most intensely fulfilled in the sacraments which, by their nature as response to God's gift, are the formal expression of openness to communion with the Father.

C. Celebration of the Whole Community

All the members of the worshipping community are potentially active subjects of the accomplishment of the sacramental celebrations. Because there is no exercise of the faith which has only an anabatic aspect, this means that, in a certain sense, all the participants are also subjects of the grace of every sacramental celebration.

1. Community as Subject of the Accomplishment of the Sacraments

All the sacramental rites express the faith of the Church, and the concrete assembly expresses this faith as its own through the communication between the individuals in which the leader has an organizing role. Because of the various roles of the members of the assembly, there is a giving and receiving. This human dialogue, expressed in common prayer, song, reading of Scripture, homily and responses, ritual gestures, signify for the eyes of faith a dialogue between the Father, through Christ in the Spirit, and the faithful.

The human giving and receiving ultimately signifies God as the giver and the community as receiver of saving grace. The community can be identified as the giver only insofar as its members ministerially offer grace to one another through the various forms of exercise of the faith. That is why the liturgy of the sacraments is always referred to God: a response of praise and thanksgiving for what God has done and is doing now in the liturgical assembly, and a petition for a new advent of the saving grace of the Holy Spirit.

2. Community as Subject of the Grace of Sacramental Celebrations

It is evident that the Eucharist is a celebration in favor of the whole assembly under the aspect of both the sacramental sacrificial offering in union with Christ and participation in the sacrament of Christ's body and blood. The other six sacraments are celebrated in favor of individual members of the Church. However, even in these cases they are forms of sacramental communication of grace to the whole community as such.

In these latter sacramental celebrations, the community's petition is mainly directed to the the obtaining of a special grace for the individual. Nevertheless it shares indirectly in the grace of the sacrament by its grateful response for the grace being offered to one of its members. In this way the community recognizes its responsibility toward the subject of the sacrament and, through its grateful response, opens itself to obtain the support of the Spirit to fulfill its responsibility to contribute to the individual subject's growth in the life of faith.

Moreover, in these sacramental celebrations the assembly is made aware that all saving grace is a gift of God, as manifested in the sacramental offer of God's personal communication to the individual in whose favor the celebration takes place. As a consequence all the participants are conditioned to recall with thanksgiving the life of faith that has been granted to them already, and to open themselves to a deepening of personal communion with the Father through Christ in the Spirit.

D. Individual Subject of the Sacraments

The individual subject, in whose favor the sacrament is accomplished, comes to the liturgy with a personal commitment in faith. But the goal is not merely to give thanks for what has been experienced as a gift of grace elsewhere. A person may enter a church building to praise God for past benefits. This is not the precise purpose of entering into the liturgical assembly to become an active subject of a sacrament.

The liturgy of a sacrament does not allow a subject merely to give thanks for a previous divine saving action. The various forms of such celebrations of the faith do not simply serve as means for external expression of grateful dispositions originating in past experiences of God's grace. Rather, through the sacramental celebrations, the previous faith commitment and grateful dispositions of the subject are caught up in the communal expression of the faith of the Church so that one's previous spiritual condition is transcended.

In the sacramental liturgy the subject of the sacrament is drawn into the Church's invocation on his or her behalf. The offer of God's grace is experienced through the liturgical language and symbolic actions. At the same time, the subject experiences the support of the Spirit to agree with the offer by gratefully acknowledging that it is a gift given apart from personal merits.

Sacraments, as epicletic activity of the Church, proclaim that the gift of grace transcends the personal commitment of the one who expresses his or her faith in the liturgical celebration, that this personal commitment itself is grounded on the participation in the faith of the Church. Hence the subject of the sacrament is helped by the liturgy to become more open to the gift of God's grace. Participating in the sacrament, in the expression of the faith of the whole Church and of the assembled community, the individual subject is enabled to transcend one's limited commitment of faith, to really experience the offer of God's grace within the ecclesial context, and to accept it gratefully. This is something that no individual is capable of doing for oneself. No one can make a sacrament for oneself in isolation from the Body of Christ.

E. Specific Efficacy of the Sacraments

According to the traditional teaching of the Church, there is an intimate relationship between the active participation in the sacraments and the personal sharing in God's grace. Since it is a question of a personal giving of God and a personal receiving on the part of the subject, the openness to God's grace measures the depth of the event of sanctification. The personal engagement of one's faith is the condition for the personal reception of God's self-communication. This is the rule for the adult Christian's fruitful sharing in the sacraments.

The exceptional case of infant baptism cannot be made the norm for the adult participation in the sacraments. Christian tradition defends the practice of infant baptism on the ground that it includes the engagement of the faith of the Church in favor of the individual. However school theology of the West, on the basis of a theological outlook that was dominated by an almost exclusively katabatic interpretation of the sacramental grace event, awarded the dialogical aspect only marginal consideration. The minimum intention for the fruitful reception of a sacrament by an adult was often phrased in negative terms, that is, the subject of the sacrament must not place an obstacle in the way of the bestowal of grace. This tended to make infant baptism the normative case for reflection on the efficacy of sacraments. Theologians could find an analogy there to support the theory that a habitual intention to receive a sacrament was sufficient for the reception of a new sacramental grace by an unconscious adult.

The concern to stress the preeminence of God's activity in the sacraments corresponds to the Christian experience of being graced by God through the sacraments. God's self-communication is simply God's work, and the ability to respond is based on the gift of faith, which is also a work of God as the dogma of justification by faith alone affirms. But the scholastic synthesis developed a theory of sacramental sign that placed it on the side of God vis-à-vis the community. Sacramental rites were depicted as objective means of grace, situated in liturgical rites that otherwise express the faith of the Church. The fatal flaw in this theology lies in the sharp distinction between the liturgical spheres of the expression of God's love (the essential sacramental rites) and the response of faith of the community (the surrounding liturgical prayer and ritual activity).

The scholastic theology of the objective efficacy of the sacraments corresponds to the patristic point of view. In both cases, the chief rites of the Church are awarded a certain objective holiness in virtue of which sanctification is communicated to apt subjects. Likewise, in both cases a central symbolic action, accompanying an associated ritual formula, is singled out as the climactic moment of the sacramental event. Finally, in both cases, the material element used in the sacramental rites is awarded a mysterious efficacy, based ultimately on the common place idea that sanctification relates to the whole person, body and spirit. Consequently it is explained that appropriate material is used to effectively signify the corporeal transformation, while the prayer of faith manifests the sanctifying action of the Holy Spirit on the human spirit. A text of Gregory of Nyssa can serve as an example of the general outlook of both the Greek and Latin writers, as well as the Syrian Monophysites.

Commenting on John 3:5: "Unless you be born of water and the Spirit," Gregory says:

> Why by the two, and the Spirit alone is not esteemed sufficient for the completion of the baptism? Man is a composite, and not simple, as we certainly know. But for this reason, on behalf of the twofold and conjoined, the related and similar medicines for the cure are appointed; for the body, which appears, water which is perceived by the senses; but for the soul, which escapes vision, the Spirit, who does not appear, who is called by faith, who comes secretly.[4]

However the Fathers of the Church did not develop a distinction between the anabatic and katabatic dimensions of the liturgy such as that found in classical scholastic theology.

A closer look at the elements of sacramental celebrations shows that they consist in human language and corporeal expression, constituted by the activity of the Church under the inspiration of the Spirit. They correspond to and express the faith of the Church. The language of the sacraments mediates knowledge of a relationship between God and believers. It announces in its own way, under the form of response to God, that grace is being communicated for the benefit of the participants.

The intention of the language of sacraments is to transform the worshipping situation, to carry the community to a new level of religious experience. In short, it aims at disclosing the mystery of God's abiding presence in the community, and eliciting the proper response. The language of liturgy represents an instance of the transformative function of the timely word, such as that described in the account of the experience of the disciples, occasioned by the conversation with the risen Lord on the road to Emmaus: "Were not our hearts burning in us as he talked" (Lk 24:32). The language of the sacraments, in its verbal and gestural forms, is performative speech. It is not simply aimed at providing information about what God has done in the past. Hence it cannot be explained as merely a means by which the participants of the liturgy recount what they have already experienced in the daily life of faith.

But the language of the sacraments is performative speech in the way peculiar to the dialogical structure of the liturgy. It announces what God is doing now in the assembly in the form of intercessory activity. The speech of the sacraments expresses the confidence of intercessory prayer made in union with the eternal intercession of Christ.

According to the old scholastic axiom, the sacraments are efficacious *ex opere operato*. When the sign is correctly placed, according to the intention of the Church, God's promise of the offer of grace is assured. The interpretation of this axiom takes a different turn when it is recognized that the sacramental word is essentially a prayer. In other words, the sacramental celebration is an infallible offer of grace because Christ unites the prayer of the Church with his heavenly prayer (Heb 7:25) and because of the promise given through the institution of the sacraments by Christ the Lord, in the Spirit.

Since the sacraments are the expression of the faith of the Church in the form of thanksgiving, praise, and invocation of the Father for the gift of the Spirit corresponding to the meaning of each one, it follows that the efficacy for the adult participants depends on the integration of one's personal subjective commitment of faith into the liturgical expression of the faith of the Church. If the participants do not agree with the faith of the Church expressed in the sacramental liturgy, there is no possibility of a personal engagement with God according to the conditions expressed in the liturgy itself. If the participants agree, they are carried along and supported by the sacrament to respond appropriately to the offer of grace.

The whole purpose of the Christian liturgy in general, and the sacraments in particular, is to enable the assembly of believers to become in act what it is by its very nature, namely, the Body of Christ. The goal of the grace event of the sacraments is no more and no less than to enable human subjects to be freed from the narrow confines of their own self-understanding, to realize that they are called to be answering subjects to God's offer of loving communion. This grace of God attains its finality when the Spirit so penetrates the bone and marrow of the Christian that he or she can take their stand as "other" over against the God of love, and respond in love with the whole people of God.

The ideal liturgy is not one in which the leader alone, through the fixed forms of liturgy, expresses openness to receive communion with God in the name of all those present. Rather, it is one in which all those present express the faith of the Church as their own. Here the word of the Book of Revelation can be cited as a succinct description of the liturgy of the saints:

> The Spirit and the bride say, "Come." Let him who hears answer, "Come." Let him who is thirsty come forward; let all who desire it accept the gift of life-giving water (Rev 22:17).

Sacraments enable the community as a whole to become active subjects responding to God, and the individual subjects, in whose favor the celebration is accomplished, to take their proper place in the community of faith. The kernel of the sacramental rites is not a "means" of grace, set over against the participants. It does not have the form of an objective institutional means of grace to be applied to willing recipients. Rather, it is the incarnation of the grace of faith in the form of an appeal to the Father through Christ in the Spirit.

As the objective expression of the faith of the Church, sacramental celebrations mediate the dispositions by which individual subjects are moved to respond in, with, and through the community's petition for the gift of the Spirit. By agreeing with this faith, the individuals are made fully subjects of the sacraments, and not merely passive objects of the sacramental bestowal of grace. Hence God's grace, mediated through the liturgy, appears in the first place as granting the dispositions of the subject to respond to the offer of grace, rather than as presupposing the dispositions as a condition for the reception of the grace of the sacraments.

As forms of communication of the faith of the Church, sacraments communicate the dispositions whereby the subjects of the sacraments are brought to a higher level of openness to the self-communication of God, resulting in a deeper integration into the mystical body of Christ.[5] But all of this depends on the commitment of the individual, under the inspiration of the Spirit, to seriously involve oneself in the sacramental celebrations of the Church of Christ.

Notes

1. The sacrament of marriage is a special instance, according to the Catholic tradition, of reciprocal ministry. According to this theology the marriage partners are ministers of the sacrament to each other. To the extent that this theology can be maintained, it offers support for the idea that marriage partners can invalidate the sacrament by their secret intention, both as "administrators " and "recipients." However, it is highly probable that the minister of the sacrament should be identified as the one who officially represents the Church in the cultic act in which the partners enter into a new relation with the ecclesial community. Eastern churches traditionally hold this point of view. Some Orthodox churches have drawn the conclusion, from the liturgical practice that Christian marriage is only possible when a priest assists with the intention to act as minister. This position is not tenable from the standpoint of the history of recognition of Christian marriages in the Orthodox tradition. But it contains a grain of truth, namely, the idea that the human situation of conjugal love is not automatically a sacramental state because the partners happened to have been baptized, but becomes so when the partners accept this human situation in their lives of faith, and in a setting that can somehow be described as ecclesial. From this point of view, it is as "recipients" of the sacrament that marriage partners can render the sacramental celebration meaningless by refusing to accept what is signified in their lives of faith.

2. W. Van Roo, DE SACRAMENTIS IN GENERE, 306-343; P. McShane, "On the Causality of the Sacraments," has carried through the approach of Van Roo to its logical conclusion.

3. F. Tillmans develops this thesis in "The Sacraments as Symbolical Reality of Faith: A Theological Programme," in H.J. Auf der Maur, et al., FIDES SACRAMENTI, SACRAMENTUM FIDEI, 253-276. The following analysis corresponds, in part, to his exposition.

4. IN DIEM LUMINUM, a sermon delivered at the feast of the Epiphany, 383 (E. Gebhardt, "In diem Luminum, vulgo in baptismum Christi oratio," in Werner Jaeger, ed., et al., GREGORII NYSSENI OPERA IX Sermones. Paris I [Leiden: Brill, 1967] 225-227).

5. The sacrament of the body and blood of Christ, the unique instance of a sacramental presence that remains after the sacramental action by which it is realized, is also a form of communication of the faith of the Church. If Christ communicates himself to the believing participants of Holy Communion, he does so through the word of faith of the Church by which the sacrament is accomplished, and which enables the response "Amen" to the invitation of the minister who announces: "The body of Christ; the blood of Christ."

Conclusion

Through the liturgy of the Church, in all its forms, the Christian assembly experiences the saving presence of God. It does so by recalling its foundation in liturgical prayer, song, and symbolic activity, namely, the once-for-all redemptive work of Christ and the sending of the Holy Spirit through whom the Church was established and believers drawn into communion with the Father through union with the risen Lord.

At the same time the Church is aware that, since the final age has come, Christ is actively present in the Spirit in a new way in all situations of the lives of Christians and all others. Hence the Church makes no sharp distinction between the spheres of the holy and profane. Christians recognize that Christ is present in all situations of life calling for the decision of faith to accept the love of God and its consequences. This places the role of the liturgy of the Church in a new light.

The liturgy of the Church is not the only place where Christ is found with his saving grace. Christ is personally present in the whole range of daily life, where there is a response of faith through witness to the gospel, and loving service of the neighbor. Moreover Christ's presence in all dimensions of the life of faith points to the time of the new and definitive presence. In the transformed world of the Kingdom of God, the people of God will continually commune with the Trinity in "spirit and truth" (Jn 4:23), through the one mediator between God and humankind, the risen Lord.

In the fulfilled kingdom of God, the special moments of the communal worship of the earthly Church, in which the Church is explicitly related to the liturgy of the Cross, and to the heavenly liturgy, will have no place. However in the age of the pilgrim people, the variety of holy encounters with the Lord in daily life of witness and service do not suffice to meet the needs of a full life of faith. Christians need to be continually supported by the community of faith. They cannot do without the liturgy in which they renew and deepen their personal commitment of faith by expressing and enlarging on it within the scope of the confident expression of the prayer of faith of the whole Church, made in union with the one High Priest, Jesus Christ, in the power of the Holy Spirit, unto the glory of the Father, the source of all blessings.

Index I: Scripture

Index II: Councils and Papal Documents

Index III: Patristic And Liturgical Sources

Index IV: Names

Index V: General Theological